Profanity, Obscenity & the Media

Melvin J. Lasky

Profanity, Obscenity & the Media

The Language of Journalism, Volume 2

Being A Second Volume,
Wherein the Language of Journalism is Examined,
Its Splendors and Miseries—
including Clichès and Trivia,
Sensationalism and Prurience,
Wit and Witlessness,
Fiction and Faction,
Pseudery and Jabberwocky,
Scoops and Hoaxes,
Racism and Sexism,
Profanity and Obscenity,
Virtue and Reality,
Culture and Anarchy—
and the Abuse of Slang, Style,
and the Habits of Writing Good Prose

 Transaction Publishers
New Brunswick (U.S.A.) and London (U.K.)

Copyright © 2005 by Transaction Publishers, New Brunswick, New Jersey.
www.transactionpub.com

All rights reserved under International and Pan-American Copyright Conventions. No part of this book may be reproduced or transmitted in any form or by
any means, electronic or mechanical, including photocopy, recording, or any
information storage and retrieval system, without prior permission in writing
from the publisher. All inquiries should be addressed to Transaction Publishers, Rutgers—The State University, 35 Berrue Circle, Piscataway, New Jersey
08854-8042. www.transactionpub.com

This book is printed on acid-free paper that meets the American National Standard for Permanence of Paper for Printed Library Materials.

Library of Congress Catalog Number: 00-034408
ISBN: 0-7658-0220-1
Printed in the United States of America

The Library of Congress has cataloged Volume 1 as follows:

Lasky, Melvin J.
    The language of journalism / Melvin J. Lasky
        p. cm.
    Includes bibliographical references and index.
    Contents: v. 1. Newspaper culture.
    ISBN 0-7658-0001-2 (v. 1. : alk. paper)
        1. Newspapers—Language. 2. Journalism—Language. I. Title.

PN4783.L37 2000 V. 2.
070.4'01'4—dc2   00-034408

"Take Care When You Get information. We Live By information, Which Exists By Faith in Others.But If the Ear is the Side-Door of Truth It is the Front-Door of Lies....the Truth Seldom Comes in Elemental Purity, Especially From Afar – there is Always Some Admixture of Moods of Those Through Whom It Has Passed. Passions Tinge and Color Whatever they touch, Sometimes Favorably, Sometimes Odiously.... Pay attention to intentions....Let Reflection Test for Falsity and Exaggeration."

—Balthasar Gracián, the Art of
Worldly Wisdom
Oraculo Manual Y Arte De Prudencia (1647)

Table of Contents

Introduction

Now that my second volume has been completed and set for publication, that infallibly mathematical half-way mark has surely been reached. At least for trilogies. And Kafka in his inscrutable way recommended it as the fateful point of no return. Now there is no turning back, but the reader–or the browser in a bookshop with this book momentarily in his hand–need not be alarmed. The momentum which was unleashed a thousand pages ago by the traumatic impulse of my father's disillusionment with the *New York Times* (fifty years or so ago) will now be carrying me and the argument to the very bitter end; and the author can give the reader an important reassurance: He need not have read the first volume of *The Language of Journalism* (2000) to be profitably provoked–and possibly persuaded–by the sequel he, or she, has in his or her hand. A neighborhood wit once coined, in the days when we went to the movies in the afternoon (mostly Saturdays) and the double-features were being shown in "continuous performance," the immortal recommendation for us, the "early-bird" matinée crowd, to the effect that "This is a film that begins in the middle…for the people who came in in the middle!" This is such a book.

I admit that with the years since the first volume appeared I have tried to develop and vary the analysis, and indeed to extend the research; and still I feel that coming closer to the end was like approaching the beginning. I was tempted–but an editor's blue pencil overruled me–to add yet another revealing motto somewhere around the thousandth page. This would, with Aristotelian authority (no less), associate everything I was saying with large Athenian ambitions and classical wisdom. The ancient credo was full of promises: "We will then show how the absurdities of speech are born from the misunderstandings of similar words for different things and different words for similar things, from garrulity and repetition, from play on words, from diminutives, from errors of pronunciation, and from barbarisms" (Aristotle, *Poetics*, c. 350 B.C.). I still have, as is obvious, wangled its interpolation here, for prefaces are also promises. But there are also obvious lessons to be learned from such belated commitments. A famous warning from one self-critical master came up with the aptest of cautions: …What one learns last in writing a book is what should have come first. Or, come to think about it, how to begin in the middle.

In my own case what might have come first, or at least very much earlier, is an unforgivably tardy awareness of how it all began, and where and why. I have often on the previous pages made reference, in personal bursts of "re-membrance," to early reading habits (to the *Times* and the *Bronx Home News*). D family traditions of literacy (my grandfather's pious addiction to his favorite local daily, my father's blue-eyed faith in his)…to my university years wherein a small group of New York students, alternately poring over cryptic medieval documents and stop-press stories in our daily newspapers, learned to detect hidden meanings (or so we thought) buried deep beneath the superficial "vis-ible surface" of reported events. My old City College classmate Irving Kristol reminded me the other day in Washington that the collegiate review I edited from our shared Alcove 2–a mag called *History Chronicle* (to which he was a contributor)–looked, sounded, and read like all the subsequent journals I had anything to do with. (It also featured, in its large double-column pages way-ward quotes, stray clips, odd footnotes, and other eclectic tidbits, printed alternately in italics and boldface, and framed by a thin-lined box.) So much for growing up, coming-of-age, and the delusions of progress and change.

Do all attempts to remember the past turn up, in agreeably familiar patterns of discovery, similarities if not identities? Is it inevitable that what we recall is shaped by such apt episodes of selective relevance? My first semi-profes-sional experience as a teenage editor of a literary magazine entitled the *Mag-pie* only strengthened our youthful foraging instincts, to steal away with a few shining bits of truth. The world was turning out to be a hard place to under-stand; and whether in the library or at the newspaper-stand, we were driven each day to come away with an item or two, underlined with apparent percep-tiveness or, even better: stabbing insights.

Looking back in the perspective of half-a-century, I think I can detect the line that took me from there to here. Novels, of course, were the stepping-stones. I remember the "newsreel" insertions which adorned John Dos Passos' *Manhattan Transfer* (and the other volumes in his *USA* trilogy), replete with artfully selected news-items.[1] I hesitate to mention Marcel Proust, but then the *madeleine* experience, now so platitudinous, seemed to be happening for the first time, at least for young readers. We would have to remember the actions and the passions of our own generation; and we were, whether we knew it or not, stocking up on little stimuli which would be on hand when memories needed to be fully recalled. An old cutting takes on new life, and becomes the illuminating context for (in Burton's seventeenth-century phrase) "*new news.*" To be sure, professional journalists in our time all had at their command their own newspaper's so-called *morgue*: presumably the place where the old dead stories could be summoned up to serve as still lively factual background. This might add a spot of color and coherence to a fast-breaking story. But where was truth? or where was art? Could newspaper culture embrace the highest values (*what*, with collections of yellowing clippings)?

I remember my first meeting with an accomplished artist–with George Grosz, a famed German painter who was forced into American exile by the Hitler régime. It was in the Russian Tea Room on Manhattan's 57th Street. He was wearing an elegant single-breasted suit (with vest) and a wide-brimmed Panama straw hat, as if in disguise or at least camouflage. His jacket pockets were stuffed with a copy of a New York evening newspaper and the jagged-edge clippings already excerpted from the morning reports. He was an inveterate clipper and collector. In his first breakthrough period in the Berlin of the 1920s Grosz had brilliantly used a miscellany of what he called *Schnipsel* (scraps) to compose his notorious *Dada-collages*. Although he was now into other things in his Manhattan office and Long Island studio, his old-style *Archiv* lived on, for there had been a widespread aesthetic recognition of the significance of bits-and-pieces, indeed there had been in fact a cultural institutionalization of the cutting.

In the case of Grosz (and so many others) it amounted to a lifelong obsession. He had begun, at the outset of his career, collecting the widest variety of *Schnipsel*, of clippings and cuttings. Once, in a letter of 1918, he wrote about also salvaging bus tickets, restaurant menus, banner headlines (mostly about German generals, Ludendorff and Hindenberg), cooking recipes, paragraphs from serialized novelettes, bread-ration coupons, stock market listings. (They all still exist, intact, in his *Nachlass* preserved in the Berlin Academy of Arts and Sciences.)

The clipping itself almost became an objet d'art in those early twentieth-century days when men of letters and art searched for new ways to root themselves in reality. Sometimes they even fancied their imagined conceits to be "*a new reality*," vicarious or virtual or whatever. In any case, they were committed to evade their lonely perch in the designated ivory tower. And thus it came to be thought that cuttings (and other bits of throw-away scraps) contained documented truths or, at least (or even more), vibrations of contemporaneity and the chaos of our modern existence. The clip was handy, preservable, and ubiquitous. It also looked good in a scholar's research *Zettel-Kästchen*, or pasted on a haphazard collage, featuring hole-punched trolley transfers, or an Aschinger menu announcing the soup-de-jour (among other price-worthy delicacies). Artists like Kurt Schwitters, Max Ernst, and Hannah Höch added meaningful pieces of flotsam and jetsam, among other aforementioned detritus of a busy day, to widespread acclaim. Art critics and historians like the authoritative Aby Warburg recognized the innovative inspiration and helped to establish avant-garde reputations.

Last but not least, there developed around this time a pioneering "clipping service" in Paris called "*Argus de la presse*." It became a prosperous cottage industry for a century or so–before the invention of *Google*, that computerized near-omniscient search-machine on the Internet–which catered to artists, writers, and very-important-persons in all walks of life. The German branches proudly referred to themselves formidably as the *Zeitungsausschnitt-Industrie*. Thousands of clients wanted cuttings about themselves, their works and activities, and/or about certain persons or subjects they were following. All the world's press was soon being creatively cannibalized, and the business of cutting-and-pasting had its years of glory. American agencies even thought of themselves as some kind of "intellectual clearing house." One even announced to its clients its motto, borrowing from Andrew Carnegie, the tycoon of steel and the patron of popular public libraries, to wit: "Nowadays every man has to read and study, to get to the basics of things in order to be equipped, in the ever sharper struggle of life, to survive."

Yesterday's newspaper was no longer "rubbish." The print media were seen by the clippers and their clients, the collectors, as–when you get right down to it–essentially a raw collection of clippable items. When they were properly cut, labeled, pasted into context and cross-referenced, it would all amount to a source of cultural strength for Carnegie-sponsored libraries and Darwinian struggles-for-existence…also in the search for truth (and sociologists like Max Weber and Georg Simmel began to recognize journalism, at its best, as a form of scholarship). It also became a source of art and even beauty when avant-garde aesthetics gave modernism its museum-keeping seal of approval. It was, moreover, taken to be a primary source of historical record…and an International Conference in the year 1908 discussed for days the value of the newspaper to historians as a body of reliable evidence. Everything seemed to be going the cut-and-paste way of the *Schnipsel*.

Proust, be it recorded, gave this phenomena a touch of his own. On occasion, when he brought himself to think of what his fellow-writers in France, especially those forlorn souls (like Sainte-Beuve) who wrote for the literary pages of the popular Paris press, were actually up to…he gasped at their soulless collaboration with a form so mechanical and repellent. In every copy of *Le Constitutionel*, over the same columns on the same page, one would find every single Monday Sainte-Beuve's *Causeries du Lundi*. The papers, still moist from the printing, were available at the local kiosk and…to be frank about it, they were (for some) rather more inviting and fetching than the brioches being dipped in the café-au-lait in the local bistro. Most astonishing of all was the miraculous repetitiousness of all those printer's-inked texts whereby the second or third copy of that morning's edition featured, lo and behold, the very same stories (and columns, and headlines) which he had just been looking at in his own copy. What would he have made of the prime-time images on our television screens? Such mass recurrence could only be rebarbative.

Proust made much of this "conceit." He reflected dourly that the same ideas and images were being transported all over the country that morning and simultaneously being inserted into the minds of a vast readership!

And yet, and yet….The "culture of the clipping," in its modern development, actually predated the moist, inked pages of the morning newspaper.

One suspects that the watershed of modern communications, its splendors and its miseries, came soon after Gutenberg's sixteenth-century invention of printing and the seventeenth-century discovery of new scientific "marvels," or facts, or truths. But what was *a fact*, and why did it have to be so short, or brief, or concise in order to be true? Possibly because the "hateful fact" would be so instrumental, as T.H. Huxley remarked, in killing so many "beautiful theories." The nitty-gritty details were proving to be the constant enemy of the airy-fairy abstractions. An item of *"new news"–viz.*, the Copernicus story and Galileo's follow-up, or Newton and Harvey on apples and blood streams– could destroy old beliefs, hoary attitudes, yesterday's assumptions. Could anyone be content anymore to be sitting quietly in his room and engaged in pure thought about the largest matters? When *experiments* were being devised all around them to establish a new and decisive kind of proof, graphic, logical and altogether incontrovertible?

It was inevitable, given the vagaries of the human mind, for men of intellect and curiosity to be of divided views on such matters. There was the faction of the fact, led by Francis Bacon who delighted in the post-Gutenberg world where knowledge could quickly be disseminated, in a compact form, with details to be listed and tabulated. Concision favored aphorism, and his *Advancement of Learning* (1605) Bacon hailed the new style, "sententious sentences," as allowing (in a glorious phrase) *"the wit more free to turn and tosse...."* But Bacon's factology was soon to be denounced as an undigested heap of details, for details could only blur the whole and true picture of reality. Even crisp brevity and short terse sentences–the "army of particulars"–were not at the heart of true knowledge. Theory, and interpretation, and well-founded general opinions were the soundest methods for the path ahead. Centuries later we can find Wittgenstein, full of ingenious abstractions, arguing that *"Die Welt zerfällt in Tatsachen* (Facts fragment the world.)"*

As far as journalists and scholars are concerned, what I have called *factology* actually divided them into two camps. For one, as a historian of the "fact culture" has written: All honest investigations "shared an emphasis on truth, an insistence on fact over fiction and imagination, a preference for firsthand and credible witnesses, and a rhetoric of impartiality"(Shapiro, *Culture of*

---

*   Ludwig Wittgenstein, *Tractatus logico-philosophicus* (1922), p. 7. In the 1922 ed.; and pp. 30-31 in the 1961 ed. In both texts it is translated mildly as "The world divides into facts." Other translators give it a more drastic touch inasmuch as the the German word *"zerfällt"* can mean *disintegration* as well as *"consists of"* or *"divides into."*

Wittgenstein presumably belonged to the *fact*-faction; but he might not have been averse to a quasi-mystical suggestion that, in giving order and coherence to the world, the division into facts could also help...in point of fact...to disintegrate it. The ideal of a good cosmic order, with everything in its proper place in the universe, is often very close to the dark vision of a coming or an accompanying catastrophe. Attractive utopias seem always to need a violent, purifying inauguration.

Fact, p. 5). The reporter of realities, whether for scientific advancement or new discovery, became in the infectious enthusiasm of Francis Bacon (and the Baconians to follow) what we would be calling a Culture Hero. He rejected "rumour and the gossip of the streets." He cited only believable eyewitnesses. He was open about his sources. He was "sober and severe" (and not "a vain-speaking and light person").

For the other camp, the search for real truths was obliged to rise above factology. Finding a mere fact was not to discover a black-on-white witness to reality, a simple and infallible guarantor of a truth about nature or human action. In short, facts were only a starting point–and we would be having to deal with the thornier, more profound problems involved in "*conjecture.hypotheses.inference*" (and the like), not to mention "*reflection.principles.theory.*"

The worship of the fact could become little more than a fetish if, in its ritualistic innocence, it misperceives (as is, alas, often the case) the small piece of reality which it hopes to record accurately and truly for all time. Errors happen.

This dualism of fact and opinion–sometimes presented as the conflict between objectivity and subjectivity, between impartiality and bias–is not, of course, as simple as it is often argued to be, for it comprises a treacherous ambiguity which has been misleading observers for well over four centuries. In the very beginning of the printed newspaper there was a sensitive early awareness of how difficult it was to report events, happenings–"new news"–accurately and justly. In 1644, as printed newspapers were beginning to come on to the scene, Richard Collings conceded (as every candid editor has ever since): "And indeed in many Papers there have been such apparent contradictions and such a thwarting of the truth by an endeavour to enlarge the story, that while the Reader turns Sceptick and finds he hath reason to suspect, he therefore doth draw often unto himself a wilde conclusion and will believe anything." But the reports from "honest hands," he insists (with perhaps a shade of noble naiveté), would be neither "defective or excessive." Still, don't we all begin this way (and doesn't it turn out to be an illusion and indeed self-deception)? A seventeenth-century journalistic contemporary of Collings valiantly promised, as every crusading or investigative reporter has ever since: "I intend…to encounter falsehood with the sword of truth. I will not endeavour to flatter the world into a belief of things that are not; but truly inform them of things that are." Yet another contemporary colleague vowed that he would represent things "as they really happen."[2] Where have we heard all this before? Such lofty ideals were not first pronounced by journalists in a London printshop but, as it happened, in the English courts of law by justice-obsessed jurists and judges. (For example, one "should not swear a thing to be so or not unless he know it to be so or not; He must not rely on Conjectures, Rumours, or Probabilities.")

The ideal intentions of honest and truthful journalism seem to be fairly constant over all time, but the lapses and deviations–to which all editors and reporters have been heir–discolor the true history of the journalistic attempt (and indeed of the scholarly historian's efforts) to "tell it like it is [or was]...." One man's moderation is another man's excess; one writer's sword of truth cuts its way, in the eyes of another, only to some "wilde conclusion." Some ambitious journalists only came to enlarge and embellish; some few others were modestly content to be lean, sparing, positivistically factual.

That ingenious mathematician and inventor Robert Hooke (1635-1703) tried to devise something which he thought was a conception of an ideal reporter, a wise and virtuous spirit who would be only devoted to matter-of-factness: "I conceive him to be no ways prejudiced or byassed, by interest, affection, hatred, fear or hope, or the vain-glory of telling strange Things, so as to make him swarve from the truth of Matter of Fact." Yet the finest English writers of the day, caught up in the passions of utopia and revolution in Cromwell's Commonwealth–I am thinking of, on the one side, John Milton and Marchamount Nedham; and, on the other, John Locke, James Howell and Thomas Hobbes–composed ringing manifestoes and well-argued pamphlets in the great debate of the day....But none were free, nor could they possibly be, from bias, interest, affection, hatred, fear or hope (or "vain-glory"). These personal qualities of mind, character and style were all just as incorrigibly "matter of fact" (or thought to be) as the date of Cromwell's death, 1658, and the subsequent return of King Charles from France, 1660.[3]

There was a strange and striking utopian element that was in the handwritten transcription of excerpts (from books and documents) as well as in the collection of cuttings (from so-called "news-books" and, later, newspapers). Here among the noteworthy and worthwhile items, all relevant and put in order, were the building blocks of a reality perceived; and implicit (or, even better, explicit) therein were truths about life and nature, or about science and society. This enthused faith, as I have suggested, was akin to a utopia of reason and progress. With each newly recorded *fact*, whether established by careful experiment, or sharper observation, or on-the-spot witnessing, we were forever moving closer to the solution of old mysteries and hitherto intractable problems. But ever since the ancient emergence in classical Greece of an enlightened rationalism no thoughtful or sophisticated person could be unaware that any such solution could itself be faulty and unwarranted and would be, in turn, susceptible to revision and/or displacement. Science corrects. It is committed to overcome an endemic human forgetfulness, the amnesia which we are embarrassed to detect in the whole repetitive history of governance with its wars and frauds, and in the pattern of error and illusion in intellectual explanation.

I myself should have known better. Some years ago, with time on my hands, I turned to the collection of cuttings from newspapers and the periodical press which I had assembled fairly systematically, as an editor and journalist in Europe and America over some forty years or so. I was confident that therein, with facts and quotations galore, lay truths about life and letters in our time which could richly fill two or three volumes on any subject and its related themes. Here, surely, was empirical evidence to buttress a thousand insights into the nature and practice of "the Language of Journalism." My personal archive was "wide-ranging" but in no way complete; there may well have been small faults, or gaping omissions, or other shortcomings and imperfections. The scissors were not always there for the cutting. (That glorious instrument which, in the memorable 1517 portrait of Erasmus of Rotterdam is seen in a corner of a bookshelf, hanging at the ready on a hook!)* And so many items had ragged edges which rendered some words tantalizingly unreadable (with dates and page numbers disagreeably absent). And, again, sometimes the mucilage paste was so irremovably sticky that the material on the other side, at first ignored but suddenly pertinent, was quite irretrievable. (Historians of the clipping have often recorded academic discussions about which glue had the proper chemical consistency for "the other side" not to be lost forever!)

And it was just about this time (1556) that a Dr. Konrad Gesner, excited in the Renaissance about how much new there was to know and grasp, recommended to all scholars "to cut cleanly"; for neatness was essential to his program of "indexing" a plethora of materials which one couldn't possibly keep in good order in one's head. He advised writing down words and phrases to remember; and categories were devised for quick classification. Thus, "cut-and-paste" became wedded to file-and-find. Dr. Gesner gave system to the whole procedure.

The man was the metaphysician of the Excerpt. He even dealt with sixteenth-century books according to his own stringent method and intellectual style (*cut the pages cleanly*). He also recommended a not-too-permanent mucilage so that the various items could be removed from one file and reinserted in another...in which context they took on additional meaning.

Alas, the good Dr. Gesner often remained stuck, as in a sticky paste, in the shortcomings of his own innovative impulses. In one instance he had to apologize to a colleague named Johann Bauhin for not answering his kind letter. It was not available for reply since Dr. G. had cut out the various passages that interested him for his files, in the favored arrangements (alphabetical or thematic). Books may have been grossly dismembered, but it was all in the service of a grand idea, a *Biblioteca Universalis*.

By the time of Francis Bacon the idiosyncratic drive to the systematization of knowledge, consigning every little scrap of a useful fact to its proper place, was approved by the master. Bacon wrote: "I hold that the diligence and pains

---

*   The painting in question was by the Flemish artist, Quentin Massys (1466-1530). See Anke Te Heesen, "Fleiss, Gedächtnis, Sitzfleisch (Diligence, Memory, and Patience)," in *Cut and Paste*, p. 147.

in collecting common Places is of great use and certainty in studying." What the pioneers of the new sciences and general intellectual enlightenment were enjoying was a miraculous extension of memory. The "storehouse of facts" was the insurance policy against that awful occasion "when if we wanted any particular Thing we could not tell where to find it."

Until the electronic and digital era of the twenty-first century this was standard intellectual practice, whether among journalists and editors or scientists, with minor personal differences. Some researchers persisted in cannibalizing printed books, tearing out and pasting up paragraphs and even whole pages. In the age of cheap paperbacks this was not too costly; but what a far cry from the personal computer's quick and clean consultation of Google, "the research machine." For my part I had long since abandoned making notes by hand, finding my own handwriting too difficult to read easily. I used to type on the 3x5 cards for my little filing box in the "typewriter room" of the British Museum, as it then was. The excerpting was noisy but quick, especially if one had noted the pages in advance. As John Locke put it (in 1706):"The Places we design to extract from are to be marked upon a piece of Paper that we may do it after we have read the Book out." I am afraid, as I have already hinted, that "*Reading out*" newspapers and magazines offered an additional pitfall when the choice excerpt on one side of the page ruined the pertinent passage on the reverse side. In the 19th-century when the "clipping services" (*Argus*, etc.) came to the aid of scholarly research with a useful division of labor (*they clipped, you collected*), all agencies learned to acquire two or three copies of all publications–so that nothing would be missed by those conscientious pair of scissors. But back in the world of Bacon and Locke, and their marvellous *Commonplace Books*, there was a nagging fear that excerpts would be missing some fresh observations not duly classifiable, some new insights and original experience.[4]

The style of research, the ways of ascertaining a fact, and the method of registering an accurate and true insight...all were preoccupations of the early modern scientists. They influenced (and were influenced by) the revolutionary progress made by Copernicus and Gutenberg and all the others. The extension of memory was one great factor, for without a handy record of mankind's trials and errors there can only be mental stagnation in which old falsities get propagated and awkward contradictions just happen to slip one's mind. The cut-and-paste technique I have mentioned above seemed to be consistently revised in order to match the revisionism of the scientific temperament. Yet each new generation was troubled by the same rather primitive difficulties. The physicist Robert Hooke, not unlike Dr. Gesner long before him, was constantly irritated about "*Mouth Glew*." Its chemical composition needed to be such that it could safely be applied on evidence of new discoveries, and thus guarantee that "they may at any time upon occasion be presently removed or altered in their Position or Order, that which was plac'd first may be plac'd middle most, or last." Ingenious, if finicky, minds of the day also concerned themselves with the paper on which the seminal cuttings were to be pasted; as well as with the *drawers* and the *closets* in which they were to be pigeonholed; and the like. In our own day historians have devoted themselves to every little apparently trivial aspect of the Great Breakthrough in science, medicine, and technology that transformed European societies. There are now histories of "cut paper" and (as they cannot help saying) "*the culture of the cutting*" in modern civilization. There are catalogues of the varieties of "collecting" and the emergence of new collectibles. There are even studies, with anatomical asides, of the *Sitzfleisch* (all those fleshy bottoms!) required for the qualities of patience and diligence to accumulate the raw material for scientific investigation and the framing of hypotheses.

German "historians of ideas" have been especially adventurous in these fields. After all, they can always (and they do) point to the wit and wisdom of Goethe, not only as a man-of-letters but also as a publicist and betimes natural scientist. On one of his journeys–making sketches, scribbling quatrains, planning novels and dramas–he was inspired to collect all the documents which might prove necessary for his ambitions. "*Die Acten*" consisted of every kind of printed page and publication he happened to come across: newspapers, weekly journals, texts of sermons locally preached, official proclamations, theater programs, catalogues (with prices), etc. In the view of Ernst Robert Curtius, Goethe was here "*cutting up the world*," each bit constituting "a slice of life." He also speculated about the road not taken–how would the Goethean ouevre have looked if the Master had decided not to *collect-and-cut* but to copy or make handwritten jottings (the way he used to do in his notebooks). Now he was collecting all the raw materials, binding them in sturdy files, arranging them in orderly fashion on nearby shelves.

The Hookes and the Lockes might have objected, but where research techniques for the use of science might confuse and confound literary work, for a man of imagination, spinning fictions, they might by indirection facilitate creativity. In any case, odd collections of marvellous details have contributed to intellectual fertility.

One question remains. Did the sensitive and curious minds seek out congenial matters of fact and impose order and meaning on them? Or did he read and cut and clip and paste and file and then find himself thunderstruck by a lightning-like illumination about...the course of history...the nature of time and space...the rise and fall of languages and cultures...the course of curses and taboos...the onset of disease and death...the tragedies of utopias and revolutions...the turning points in the arts of logic and explanation...the origins of the species and the very laws of motion in the universe?

Clippings in their collectivity needed to be handled with special care. Obviously: a single story, a valued piece of "new news," may or may not be completely accurate. A hundred excerpts from the daily and periodical press are surely replete with errors, contradictions, mistranslations and misunder-standings, and worse.

1. When the collector assembled his archive out of personal, and indeed romantical, inspiration, it turned out to be mostly a fairly utilitarian stratagem with hardly a pretence at the scientific or the scholarly purposes which elated the early founding fathers of the cutting (Bacon, Locke, et al.). Theodor Fontane, that superb nineteenth-century novelist of Berlin and Mark Brandenburg, attested to the high value of the growing archives in his day, as part of a critical effort to recover the past and capture realities. But so far as he was concerned he used the technique to supply what he called *Kolorit*, mean-ing the colorful details, the warmth and liveliness that the broad themes in his own writing needed to have. Fontane's *oeuvre* remains rich and readable; but how much of its meaningful background is still true, the way it actually and truly was?…Clippings yellow, crinkle, fall apart. Only art and the imagination survive. And it is practically irrelevant if the fact-driven author got, say, "Fehrbellin" (where Kleist's hero, the Prinz von Homburg, famously defied all the enemies of Brandenburg) exactly or quite right. If all the facts were con-trived, or imagined, would not the art (as in Shakespeare) still have been permanent?

2. When the collector assembles his archive out of motives which are pro-fessional and intellectual, closely linked with a general philosophy and a committed scientific thesis of one shade or another, it could turn out to be an assemblage of arguable evidence, a secret weapon in a war of ideas, massive in its bias, and infatuating in its expansiveness. More often than not, it all adds up to what the collector (or his backers) intended the end-sum to be. The ever-growing collection of cuttings becomes a huge article of faith: polemical, dogmatic, tautological. At one extreme it has all the qualities of a charlatanry; at the other an exercise, at once gallant and futile, in self-fulfilling research. In a previous book I cautioned (essentially myself) against the dangers of the collectible-syndrome: "…the fragments which he brings back from his search were perhaps strung together long before in his own mind." This, I suspected, was the basic solipsism of the intellectual historian. "One must look if one is to find, but one may be always finding what one is looking for…."[5]

I offer two brief examples of this collectible-syndrome, illustrating the cut-and-paste folly of two disoriented scientists in our time, inveterate clippers in their own way, with whom fate dealt badly…in "the most unkindest cutting of all": news of one's own error and imminent oblivion.

Einstein remains world-famous; nobody, or hardly anybody, remembers Professor Otto Gehrcke (1878-1960). For half a century and more Gehrcke stalked his colleague, his fellow-physicist, the Nobel prize winner (in 1921) Albert Einstein. It wasn't as if he hated or resented the man, as a success, or a celebrity, or even as a Jew (and the Berlin of their day was rife with anti-Semitism). He just thought he was plain wrong. And he proceeded relentlessly, with the energy and dedication of an Inspector Javert pursuing Jean Valjean, to accumulate the evidence to prove to the world that the so-called *Theory of Relativity* was a snare and a delusion, and that everybody involved had been mistaken, misled, and grievously manipulated.

At the heart of Professor Gehrcke's campaign was his *Archiv*, an exhaustive (yet ever expanding) collection of newspaper cuttings that purported to document the fraud which had been perpetrated on a gullible public opinion. His *Archiv* contained thousands of items about "the Father of Relativity." Every little *Schnipsel* about the man and his work was cut out and filed in his deadly collection. It grew and grew, and became a "clearing house" for a great and remorseless polemic. Other more temperate physicists have come on to the scientific scene as critics of Einstein's relativity: and they offered alternative field theories to explain time and space, light and motion, and other cosmic fundamentals of the universe. But Gehrcke is as good as forgotten. His vast collection of cuttings gathers dust in the Library of the Max Planck Institute for the History of Science. The last newspaper clipping is from 1955, the date of Einstein's death in Princeton, New Jersey.

The scissors were the weapon...not to cause mayhem but to mythologize, to demonize. There were many sophisticated men of science who believed (like Gehrcke) that only *experimental* physics could come up with something true and valid about the cosmos. Theoretical physicists (like Einstein) could come up only with...just that: finely-spun theories which would never be proved and could only be insinuated into world opinion by egregious methods of *mass suggestion* linked to the usual and nefarious techniques of press (later: media) *manipulation*. Today it would be ascribed to a species of sinister *conspiracy*, with the usual suspects to be rounded up (and rounded on).

Einstein had it more difficult than Darwin. The opponents of Relativity were indisputably of a higher quality (in terms of scientific credentials) than the enemies of the idea of Evolution. Dr. Gehrcke himself was a physicist of repute and distinction, popular among students of the Berlin University. He did significant research that, in one case, presaged the "Atom Model" of Niels Bohr and, in another, the discovery of the Isotope (by Francis Aston).

But factionalism makes for divided camps even among the most reasonable of rationalists: and Gehrcke railed against the "*phantastische Theorien*" and "*uferlose* [boundless] *Spekulationen*" which, wrapped by Einstein in formal mathematics, stood truth and reality upside-down. Why had Einstein become so "popular," indeed emerging as early as the 1920s as a media star? But for a while the counter-movement also enjoyed publicity and notoriety. The distinguished Max von Laue was alarmed at the "mass meetings" against Einstein with their populistic demagogy and undertones of illiberal anti-Semitism.

But those were not Dr. Gehrcke's weapons. His collection of clippings were the thing. They functioned almost like voodoo pieces in a secret tribal vendetta. He expanded his *Archiv* avidly. It would all contribute to a devastating refutation–exposing the phenomenon of *Massen-Suggestion* in the popularity of Einstein's dubious ideas of time and space. In this great debate when would the rebuttal finally come? All were waiting for the knockdown rejoinder. But the *Archiv* was evidently not yet ready to be "written up." Much was, at the moment, "unsorted" and "not yet worked through."

The historian of Gehrcke's collection has speculated about why Professor Otto Gehrcke hadn't ever fulfilled his promise. Obviously, in the year 1933 with the Nazis coming to power, he could easily have obtained lavish governmental support. Hitler's anti-Semitism had consistently targeted "Jewish science." But Gehrcke was not a Nazi, not a *NSDAP* party member nor, as far as we know, any kind of an anti-Semite in his attitudes. He had nothing against the Jews; he just had something against Albert Einstein. And he hated his Theory, which he called, in a lecture at Heidelberg University (in 1936), "the rottenest [*allerfäulste*] fruit on the tree of scientific explanation."

In 1945, when World War II ended, with Albert Einstein in victorious America and Gehrcke in defeated Germany, the United States gave protection and shelter to a great many leading scientists in Central and Eastern Europe. Gehrcke was not among them. He remained in the Communist East, taught at Jena University, and died in the DDR in January 1960. He had been nominated for high prizes but received none: his "Einstein" campaign always stood in the way. His *Archiv*, so sedulously cultivated for a lifetime, impressed few and convinced nobody. It was a fetish, but evidently had no voodoo or other black-magical powers to harm Einstein; and, in the end, it boomeranged against himself. His clippings had no cutting edge.

Lenin's connection with the cut-and-paste phenomenon that has been haunting us is a posthumous story, and has something to do with Leon Trotsky which makes it all the more ideologically serendipitous. The Bolsheviks had been in mourning ever since the death of their great leader in 1924. Stalin was sorely tempted to contrive some invincible claim to immortality for the...well, immortal Father of the Revolution. In the first place, Comrade Lenin was not to be buried like ordinary mortals (like even Karl Marx, under his heavy London headstone in Highgate soil). He was to be preserved, and to be exhibited; and to be present, and be forever among us. Nor was this a more romantic flourish of sentimentalism. It was a deserved tribute to a *very superior person*, the very first in a vanguard of New Men. The socialist movement and the inauguration of the communist society constituted a great turning point for the human race; and Marxism promised (and Trotsky predicted) that ordinary mortals, come the revolution, would acquire the stature of a Kant or a Goethe or a Renaissance Man (Michelangelo, Leonardo, Galileo, take your pick). Lenin's greatness illustrated it, but what could prove it beyond all doubt?

An invitation went out from Moscow to a well-known professor of anatomy who was considered the foremost brain specialist of the day. He was Dr. Oscar Vogt, a director of the prestigious Kaiser Wilhelm Institute in Berlin, Germany's main agency for scientific research. Vogt was at the time the world's greatest authority on his subject, and the honorific invitation to the Kremlin called for a press conference (and not a mere notice on the calendar of academic events). The good professor was enamoured of newspapers, loved to give interviews; and this addiction to news and publicity may have proved to be his undoing. In all the years he devoted to "Lenin's brain" the headlines in the press were his favorite means of communication (and not the article in a scientific journal or a lecture in the academy).

In 1925 was Dr. Vogt's first stab at the preserved form of the Bolshevik leader. Several years later, on the occasion of the tenth anniversary of the "October Revolution" (which was in November), the Bolsheviks opened a new Moscow Institute for Brain Research, with Vogt giving the inaugural lecture. So what else was new? Well, the man had been conducting microscopic examinations for years, and from what I gather from the accounts of his work, the techniques of surgical segmentation allowed him to compare piece for piece. He found the "*third segment*" rather larger which might suggest that the "*pyramidal cells*" found therein could have led to, or might have produced, exceptional, highly developed "*associative faculties*." Whether this was a factor in Lenin's great 1905 victory in the Russian Social Democratic Party ("Bolshevik" means majority)–or in his ingenious persuasion of the Kaiser's government to allow him to return home from Zurich to make the 1917 revolution–or in his well-timed strategy to liquidate the democratically elected Duma and seize exclusive power for his Soviet cadres…these are matters which are surely beyond the ken of surgery and biology and any kind of genetic determinism.

Nevertheless, *Pravda* made the most of it. And given Dr. Vogt's touch for publicity, the world press had a sensational story. For the Kremlin its Lenin Cult had another bit of iconic good news, and the doctrine of "historical materialism" had another historic instance of material causation. "Lenin's genius" could have been–indeed *was*–embedded somewhere in the brain's cortical cells between the pyramid and the segment. Skillful Comintern propagandists, like the legendary Willi Muenzenberg, made sure that the tentativenss of the scientific-clinical language, with its *may*'s and *could have*'s and hypothetical *possible*'s, was blurred as the headlines and *feuilletons* oversimplified the tale of a wondrous breakthrough.

Dr. Vogt himself contributed freely to the Party newspapers, and his articles served as a further blow to Marxism's philosophical enemies, *i.e.* to any kind of "metaphysics" or "body-mind dualism." The theme of Lenin's brain was often coupled with John Reed's famous paeans of praise for Lenin's genius in directing the "ten days that shook the world." New editions of Reed's reportage–*now even truer than ever*–rolled off the presses.

Vogt's *Institut* kept busy. By 1929 he was able to report that he had already assembled in his laboratories some dozen "*élite brains*" to deepen the neurological research in his quest for the cells, or the genes, that made men great. His Berlin base, the Kaiser Wilhelm Institute, also flourished; and Vogt now headed "the largest brain research center in the world." His preference, rare among practicing scientists, for the public press conference remained; he thought he could highlight and underline what he wanted to say; but what reporters and editors made of his story surprised but rarely upset him. He thought he was using the press for the purposes of scientific enlightenment; but the press was using him for yet another beguiling, exotic feature. As for his *Archiv* it appeared to be regularly enriched by the addition of another choice item, a veritable scoop, sometimes a sensation. He spent much time collecting every clipping, every newspaper feature on the subject since he had his unexpected invitation to Moscow. He was widely, if loosely, called "a Leninist," and the charges ultimately led to his expulsion from his Berlin Institut as a pro-Soviet propagandist. But his Leninism was not in his ideology (his own views were said to be dry and neutral)–it was a confused mix of politics and vanity, of eugenics and socialism. More than that, observers even noted that Oscar Vogt began to resemble Lenin more and more: the balding head, the goatee beard, the angular eyebrows; photo-editors had a habit of "twinning them together."

Dr. Vogt began to rue the day he thought of giving his first press conference...and yet, even in his last days, he could not resist the temptation. After the war he was approached by Manuel Gasser, a Swiss editor and intellectual whom I knew in the Berlin of the 1940s. He was asked to contribute a piece about how Germans view "The German Character" now that the evil Nazi régime was no more. (Hadn't Lenin, and stolid old Stalin, proved themselves "brainier"?) He obliged, and there was yet another clipping to add to his collection. His article in the Swiss monthly *Du* went on, and on, as of old, about the configurations of the brain...and what they might have signified. Wasn't it all there, in the crevices? The evil, the crimes? Vogt's biographer sadly concluded that this is what comes from cultivating a lifelong addiction to clippings and cuttings.[6] He came to believe everything he had been reading on the subject.

For a previous book of mine I collected over some ten years innumerable "cuttings," enough to buttress the main theses about utopians and their revolutionary enthusiasms with some hundred pages of footnotes. I had collected old newspapers and new books, as well as recondite articles and obscure pamphlets. Shelves groaned under weighty volumes; overstuffed filing cabinets refused to close. Halfway into the manuscript I changed the system from an over-complicated thematic arrangement to an over-simple alphabetical orderliness. I now knew where to find Tolstoy's notion of an "*Ant Brotherhood*" as a metaphor for a good and perfect society (– under *A*)...and how to locate Jacob Talmon's views about Zionism and its half-dream half-nightmare (– under *Z*). All else between *A* and *Z* fell easily into place; but I sometimes felt I had lost grip on the sequence of the centuries, for Condorcet came long after Camus, and Dante's vision of the Twofold Paradise was digitally entangled with (under *J*? under *F*?) Joachim of Fiore's medieval hope for a Third *Reich*....

All these snares were as nothing compared to the complexities which now had assailed me with my half-century's collection of cuttings purported to be at once a topical history of my own times and a documentation (replete with by-lines and headlines, scoops and quotes) of what during, roughly, these eight decades has happened to the language of journalism.

Not much! I hear the cynics cry. *Not much that we have not encountered before!* add the historians, keepers of all our experiences.

My reader can now presumably judge whether or not the clippings I have assembled, haphazardly preserved, and annotated at length, took on, subtly over the years, a predetermined shape, tendentious and even manipulated. Or rather, whether "the last archive" (before, that is, Google) did in fact hand-pick useful and arresting old-fangled evidence for greater understanding and insight into the language of journalism and "what the papers say."

In any case, what has remained obvious and robust over all those years is, as I must admit, that confessional moment when the most learned intellectual of the day, Pierre Bayle (1647-1706), conceded (and I have cited his letter of 1673 before): "I recognize quite plainly that my insatiable craving for news is one of those inveterate diseases that set all treatment at defiance. It's dropsy, that's what it is. The more you give it, the more it wants." [7] Somewhere between the addiction and the excess lie the seeds of a newspaper culture.

London/Berlin   M.J.L.
October 2003

Part 1

Towards a Theory of Journalistic Malpractice

"I recognize quite plainly that my insatiable craving for news [mon insatiabilité de nouvelles] is one of those inveterate diseases that defy all treatment. It's dropsy, that's what it is. The more you give it, the more it wants. [C'est une hydropsie toute pure; plus on lui fournit, plus elle demande."]
—Pierre Bayle, letter (Paris, 27 February 1673)

"Professionally you try to get as close to things as possible, but never to the point of involvement. If journalism were a philosophy rather than a trade, it would say there is no order in the universe, no discernible meaning, without...the daily paper. So it's a monumental duty we wretches have who slug the chaos into sentences arranged in columns on a page of newsprint. If we're to see things as they are and make our deadlines, we had better not get (personally) involved."
—E.L. Doctorow, The Waterworks (1994)

"I'm with you on the free press. It's the newspapers I can't stand."
—Tom Stoppard,"Night and Day" (1978)

1

From A. N. Whitehead to Irving Kristol

Illusions and Self-Deception

If our subject is what it is programmatically set out to be, "our newspaper culture," or "Culture and the Media," then I confess that I am myself not so sure I know what it really amounts to. "*Media*" is probably unproblematical. It used to be known as the Press, until television came along; and although no channel or station or newspaper is ever referred to as "a medium"—the spiritualists at all the séances in the world would rise up and protest!—"media," in the plural, is clear and understandable enough. We know the messages of the media: information, knowledge, interpretation, analysis, criticism, and last but not least: entertainment. But what has "culture" to do with it?

We could, I suppose, deal with the culture of the media professionals. It's an approach not very different from Margaret Mead's among the Samoans when she was investigating the culture of the native tribes. For among the tribes of media men and women there are also customs and mores, rituals and taboos, which call out for anthropological classification. But if field an-thropology could take us too far afield, perhaps homespun aesthetics is closer.

We could just as easily discourse on the subject of how well in the media such cultural subjects as Sunday painting, music, local poetry, community architecture, and the like are treated (if at all), and the extent to which man's artistic aspirations are being reported, recorded, criticized, evaluated, and perhaps (ultimately) encouraged. Some corners of the media might come away with fairly good marks—some of the best American newspapers for their meticulous reporting at length and in depth (especially the *Wall Street Journal*); the *BBC-TV* channels for their excellent theater; the London *Times* for its "TLS" (*Times Literary Supplement*); the best Italian newspapers for their *terza pagina,* their "third page," replete with elegant features; in Frankfurt the *Frank-furter Allgemeine Zeitung* for its formidable *feuilleton;* the Swedish television for its devotion at great and admirable length to its indigenous cinematic genius Ingmar Bergman.

One could go on, and then break to disburse the bad marks: to the popular low-quality press in each of our countries in whose sensational columns there is rarely any place for anything but sex and crime, violence, and murder, weeping mothers and/or sadistic fathers; or to the more popular, that is, most highly "rated," television programmes which aspire to nothing higher than the lowest common denominator of thrills and gags which catch and hold the short attention span of tens of millions of viewers, all teetering on the edge of uneasy boredom, with dangerous remote control switches at their fingertips. Is this our theme? Perhaps; perhaps not. I hope the reader of my first volume, published in 2000, will benevolently give me the benefit of any doubts.

All these matters are surely part of a great problem which has been generally set for us. Who the makers of the media messages are, what their properties and characteristics are, their ideas and their *idées fixes*, their conspicuous virtues and natural vices—all this is an aspect of valuable current anthropology, of the "sociology of knowledge" or the sociology of the knowledge industry. And, further, the attention (or lack of attention) which is being paid in our increasingly literate, increasingly educated societies to what in more old-fashioned times used to be called "the higher things"—this, doubtless, goes to the heart of such matters as liberal values, democratic ethos, human ideals, social ethics, and what Walter Lippmann referred to as "the public philosophy."

Is the subject really so wide as to embrace anthropology, economics, psychology, sociology, and philosophy (not to mention journalism)?

One philosopher, the great Alfred North Whitehead, wrote the following (in his *Aims of Education*, 1929) about the meaning of culture which has been giving us so much trouble in these pages (and will give us even more, in the third and concluding volume to come):

> Culture is activity of thought, and receptiveness to beauty and human feeling. Scraps of information have nothing to do with it. A merely well-informed man is the most useless bore on God's earth. What we should aim at producing is men who possess both culture and expert knowledge in some special direction. Their expert knowledge will give them the ground to start from, and their culture will lead them as deep as philosophy and as high as art.

This is a noble statement, but more than a little naive in its utopian innocence of the early years of the twentieth century. We have indeed produced several generations of men, especially in the media, who have "special knowledge in some special direction," superb technicians of film and of typography, experts in communication—but have they, or we, been led to realms "*as deep as philosophy*" and "*as high as art*"? More often to depths as low as slanderous gossip and to levels as shallow as soap opera.

It is this aspect of liberal and humane innocence which engages me: all our illusions about information and expertise; our self-deception about literacy and mass communication; our careless mistakes and grievous errors about the useful and constructive function of press and television–or "media"–in a democratic culture which is increasingly offering more treacherous traps than the golden opportunities for utopian progress which Whitehead surmised. It is to this darker aspect of the theme of "Our Newspaper Culture" that I want to turn.

Still, before moving from A. N. Whitehead to, say, Irving Kristol–a City College classmate of mine in the New York of the 1930s (and my predecessor as American editor of *Encounter* in London) whose writing career managed to encapsulate the zeitgeist of the century–I venture a few remarks about the connections between the first and second volumes.

Hard Facts and Soft Future

In the development of Western culture from its modern beginnings—some put it in the English seventeenth century, in the time of Cromwell's Revolution, accompanied as it was by brilliant pamphleteers and newssheets (a few written and edited by no less than John Milton); others put it in the French eighteenth century in the time of the *philosophes* of the Enlightenment and the radical politics of Condorcet, Danton, and Robespierre—we can locate the special qualities which characterize the spirit of our modern media.

Here was *urgency*, and *public-spiritedness;* here was *new information* about the way we live and how society is thought to function; here was a new note of *criticism* and *candid communication,* disseminated often at great personal risks for writers and editors; here were *innovative* forms of the written word and the "broadcasting" of various opinions, often *dissenting* and *dangerous.*

Each developing nation came to have its own "culture heroes": men who went to prison for writing as they pleased, for defending the emerging "rights of a free press." The name of the eighteenth-century German émigré to America, John Peter Zenger, only stands for many who over the centuries fought for the right to tell truths; his trial and acquittal of the charge of "libel" is considered the classic landmark.*

But if we move forward in time to our own day we note that this critical spirit has become an increasingly relentless one. In the past it helped to open up windows in a fairly closed society. Is it, in its systematic devotion to airing every issue, blowing a cold wind into every nook and corner, still opening windows–or smashing them? We must be candid enough to ask of ourselves self-critical questions like these.

---

*   On the occasion of the 250th anniversary of the Zenger libel trial (4 August 1735), the U.S. press showed itself to be pompously untroubled. *The New York Times* proposed a "toast to the Zenger jury" on behalf of the "American idea": "The freedom of the press to challenge authority and convey complaints of the citizenry is indispensable in a free society." Too true. But has nothing happened in the 250 years to raise an eyebrow of self-critical questioning?

The cultural context in which our media have developed has, as I have already suggested, shaped them into a necessarily critical force, subversive of conventional attitudes and, more than that, of existing institutions. For if there is to be progress, *le progrès, Fortschritt*—a basic ideal in our Western pantheon of values—then we have to move forward to the *better* from the *bad*. Distressing evils are in the present; fine hopes are in the future...but only if we proceed to right wrongs, expose malefactors, improve faulty institutions, ameliorate our changing society. C. S. Lewis, no man to be in tune with modern fashions of thought, curtly dismissed the contemporary class of intellectuals precisely because "we have trained them to think of the Future as a promised land which favoured heroes attain..." What he loosely called "the general movement of our time" had the effect of fixing

> men's affections on the Future, on the very core of temporality. Hence nearly all vices are rooted in the future. Gratitude looks to the past and love to the present; fear, avarice, lust, and ambition look ahead....We want a whole race perpetually in pursuit of the rainbow's end, never honest nor kind, nor happy *now*, but always using as mere fuel wherewith to heap on the altar of the future every real gift which is offered them in the present.[1]

Here, then, is the general proposition from which our media have deduced its essential maxim: good news is no news. Only bad news makes headlines, interests curious and impatient readers, recaptures colorfully the kaleidoscope of fast-moving reality. The syndrome is familiar: "Man Bites Dog," not "Dog Bites Man," is the call which must catch the attention of us all.

As a result we have had throughout the twentieth century, in the democratic communities of the world which have enjoyed a more-or-less free press, an unending cascade of devastating criticism.

We know about the horror of mounting crime; the dirt in the hospitals; the child abuse in the homes; the corruption of the police; the wastage of millions in the military establishments; bribery in high and low government places; the monstrous hypocrisy of Northern affluence in a world of Southern poverty; the swindles of financiers and the greed of doctors and lawyers; the miseries of prison life in our jails; the blackboard jungles and functional illiteracy in our schools; the muggings in our parks and the gang warfare in our streets; the pollution of our environment; the insidious drug addictions in our slums. One could go on to the point of exhaustion. And my point is that it is a wonder of our lives, almost a psycho-social miracle, that we can get up each day and survive yet another round of doom and despair.

I am not trying to deride this, only to explain it. Whether it is desirable or not in the *abstract* (and we do not live in the abstract), it is inevitable in the here-and-now and it is sturdily reinforced, for better or worse, by the ethos of our Western culture—the truth will make us free. The dark side of this faith is what I want to touch upon in passing.

In the first place I am not at all certain that it is "the truth," that is, the whole truth, and nothing but the truth, which is being told about the virtues and vices of our mixed democratic societies; I will return to this in a moment. In the second place, I am not sure that these so-called truths are invariably making us more "free," or more strong and resilient, as liberal and humane societies. I have been in bookshops in at least a dozen world-capitals where there are innumerable shelves of books on all four walls—fiction as well as non-fiction—which in this spirit criticize, and expose, and indeed almost annihilate the very social-political foundations of Western societies. Are we willing to argue that all this is, invariably, an unqualified source of strength?

We, at least most of my readers, are writers, critical journalists, sceptical editors, independent intellectuals–and each of us has often dwelt on the "negative side" of our own cultures and governments. We are justifiably proud of efforts to tell us *what has gone wrong*–I myself am groping towards that kind of critical position in this chapter. But I have also come to the unhappy feeling that we in the West all too easily say, "Of course we are relentlessly critical— therefore ours is a healthy society!" I too once believed that, and am now beginning to disbelieve it. More and more it is, I feel, like saying that because there are a good dozen brilliant surgeons on hand to analyze a case of cancer, therefore the case of cancer isn't really as bad as it originally was! I know that this is the faith that we in the democracies live by; I am just wondering whether the faith isn't misplaced. Writers have made a fetish of "swimming against the tide"; but there is also a danger of drowning. André Gide used to preach that "the truth wounds only to cure"; but is the wounded patient always so lucky? I doubt it.

As in certain doctor-patient relations, the result of careless and blunt truth telling does not reinforce the will to live but induces despair. In the case of the United States, the twentieth-century decades from "the Muckrakers" to the Ideologists of a "sinful, evil America" brought a chronically cheerful population to a state of such melancholy that public-opinion polls revealed that for the first time–it deeply depressed President Jimmy Carter in 1978–the old Yankee optimism was giving way to despairing feelings that the future would bring nothing good at all for the children. Despite a brief burst of passing self-confidence during the Ronald Reagan years, an unprecedented note of pessimism still obtains in the national temper.

This, then, is my first question about the relations between our cultural tradition and the spirit of the media. Is the balance right between the ethical and philosophical commitment to maintaining (and, if you will, "improving") a free, changing, democratic society—and I take it that this is what our media-makers as citizens are publicly committed to—and the actual practice of cameramen, thrusting mike-in-hand interviewers, and stop-press headline writ-ers? Put another way, is the balance right between the primary responsible civic engagement and the traditional century-old role of the intelligentsia as a radical avant-garde, the journalist as the gadfly of the state, and our media corps *en masse* as a permanent, relentless oppo-sition to established institutions, to everything that is and has ever been?

I ask the question; I am not alone in the Western world in asking for an historic reconsideration. Dogs do bite men; and if thereafter no cases of rabies are ever registered, as in the British Isles, then it is good reportable news. Neo-Nazis are not always "on the march again" in Germany; and when a peaceful constitutional order stabilized itself over five decades, as in the Bonn Republic, then it should have been registered (it was infrequently so, and then only grudgingly), even at the expense of losing on occasion a dozen columnal inches of reportage on Bavarian neo-Nazis or Brandenburg skinheads and their ugly hate campaigns against "foreigners." Not every bark and bite, grunt and groan of an interviewed IRA terrorist or Shi'ite kidnapper contributes something new to the public understanding.

Isn't there some virtue in a balanced overview which corrects the distortions of thousands of scraps of bad news? Not if the media is consecrated to some specious formula of (to use the popular American phrase of the day, a formula as mindless as it is ungrammatical) "telling it like it is." A few facts, sometimes even a great many, are being confounded with the whole truth.

This short-tempered impatience with established institutions, flaring up from small irritations to large conclusions, may well be an American habit but if fits suitably into the mood of other national alienations. In one case it emerges as an irascible radicalism; in the other, a world-weary cynicism–as in this dejected rhetorical question asked by an English columnist after having viewed the traditional residence of Great Britain's old Foreign Office, now restored and refurbished. He noted "how the ornate Victorian decoration of this temple to Empire had been repeatedly vandalized," of how the interiors had been scrubbed with pumice because the colors and gilding were deemed vulgar. He was aghast with disbelief at how "everything was hidden behind false ceilings and partition walls." Could there be prospects for a national destiny when the vandals are amongst us?

> How can we rely on the inhabitants to defend Britain's interests around the world, when they can't even be trusted to look after a few painted ceilings and cornices properly? (Joe Joseph, in the *Times*, 14 August 1997, p. 43.)

For want of an imperial cornice all hope was lost. How defeatist can one get?

Adversarial Culture

My second consideration follows on from what has just been said: for the basic aspect of our modern culture, bearing upon it a relationship to the media is that—to use the idea made famous by the late Columbia University literary critic, Lionel Trilling—it is *adversarial*.

The notion of an "adversary culture" has become part of our common vocabulary; and it is an additional factor to those which have been mentioned—the idea of Progress; the loyalty of the ideals of "1789 and all that"; the pride in the early martyrs of heroic liberation struggles—to explain the mood of discontent and disaffection which colors our contemporary temperament. Endemic to our modern culture is "*nay*-saying," never "*yea*-saying." If the balance of truth, dictated by moderation, dispassion, and reason, lies somewhere in the middle, then so much the worse for the middle: it was always a "centre that cannot hold." The New York (and now Washington) publicist Irving Kristol has summed up the American experience, and in citing it I feel confident that its validity extends, *mutatis mutandis*, to most places in Western society (and in other continents which have emulated certain Western patterns and habits, such as India, Japan, etc.).

> It is hardly to be denied that the culture that educates us—the patterns of perception and thought our children absorb in their schools, at every level—is unfriendly (at the least) to the commercial civilisation, the bourgeois civilisation, within which most of us live and work. When we send our sons and daughters to college, we may expect that by the time they are graduated they are likely to have a lower opinion of our social and economic order than when they entered. We know this from opinion poll data; we know from our own experience.
>
> We are used to this fact of our lives, we take it so for granted, that we fail to realise how extraordinary it is. Has there ever been, in all recorded history, a civilisation whose culture was at odds with the values and ideals of that civilisation itself?*

It would take us too far afield to follow this argument all the way to the explanation of the "anti-bourgeois" or anti-Establishment ideology which is the cultural coloration of many (certainly not *all*) sectors of our media. But one caution is worth making, in order to forfend any heated discussion based on misunderstandings. It is *not* uncommon that a culture will be critical of the civilization that sustains it, and always critical of the failure of this civilization to realize perfectly the ideals that it claims as an inspiration. As Kristol points out, "Such criticism is implicit or explicit in Aristophanes and Euripides, in Dante and Shakespeare. But to take an adversary posture towards the ideals them-selves? That is unprecedented."

One need not go so far. There is an impulse in the adversary culture—and it is this which is my concern, and not the secret advocacy of hidden new ideals of some "alternative culture" or ideal society—which can have its stop at the half-way station of nihilism. All social forms and human arrangements must be unmasked; all myths demythologized; all politicians exposed (except a few, very favorite sons, noble warriors in the common cause); and all present policies rejected for their confusions, inconsistencies, and incoherencies.

---

*   Irving Kristol, "The Adversary Culture of Intellectuals," *Encounter* (October 1979), pp. 5-14. See also his stimulating, more recent essay on the "*Counter-Cultures*," *Commentary* (December 1994), pp. 35-39.

One must conclude, after reading the celebrated investigative reporting of the last few decades, that if only society were to be conducted by our intellectual critics, our journalists, our crusading editors, our columnist-pundits, all would suddenly be well—foreign policies would be thoughtful and effective, economic programs would be scientific and realistic, arts policies would lead to a veritable cultural renaissance. Nothing is ever seen as problematic, difficult, recalcitrant.

Implicit in radical negation is the prospect of some easy utopian solution. "Reagan's racism" was responsible for lingering black poverty in the U.S.A.; how easy it would be to make the old Negro ghettos flower in humanism *if only* our ethnic theories would prevail. "Kohl's philistinism" has been responsible for the dull and uninspired role of Germany in the world today; *if only* our "*Kulturkritik*" would take power. "Thatcher's hard-heartedness" and "Major's mediocrity" were responsible for the British industrial decline into unemployment and class strife; *if only* our neo-Keynesian social formula of planned growth would be adopted.

I have now, I believe, roughly summarized a hundred articles in the British press, a thousand editorials in the German and American newspapers, and innumerable hours of television documentaries on all the little milky screens of the electronic world. Mind you, I am not here concerned with the politics, Left or Right, of these matters, only with the mind-set of an adversarial culture which dictates certain attitudes and patterns of judgment. And these are, of course, reflected and enlarged in the customs-and-mores of our newspaper culture. "*Against*" is what we must be. It's the duty of the opposition to oppose.

"Sensations": From Silent Images to Talking Pictures

The controversies over the f-word, in many of its camouflages or orthographic variants, begin of course on the semantic level–its raw, rude reality as it is spoken or written–but remain only briefly there. The argument becomes elevated quickly to one of good taste, or proper morality, or unseemly behavior in-the-presence-of-children, or half-a-dozen other civic or ecclesiastical grounds which emerge to justify outrage, offense, embarrassment, censorship, or diffuse general hostility.

Rarely are the strong feelings clustered about technical standards of style or the writing of good, effective prose. Our liberal ideology which has for so very long attached itself to "free speech" for "the language of common men" also guarantees that cursing and swearing become grave matters of large socio-cultural consideration. Chaucer, Shakespeare and D. H. Lawrence (and the likes of, say, Hubert Selby or James Kelman) have to be defended with the moral passion of the violated human rights of Captain Dreyfus or Sacco and Vanzetti. Unfettered expression was a great and good cause; hence the f-word was a brave flag, and zealous bands of libertarians–quite untroubled, as in our

own day, by uncouth pornographers at the extreme wings–waved it courageously. Prizes were awarded to novels which exceeded hitherto known levels
of obscenity-per-page. But could it be that a thousand cumulative expletives
merely attest to a boring, uninspired sense of diction? Isn't one justified in
suspecting that the mechanical repetitiveness only betrays a pseudo-literate
writer with a poverty-stricken vocabulary? Not at all! Rude literary achievement amounted to a cry of anguish, or a protest against established genteel
euphemisms, or a plea for an alternative sexuality. It as a harbinger of a richer
speaking relationship in a new, different and surely better society.

To enter the plea of seriousness, or of innovation in the cause of high
creativity, is to be exempt from all critical reprisal. In the case of the very latest
"works of art"–say, the celebrated Saatchi collection, exhibited as "*Sensa-
tions*" (London, 1997; New York, 1999)–the local politicians (*viz.*, New York's
Mayor Rudolph Giuliani huffed and puffed–and cut off public funds for the
Brooklyn Museum). In characteristic dissent and protest the intelligentsia–
among them: Susan Sontag, Nadine Gordimer, Arthur Miller, Norman Mailer,
Joan Didion, William Styron, E.L. Doctorow, et al.–rallied to the defense of
Chris Ofili's *Black Madonna*, decorated with porno stick-ons, as well as to
Damien Hirst's stuffed sheep or mummified horses (or whatever). Here is what
one mainline Manhattan art critic wrote about the "lightning rod of the show,"
that is, Ofili's *The Holy Virgin Mary*. The work was eagerly acquired by Saatchi
(in 1996) during one of the professional Westminster pauses from spin politics
when he could tour the "most 'sensational' London studios." (The Saatchi
brothers ran the leading British advertising agency and helped, famously, to
create the political ad campaigns which put the Tories into power in several
national elections.*)

> The work, which has now been placed behind plexiglas, with a velvet rope in front and
> a guard standing by to protect it from any angry viewers, is a perfectly competent
> rendering of a Christian icon–a central figure on a ground of gold. The drawing of an
> African Mary [Ofili is of Nigerian descent] is plausible, but there is no real depth, no
> great feeling in the line. You might pass right by if it were not for Ofili's strategy to

---

*   A spin doctor's medicine is, of course, admirably non-partisan. Reporting from the
British Labour Party conference at the time, the *Sunday Times* recorded that "half of
the 6,000 attendees at Bournemouth were lobbyists and businessmen. Lord Saatchi
was, of course, entertaining in style...."

This appeared to be a distinctly significant change in rhetorical style in a traditional political culture; but reporters often spot a trend when it's only a matter of a
temporary speechwriter's passing mood. Still, these tropes seem to be playing and
playing. At the same Labour Party conference in Bournemouth, Tony Blair (subsequently Prime Minister) was still heard to be "dropping his *aitches*," inserting
conversational "*yer knows*," and "leaving out verbs by the truckload as we get the
full Tony with the sincerely crinkled chin..." (*Sunday Times*, 10 October 1999, p. 20).
Everything, including high styles of art and simulations of low accents, appears to be
calculated. A winning strategy is all.

shove the voltage up by adorning it with a pattern of cutouts from porn mags of women's crotches and then adding to the rhythm of the work with clumps of elephant dung. Interpretations reach too glibly for the symbolism of this Virgin in a cloud of sex parts as an emblem of the sacred's overcoming the profane, of the elephant manure as an African symbol of regeneration that adds lust to Madonna's beneficence. And so it maybe....[2]

The politicos–and, evidently, many agitated Brooklyn viewers–retaliated, as in all such altercations, with accusing fingers. Merely *"competent,"* they cried? Only *"plausible,"* in a Museum which is said to be "one of the finest in the land"? What became of excellence and integrity? As for "regenerating dung" (Ofili's inspired additive to his provocative *Virgin Mary*), would it work as well on a floating figure of Nelson Mandela or of Bishop Tutu, immersed in Plexiglas jars of sea-green (especially treated by the artist) urine, symbolizing the profane's compromise with the sacred on behalf of multicultural beneficences?

Since the contemporary "turning-points" of Andy Warhol, Jasper Johns, and Robert Mapplethorpe, everybody has been coming up with their own brand of soup-cans, national flags, and faded film negatives in outbursts of do-it-yourself artistry. It appeared to some to be an easy kind of knack, quickly mastered by clever young semi-professionals in the two or three generations since the old avant-garde had become the new establishment in our museums, galleries, and auction houses. One New York reviewer suggested in his critique of *"Sensations"* that the perceptive Clement Greenberg already in his own day had detected what was happening; and he put a remark of Greenberg in 1969 as a motto at the head of his piece –

Today everybody innovates. Deliberately, methodically. And the innovations are deliberately and methodically made startling. Only it now turns out not to be true that all startling art is necessarily innovative or new art.... It has become apparent that art can have a startling impact without really being or saying anything startling–or new. The character itself of being startling, spectacular, or upsetting has become conventionalized, part of safe good taste.[3]

Part-time artistry or not, the jocularity helped to overlook that serious money–and therefore some kind of makeshift aesthetic commitment to its cash value–was involved in the sale of such works. Shortly thereafter there was indeed a Sotheby auction of a painting by one of the Saatchi/*Sensations* stars. A newspaper story added gossip about a personal feud between artist and owner, and so the item almost made its extravagant estimate of £200,000.

"CHEF'S £200,000 PAINTING ROW SET TO BOIL OVER"

The story (with colored illustrations) narrated details of a nasty personal and legal quarrel between Damien Hirst and his former friend, a celebrated

London chef (Marco Pierre White) who–in an act of solidarity with a "new trend" in contemporary art–paid the artist vast sums to exhibit several "authentic Damien Hirsts" in his West End restaurants. Several of Hirst's controversial "spot" paintings were involved (*viz.*, a toilet's medicine-chest full of surgical instruments, a cow's head submerged in formaldehyde). As White testified, "Customers didn't like his art so I got rid of it."

This English reaction contrasts sharply to the dictum of an American juror who justified his vote in the Mapplethorpe obscenity trial; he said he didn't like the "offensive" photographs in question but "If people say it's art, then I have to go along with it." Curious, this transvaluation of values–in England, the familiar common man's maxim ("*...but I know what I like*") came to prevail while in the U.S.A. a class-colored deference of old Anglo-Saxon snobbish provenance protected elitarian wilfulness. In any case, whether meekly accepted as high art by the popular masses of uncertain taste or bitterly deemed distasteful and unsuitable for the walls of fine restaurants, the Hirst painting was sold for £177,000 at Sotheby's in London. The sale occurred on the evening of 9 December 1999, only a month or two after the "*Sensations*" exhibit had opened at the Brooklyn Museum in New York City.[4]

Needless to say, the lingering smell of scandal which inevitably attached itself to the controversy of Ofili's use of dung in his canvases only helped the commercial value of his work. In New York auctions of contemporary arts during May 2001–in which other paintings favored by Charles Saatchi failed to sell, including Damien Hirst's stainless-steel cabinet with surgical instruments, Gary Hume's *Four Colored Doors*–a 1997 elephant-dung painting by Ofili sold for $211,500. One Art Sales reporter described it as "glittering," which suggests that the dung had been especially treated and that the additives evidently were capable of being organically dissolved in order to produce an element of iridescence.[5]

By this time the Brooklyn polemics about the sacrilegious character of dung on a painting of a religious theme had relaxed and had taken on another extra-cultural African significance. It was not only the rarity and the quality of the elephantine excrement which could be argued in Ofili's favor. The fact is that in many African communities to use turds to write a welcoming word of greeting or congratulation is to give a heartfelt gesture of tribal affection. I myself have seen such a one; and even if it didn't "glitter," its color and calligraphy were impressive. Michael Palin, a famed roving reporter, was so greeted in South Africa when he returned, after a long absence, to visit a Soweto family he had known in London. The scene formed a touching climax to his widely shown travelogue film (*BBC World*, May 2000). I would have been interested to have had a "faecal footnote" which indicated the source of the ingredients so traditionally employed (elephantine, b—s—, whatever). Alas, no further information happened to be available.

Time's critic and the intellectual cohort was reflecting established opinion, since a New York poll suggested that the Mayor's opposition had gone "too far" and that "art" (if it was art) "should be free." In the absence of the redoubtable Robert Hughes* who was *Time*'s arbiter of modern taste (ever since his classic work *The Shock of the New*, 1980) we were only offered familiar old apologies, e.g., that "work once seen as scandalous takes on new meaning as culture is rocked by alien, disquieting expressions and then slowly evolves...." Evolves, presumably, to the next alien, scandalous work. Its impressive competence, crowned with slender plausibility, would always warrant "respect"...unless one were to choose, inexplicably, to remain behind with the rear-guard...forever longing for *objets d'art* of a kind and character which no new, young, restless spirit, relentlessly confronting the world's realities in his studio, is ever prepared to offer. Could the zeitgeist allow it? Hardly likely. Not via his private patrons and avid collectors who are convinced they *know* the pattern of evolution–and not via a curator of any great public museum who is selflessly dedicated to new works as they rock on to take on their new meanings. Not even in Brooklyn.

In Manhattan the director of the Metropolitan Museum of Art, Philippe de Montebello, made a singular effort to restore the city's raging controversy to an aesthetic level. What of the "relative merits" of the Saatchi collection as Art–and not, as he waspishly put it, as "a meaningful challenge to the turpitude of quotidian existence"? He was, for one, on the side of the mayor and his "astute critical acumen." But the bureaucratic effort at censorship was regrettable; for it gave undue notoriety to artists who deserve to be obscure or to be forgotten. A politician should not have used his official power to cut the Brooklyn Museum's public funding and to dismiss its Board. Nevertheless, at least one voice among the thirty cultural institutions of New York which had joined the protest went on from the issues of constitutional law–crudely put: Can majority-taxpayer's money be used to finance minority-taste culture?–to the heart of the matter which had so "rocked" the newspaper culture.

> In the end [wrote Philippe de Montebello], what remains terribly disturbing to me is that so many people, serious and sensitive individuals, are so cowed by the art establishment or so frightened at being labeled Philistines that they dare not speak out and express their dislike for works that they find either repulsive or unaesthetic or both.[6]

---

* Alas, Hughes was "indisposed in Australia," and unable to do *Time*'s stint. He was still badly injured after a near-fatal automobile accident which left him in a month-long coma (with, as he tells it, Goya-esque nightmares, which might conceivably influence the on-going debate one way or another). See: Robert Hughes, "In Death's Throat," *Time*, 11 October 1999, pp. 137-38. Such "accidents" sometimes play a significant role in the formation of public opinion: by-lines are important and persuasive.

One conservative political columnist of the *New York Times*, William Safire, hastened to underline the gravity of the dilemma in which freedom of expression is right but public payment for it is not an entitlement. For is not all civic spending "accountable" to the people and its elected representatives?

Believers in the unfettered right of expression–they constitute nowadays a broader front than artists representing their cult of erotic expressionism–are forever trying "to drive the yahoos from the temple." If the public museums, as Safire warned, win in the high federal courts (as well they might), if they insist on "the right to offend egregiously"–which is to say, without being punished by losing their subsidies–then…they will surely lose their subsidies beforehand.

The likely end result? If the contemporary art world is not absolutely, irredeemably enslaved by Mammon–or that part of his gold which is dispensed in public subsidies–then the "Sensations" of the Art World will be going entirely private. Governments are stingy; but our billionaires are richer, and indeed rather more generous. Safire's nightmare will be, in the future, commercially sponsored:

> Let's assume the curator of the National Gallery in Washington came up with a show called "Outrage." It featured a statue of Moses wearing a Nazi swastika on his chest, a painting of a violent Reverend Martin Luther King, Jr. forcing Elizabeth Cady Stanton into submission, and an avant-garde collage of the cutest puppy you ever saw being tortured to death by a sadistic homosexual….

In the spirit of Mort Sahl, Safire contends that there's nobody now he hasn't offended. It will be quite enough to round out the usual rumpus, even if a few elements are conspicuous by their absence.

For one, he's overlooked the defecatory dopesters, and their vested interest in the excremental market. Without sympathetic public support the artist's steady guaranteed supply, whether zoo-fresh or deep-frozen, is not likely to be stable or inflation free.

For another, the spirit of the zeitgeist is missed out; and that strict determinant of all worldly things includes the inevitable conspiratorial element in every sinister development. Newspapers for several generations now have been rife with the rumor that "modern art"–praised for its Picasso brilliance, denigrated for its Pollock foot-work–has been (mostly) a manipulated affair, foisted upon the gullible, impressionable public, by hidden hands which are pulling strings and making money. Here, too, the scoop never fails to turn up:

MAYOR OF NEW YORK
SMELLS AN ARTISTIC RAT

The local correspondent of the London *Times* "told all" under this headline to the effect that "there is a more sinister plot involving the museum, its

sponsor, Christie's auction house, and the collection's owner, Charles Saatchi."
If true, the argument over *Sensations* will have its day in court and at the
moment looks like "developing into an epic clash between a former Mafia-
prosecutor (Mayor Giuliani) and the London ad-man (Saatchi)." Was there, in
point of fact, an art-world conspiracy to boost the value of the Saatchi collection and indeed to drive up prices at future auctions of his sensations of choice?
Did he contribute a large donation to the Museum on a "commercial" understanding? Denials all along the line...for conspiracies are by their very nature
hard to pin down. Patrons as well as auctioneers insist that everybody was in it
just for the art, and sensations are what you get when you're trying to champion talented new artists.

Now, which part of the ubiquitous zeitgeist do you want to run with?...that
all social progress and cultural innovation features "the shock of the new"?
Or: that it's all a put-up job? Adversarial culture clashes will in certain heated
moments seek out semantics that will give one side or another some advantage
in the rough-and-tumble of the contest. Even art critics and museum directors
have been known to lose their cool.

A Brooklyn Museum curator was strangely casual about it all when he was
quoted as saying smirkily, "Dung happens." No, it doesn't any more. In a
globalized economy, it has to be planned, or managed, or cornered, or bought
among the market's futures at some risk.[7]

The respect for which the *Time* critic called is, at any rate, a grudging one in
the case of Damien Hirst who has been vilified by animal-rights groups in
London and New York for his sculptures incorporating dead animals sliced
down their middle (or sideways) and displayed in all their "forensic grimness"
inside formaldehyde-filled cases. The famous piece which first earned him
notoriety was also among Saatchi's "*Sensations*" exhibited in Brooklyn. Its
vitrine was still full of maggots and flies that swarmed over the bloodied head
of a cow.

At this point in Brooklyn the quest for meaning began anew. But our newspaper art critics usually write of this in the standard journalistic staccato which
assigns meaningfulness to works of art–as well as to other literary events and
other cultural happenings–by recycling earnest bits of the vocabulary of aesthetics or of philosophy and coming up with...well, "meaningfulness." It appears to be a high-minded justification for grimly spirited hi-jinks that can be
played by the numbers.

Consider Rachel Whiteread, another artist among "*Sensations*," who produces objects which are "eerie, elegant, and refined" (which means, in translation, no offal, no snapshots of genitals, and the like). In effect they constitute
"a tranquil hymn to loss and absence." Domestic items like a plaster cast of a
room or the underside of a humble chair "evoke the sense of departed souls
who once sat among us." I once saw in Vienna Ms. Whiteread's display of
plastic casts of nameless volumes which were the stand-ins of humble prayer-

books of pious Jews...and they were supposed to be evoking, in a Holocaust memorial, the sense of departed souls who etc. etc.

In the case of the latest "sensational" work of Ms. Rachel Whiteread, the extravagant press reaction to her subsequent private exhibition–in London's Serpentine Gallery (June 2001) of "Unseen Voids"–almost established her as "the most important British sculptor of her generation." A good deal of fashionable gobbledygook managed effectively to camouflage the insular element of chauvinistic exaggeration–after all, the passing of Henry Moore left a huge gap in the nation's artistic pride. It won't be filled by the sheer obscurantism which is still coming out of "Pseud's Corner."

If art–as we are instructed–is a form of memory and, in painting, the passing forms of life and thought are fixed in pigment, then Ms. Whiteread's sculptures immortalize space that had previously been invisible or neglected...under floors, inside beds, within walls. But rather than modelling or carving them, she makes casts. These are supposed to make solid the voids that are "underneath" the floor or "behind" the bookshelf...and all of which, as one critic wrote, makes them "spectral" and "touching." This is rather far away from the "witty points" that were being made by Claes Oldenburg with his soft telephones and hard hamburgers. Here, in Ms. Whiteread's first work in the Serpentine–the cast of a floor in iron–you should always be conscious of the object from which it was cast ("the ridges being the indentations in the original"). It might have been about "weight and mass"; but no, it is about "absence," namely about "the phantom of the vanished floor from which it was cast." Also about the marks from the surface of the stairs (in the massive *Untitled [Upstairs]*). Finally: the bookshelf-casts reveal the leftover pastel-colored marks from the books' covers and pages....

And so back to her Holocaust Memorial which she made for the Juden-Platz in Vienna. The art critic of the *Daily Telegraph* had his enthusiasm slightly dampened by its "slick, polished finish." His remarkable phrase for a work which he concedes "has gone wrong" is: "*a qualified success.*" This is, I suspect, a euphemism for an "*unqualified failure.*" Words fail all of us, art even more so. The books, holy to a murdered people, are pale, vague, and indifferent. The temple which houses them is smooth and colorless. The memory of the Holocaust and its associated sentiments is absent, invisible, forgotten without a mark or trace. Except in a programmatic note–on the floors; on the steps; on the walls!–which reminds of Auschwitz, Buchenwald, and all the other death camps, in alphabetical order. There is no sense in sensations.[8]

The interpretations are interchangeable, and one item–say, "the variously colored blocks shining softly under a skylight like a plot of grave markers"–can serve for sacred literary texts in Austria and eerie steles in Germany where they were enlisted to compete with another Holocaust sculptor's thousand grave-markers in a Berlin "garden of remembrance." But, oh yes, Hirst's number with maggots and flies: "It's [writes S.H. Madoff in *Time*] a little pocket of hell: nauseating, unerringly brutal, but its shock looks death terribly in the face. Not silly, not shallow, not shock for shock's sake." Other critics differ– and the parrying thrust says: *not* serious, not thoughtful, not art for art's sake. Perhaps art for the sake of...*sensations*? Still, one American defender of such cynical sensationalism could not evade the basic questions (and he put them without providing any answers): "Should the largesse of public funding be allowed to circumscribe free speech? Can unhindered expression, in its turn, become sheer offense? And how ironclad are the constitutional protections for edgy art that may amount to hate speech?..."

Art News and New Art

New York defenders of the London sensations avoided most of these issues raised in the stormy media debates.*

Nor was it a matter of Anglo-American cultural solidarity (didn't *we* defend Joyce and Lawrence and Oscar Wilde?). For, obviously, any Manhattan curator or resident gallerist could put together from the current or recent efforts in bohemian So-Ho studios a similar collection (at least as pertinent as Safire's proposed "*Outrage*," above). What if it were to confirm that contemporary artists had become so alienated from a repellent established society as to be creatively obsessed with hate symbols, *e.g.* fiery crosses from the KKK, even more crooked swastikas from the neo-Nazis? Can works hanging on straight painted walls, even with disagreeable substances stuck on and little smutty cuttings attached, ever constitute Mr. Justice Holmes' "a clear and present danger" calling out for public intervention?

A native collection of New York sensations would, I surmise, feature perhaps a little less manure, a little more passed waters. Scatological imagery changes from place to place, even if the basics necessarily remain the same. One would expect a little less Jesus-bashing and, possibly, an uncontrollable obsession or two with Mahomet and his Islamic sheriffs (in the robust spirit of Salman Rushdie). Or an innovative spiritual turn to confronting the ten thousand faces of Buddha. At any event and in any case, the fundamentalists of modern art are unwaveringly persuaded that, as in the headline in the *New York Times* –

---

*   The international press also preferred to "evade issues"; making jokes was more agreeable. In the London *Sunday Times*, Jeremy Clarkson discussed the new post of Mayor of London (now filled by unpredictable Ken Livingstone) and cracked: "...I suppose like the Mayor of New York he could try to stop Damien Hirst from hanging a pig's testicles in an art gallery but this is hardly a full-time job...." (*Sunday Times*, 10 October 1999, p. 19).

CONTEMPORARY ART SENDS
A MESSAGE WORTH HEARING

How could it not? What would be the criteria for judging a message vapid…or puerile…and not worth listening to or looking at? For Glenn D. Lowry, the director of the Museum of Modern Art in New York, the worthiness is built in, and its cultural importance is a given quite by definition. Lowry writes in the *Times* as if we were all ensconced at the turn of an old century with nudes on all sides descending staircases –

> Innovation in the arts occurs by pushing the boundaries of aesthetic and social norms, by reconfiguring what we see and know. Monet and Cezanne did this, as did Picasso and Pollock. I would argue that many others are continuing to do it today.

The question is circuitously resolved by the old metropolitan habit of answering a question with a question:

> What is it about society [Lowry writes] that makes so many of us intolerant of contemporary art? Why are we so quick to condemn that which we do not understand, to dismiss that which forces us to confront disturbing issues?

The studio slipper should sometimes be on the other foot. What is it about contemporary art that makes so many artists intolerant of any and all values in a multivalent society which they do not understand or respect? Why are they so quick to break up norms and boundaries in order to make a sensation, to outrage and scandalize, or otherwise disturb? Shouldn't respect be a matter of reciprocity?

> Many of the artists whose work has recently been attacked deserve our respect. They may not be welcome at every museum in New York, but they should be. Their work is serious, thoughtful and daring, and time will tell if it is also enduring.

Its durability might well come to depend on several non-aesthetic factors, namely on the vaporization rates of formaldehyde in open jars or the decomposition of dung (and its smell-by date).

The mayor had originally taken the high ground that the art of "sensations" could not and should not be supported by public money for it was taken to be "offensive" and "sacrilegious." The follow-up argument, based on financial material which had been dug up by *New York Times* reporters, had put the Brooklyn Museum in a rather more shady light. The money that had exchanged hands was, perhaps, unusual, and possibly unethical. But Judge Nina Gerson in the U.S. District Court in Brooklyn was single-mindedly concerned with guaranteed constitutional freedoms under the First Amendment; and she was positively Jeffersonian when she cited a long line of legal precedents that forbade public officials to use their control of government funds to punish unpopular or offensive speech. These were old quarrels, and in our own time legislators had vainly tried to deny film licenses to motion pictures thought to be sacrilegious. Ofili's dung-decorated Madonna may have gone "too far" in one heretical or blasphemous direction; but, on the other hand, the Museum was full of paintings rich in Christian piety and orthodox reverence. The judge was adamant on this issue, and the lady was not for turning. As she wrote in the decision that spelled defeat for the mayor, "if anything, it is the mayor and the city who by their actions have threatened the neutrality required of government in the sphere of religion."[9] Perhaps Rudy Giuliani, a Roman Catholic, had been badly advised to base his case on the sensitivities of a minority religious group…where the silent secular majority had long cultivated an indifference to the issues of theological divisiveness.

"There is no federal constitutional issue more grave," the judge wrote in her thirty-eight-page decision, "than the effort by government officials to censor works of expression and to threaten the vitality of a major cultural institution as punishment for failing to abide by governmental demands for orthodoxy."

Where were the demands? What was the orthodoxy? Many New Yorkers had yawned at the plethora of sophomoric works of insipid expression. They only exhibited the lifeless non-vitality of major cultural institutions which were failing to exercise the aesthetic demands for intellectual coherence and mature critical acumen. But where was the law against bad art? Who was still around to want to remove nasty pictures from a museum wall? Certainly not Judge Nina Gerson. Her judgment in the dispute made the front page of the *New York Times*, and in the elegant old pyramid of its one-column headline it told the whole story of a famous victory:

GIULIANI ORDERED
TO RESTORE FUNDS
FOR ART MUSEUM
First Amendment Cited

Ruling Says That Mayor Must
Stop Pursuing Eviction –
City Planning to Appeal

The *New York Times* was, within its well-known limits, behaving impeccably. On the Sunday before the judge's decision (on the Monday) it had published more evidence than the mayor had been aware of that the financing of the Brooklyn Museum's exhibition was distinctly irregular. Companies and individuals with a direct commercial interest in the works of the young British artists in the exhibition had contributed substantial sums of money "to get the show on the road." Saatchi himself had pledged $160,000 (and it was concealed from the public); the auction-house, Christie's, chipped in $50,000. Museum officials had solicited hundreds of thousands of dollars in other donations. David Bowie, the pop star, topped up the kitty "substantially" (his Internet company was awarded the right to display "*Sensations*").

The muckraking came a few hours too late. The judge had already written her long piece of prose, and she wouldn't postpone her judgment. On the Tuesday the mayor accused her of "rushing to issue her ruling…to block lawyers from fully investigating the finances…." Whereupon the Museum's lawyer counterattacked by charging that "if he [the mayor] were in England he would be in prison tonight for contempt of court…." By Wednesday it was all too late.

Was it always so? Bad art makes for bad law and even worse controversy. Even the journalism entangles itself in large issues which cannot be resolved in the rush to make a deadline. The *Times'* arts reporter (Michael Kimmelman), as the curtain rang down on the story, delivered a final word of Solomonic judgement which was as wise as it was indecisive. "IN THE END," as his headline pronounced, "'SENSATIONS' IS LESS THE ART THAN THE MONEY."

> What Brooklyn did by soliciting money from people with direct financial involvement in the works of the exhibition was at the dubious extreme of museum practice, if it wasn't unethical, and it certainly makes a very bad impression by creating the image that Brooklyn is for sale. The museum was additionally foolish to have dissembled about the financing.

Yet, on the other hand, this is the way things are, for

> This is a capitalist country. Museums must depend on private support, and private contributors have their own interests….The problem stems from the puritanical American supposition that culture is pure and money is corrupt….But this isn't an ideal world.

Newspapers, alas, take a shorter perspective, assuming that an item of news must thereby be new.[10]

To be sure, newspaper journalists–even in the finest of feature pages–are not generally called upon to explore the intellectual presuppositions at the root of their critical judgements. A review is a review is a review. But sometimes large implications peep out of daily stints that cover what is new in the arts, and the reviewer of an exhibition of paintings in Brooklyn may not, if one probes long enough, be exactly in the same aesthetico-metaphysical camp as the reporter who is writing about the première of Busoni's *Doktor Faust* at the Metropolitan Opera. The "revival" (as a new production of an older work is curiously called) was appreciated and indeed welcomed by a *Times* critic, even though it was offering "painful truths"–among which were the tragic inadequacy of utopian "Faustian" aspirations and the importance of received tradition. As the perceptive Edward Rothstein concisely remarked in the *New*

York Times, hinting at his deviance from the conventional correctness of the Manhattan establishment: "But the novelty of novelty has started to wear thin." Should this precept spread from the halls of music to the art galleries of museums, small fortunes in the cash value of novel and innovative art objects would be wiped off the current market prices.

> Busoni's opera is a solemn rebuke, a declaration…that a tradition provides the foundation for future innovation. This might seem a stodgy, old-fashioned response to the avant-gardist demands of artistic revolution. But it remains as vital as the forces opposing it.

Going on about "the tradition thing" too long may mean civil war among the forward-looking Faustians and the stuffy anti-Faustians writing in Times Square.[11]

The images of sensational art have spoken for themselves, but their so-called obscenity up until very recently was curiously wordless. Titles of pictures or sculptures or installations have been conventionally classical, ranging from modest labels ("Landscape," "Portrait of My Mother") to a witty or vague allusiveness ("The Pillars of Society"). What profanation there occurred was in the image or the idea, not the word. Art critics, whether *pro* or *contra*, could safely vent their reactions in family newspapers, without having to refer to works officially identified with four-letter words. If the avant-garde taboo-breaking artists were content to make their statements with ingredients like *urine* or with *dung*, so be it. These were not cowardly circumlocutions, but in point of lexical fact accurate, the real thing. The controversial and sensational breakthrough was optical, not verbal. This isolationist mind-set or particularist art-set was unnatural and of short duration. Some strong or complex works almost cried out for a clue. We have already seen the breakaway aesthetic faction devoted to the art of *piss*--flowers. And I suspect I have missed one or two Chelsea or SoHo shows which suggested why *turds*, by their very shape and color, really belonged to the realist representation of a fruity *nature morte*.

After the brouhaha in Manhattan and Brooklyn over the Saatchi *Sensations*…the dogs kept on barking…and the caravan moved on. In this case: back to London, and to the sources of renewal and innovation. What we needed obviously was a new interaction between word and image, a move forward from mere artistic profanation in order to reinforce the literary profanity which was all the rage. Art would move beyond color and paint and pattern (and even, see above, smell) It would, at long last, be linked to the matching vocabulary which would give a sound-track to the hitherto silent perception of sensational truth-telling. Back in London, Saatchi and the Royal Academy led the way…as a pace-making avant-garde properly should. After the sacramental symbols of formal religion, we have the fresh targets of secular themes–from flags of patriotism to national memorials or to the life-and-death customs which have arrogated to themselves the hushed respect and immunities of the sacrosanct.

We are about to move from Golgotha to Auschwitz. The Saatchi collection is progressing from the virtual virginity of deviant Madonnas to visible and pronounceable obscenities of the Holocaust. What was once considered low language can be used to point up high art. The first to come with the good news was the *Sunday Telegraph* whose Arts Correspondent (6 February 2000) reported –

SAATCHI BUYS HELL ON EARTH
Royal Academy to show apocalyptic vision featuring Nazis

The vision was said to be (few at the time had yet seen it) a giant sculpture of hell. It featured an effigy–just to be topical–of the physically challenged Professor Stephen Hawking…not old Albert Einstein, a Jew…among a writhing mass of Nazis and Hell's Angels. It was intended to fill an entire gallery in the Royal Academy on Piccadilly, and it was called, following an ingenious verbal trick devised by the playwright Mark Ravenhill, "F****** Hell." Covering some twenty-eight square feet, it was the culmination of several years' work by the artists Jake (thirty-three) and Dinos Chapman (thirty-eight), and is made up of thousands of figures in various stages of decomposition and mutilation. Needless to say, it has already been sold "to the art collector and advertisement mogul Charles Saatchi," and at £500,000 now forms the most expensive piece in his collection: "'This is a killer piece–literally,' said Mr. Saatchi." And with characteristic generosity he is lending the piece to the gallery for a forthcoming exhibition. The art-critical voices in the community were prompt in their encomia. One of the curators of the show, Max Wigram, pronounced: "*F****** Hell* is a beautifully made intelligent work, which has all the fantastical qualities of Hieronymous Bosch. It may well turn out to be one of the most important pieces of sculpture of this era." It was not less important because the tableau was born of a dream–Freud reinforcing Hawking–that one of the brother artists had one night. As Dinos Chapman explained the aesthetico-neurotico-nocturnal inspiration: "One's subconscious is populated by people you've murdered. Everybody dreams of destroying surrounding people." Whether this homicidal message was the one that attracted Saatchi can only be surmised. The various sections of the sculpture (nine in all) are vivid enough. A volcano spews out Nazis who are savaged in unspeakable fashion by grotesquely mutilated humans. A model of Auschwitz concentration camp is complete with gas chambers and people being shovelled into ovens. But another section is modelled "like the Parthenon"…surrounded by trees upon which bodies have been skewered. According to the newspaper report, "the most repellent" section is "The Pit of Death" which the artist wanted to be "like a Bacchanalian orgy of flesh."[12]

What repels can also educate. The man who brokered the deal to sell the work to Charles Saatchi, a Mr. Jay Jopling, ventured the opinion that "this piece is an unbelievable opus"–which, in his verbal insensitivity, put him at risk of being an unbeliever, even a culpable Holocaust-denier (a crime in post-Hitler Germany).*

At any rate,"*F****** Hell*" is at the very least our prize example of *participatory obscenity*–I am not sure whether the asterisks were the idea of the newspaper editors or of the Chapmans, or whether they and the Royal Academy curators will go all the way, will indeed come clean in the exhibition's official catalogue. At best it is participatory genocide, or a do-it-yourself atrocity. Doesn't everybody dream of murdering everybody?

American novels and crime stories, especially their Hollywood film versions, almost always cause similar difficulties for certain "poets of profanity"– Elmore Leonard, Quentin Tarantino, et al. They are rendered in a vernacular allusiveness which is artificial, arbitrary, and consistently wide of the mark– anatomically, sexually, or otherwise (with the freaking f-word usually becoming excremental).

Of Nihilism and Mendacity

Some go on from there, go as far as one could go—even further, and without the ultimate limit (wise and witty, as surrealistically propounded by Jean Cocteau) of knowing how "too far" one should go. The penchant for limitlessness, as so many philosophers of history and politics have been aware, can be the prelude to decadence and decline.

The surprise is that one of the most extreme formulations of the dictum, as applied to jour-nalism, should have come from England which has for centuries prided itself on the civilized restraints of a moderate political culture. I refer to the editorial injunction to the journalists of noth-ing less august and establishmentarian than the *Times*: "Find out why the lying bastards are lying!" This is the famous phrase of an editor of the *Times*, Louis Heren, who received it as "advice given him early in his career by...a correspondent of the *Daily Worker* [the Communist daily in London]: 'Always ask yourself why these lying bastards are lying to you.'" (And in his recent obituaries, reviewing his life and career, it was much quoted as a classic newspaper

---

*   As for the obscenity in the title, *Die Welt* referred to it in the original English. In the newspaper's standard German orthography it comes out as "*F...Hell*," *i.e.* with dots or periods, known as *full stops*, and one doesn't usually count them. The approximate translation is helpfully added: "*auf deutsch etwa 'Scheiss-Hölle'.*" This is an inadequate but inevitable translation, given the fact that the *F*-word and the s-word have different specific gravities in Anglo-German translations of coarse slang.

precept).*[13] Heren was for many years the deputy editor of the *Times*; but born as he was in London's East End, on the "other side of the tracks," he rarely reflected establishment values. He was an emotional, impassioned journalist, and often gave way to his prejudices with cockney self-assurance. He loved Singapore, and we once fell out when I declined to publish his piece of commissioned reportage in *Encounter* as being conspicuously uncritical of the dic-tatorial ways of the charming and brilliant Singapore patriarch, Mr. Lee Kuan Yew, of whom he was fond.

He also had another pet hatred: the postwar Germans. The prejudice was flagrant although, or perhaps *because*–as I once was so careless to taunt him, these psychic turnabouts occurring so often in ex-Teutonic families–he had a maternal grandfather who was a German. I was on occasion rudely critical of his dispatches to the *Times* from Bonn in the 1950s. One textbook example of bias I give from memory.

We had been sitting together in the Press Balcony of the *Bundestag* in the early years of the Konrad Adenauer administration, listening to the *Kanzler* give a defense of the new military pro-NATO policy he had promised to Western Allies to pursue. In the story which Louis Heren then wired to the *Times*, his "lead," the opening paragraph, ran something like this: With the obtuseness and confusion that have marked Dr. Adenauer's recent performances, the chancellor yesterday in a speech to the *Bundestag* stuttered his way to a new crisis in his shaky coalition.... etc., etc.

I was there, as I say; and I was aware that Dr. Adenauer (then in his eighties) had slipped up momentarily in turning the pages of his prepared parliamentary text; I saw, and heard, nothing more than that. *Der Kanzler* was, otherwise, his usual self-assured sovereign self; and the vote of confidence after the debate went, as ex-pected, his triumphant way. From the *Times* one could not learn how pleased the NATO Alliance was to be strengthened decisively in this "shaky" manner. (Ultimately, forty years later, it tipped the balance for a re-united Germany and the end of the Cold War as we had known it for forty years.)

This is not the place to unravel the pattern of prejudice which might explain why one "lying bastard" (if all were lying, who exempted us journalists?) was being economical with the truth. Which in his own eyes, and evidently those of his editors, he was not. Apart from the corruptibles and the

---

*   The former editor of *The Times*, William Rees-Mogg (under whom Louis Heren was deputy-editor) pays handsome tribute to "a great correspondent" who served in Bonn and Washington and Malaya, "angering Chancellor Adenauer and General Templer [the British commander in the Malay emergency] about equally."

But he got on famously with President Lyndon B. Johnson who also had his pet hatreds, e.g. "the Georgetown intellectuals." As Rees-Mogg notes in *The Times* (30 January 1995), .".Louis did not live in Georgetown and he did not see himself as an intellectual." Hence some prevaricating politicians get to be exempted.

ignoramuses, professional journalists only play fast and loose with a story–its facts, its deeper meaning–when the committed truths they were serving are adversarial.

The classic example—apart from the case of the premeditated misreporting of the Soviet Union in the 1920s and 1930s, famously exposed by Malcolm Muggeridge and Eugene Lyons in their muckraking journalistic memoirs—is the Vietnam War. The distortions of the American and the British press are by now well documented. I myself published one journalist's eyewitness critique of his colleagues in Saigon's foreign press corps, the revealing memoir by Robert S. Elegant in *Encounter* (to which I will return in volume 3). Subsequently, a handful of chastened journalists have conceded, in remarkable self-criticisms, the error of their ways. Stanley Karnow, author of a standard U.S. history of the Vietnam War, once asked himself bemusedly why he had trusted Saigon sources that were so obviously "agents of influence," peddling Hanoi-inspired stories. Julian Pettifer, the British war correspondent for ITV, puzzled embarrassedly over the question of why, and how, he had persuaded himself to "report what was obviously not so."[14]

My point should not get lost in the polemical mood of *tu quoque*. There will always be a virtual class struggle between regimes in power and an independent press, between established authorities in war or peace and inquiring reporters buzzing around as gadflies-of-the-state. But, alas, few on either side retreat from their fixed positions in the crossfire of mutual recriminations. Mendacity seems always to be on the other side of the trenches.

So it is no surprise (to return to our original theme) that a recent headline in the *Guardian* (8 February 1995) insisted:

"NO MERCY FOR LYING BASTARDS"

This was the short message that John Mortimer, Q.C., eminent lawyer and playwright, was eager to get across "in the spirit of the late Louis Heren." It was also a reply to the argument of the head of the BBC, John Birt, who had acknowledged that both his TV- and radio interviewers, as well as the inquisitors for the print press, were "too hard" on politicians:

> Interviewers [in the Birt thesis which infuriated Mortimer] sneer at politicians, subject them to disorienting opening questions and fail to listen; the conse-quence is that our political masters are seen as behaving badly and earn, unfairly,...the nation's distaste.

Nothing, in Mortimer's judgment, could be further from the case. He invoked the whole Western tradition in rebuttal, and also his own personal sharp-shooting experience. Had not Socrates advanced philosophy by tirelessly asking awkward questions? And had not he him-self, i.e. John Mortimer, a successful Queen's Counsel, proved himself triumphant in so many courtrooms by relentlessly, even monotonously, pressing his partisan point? "Restraint" was not the word for his style of cross-examination. Being fair and just and ob-jective was not on the legal agenda.

No matter that, in the end—in sharp contrast to the opinionated editorial page or the probing political broadcast—the gladiatorial contest in the court-room trial concludes definitively, in a decision which should be an approximation of justice and juridical ethics. For the adversarial lawyer, as for the partisan journalist, scoring and winning may not be everything in life, but what else is there?

Well, for one thing there is fun and entertainment. Can that be the exclusive brief for the television medium? Journalists, as Mortimer insists, should be single-mindedly occupied in the exposing of sleaze and incompetence. If making fun of politicians and squeezing entertainment out of public scandals and embarrassment in all the highest places is part of the assignment, so be it. Society is failing humankind—and "anything goes" to make the point. Lawyer Mortimer's summing-up is worthy of the playwright's eloquence:

> There are many serious and important things in life, love, happiness and art. There are great political issues of justice, secure employment and proper education, the relief of poverty and the sensible approach to crime. While none of these great problems are being addressed, it is only possible, much to Mr Birt's sadness and regret, for us to regard politics as part of light entertainment. Any deeper significance it may have seems to me to be provided mainly by the journalists.

If only we could be sure that the journalists, unlike the politicians, were not "lying bastards," that they were (if a little on the unrestrained side) always advocates of demonstrable truths! If only the world of radical criticism were conspicuously marked by probity rather than sleaze, by enviable workaday virtues rather than incompetence!

Given the suspicion, if not the certainty, that all are "lying bastards," then it is an illegitimate system of total mendacity that we have to be dealing with; and, consequently, the unmasking of the sleaze, the incompetence, and the sheer indifference to urgent human needs, must necessarily be of a far-reaching magnitude. So we are told: It just will not do to take on a bit of muckraking here and there—the wholeness of the evil (and the struggle against it) must be confronted. We must all be revolutionaries now.

One or another of these views I put, with fair regularity, before editors and journalists at international conferences throughout the 1970s and 1980s. I am afraid such interventions had little persuasive effect, and I remained in a misunderstood minority. My criticism of the Western intelligentsia earned me the sobriquet "anti-intellectual" (from no less than the editor of the *Economist*, then Donald Tyerman, formerly an editor of the *Times*). The general argument was narrowly interpreted as some sort of patriotic or conservative defense of the status quo in America and Western Europe which would in effect only serve to bolster a species of Cold War ideology–but, in the end, it would stifle the free press which could only fulfill its liberal Jeffersonian duty by being relentlessly critical. Yet how could democracy under challenge defend itself with any self-confidence if it appeared every day, after the morning editions (and especially after the evening news), to be a worthless thing of shreds-and-patches?

The Cold War ended, and the "parameters" or the "paradigms" of our climate of opinion changed radically. I take it that the message I have been trying to convey has now become conventional wisdom. The ombudsman of the *Washington Post* is the guardian of the paper's precious values, defender of ethical standards, incorruptible judge of journalistic malpractice. In that capacity Geneva Overholser warned (in July 1996) the professional apostles of bad news of the large and sensational errors of their ways. They were so eager to spot when things go wrong, and so pleased when the exceptional ("a defining characteristic of the news") turns out to be alarmingly negative. A newspaper editor's news-judgment may be, from case to case, impeccably professional; but Overholser suspects that all this "will hardly give readers an accurate view of what is going on around them."

What, there is an alternative?–positive stories?–uplift with namby-pamby do-gooders? Well, yes. "The press doesn't tell nearly enough substantial stories about things that work, innovations, citizens who act, problems that are solved." One gets the impression that it took a whole generation, calculated in the old way (thirty-three years or so), to emerge from a hard-bitten adversarial temperament which unhappily allied itself in the 1960s to an ideology of Nihilism-now and Utopia-later. Reading Geneva Overholser, pronouncing as the ombudsman of the *Washington Post*–which instituted the admirable position so that the paper's work could be criticized honestly–I no longer feel alone.

> It is hard to read an American newspaper today and not come away with a feeling that nothing works–not politics, not government, not the economy. Certainly not schools or cities. And television news, with its *'If it bleeds, it leads'* philosophy, is even worse.[15]

But the nihilism is inevitable if a banal sense of balance or evenhandedness does not function to dull the sensationalism of each day's scandalous big story. The extremism is emphasized by the general impression of "nothing working," and by the professional commitment of journalists to expose it all or "let it all hang out." A chapter in the history of contemporary alienation may well be nearing its turning point.

Here, as so often in the past, we are enjoined to think systematically, and not in terms of small reforms in a sustained effort over generations to ameliorate the human condition. The dream is of an organic change, a "revolution" in the old-fashioned sense of the word. As Brecht used to say, little changes are the enemy of big changes. To be sure, after 1989, in the aftermath of the collapse of socialism and other utopian perspectives, the ideology of total change has been almost altogether discredited. Yet the feeling still runs strong in Western societies that evil–corrupt institutions, inhumane practices, sordid and selfish habits, all in "a world we never made"–is omnipresent. What else should journalists on serious newspapers do but rush to tell all the truths that will make us free?

Thus, our old troubled question about ends and means returns: Can we trust the cadres of our adversarial culture when they justify the means of nihilism in order to achieve the ends of "love, happiness, and art"?

If not, then it may be enough to be getting on with to justify "opportunism," simply to rationalize as best one can the fallibility of the great game in which we all win some and lose some. One can even do without the Jeffersonian pretense of noble efforts of a Fourth Estate committed to the efforts of a free press on behalf of liberty and truth. As in the following story of Adolf Hitler.

2

The Little Lie and the Big Story

Hitler's Hoax

The memorable unmasking of the forged Hitler diaries was an international scandal, for the hoax was sold to many newspapers and magazines around the world. It involved, in its origins, the copyright owned by the Hamburg weekly, *Stern*, whose editors had apparently unearthed the "long-lost manuscripts" of *Der Führer,* had them "authenticated," and launched with great *éclat* its ill-fated scoop.

Why it should have been believed escaped me at the time. *Stern* had an entirely unwarranted reputation for "serious journalism." It had always been addicted to sensationalism, although its crusading liberal-left bias on home and foreign affairs gave it in some European circles a semblance of ideological earnestness. On its sensational side it had often gone too far and has had to pay substantial libel damages. Many of its "exposés" have in turn been exposed, *viz.* its use of "secret documents" fed to the editors by the old *KGB* in Moscow (most dubiously in the questionable material which allegedly exposed Solzhenitsyn's private life).

Its professional irresponsibility—coupled with its technical ingenuity—has doubtless contributed to its profitable circulation successes; at nearly two million weekly copies it was the largest picture magazine in the West since *Life* and *Look* went out of business or regular distribution. It always gets the photo-of-the-day or the flash-of-the-week, at great expense to its publishers, considerable risk to its correspondents, and mortal danger to its conscience (often slightly troubled by erratic captions and non-existent textual documentation).

The "Hitler Diaries" scandal was the high (or low) point of its post-War career. If they were authentic, *Stern* had the greatest scoop-of-the century; if they were not, they would publish (and they did!) the biggest "inside story" of the biggest hoax-of-the-century. Heads they win, tails the readers lose. The

31

two chief editors who were the "guilty men" of *Stern* were each paid, in the end, three million marks for their services and resignations.*

Of *Stern*'s foreign partners, the *Sunday Times* in London bought the forgeries; and then offered a humble apology in the *Times* for its error in publishing (on the self-admittedly faulty advice of Professor Hugh Trevor-Roper) a first Diary installment which would begin to "revise our whole view of the Hitler epoch." It would have been no small achievement if it had: our newspaper culture is nothing if not meaningful, truthful.

There was also an American side to the story. Mrs. Katharine Graham's *Washington Post/Newsweek* combine had also purchased the forgeries—"crude and obvious," according to the handwriting experts who finally dismissed the sixty-volume counterfeit for which millions of marks, pounds, and dollars had been paid out. But *Newsweek* neither exposed itself and drew certain editorial consequences, as did *Stern*–nor did it apologize, as did the *Times* in London. It brazened it out, and hung in there tough (to borrow the Watergate phrases from the *Washington Post*'s favorite villain, ex-President Nixon).

The whole explosive matter was broached subsequently at the annual shareholders' meeting, at which Mrs. Graham (still outmodedly referred to as "the chairman" of the *Washington Post* Company) officially reported, "Quality is an ever-present goal as we exercise the craft of journalism. It's reflected in the pursuit of accuracy, fairness, completeness, and truth."

It occurred to more than one shareholder that if these ideals were being pursued, the *Post/Newsweek* editors were frequently failing to catch up with them. Memories are still fresh of the Janet Cooke "junky" story which won a Pulitzer Prize award (in 1981) for the *Post*–until it turned out to be a shameless piece of contrived fiction. Editor Ben Bradlee then made the classic remark: "Well, it might have been true." So could the tale of flying horses, if they had wings. But I wouldn't want to put it on the front page.

Among the objections was one registered by Arnaud de Borchgrave, veteran *Newsweek* correspondent and (with Robert Moss) author of the *Spike*, a best-selling novel about low corrupt practices in highminded journalism. According to the transcript of the shareholders' meeting on 13 May 1983 (as published in Reed Irvine's *Accuracy in the Media* bulletin of June 1983), Borchgrave said, and the historic text is worth preserving:

---

*   There is an excellent, richly detailed book on the subject by Robert Harris, chronicling the diligent researches and handwriting coups of the forger, Konrad Kujau (subsequently arrested, tried and sentenced to four years imprisonment for his ingenious fraudulence), and also the melodramatic efforts of the literary agent and go-between to "plant" the manuscripts (in the dark of the night, deep in the earth, under a tree). See: Robert Harris, *Selling Hitler: the Story of the Hitler Diaries* (1986, Faber, London). There was also a piece of "cinematic faction," a rather funny German feature film, starring Goetz George, entitled odoriferously *Schtonk!* (1992).

I am sure it will come as no surprise to the management of the *Washington Post* Company if I tell you that *Newsweek*'s treatment of the Hitler diary forgery has deeply shocked the journalistic fraternity—not to mention the public at large. Nothing like it has been seen since the Janet Cooke scandal in the *Washington Post*. If any high-ranking government official had been guilty of such a grievous error of judgment, the *Washington Post* would have demanded his or her resignation.

The so-called 'Hitler Diaries' were palpable forgeries from the word go, and I said so publicly on radio and television three hours after the story first broke. Not only did *Newsweek*'s two top editors decide to devote a 13-page cover story to the scam, but the 39-column story itself repeatedly conveyed the im-pression that the diaries were authentic. This is a clear case of unaccountable media power out of control.

The *Sunday Times* apologized for buying into the scam; two top editors of *Stern* resigned for their part in perpetrating the scam, and the reporter respon-sible has been fired and is being sued by his former employer. Bob McCloskey, the *Washington Post* ombudsman, was appalled by *Newsweek*'s conduct. Nowhere in its follow-up cover story did *Newsweek* acknowledge that its original cover misled its readers. *Newsweek* even went so far as to say that the diaries were of tremendous historical significance, whether they were genuine or not. That is the most ludicrous statement I have ever seen in *Newsweek* and I spent 30 years on the magazine. I have seen four *Newsweek* editors fired over the last 10 years for what were minor misdemeanours compared to this latest scandal.

So my question to the management of the *Washington Post* Company is whether any editor at *Newsweek* who was responsible for this fiasco has submitted his resigna-tion. If not, does management plan to dismiss the editors responsible? And if not, why not?"

The following reply by Mrs. Graham was recorded:

MRS GRAHAM: The answer to your question, Arnaud, as you know, is that no resigna-tions have either been submitted or asked for. The editors' statement, and I agree with them, is that the diaries *were* an interesting story—that it was an interesting story whether they were true or false, and, of course, you have to ask the question, were they forgeries. But the fact that they had surfaced and they were circulated has made a cover story. It also ran on the front page of the *New York Times* for several days. It ran on the front page of most other publications, and the decision to make it a cover story was a decision which I wouldn't disagree with.

At this point, another shareholder–who happened to be Reed Irvine–ex-pressed astonishment that such an "obviously terrible *faux pas*" could still be defended.

REED IRVINE: Mr Maynard Parker [editor of *Newsweek*], on the night before the German government revealed the evidence that these were terrible forgeries, said on Hodding Carter's TV program, 'Inside Story', that these diaries were a find of tremen-dous historical significance that would make a great story, and that's why they played it that way.

Obviously they were not a find of tremendous historical significance, and (as Arnaud said) they were a tremendous embarrassment to anyone who considered them in that light. While *Newsweek* alerted us to the fact that they weren't authenticated, [*Newsweek* was] certainly leaning heavily in that direction.... I think that Mr Parker, who put himself way out on that limb, certainly made him-self very vulnerable.... I suggest that maybe you need a new editor of the month at *Newsweek*.

MRS GRAHAM: We disagree.

What we are left with is a wide-open Pandora's box devoted to the horrendous new principle in contemporary journalism that stories are "interesting" whether or not they are "true or false."

In a recent exchange with the editor of the *Times* (London) I suggested, in connection with the contemporary reporting of wars and civil strife (from Vietnam to the Lebanon), a serious degeneration of both moral and professional standards in the dissemination of news in our Western media. It would seem to be not merely a matter of distortion, partisanship, misinterpretation, and alien bias. It is becoming now a matter of the value of truth itself. The hunger for sensation is devouring the appetite for facts–for news–for the real thing, authenticated, double-checked, incontrovertible. Everything is becoming permissible; and anything can be taken for true, if it "*could* be true" and is held to be "*interesting*" enough.

The *Führer* might well have enjoyed the postwar spectacle of how his doctrine of "the Big Lie" became usefully transmogrified into the credo of "the Big Story." Evelyn Waugh once thought it all very humorous and made (in his witty novels, *Scoop* and *Black Mischief*) good jokes of it. It no longer is funny.

A Counterfeiter's Fiction

The relentless pursuit of a "scoop," often associated with checkbook journalism, is of course endemic in both the print and electronic media. When newspapers get into circulation troubles and become more desperate for some "inside story," for a "missing" photograph, for a revealing memoir by a killer, a terrorist, a rapist or other villain, they will be prepared to pay more money for an "exclusive" than even the prospering TV moguls.

In the affair of *Stern* and the counterfeit *Hitler Diaries*–extensive handwritten notebooks–the hoax was a natural temptation for the press which is in the business of publishing printed matter, by the *Führer* or by any other hand. Sensational picture stories–which used to go, in the old days, to *Life*, or *Look* or (in Britain) to *Picture Post*,—wend their way towards the television stations, and film editors there have proved themselves to be no less gullible or, as the case may be, cynical and irresponsible. The scandal of the journalistic fraud and its deception of public opinion are equally distasteful. I do not suppose that the German scene is any more outrageous than any other, but it could be that its small band of tricksters are not as skillful and subtle as their Anglo-American counterparts and, accordingly, provide more perfidious material for the student of mendacious malpractice. Nor can, especially here, a dramatic dichotomy be drawn between the press and the box, between news-paper journalism and television reportage. The culpability for the dissemina-tion of "bogus pictures" with the narrator's accompanying soundtrack text of even more fraudulence (picture-shots lie singly, words go on and on) had to be shared between publishers and producers. Most of the specious German docu-mentaries in question had been prepared for prime-time evening TV broad-casts and sponsored by mainline newspapers and magazines.

Our friends at the weekly *Stern* magazine of Hamburg were, again, the main victims and unfortunate accomplices. *Stern* has for many years now been involved in regular Television News-Features, offering what purported to be serious, accurate, and important film clips on all the topical themes in world affairs–one night the bloody war in Bosnia or Chechnya, the next night the scandal of toxic British beef or the sinister machinations of German arms manufacturers. Similar programs are broadcast by the newsweekly, *Der Spiegel*; the cultural weekly, *Die Zeit*; and the distinguished daily, *Süddeutsche Zeitung*. All of them, to one extent or another, participated in the fraud...and were obliged to offer embarrassed public apologies for their editorial waywardness.

The *Stern* bore the brunt of the humiliation, for it had broadcast more film footage of men and events that (as it was discreetly put) "were not what they purported to be." The popular presenter of the program was a star performer on the German entertainment scene with the unfortunate name of Gunther Jauch–bad luck had it that when lightning struck twice in the *Stern* "*Redaktion,*" the whole country remembered the old *Hitler-Diary*-scandal of Konrad Kujau's forgeries, and every punster in the land was doing poor Gunther down by calling him "*Kujauch.*" But he tried to recover some poise and a bit of reputa-tion by exposing–naturally, on prime time, on his own program–the real cul-prit, a young cameraman who had been concocting counterfeit documentary clips for many years, who was energetic and resourceful and ruthless, and who suddenly became the most notorious counterfeiter since Meegeren stopped painting his forged Vermeers. Michael Born, they all avowed, would never be employed again. He had been delivering damaged goods. He was put under arrest and tried; a court in Koblenz convicted and sentenced him (in December 1996) to four years in jail.

Editors, in defending their role as purveyors of sleaze, usually use the rationalization that they are only offering the readers what they want and expect. Herr Born echoed the pretext, and had on offer all the "terrific stories" that a TV film editor desperately needed before the evening news stole all the headlines. Did you want to view with alarm the nefarious doings on the Far Right? He had just the dreadful clip of a secret Neo-Nazi meeting–or, if that was old stuff, ten minutes of frightening footage of the Ku Klux Klan and its first midnight bonfires in its "secret invasion" of the German scene. Michael Born rounded up all the actors, got tailors to work on fashioning the white sheets, found a carpenter to make ominous wooden crosses, and bought several boxes of fire-lighters. The Klan shots in a remote Bavarian field were realistic, especially when his hand-held camera seemed to be trembling in fear. Or, for some variety, German exchange students at an English-language school in Eastbourne wasting the taxpayers' money by going on wild sprees and binges. The Eastbourne school has already filed a lawsuit for damages.

Well, what about a "human interest" story for a change? He offered: Poor exploited children in Pakistan, working to produce rugs for our big-city department stores. Animal interest? He had: Trigger-happy German hunting-clubs shooting innocent cats. Terrorism? On hand were: Militant Kurd refugees piecing together a homemade bomb somewhere in the German underground. Drug drama? You could take away: Cocaine smugglers crossing the Swiss frontier under the cover of night. Born had a good circle of helpful friends who obliged him by playing the roles of dealers, hunters, bombsters, and rug-salesmen. The cats were collected from a friendly neighborhood animal refuge.

How long could this last? For longer than it did, since the demand was so great and the supply was delivered with such professional dispatch that reputations were made. Here were dramatic documentary films in the enlightened public interest, and the public non-commercial channels, *ARD* and *ZDF*, were attracted and exhibited some of Born's sensational footage that was not already gobbled up by the private stations. But it all came to a notorious and disgraceful end when the police got into the act–on a hot tip from a disgruntled actor who had not been paid for his various stints–and began to look for the illegal klansmen, the sinister dealers, the criminal cat-killers. They only found a cameraman, a small studio, but with enough cans of film to contrive a whole Documentary History of Our Times.

In the aftermath Michael Born's defense attorney began arguing Jesuitically that the film clips were *not* (repeat: not) "fake"; they were *actual* pictures, *well* photographed with *real* scenes; but they were, he conceded, falsely labelled and thus misleading. (Which misdemeanor called for a lesser charge and a lighter punishment.) The perpetrator himself put the blame squarely on "the culture" and its "unbearable pressure to dramatize the news." The TV-producers (including "Kujauch") added: You know, there is so much drama in the world, so much nastiness and danger, how can one be expected to know the real thing? As an afterthought, the German *feuilletonists* took the large view, and concluded in the long perspective that it's all probably worse in America–for hadn't Janet Cooke written a phoney drug story, bogus from beginning to end, for the *Washington Post* and won a Pulitzer Prize for it?

In this mood the slangy word "*fake*" (in English) was regularly used in the courtroom and in the newspaper trial reports. It was yet another Anglicism to relieve the German language's burden of guilt, possibly compensating for its reluctance to call a spade a spade, although the sound of "*fayk*" (sometimes pronounced *fahkuh*) and the sight of "*ge-faket*" is punishing enough. At the very least, as the trial judge conceded, the hapless Herr Born deserved a little credit for having "raised a very important media issue for public debate."[1]

Criminology and jurisprudence, thus, were hard put to deal with the tragedy of truth and reality; high-flying German philosophy was more likely to come to terms with it (and, in a moment, we will be describing the "metaphysics" of the debate as it raged in the newspapers). In point of fact, the Koblenz judge's conviction of the counterfeiter in this case was less for his disservices to the general code of honesty in the journalistic profession and more for perpetrating the other incidental infractions in his meteoric TV career: such as driving his film truck without a proper license; flagrant cruelty to animals (those ill-fated cats); possession of illegal weapons (those armed smugglers!); photographing a blank piece of paper and pretending that it was an official legal document; and–most grievously (and here the German law is, for well-known reasons, famously tough)–having his Ku Klux Klansmen shout, in public incitement, anti-Semitic slogans.

Mysteries of the Piltdown Forgery

Our press has always had its corps of Monday-morning quarterbacks who were wise after the event, and avid to score points where on the wayward afternoon only errors, fumbles, and wild throws had obtained. Careful and knowledgeable newspaper readers will find it easy to spot mistakes in any of their favorite publications; and I can recall the challenge to an assemblage of senior editors by that Scotsman of supreme knowledgeability, Professor Sir Denis Brogan, who promised to find a dozen *faux pas* in a quarter-of-an-hour's perusal of any of their own daily papers. It was at an International Press Institute conference in Paris in the mid-1950s; and Brogan brilliantly pulled it off, to the embarrassment of the IFI's representatives of the Manchester *Guardian* (Alastair Hetherington), the London *Times* (Donald Tyerman), and the *New York Times* (Lester Markel). But then nobody could read as fast, and knew as much–stored for instantaneous retrieval in a phenomenal memory–as Denis W. Brogan, historian, journalist, and all-knowing fact-checker.*

---

*   Denis W. Brogan (1900-1974), professor of political science at Peterhouse College, Cambridge University. Author of an excellent work on French history *The French Nation* (1957) and innumerable works on the U.S.A., among them *Introduction to American Politics* (1954), *The American Political System* (1933) and *The American Character* (1945). Also a learned work on *The English People* (1943). His *Price of Revolution* (1951) is, like everything he wrote, incisive and witty.

I should also mention copious articles and essays that were incomparable for their sound, if sometimes recondite, information. On the day after the Kennedy assassination he remarked to me that the old Italian rifle that the Dallas police initially said that Lee Harvey Oswald had used was quite incapable of that range and accuracy. He was right; the F.B.I. later corrected the identification of the assassin's weapon. Sir Denis explained to me, when I challenged him as to how he could possibly know such a thing, that he had when very young read an illustrated guide in

In the examples I have cited where "a little knowledge" led reporters astray–and where, presumably, a little more knowledge would have helped them to get it right–there are also distorting factors such as bluff, vanity, and intellectual pretension which compound themselves with sheer ignorance. There is, frequently, in such exercises an element of academic arrogance which drives highbrows to sit in critical judgement of the low cultural levels of middlebrows. I may be excused from this bit of hubris by my next example which is a personal confession to an egregious error; and my own self-criticism may highlight the vulnerabilities of all journalists who answer the call to make meaningful sense of things in the world around us. In the uncovering of few stories is there such a preponderance of evidence and logical connections as to obviate any and all likelihood of fallacy and fallibility. We establish one set of facts, and miss out on another. We make reasonable assumptions, which turn out to be presumptuous. A coherent interpretation, or a cogent analysis, in an attractive effort to say something true and useful, all run into grievous difficulties when something contradictory, such as life is with its little ongoing surprises, upsets the whole apple-cart.

It was some time in the spring of 1955, on one of my visits to England, that I began to be interested in the "mystery" of that triumph of British anthropology (or was it paleontology?) known as *Eoanthropus Dawsoni*, dubbed popularly "the Piltdown Man." A discreet silence had lately descended on our oldest ancestor, in fact he had effectively disappeared; and all references to him were removed from the various British museums. When I took the train from Victoria Station to Uckfield in East Sussex I was not quite sure what "Piltdown" stood for (the digger? the dig?); and it turned out to be a tiny village where I received further directions. For at the Piltdown pubs the whole subject was still a matter of local pride. One pub was signposted with a grisly skull that looked like an ad for a notorious pirate flagship; the other had a related illustration of a hairy prehistoric man with a rock as a weapon in his left hand, and behind him lurked a menacing dinosaur. The primitive drama, which had featured the local squire of Barkham Manor where he had discovered "Dawson's Man," was still playing. It was a touch of Spielberg's "Jurassic Park" *avant la lettre*.

In 1912 when the story first broke it was a world sensation. Darwin had, when he worked on his Theory of Evolution, almost no fossils at hand; and he

---

his father's library to all the ordnance used in World War I. Memorable was Sir Denis Brogan's article on the Kennedy assassination, in *Encounter* Magazine, "The Presidency," January 1964, pp. 3-7. Since he knew so much about the Mannigfacher-Carracano rifle, with or without Oswald's long-distance gun sight, I quickly commissioned him on that occasion (lunch at the Reform Club in London) to do this article when his memory was so fresh....

He was knighted in 1963 – as the Cambridge word had it – "for omniscience."

and Huxley speculated about the "missing link" in the great chain of being. And suddenly he turned up...courtesy of Charles Dawson, an amateur geologist–accompanied at times by Pierre Teilhard de Chardin, a young Frenchman who later gained fame as a Catholic philosopher–both puttering around in his fields. They found a bone here, another fragment there, and then a piece of skull (first thought by some dim-witted Sussex farmer to be a cocoanut–alas poor Yorick!) that appeared to fit together with an impressive jawbone. This seemed to be a historic breakthrough: "the First Englishman," and the substantial instrument (carved out of some poor elephant's tusk) that had been found at his side was referred to locally as his "cricket bat." The old boy was English to the nines.

But the whole picture had more than a few puzzling distortions. A cranial "coherence" was lacking as the skull, more or less human, fitted awkwardly with a curiously ape- or gorilla-like jawbone. The big brain of *pithecanthropus erectus* had developed, so modern scientists had always argued, only slowly and indeed belatedly–*i.e.*, after mandibles and teeth etc. took on a human appearance. Had Dawson dug up the remains of not one ancient creature but two? Doubts grew. If he was the first Englishman he was perhaps a very eccentric sort of aged gentleman, a peculiar exception to the hereditary evolutionary rule, in an old line that led nowhere.

Skepticism ultimately led to scientific proof and refutation: the "discovery" by Dawson was disproved as a fake, a hoax, a fraud. The way it was perpetrated was demonstrated by carbon and other laboratory testing which revealed that some of the pieces had been artificially stained, were only centuries old, were imported from North Africa and planted in a river-bed of the Piltdown moors....Dawson had died in 1916 and thus could not stand interrogation. But an Oxford anthropologist, J. S. Weiner, had all the answers–or most of them–by the 1950s and his evidence from additional fluorine tests and the comparative figures of radioactivity from the Geiger counter all underlined, cruel to say, the swindle. Dr. Weiner talked about its "cleverness" and it seemed only a typical English understatement. Old colleagues recalled that Dawson had a reputation of being "a Sussex magician," and one of his neighbors at nearby Lewes talked darkly about his "low ambitions" and ominously quoted a line from *Macbeth*: "*Let not light see my black and deep desires.*"

The most recent historian of what he calls "the Science Fraud of the Century" summons up evangelical wrath at the very thought of the Piltdown affair: "The Piltdown fraud was nothing short of despicable, an ugly trick played by a warped and unscrupulous mind on unsuspecting scholars."[2]

My own contribution to the story was small; but, striving as we all are tempted to do for the larger coherence, I attempted to place the dramatic episode in an overarching cultural context. If Shakespeare came into it, then Goethe with his "Faustianism" was not far behind. The motivation for the grand pseudo-scientific conspiracy to coax nature a little bit along–to round out and complete in agreeable fashion the missing picture of human evolution–seemed to cry out for theology as well as literature, for ideology as well as ambition. In fact I expatiated on Dawson's Christianity when I found out that he had pieced the skull together to emphasize Piltdown Man's *"angelic forehead"* (rather than his base gluttonous features).* More than that, I dwelled on his love of "God and Country," and I underlined his patriotic sensibilities which had been wounded by the discoveries by foreigners–Germans!—the latest being *Homo Heidelbergiensis* of 1912; and these, mind you, were the years of intense Anglo-German rivalry which had been overheating to a European power-political contest between Civilization and *Kultur.* I subsequently asked the Piltdown bartender whether, in the light of the exposés, he wouldn't be taking down his "prehistoric" pub signs. With a mixture of fair play to whomever might have been buried in the Piltdown gravel 50,000 years ago and a slightly alcoholized indifference to the realities, he said no, they would remain, for "the old boy had made history, didn't he?...One way or another."

There was a third way still to come. Only recently, some forty years later (1996), a canvas traveling-trunk with the initials of Martin A. C. Hinton was found at London's Natural History Museum (where Hinton had been curator in 1912), and it has given the story yet another twist. Not Dawson–whose religious and nationalistic inspiration had been a many-splendored thing–but Hinton was the culprit. And he evidently had been essentially motivated by nothing more substantial than his own eccentricity and an overripe schoolboy prankishness. (In the 1935 edition of *Who's Who* he dropped a hint as to his own interest in hoaxes, and that he had studied many of them.)

Hinton's re-discovered trunk contained bones, stained and carved in the same fashion as the forged fossils and assorted artefacts which had deceived so many great minds in classical paleo-anthropology. This was the tool-kit for the hoax which had been intended to (and did) embarrass the Keeper of Geology of the Museum, Professor Arthur Smith Wood. Professor Wood was a pompous and stuffy character, and such an elaborate practical joke would be a way of getting back at him. Wood defended the Piltdown Man to the end, publishing a book in 1948 called *The Earliest Englishman.* But Hinton had also preserved in that incriminating trunk several glass test tubes containing stained teeth which he had evidently been treating with his very own concoction of iron, manganese and chromium.

In a letter written by Martin Hinton after the fraud was exposed, he speculated: "The temptation to invent such a discovery of an ape-like man in a Wealden gravel might have proved irresistible to some unbalanced member of

---

*   When a translation of my "Letter from Piltdown" appeared in *Der Monat* (September 1955), there was a printer's error – the Germans call it the *Druckteufel* at work, the printer's deviltry. It transformed the *engelhaft* ("angelic") into *ekelhaft* ("loathesome"). So if there was Faust, there was also Mephisto, and somebody up there just didn't like the story in any shape or form.

old Ben Harrison's circle" (a reference to his Sussex-based geologist colleagues). An editor of *Nature* commented: "This reads as almost a signed confession."

Hinton was obviously fascinated–to the point of unbalance?—with his bogus Piltdown specimens which, on careful examination, had betrayed their true age and artificial coloring. At the age of sixteen Hinton had published a paper–in which Sherlock Holmes could have detected all the telltale clues–showing "how fossils in river gravels would be impregnated with oxides of iron and manganese, staining them a chocolate brown colour."

So did the *dramatis personae* of the hoax drama have their roles redefined. Charles Dawson was an innocent dupe, an amateur geologist who had little or nothing to do with it. Arthur Smith Wood was felt to be an incompetent Museum keeper and could be taken in. The young Frenchman (to whom I will return in a moment) had struck a blow for an *entente cordiale*. Martin Hinton was one of those office jokesters who go to a lot of trouble to get the last laugh.

And where did it leave me? An opinionated journalist easily tempted to jump to conclusions? a gullible intellectual, forearmed only with "a little bit of knowledge" (and, as time would tell, not enough)? Theology can offer less than divine guidance; patriotism may be the last refuge of a scoundrel; but not all villainy is loftily inspired. My account was, in its way, ingenious and convincing but it did not exactly turn out to be true. I did not reckon with a dusty, unopened trunk in a dark cellar, a Pandora's box of unexpected evidence. In the 1950s I over-associated the dramatic and indubitable evidence we already had with the larger movements of ideas and politics. And like Tennyson's flower-in-the-crannied wall, I connected everything with everything else. Sometimes the sufficient explanation is small, casual, eccentric, isolated. The warning to all who want always to be plugged in: Only disconnect.

It was Tom Wolfe, no less–the father of "the New Journalism" (a spectacular mid-twentieth-century phenomenon)–who renewed my attention to the odd fact that the young Teilhard de Chardin (1881-1955) had been associated with the Piltdown dig. Wolfe, who has an undiminished reportorial appetite for recondite and suggestive details, writes in his most recent book, *Hooking Up* (2000): "At the age of 32 he had been the French star of the most sensational archaeological find of all time, the Piltdown Man, the so-called missing link in the evolution of ape to man, in a dig near Lewes, England, led by the Englishman Chalres Dawson." Presumably the same pseudo-theological feature that inspired Dawson–the "angelic forehead"–led Teilhard astray, although he went on, as an adventurous Jesuit priest, to spin other transcendental theories of which Tom Wolfe offers an incisive, if wry, account:

> In 1953, two years before his death, he suffered one especially cruel blow. It was discovered that the Piltdown man had been, in fact, a colossal hoax pulled off by

Charles Dawson, who had hidden various doctored ape and human bones like Easter eggs for Teilhard and others to find. He was in an acute state of depression when he died of cerebral hemorrhage at the age of seventy-four, still in exile. His final abode was a dim little room in the Hotel Fourteen on East Sixtieth Street in Manhattan, with a single window looking out on a filthy air shaft composed, in part, of a blank exterior wall of the Copacabana nightclub.

This bit of biographical melodrama is told in a chapter entitled (characteristically), "Digibabble, Fairy Dust and the Human Anthill" which hooks up somehow for the author of *Radical Chic & Mau-Mauing the Flak Catchers* with Teilhard de Chardin's *"noösphere,"* Marshall McLuhan's *"Gutenberg Galaxy,"* and Edwin O. Wilson's *"Darwinian myrmecology."*

It takes all the wiles of the master of the New Journalism to make of all this a coherent episode in intellectual history. When properly *"hard-wired," "dialed up,"* and *"digitally connected,"* it should go a long way to explaining almost everything in our time. "Mere research protocol drudge though I may be," Tom Wolfe promises a new installment entitled *"The Human Comedy."* Meanwhile, the human tragedy suggests that hoaxes hurt, and counterfeiting can kill. Poor Teilhard, poor Dawson.[3]

3

Difficulties in Grappling with Reality

The Reporter Rearranges the Scene

The counterfeit question is not merely a matter of the inaccurate labeling of a media product nor a distortion of the external realities which should be, in all honesty, faithfully transmitted. It also impinges on a whole host of political issues, including civil liberties which are thought to include an inalienable human right "to access" real as well as virtual reality. Could Janet Cooke have been prosecuted in Washington as Michael Born, the German hoaxter, was in Koblenz–for fraudulence or *Betrug?* Legal systems differ, but should our media communications systems continue to be sheltered behind an absolute guarantee of freedom-of-the-press under which the freedom to distort, to misrepresent, and even to fabricate, may be deemed to be defensible and legally excusable?

Under the totalitarian systems, to be sure, the revolutionary regime always arrogated to itself the absolute right to adjust any fact in the press, any picture on the screen, any entry in an encyclopaedia, any aspect of reactionary reality which failed to comply with whatever the Party line happened to be over long periods of tyrannical rule. What Trotsky called "the Stalin school of falsification" rewrote Soviet history every few years–and indeed retouched historic photographs (Trotsky was no longer seen standing on any platform alongside Lenin). Autocratic vanities were appeased, and orthodox images touched up to remain pure.

The Chinese regime trod a not dissimilar path although the directional marking signs read a little differently from the Russian. Stalin in that most elaborate of modern-day hoaxes, his "Show Trials" of 1936-38, used a Byzantine technique of a churchly confessional which, I have always thought, goes back to the way that mortal sin and guilt, or suspicions thereof, were handled in Stalin's own religious childhood and in his theological training in a Georgian seminary.[1]

The men of the Beijing regime also allow a thousand lies to bloom, but pay–with a traditional Confucian finickiness to detail–rather more attention to every petal, to every color of the artificial flowers they fabricate. A recent Reuters dispatch calls our attention to the fastidious absurdity to which they are prepared to go in order to maintain their monolithic fictions. Mao's memory is still revered, and his portrait hangs everywhere. But filmmakers have been "adjusting" the soundtrack of the documentary movies of yesteryear. It is well known that Mao spoke in a heavily accented local dialect. Today he can be heard speaking elegantly in "measured tones of standard Mandarin Chinese" (according to a report in the *China Youth Daily*) so that the new generations of youth will have no difficulty with the guttural thickness of the Great Helmsman's voice as it once was. Voices have been switched as new soundtracks dubbed traditional films to give Mao a Mandarin accent he never had in real life. The new speaking style follows the revised injunctions of "linguistic correctness"; for as the Chinese newspaper said, "Language should not be an obstacle in the way of a people's appreciation of the beautiful." Beauty, at least in statist politics, needs an official stamp of approval, regularly renewed.[2]

In the West, with open societies affording recourse to the rule of law, such legerdemain always winds up before a judge in a courtroom full of complaints and counter-charges. One might have thought it was a small matter whether the French photographer Robert Doisneau (1912-1994) had "touched up" or otherwise contrived at the beauty of his artistic snapshot featuring a couple on a Paris bridge impulsively kissing. But "The Kiss" had been published in *Life* Magazine in its day as a classic *Magnum* photo-document, and subsequently it sold a half-million copies in the form of a large-sized poster. Recently a couple in the French provinces turned up who said they had been in Paris on that very day and were indeed the young lovers caught kissing by Doisneau; and they sued to get their share of the Doisneau royalties. The famous photographer of "life's little incidents" fought the case but his denial of that aging couple's claim included startling evidence of the actual couple–Paris models hired and dressed for the occasion!–whom he had employed on that day to pose for the "spontaneous photo" of love in the Paris springtime. The artist won the case, but in the process lost his credo of photographic verisimilitude. Pictures were once again shown not to be what they seemed to be. Like writers and other wordsmiths, photographers can lie with the best of them.[3]

Are there professional rationalizations which offer a plausible way out? Two are common and still current. The first is the journalistic apologia for the Higher Hoax which argues that a minor detail or two may well be counterfeit, added only to help the truth along, but the end-effect is real, authentic, true. This is threadbare casuistry. The other excuse is the defense of the victim who claims the innocence of "cultural victimization": namely, that it is *society,* the environment in all its pragmatic manipulation which is responsible for such very normal practices. Indeed our whole culture is a kaleidoscopic apparatus for making an artificial pattern of various bits and pieces of reality. As a matter of fact, such a defense was put forth in Koblenz on behalf of Michael Born's dramatized pseudo-documentaries.

A hundred times a year the front page of your favorite newspaper publishes a photograph of two or more world statesmen, or a couple of leading local personalities, meeting, shaking hands, smiling, chatting affably or whispering gravely, all in poses which were a routine demand of working photographers. They were creating their own photo-opportunities, not a frame of which can be considered as genuine, as an actual picture of a real–*i.e.*, unrehearsed, unarranged–happening. The fateful process begins with such incidental dressing-up of casual matters to give them an added semblance of meaning or drama; and it enlarges itself from there. Dramatic on-the-spot television news footage often reconstructs small scenes–a purposeful walk through a corridor, a rueful glance through the window, a hectic grab at the telephone–which could have happened, might well have happened, but here each pose is dutifully repeated or acted out for the benefit of the cameras. Eyewitnesses offering on-the-spot testimony are moved about to obtain maximum pictorial effect, and there are whole scenes in wars and other catastrophes in which the news-item is placed in a quasi-realistic context with a contrived backdrop.

A famous scene in the Vietnam war was subject to stormy controversy–many years later–when the correspondent of the *Los Angeles Times* (Robert Elegant) revealed its "inside story." The horrific setting afire of a Vietnam village by a GI wielding his Zippo lighter–which was lent to him by the TV team–had all been arranged by the American TV correspondent after properly positioning his cameras to record the incendiarism in the (deserted) village. There was another memorable "grisly incident" of the Viet Cong prisoner who was supposed to have been pushed out of a helicopter to encourage his fellow-POWs to talk. No such incident was ever confirmed; but there *was* a photograph which had been "staged" with a corpse, and it was accompanied by an invented story. "The imagined event," as an historian records, "was given wide coverage."[4]

Sometimes the justification appears to be in the interests of a higher truth, sometimes in order to appease the needs of being entertaining; sometimes both at once, as in the plaintive cry of Herr Born to the effect that there is no point in covering seriously what's happening in society and the world if there's nobody out there–amused, or bemused–listening and watching. Only the sensational–ever more outlandish and outrageous–will attract mass viewing. The melodrama, hopefully involving a little filmable catastrophe, is the thing that'll catch our attention span on the wing.

So was Michael Born driven to do an alarming feature about the latest sinister turn in drug trafficking which starred something called a "Colorado toad." It was an astonishing creature whose secretions have a hallucinogenic effect: and one saw an unfortunate German youngster licking the toad's secretions for a desperate fix. The film was done with a real *Kröte* (although it looked like a local frog), but what was licked in the studio was a drop or two of condensed milk.[5]

After such knowledge, what forgiveness? But as in some enlightened schools of jurisprudence, not to the criminal accrues the guilt but to the environment, to the "whole culture" which is held to induce such waywardness. I heard during the sensational Koblenz trial of Herr Born one melancholy journalist express the conviction that what Television is doing is Destroying Reality, for we no longer see what *exists* or what *is,* what takes place or happens. Our sight–and all its sightings, whatever the optics–has become flawed. Our perception is having to make do with a diminishing sense of the realities out there–we just happen to be under the impression that we are looking at them, and registering, and perceiving.

Be that as it may, the accompanying trouble is professional and intellectual, in the journalistic tendency of serious commentators to view with apocalyptic alarm and to jump to quasi-metaphysical conclusions. This is especially so in the leading German papers where readers are subjected to regular coverage of the abstruse doings among academic philosophers as if Kant and Nietzsche were still among us.

Such over-arching speculativeness, as if we are now getting to know the whole truth even about the quintessential lie, leaves the door open for the quick and easy entry of nihilism. Nothing can be believed any more, *nothing* should be given credence. Facts and famous images blur into a deceptive mélange. Patriotic flag-waving Marianne never flourished a French *tricouleur* on any revolutionary barricade nor did the U.S. Marines ever raise the Star-Spangled Banner on Iwo Jima in that famous stance of heroic pathos. Even Robert Capa's historic *Magnum* photos of the Spanish Civil War in the 1930s were as "imagined" as Goya's. Sculptors are liars; painters prevaricate; and philosophers are fools if they think that falsification is not "*system-immanent*" and hence inevitable in any act of cognition. The new credo, worthy of a Kant or a Hegel in its abstraction, reads (and I am quoting from one German newspaper driven to exploring the deeper dialectical meaning of journalistic fakes)– "*Erst in der Inszenierung findet sich die Wirklichkeit zu sich selbst*" (roughly: Only in the staging can reality truly find itself). The seductive paradox is that, if realism does not consist in simply copying reality but actually reveals what could be possible, then true television (*fernsehen*) can also be–perhaps only be–found in so-called simulation. We are all counterfeiters now.

Accordingly the Born affair–with a knowing side-glance at Konrad Kujau and Janet Cooke and so many others–is being elevated to the general thesis that the borderline between fiction and reality disappears the moment somebody picks up a camera. There are some extremists on the scene (but, for obvious reasons, not in the press) who extend this to the moment any journalist picks up a pen and a notebook to cover a fast-breaking story. Taken together, all such charges and additional methodological suspicions amount to a variant of Heisenberg's law–the Intrusion of the Observer necessarily influences the Event. Regardless of the medium represented, a reporter's mere presence affects the perception of reality.

Are there any exceptions? Art alone, in its higher forms, is seen to have a legitimacy, for it alone can create real things anew. It gives us palpable truths with a life and a validity of their own, true unto themselves. But what is creative freedom for the artist is mischievous manipulation for the reporter: for where the artist perceives, the reporter deceives.

And so, I am afraid, does a truth-telling tradition of several thousand years of critical-historiographical efforts to get at the facts–and to establish and record some stories with verisimilitude–simply go out of the window. Any presentation of reality, trying to get the measure of the size and shape of the external world and its happenings, is an erratic, subjective enterprise. Reality, as we are instructed by that serious Munich newspaper (the *Süddeutsche Zeitung* which often stretches the philosophic wits of its usually earthier Bavarian readers): "reality is that to which we respond emotionally and comprehend rationally and is not necessarily identical with what anybody else has registered." If true, all of our newspapers–old-fashioned mirrors of grubby realities–are slowly putting themselves out of business.[6]

I am moved to recall the famous case of the Cottingley Fairies in 1917–the photographs of those little English girls being fêted by a fleet of fairies (dancing, with wings and magic wands) which were so well done that they convinced Arthur Conan Doyle...although his Sherlock Holmes would have looked closely into the original negatives which even the Kodak Company had authenticated and come to the logical and irrefutable conclusion (as others did) that it was all a fake, a put-up job, a flimsy bit of whimsy. Still, the believers continue to believe. The fairies *were* there, in Yorkshire or wherever, the fairies do exist–"but we're just too stupid to see them." As one journalist put it, summing up the closed circle of supernatural faith, namely that we are surrounded by countless winged nature spirits who are invisible to us simply because of our lack of faith: "Remember, you have to believe in fairies before you can see them–a brilliantly watertight, essentially Stalinist alibi for the little folk." (Bryan Appleyard, "A little of what you fancy" in the "Culture" section of the *Sunday Times*, 2 November 1997, p. 2).

One can follow the trail in both directions, the high road to grievous falsification, the low road to trivial fibbery. It would be humorless to deny that the contemporary penchant for hoaxes does not, with high-spirited frequency, embrace an element of nice, indecent fun. The spoofing that goes with a practical joke, mixes a touch of masquerade with a talent for hoodwinking. There may be a bit of money to be had from it on the side; but then there is also a certain passion to expose gullibility. Nevertheless, the consequences are patently unfunny.

In Paris, a satirical comedy group was hauled into the French court-room for publishing a "send-up version" of Éditions du Seuil's best-selling book, *Sophie's World*, complete with counterfeit philosophical passages. What the prospering copyright-holder considered to be serious plagiarism, undermining his sales and profits, the amateur plagiarists thought parody and irony, a light-hearted effort to "take the mickey out" of an overblown attempt to communicate to young Sophie two thousand years of philosophy from Socrates to Sartre. As one newspaper headline put it –

SOPHIE THE PHILOSOPHICAL SPOOF
HITS A LEGAL PARADOX
("Sophie," *Sunday Times*, 22 June 1997, p. 24.)

Judges and lawyers and other grave guardians of public morality have warned that the spoof may be innocent in intention but dastardly in its popularization of a fraudulence that is corrupting the cultural environment.

What of the tricksters–from publicity-seekers (desperate for "fifteen minutes of fame") to pathological liars–who go on to the European and American chat shows, taking on false names, and tell their equally fictitious tales? There were recently the nasty confessions of a loan shark (on the BBC's daytime chat show, *Kilroy*) and, a few weeks later, a homeowner who had tortured a burglar whom he had caught in the act. Both were narrated by the very theatrical Dave Smith, thirty-eight, who said he took a pleasurable satisfaction in outwitting TV researchers so very pressed to produce colorful stories. But the police moved into action when a self-proclaimed "paedophile" confessed on live camera to molesting seventeen boys in the past few years. (He made up the grisly tale and was later released on bail.)

The Smith career illustrates the clash of two cultures, the confrontation between the cynical storytellers and the naive listeners. It is also a class struggle between the chattering class of TV sensational journalism and the couch potatoes finally driven to rise up and strike back. Dave Smith, for one, was inspired by a certain spirit of spite, for he had been

> struck by how desperate these people were to make interesting TV and get the audience het up....Each time I have rung up and spun them lies, you can feel the researchers' ears prick up because you're fitting in their theme...None of my claims have ever been checked....If you've got the nerve, you're in.

Outrageous claims are, of course, the staple of such popular programs, and the grotesquerie of tale of one confession leads to yet another concoction making for even more dynamic, high-rated television. To be sure, a few are comical (even memorably so): *e.g.* New York's unforgettable "Clifford G. Prout" who had launched a grim nationwide campaign for animals to be clothed. "Prout" was, as is now known, Alan Abel, a professional hoaxer in New York for more than thirty years; and he insisted that his motivation throughout had been simply the love of performing, elevated by an occasional urge "to prick at pomposity." His record can stand up with the best of them:

> Mr. Abel's later spoofs included portraying a man prepared to lease a kidney for 99 years (to sidestep the U.S. ban on selling body organs) and a televised appearance of the Ku Klux Klan orchestra. This featured 85 musicians playing the classical music of "a kinder, softer clan"

Safeguards against such foolishness can, conceivably, be devised; but they are not likely to be foolproof.

A vast and incredible gullibility is abroad in the land, fed by spoofs and jokes, lies and fantasies, an endless series of sinful adventures, real or imagined. What loses out, in the end, is a modest devotion to truth and factuality. What is winning, at the moment, is an addiction to make-believe, laced with a large shot of mendacity.

("Hoaxers home in on gullible chat shows," *Sunday Telegraph*, 22 June 1997.)

Hoaxes lead to scoops when the story is fresh. It is headline news when the fraudsters are practically caught in the act–the perpetrators are exposed, and the dupes can still be shocked into anger at the deception or shame at their naiveté. A quieter narrative emerges when historians and scientists get around, years and indeed centuries later, to establishing the counterfeit nature of, say, the "Donation of Constantine" (*circa* eighth century A.D.) or the "Piltdown Man." Most of these scholarly exercises remain largely in the circles of academe; and sensation-hungry or gullible editors can count on an open wide-eyed reception for the next improbable feature which should have been spotted by an alert readership as quickly as a capricious news-item on April Fool's Day.

I can recall the heady days in the 1960s when LSD came into vogue from the California of the "Summer of Love" to the Chelsea of "swinging London." Most of what has been recorded of those years, the so-called hippie decade, can be classified as "misperceptions," self-serving legends of nostalgia, and in at least one or two curious cases of paradoxical misinterpretation and high-spirited myth-making.

For my own sins I have been credited with the phrase of "*swinging London*" which puts me out somewhat when tabloid features pick it up and even the BBC can carry it in its quiz programs. I happened to say it to Horace Judson, now a distinguished historian of science, but then a young and newly appointed London correspondent for *Time* Magazine. One of his first assignments was to do a *Time* cover story on "the new scene" and he came, as he said, to "pick my brain" and chat with me in the *Encounter* office. Since my magazine, at the time, was so hopelessly cosmopolitan I hardly paid attention to my own bailiwick and was, I am afraid, not very forthcoming about "a new London," said to be jumping with sex, drugs, and rock 'n' roll. I was not so very "*with it*" that I could to keep *Time* readers *au courant* with the up-to-minute trendiness that weekly news rhythms demand.

"Well," I recall saying to Judson, waving my arms at the Haymarket windows in our editorial attic (in the direction of. presumably, Chelsea to the west), "Somewhere out there London is swinging!"

Time quoted the phrase in its cover story (15 April 1966) as if I knew what I was talking about; and the rest is history, or a minor paradox thereof. The nonplussed contestants in a popular BBC quiz program gave the question a pass when they were asked about the origins of the by then fashionable buzzword of the pop community. Angus McGill had documented it by quoting me as quoted in *Time* in a long account in the *Evening Standard* of the 1960s, "When Every One Loved London." I imagine the BBC had this cutting in its morgue (and possibly in its data-base) although the ascription is dubious. (Hadn't I skeptically implied: Really "*swinging? No way!*"). The quiz question was impossibly hard.

Our chat about the drug scene brought us from *LSD* (and the Beatles' "Lucy in the Sky with Diamonds") to something called *FDA* which, one had heard, was the next big super-hallucinogen. Whether it was or not I had no reliable knowledge; but I had picked up the tidbit in Manhattan from a sheet called the *East Village Other*, and I should have suspected that its editors were sharing their "high" with the readers, not their low-down. Now it can be told. In Paul Krassner's memoir of "the Summer of Love," the author remembers affectionately "the afternoon of Oct. 6, 1966, the day LSD became illegal," when he stood with thousands of young people who had "gathered for the purpose of simultaneously swallowing tabs of *LSD* in front of the police."

What, then, was *FDA?* It was supposed to contain (like *LSD*) something called "*serontin*" and it was a concoction made from smoked banana skins. It was worth waiting for some thirty years to learn the truth of "the Great Banana Hoax." As Krassner recalls, the news about *FDA* was featured in the so-called underground papers (fed by an "Underground Press Syndicate") and it quickly became known nationwide that you could get high legally from smoking the smoked dried banana skins:

> In San Francisco, there was a banana smoke-in, and one entrepreneur started a successful mail-order banana powder business. Federal agents headed for their own laboratories, cooking, scraping and grinding 30 pounds of bananas according to a recipe published in the underground papers. For three weeks, the Food & Drug Administration tried to 'smoke' the dried banana peels.

Time Magazine duly reported the new craze. No matter that the stuff didn't work (strictly speaking, didn't even exist). It was all in the spirit of cosmic hi-jinks, and if the fun-and-games are largely over, many of that '68 generation remain loyal (as does Paul Krassner) to its "world revolutionary ideals": namely, "the pursuit of joy and the expansion of consciousness."

Ours has just been expanded with a story of a splendid spoof. Unlike in the militant "Days of Rage" in the good old times, nobody got hurt, nobody was laid low or even turned on high. Effervescence was short-lived; and after a while the happy hoaxters grew weary. It wasn't the first time in history, nor the last, when utopia and revolution fizzled out.[7]

There is in all this–from the well-meaning fraudulence in science to the cynical fakery of media tabloidists–a deeper sub-stratum of human behavior, a drive to deceive or to indulge in habitual hoaxing, fostered by any society which offers rewards of fame or fortune to messengers with marketable news. P. T. Barnum may not have gotten it exactly, statistically right–in his aphorism about a sucker being born every minute and two to take him–but the *rubes*, and their gullible friends among the *palookas* and the *greenhorns*, will always be with us. Circuses nowadays are more closely regulated by safety and fair-trade inspectors; and Press & Broadcasting Councils in many lands are busy establishing and defending standards of reportage which would guarantee a certain level of accuracy and truth-telling. The Barnums are beginning to have it slightly more difficult these days.

Still, there would seem to be a persistent "cultural addiction" to certain forms of counterfeit in our societies; and once hooked our communicators will be happy to operate as dealers in a gray market in which usable stuff will be easy to get and to fix. In London one television producer–she had been found to have faked scenes in a documentary film about "rent boys"–charged that program-makers were continuing to turn a blind eye to hoaxes (which include the appearance of actors masquerading as "authentic witnesses"), telling the stories. At the Edinburgh International Television Festival (1999) a seminar called "*Liar, Liar, Pants on Fire!*" heard evidence that little had changed despite pledges to tighten standards. One BBC spokesman (and the BBC has not been guiltless) declared that if program-makers let faking go unchecked it could become "a cancer that will spread throughout television." One faked picture obviates the necessity of forging a thousand words of spurious text.

The excuse is the ineluctable apology of an entertainment culture where everything must amuse and anything goes: "We were only joking." Critics have pointed out that it was dangerous to pretend that fakery on light-hearted programs (chat shows, and the like) was any more acceptable than on serious news broadcasts and documentaries. The distinction is untenable. If one is passing off testimony which is inaccurate, untrue, and knowingly non-factual, one is "on a slippery slope," and the nihilistic trend is to audience mistrust and general cynicism.[8]

Now that the Americans have invented "virtual reality"–and exported it (or the means of transmitting it) to the rest of the world–they find themselves, willy-nilly, involved in an abstract, intellectual, and even metaphysical discussion of lies, deceptions, and the nature of the realities pictured on the television screen. True, it is relatively unencumbered with the philosophical baggage which experienced European journalists–an Umberto Eco, in his Italian columns; a Jean-François Revel, in his Paris commentaries–bring to everyday media problems. But, for all that, there remains a pragmatic earnestness which makes even the most light-hearted transatlantic naïveté an instructive experience.

One American headline recently read:

TV'S FULL OF DECEPTIONS
SO WHO NOTICES THE LIES?

For one, Daniel Schorr. He reported from Europe for many of the post-War years, and concluded his career with CBS television with major assignments for National Public Radio. I remember in his Central European years his arrival in Berlin from Yugoslavia to do an interview with the East German Communist leader, Walter Ulbricht. He was at that time a rather young and very committed political correspondent, and he had prepared a clip-board of rather sharp, provocative questions. Ulbricht was so provoked. He lost his temper with Dan Schorr, raged at him and stalked out of the room. Calm was subsequently restored; and the edited CBS interview as shown in the U.S. was, in the end, nice and lively and quite instructive.

Some time later I was interested to learn that Dan Schorr had been congratulated on his "composure" during the stormy filming sessions by no less than the chairman of the Columbia Broadcasting System, William Paley. "*Composure?*" But nobody had been composed. Long shots and close-ups had been skilfully edited in the TV studios, and an additional series of what are called "listening poses" were also inter-cut to make a montage which reflected what both sides in East Berlin considered a useful exchange of views. Not even Bill Paley had realized that he was presiding over such a "movieland world." When Dan Schorr explained to him what had transpired–and how indeed television news is inevitably affected by the camera-eye's optics and the studio climate of make-believe–Paley could only ask, somewhat aghast (it was only the early years of TV), "But was that *honest?*" To which the reply was that it was conventional.

Everybody has learned much since then, especially about how the conventions of contemporary newsgathering have introduced the use of deception as an investigative tool, not to mention the shady habits of melodramatic reenactments. It was a long journey since, as Schorr says, "I came to understand the clever technology that enabled one to be seen standing in the halls of Congress while actually against a blue screen in the studio. A harmless little lie." But there is, as we all have come to know, "a seamless line between the small and the large deception," between the innocuous pictorial backdrop and, say, the splicing-together of isolated sentences in conflicting interviews to make a large and lethal political point against a high public person. It is only a step onward to staging an explosion in order to illustrate a headline and employing actors as extras to fill out a crowd scene. I remember seeing in Washington–and being rather taken in–a documentary film about a confessed American espionage agent where he could be seen handing a briefcase to a Soviet agent on a Vienna street. The ABC network, to maximalize gullibility, neglected to say that this was "a simulation."

I have followed the career of my friend Daniel Schorr since he went into broadcasting in 1953, and memorable was his story of the one-liner he had first received as advice from a cynical CBS producer: "The secret of success is *sincerity*–if you can fake that, you've got it made!" Schorr, and so many others among his American colleagues, declined the advice, and "made it" by being seriously sincere. They may well be virtually isolated in the new realities. As Schorr writes (in 1997), "Let me answer the question, 'Should journalists lie?' with another question: In a medium so laden with mendacity, do you think they are really aware of what a lie is?" European philosophical experience may favor approaching these questions as a matter of epistemology, going on to explore the virtual nature of knowledge. What some critics consider to be American naïveté may suggest that it is also a personal matter of simple ethics. What is at stake is holding virtually fast to certain practical precepts of truth telling.

One final incident to suggest the entanglements of fact and image in what the papers have been reporting, and the darkening shadow of their discreditable delinquency.

The *Sun* newspaper had a scoop. As so often in the London tabloid world, it concerned British royalty; and in this case the main character was, yet again, Her Royal Highness (as she then was) Princess Diana. A videocassette, sensational and scandalous, pictured an intimate love scene between the philandering unfortunate Princess and one of her male lovers. Why had it found its way to the print media and not to the electronic media? How had it reached the front-page of a newspaper which promptly gave it six other full pages as a "world exclusive"? Well, the videocassette was of rather poor viewing quality, too dark and too grainy for most television screens. Indeed it was also too brief to make substantial TV fare (only some seventy seconds of a curtained bedroom scene featuring two semi-nude bodies). This was far too meager for the voracious appetite of TV-muckrakers, and thus it wound up as a Fleet Street scoop since a newspaper can feed very well on the dozen enlargements of apparently revealing still photographs.

The *Sun*'s old-fashioned press competition, in its upstaged chagrin, immediately went into its investigative mode; and within twenty-four hours other
rival tabloids (the *Mirror* leading the pack) had unmasked the *Sun*'s videocassette as a hoax which used look-alike models. The hoaxter had concealed his
mendacity with poor-quality photography which could be sold as only "natural," what with his secret hand-held camera being precariously positioned in
nearby bushes. Names, studio addresses, mannequins' confessions were disclosed. The BBC and ITV small-screen competitors left well enough alone,
but the *Daily Mirror*–which, not having itself bought the video cassette, had
led the crusade for the truth and the real (non-existent) facts–actually managed to gloat for a week.[9]

Every other newspaper editor consoled himself with his piece of luck: but
for the size of the escalating amount in this kind of checkbook journalism,
there goeth he. Meanwhile, there was time for the murmurings of the usual
morality of our Fourth Estate: *Responsibility...Respect for Privacy...Accuracy.*
I imagine they also serve some good purpose who only stand and wait and do
lip-service to noble catch-words.

Janet Cooke and the Color of Truth

There is a special tragicomic aspect to the Janet Cooke story, to which I
have already made passing reference, which adds to the central hoax of its
being a believable forgery. It touches on some other themes in our account of
the newspaper culture: (a) the ironic twists of an unusual black usage of the n-
word; (b) the excessive ethnic over-load of making a "culture" of a skin color;
and (c) the problem of writing good prose when big-town journalists are caught
between the pressures of *jive* (black English or any kind of local vernacular)
and profanity (or the demotic use of the whole f-word world).

Some fifteen years have gone by since the Pulitzer jury admitted that it was
"taken in," and the editors of the *Washington Post* criticized themselves for
misleading the readership by not double-checking a story which they had
carelessly published and then proudly submitted for a great prize. They were
especially contrite for having accepted the Janet Cooke account of
"*Jimmy's World*" (all about the horror of a black eight-year-old heroin
addict) as "the truth" only because it sounded as if it could be true., and
was written by an "insider" as if blackness conferred automatic expertise.
Ms. Cooke thus became the first Pulitzer Prize-winner who was forced to
return U.S. journalism's highest honor. She became, to quote one recent
account of the affair, "one of the most infamous figures in journalism," her
infamy cutting across such diverse issues as "plagiarism and fabrication,
anonymity and unnamed sources, minority recruitment, newsroom ethics,
resumé fraud, the precarious practice of New Journalism." Small wonder that
the estimable ombudsman of the *Washington Post* published an 18,000-word
investigation into its "disgrace" which took on for a moment–as Warhol might

say, infamous for only fifteen minutes–the Dreiseresque force of an American tragedy.

Now there is an additional scandal which is adding to the burden of the old "Negro" community, then (in 1981) the "black" minority–a majority in Washington, D.C.–or what is now known as the African-American culture. Apparently, as Ms. Donna Britt reported in the *Washington Post*, the African-American journalist who had become "our best-known liar" has just scandalized her brothers and sisters yet again by recording her "confessions" (presumably true relevations behind all the fabrications she had devised). She has also succeeded in selling her life-story for $1.6 million dollars to a Hollywood studio planning to make a feature film. She was not content to being "an embarrassment and an outrage" to her people; she was now going to "cash in" in a big way. As Ms. Britt moralized about the "lessons to be learned from the ironies":

> People of every color lie, some egregiously. So why does the Cooke scandal still smart? Because her hoax made me and other black writers feel as awful as a stranger's act possibly could....Many of us [had] felt pride and kinship. Now the scandal was painful...excruciating.

Yet the lesson that some others would draw from the Cooke case was almost the very opposite that impressed itself on the troubled corps of "African-American reporters."

There is a price to be paid for "relating to" a successful Brother-or-Sister. I have referred to it as an ethnic over-load, and it is a burden under which you can often sink to your knees. One invests racially in "pride"–in special feelings of "kinship" with successful prototypes emerging from your "neighborhood," from your kind of ghetto–and it is at great emotional risk. Some of the go-getters may turn out to be gangsters who rob and kill (like Lepke Buchalter from Brooklyn's Murder, Inc.)–and what are all New York Jews supposed to do, go into ethnic sack-cloth and ashes? The psychic profit one can get from "relating to" an Einstein or a Saul Bellow–or to a Wojtyla or Mother Theresa, or to a General Powell or a Paul Robeson–is more than nullified when a nice Jewish boy is exposed as a crook, a famously pious Bishop as a seducer of teen-age choristers, a Black stockbroker (or big by-line reporter like Ms. Cooke) as a shady fixer. All such pride goeth before a fall. Ethnic ideologies, whether on behalf of racial or religious minorities, appear to demand role models framed in an extravagant spirit of hero-worship. If the press is not sufficiently free and honest–and, on suitable occasions, politically incorrect enough–to report the true and full story, letting the chips fall where they may, a relentlessly regular series of disappointments will come to dismay and disenchant. The herd of the faithful and true believers will be "painfully, excruciatingly" disabused of the illicit sense of solidarity. "Those who feel linked to strangers' triumphs," Donna Britt admits, "will feel just as linked to their defeats."

Ms. Britt, reconsidering the Janet Cooke story in the *Washington Post*, makes an earnest effort to unlink herself with a stranger's defeat. She finds that "the lie still rankles"; but she looks away from finding the fault in ourselves, only in the stars that failed to twinkle in an astrally correct way. Even before she became "a black scam artist" Ms. Cooke was apparently not worth "relating to" or "identifying with." She was not authentically one of us; she never really belonged. One of her editors at the *Post*, another "light-skinned black," thought Janet Cooke useless as a reporter in the Washington neighborhoods; she couldn't really "go out in the street and talk to the people." After all, "she didn't speak the language."

The required language was, of course, jive; and she was too well educated (Vassar, Phi Beta Kappa) to get it right. In writing "Jimmy's" story she was first caught out by writing "*I be goin'*" when everybody else knew that blacks in D.C. ghettoes didn't say that but "*I goin'*," and consequently her dialogue, as her critics wrote, "sounded like a white person imitating jive."

Whiteness was the fault-line. Black, as John Updike fantasized, is a shade of brown–"so is white, if you look." As a schoolgirl Janet Cooke, a product of an ambitious middle-class Negro family, used to be doused with baby-powder by black class-mates "so she would look the color she acted." She herself recited a childish bedtime prayer to become different, to "wake up blonde." She did become distinctive, at least in chromatic style. On one of her first trips to "the ghetto," only several miles from the White House in mid-Washington, "a kid looked her up and down and asked, 'What kinda nigger are you?'"

The self-confident reply was: "The kind you've never met in your life, young man." She became unique. She felt, as she tells it, "a new sense of purpose" welling up inside her: "My goal was to create Supernigger." Alas, she only succeeded in adding a small if colorful footnote to Whitey's own long and checkered history of faking, hoaxing, and pretending.

Yet she was, in her way, destined to play the role for which she had created herself as the role model. American journalism awaited its new star casting, compensating for ages of discrimination when blacks played only clowns on the studio set; and here is a former *Washington Post* writer's description of her triumphal entrance:

> She sashayed into the acre-square newsroom of the *Washington Post* on the third day of 1980, wearing a red wool suit over a white silk shirt, the neck opened casually to the second button, exposing a thin gold chain, a teasing glimpse of lingerie, the slight swell of a milk-chocolate breast. Her long acrylic nails gleaming in the hard fluorescent light, she made her way down a long aisle between the desk pods of the Metro section toward the Weekly.
>
> As she passed, heads turned, eyes bugged. People swiveled around and watched the pleasing sway of her hip, the jaunty bounce of her Marie Antoinette ringlets, a mass of dark, lacquered curls that trailed past her shoulder blades. For years the customary

greeting in the newsroom had been 'What's the gossip?' At the moment, this clearly was it.

Her name was Janet Cooke.

The self-parodic quality of the prose has to be set in counter-balance to the pastiche of profanity which provided the sound-track of *Washington Post* conversation. According to the reportage of Mike Sager (a colleague who befriended and indeed loved the beauteous girl), this began as "a fuckin' wet dream" for the men who were running the paper (i.e., Ben Bradlee & Co.). There was a bit of difficulty finding her a place to sit, and she said: "Jesus Christ, this is the *Washington fucking Post*. Can't they find me a desk?" But she landed a spot, for she had learned in a disciplined family how to be aggressive, how to get her way, how to sound like a real American rebel. "Janet began to think. Fuck it, Daddy. I'm going to open the front door." And when the time came for her big chance, a golden assignment to write the tragedy of "Jimmy"; most everybody in the acre-square newsroom was "ecstatic"–"That's a fuckin' front-page story!" An alternative way of putting this highest of journalistic expectations is (again quoting Sager) "what [Pulitzer-Prize winning Bob] Woodward would call a 'Holy Shit' story, the most precious coin of the realm." But it was not to be. After she was pressed to confess she even admitted to herself, "I'm really fucked up." And when she had to stand before Ben Bradlee, in his big office with its executive desk, it was (of all things) "four French words [that] echoed in her mind. They translated, 'Go fuck yourself'."

After such eloquence in the newsroom, what room for elegance in the newspaper? Here is one passage from Janet Cooke's *Washington Post* text, for what is finally published in the paper is surely the *raison d'être* for all the to'ing and fro'ing, the sashaying and the gossip, the literary ambition and the rough repartee.

> Jimmy is 8 years old and a third-generation heroin addict, a precocious little boy with sandy hair, velvety brown eyes and needle marks freckling the baby-smooth skin of his brown arms.
>
> He nestles in a large, beige reclining chair in the living room of his comfortably furnished home in Southeast Washington. There is an almost cherubic expression on his small, round face as he talks about life–clothes, money, the Baltimore Orioles.

The prose here seems also to be sashaying through the *Post* newsroom, teasing here and slightly swelling there, with its soft casual openings and a sudden gleam in the hard light: "The needle slides into the boy's soft skin like a straw pushed into the center of a freshly baked cake."

This kind of colorized writing, praised and prized, is the price to be paid for all the fun and hi-jinks that is to be had in all the newsrooms of the great newspapers in the land. For many readers it will seem a punishment for sins not of our doing.

Not a line of jive in a thousand words? Not an expletive to highlight an emotion or strike an attitude? This seems to be a most unnatural way of writing, especially for devotees of what Ted Bernstein used to call (and he was agin' it) the Write-As-You-Talk school of journalism. The "common language" as truly spoken by men (and, increasingly, women) is left to be recaptured only in scrupulously transcribed quotations, and then only with a self-conscious sense of difference and distance–sometimes, as we have seen, suggesting élite dismay, more often nowadays signalling the popularistic solidarity of the high avant-garde with the low demotic. Speak like Henry Miller, write like John Milton. Good "Holy" stories for the golden front page have to have a formal cadence which sounds like natural rhythms; and they have to be, as Hemingway never tired of saying, lean and clean and with only an occasional touch of color to break up the black and white. One way or the other, alas, they tend to turn out to be contrived prevarications, pieces of virtual non-fiction, fables (and not history) which we can disagree on.

The final impression of Janet Cooke's "confession" after some fifteen years of inner exile–as recorded by Mike Sager in the January 1996 *GQ* magazine, and reinforced by the harsher African-American re-evaluations it prompted–is that the poor little rich girl has served her penance but was still in excommunication. She was in her way, if one were tempted by the fashionable search for roots (one's own and other people's too), a grand-daughter of Uncle Tom; but Harriet Beecher Stowe has not yet come back into vogue. She is taken to be, in the chromatically correct metaphor of racial ideologists for whom color is a whole culture, an "*Oriole cookie*." An "*oreo*" is derived from a popular chocolate-and-cream biscuit that was "black on the outside and white on the inside." Her youthful rise to the top of the preponderantly white profession of journalism was a "scam" in its own right, for she had been "adroitly manipulating racial-gender tensions":

> To us and, by all appearances, to Ms. Cooke herself, Race mattered so much to her she seems to have run screaming from it, telling *GQ* that she never had a black female friend or dated a black man. It mattered enough that when falsifying her resumé [in her job-application to the *Post*], she created "Supernigger"–her term for a prize-winning Ivy-League-educated black reporter irresistible to white editors.

One must double-check whether, in the record of first usages, the woman is at least given credit for the black original coinage of an n-word variant in its *Super* mode.

In any event, happy is the tribe that never suffers the shame of fallen heroes (or heroines).[10]

The Duping of Hersh's "Camelot"

Some of the greatest fakes never see the light of day. Forgers were busy, greed was high, as the market for counterfeit was researched for its maximum gullibility. Then, some small error–a leak or even, perhaps, a cynical skeptical remark by some outside source–upsets the inside conspirators and the whole audacious project is abandoned. This is what can be called preventive de-bunking, and it often consigns prematurely the best-laid plans for a scoop or a sensation to the garbage can of virtual history.

Nowadays the outing of the inside story of a hoax-that-almost-was is itself a saleable item, if not as lucratively so as the original fake, premeditated with such tireless ingenuity. Accordingly, there are very good films about counter-feiting documentary television news, and fascinating articles about would-be scoops which came close to bamboozling a nation. A long essay in *Vanity Fair* is a recent example of the latter wherein Robert Sam Anson did a muckraking job on one of the most celebrated muckrakers of the day–Seymour Hersh and his self-censored best-selling *The Dark Side of Camelot* (1997). Several hun-dred pages of scandalizing sensations fell by the wayside as a long-awaited book by a famous investigative reporter emerged in a glossy tale of "debt, deception, and frantic deal-making."[11]

It all began, as all such stories do, with the breathtaking discovery of a historic unknown collection of important records which would–when authen-ticated, annotated, analyzed and finally published–change utterly our exist-ing views on certain famous men and events. As *Newsweek* reported, "it was an investigative reporter's dream come true: a trove of documents." History is always waiting to be rewritten, and an inspired investigator comes regularly and conveniently with new light and perspectives often based on such trea-sure troves. When the *New York Times* desired to compete with the *Washington Post*, who had the Woodward and Bernstein duo on its team to come up with "Deep Throat" scoops (Nixon's Watergate, etc.), it hired Seymour Hersh who had, similarly, exposed high-ranking generals and powerful politicians, with-out fear or favor (the My Lai massacre in Vietnam, and the like). Harrison Salisbury, who wrote a history of the *Times*, proudly called Hersh "a Vesuvius of a reporter," fiery, colorful, explosive, deadly.

What moved Hersh to yet another round of spectacular fireworks was the "secret papers" of a lawyer named Lawrence Cusack who had been a confiden-tial counselor to many prominent Americans (*viz.*, Cardinal Spellman) and had served the Kennedy family (President John, brother Bobby, among others). Cusack died in 1985, and his son had been offering as "private Kennediana" some items he had found in his father's papers which collectors, through a memorabilia merchant named Thomas C. McCloud and other dealers, were gobbling up at relatively high prices. If Hersh were willing to go along and write up the story, the Cusack collection would only increase its value (especially the lurid pieces involving Marilyn Monroe and the so-called White House black-mail melodrama before her sudden, tragic death in Hollywood in 1962). Here was enough scandal–sex, ruin, vice, corruption, and other improprieties–to illuminate "the dark side of Camelot." In addition to which it represented a high-minded tale of low-life intrigue which ought to shake the consciences of millions of Americans who had given the martyred President Kennedy (and all of his Camelot knights-of-the-round-table) so much support, enthusiasm, and starry-eyed devotion. It was not so much a matter of "doing dirt" on celebrities and making them infamous for 15 minutes, as cleaning up the record. Telling the truth and making us free–free of illusions and deceptions, and worse.

I considered for a while registering this whole "dark side of investigative reporting" elsewhere in this book, namely in the chapters devoted to the f-word, s-word and other obscenities; for it appears to need the context of expletives and scatological reference without which this kind of research cannot be appropriately conducted. I don't know how a Charles Beard responded when he first came across the carton of eighteenth-century U.S. financial documents which led to his radical *An Economic Interpretation of the Constitution of the United States* (1913). Or when Theodor Mommsen first assembled his archaeological evidence, especially the Mediterranean inscriptions, to shape his revised version of the *History of Rome* (3 vols., 1854-1855). When Hersh made his first assessment of the "Cusack papers" which would reverse almost every received notion of the Kennedy-*Camelot* years, he enthused that it was all "insane shit," which expressed the acme of a reporter's enthusiasm. The s-word remained the measure of all things, good or bad, as far as historiography and its methodological rules are concerned. When little doubts began to plague the big U.S. television networks which had given him million-dollar advances to fly where no man had flown before–some, if not all, of the documents seemed to be of questionable authenticity. The "insane" richness of the materials seemed to fade away. Fears were obsessive that what they were handling was indeed "full of shit." A suggestion that a completely different work might be written for the best-selling lists and for the TV screen, namely, an exposé of the collapse of communism, was greeted with the apodictic remark, "No one gives a fuck for the Cold War." Which was not quite the case with Marilyn Monroe, for obvious reasons.

Well, to the extent that one was taking conscientious trouble to "check out" the Cusack documents, hesitations mounted. One senior knight at the Camelot round-table, Theodore Sorensen (Kennedy's speech-writer), examined the handwritten letters of the President and opined that it *"looked like"* Kennedy's writing–but that, after all, was the very point of *"good forgeries."* When Ben Bradlee, the experienced *Washington Post* editor, was shown the evidence, he only said, "Where is Hersh getting all this crap?"

The integrity of the Cusack collection was the decisive problem. Hersh saw it only piece by piece. Nice and juicy bits trickled out onto the market. Sales were good (four million dollars worth) to "history buffs"; contracts were signed for paperback rights, foreign translations, feature-film options, and all the profitable rest.

Then, finally, the technicians in the laboratories of Manhattan began to take over. The s- and f-word babble gave way to a different vocabulary of expertise. The investors just *had* to know: to be *sure,* to be really convinced that "this stuff is good, not just that it ain't bad."

The technical analysis was exhaustive. How important were the little "textual errors"? A postal zip code in a Marilyn Monroe letter appeared on the envelope several years before such numbers came into practice. There were hidden bank-account numbers that simply didn't exist. There was a total lack of fingerprints on supposed original private letters from the White House. (Maybe a secretary had wiped them clean? "Oh, shit!" Hersh said.)

How long did it take until the threadbare case for the documents that secretly held "the Full, Untold, True story" fell apart? As in other famous Washington cases–notably, the Alger Hiss/Whittaker Chambers "*Woodstock* typewriter"–the machine in question was central. Could one pinpoint the work of a ball-style IBM Selectric typewriter? Could its characters be "lifted off"? No point in that, since IBM had brought out the model supposedly involved some ten years later than the documents which were purported to have been typed on it! And what about the plastic ribbon on Marilyn Monroe's personal machine? It was used for the infamous "blackmail letter" to the Kennedys (who were to fork out a huge cash payment–to her mother–to buy Marilyn's discreet silence). But this type of ribbon had been invented only several years later! The microscopic analysis went into such matters as the shape of commas and question marks, and the spacing between alphabetic letters. Last but not least, the paper itself. Stationery can be dated accurately. Nothing matched, fitted in with the dates. Every inquiry turned out to produce "glitches." Hersh had been duped. He hurriedly excised some 265 pages of documentation which had served to illuminate the real truth of Camelot, its "dark side," nay, its Stygian blackness. *Newsweek* rushed to expose "the JFK-Marilyn Hoax": "It was a sizzling scoop–a famous reporter finds a secret stash of papers linking Kennedy, Monroe and the mob. One problem: the documents were fakes."

What remained after the cleanout was readable enough, and promptly made the U.S. best-seller lists. The Book-of-the-Month Club, which had paid a half-million dollar advance, still picked it as its first selection. Newspapermen grudgingly conceded that not all Hersh's "wild stories" were made out of whole cloth or of bits of anachronistic plastic. The *New York Times'* reviewer attested,

> Quotations in *The Dark Side of Camelot* are almost fully attributed. The book includes material from unpublished memoirs, newly opened FBI files and 14 previously unheard tapes of President Kennedy's conversations. The chapter notes cover 16 pages, but there is not the rigorous footnoting favored by historians.
> "Who wants to write a book for historians?" Mr. Hersh said.[12]

More critical reviewers contend rudely that he had written a book for "suckers," assembling a dozen flimsily substantiated claims, a hundred dubious vaguely-remembered anecdotes (in the questionable style of "recovered memory"), all heated up in half-baked speculation which could tax the gull-ibility of even the most ignorant and naive. One historian (Gary Wills) imp-ishly remarked that he was prepared to believe nine bad things about John Kennedy before breakfast–"until Mr. Hersh adds a tenth, and that makes me begin to wondering about the first nine."

> He tells us [Professor Wills adds] so many unbelievable things he says we never knew that we begin to doubt all the things we thought we knew. (Gary Wills' point-by-point critique of the Hersh book, "A Second Assassination," is in the *New York Review of Books*, 18 December 1997, pp. 4-8.)

He goes on to picture the author "positively salivating" over the Camelot sex stories (from the listing of all the mistresses being secretly smuggled into the White House to the recapitulation of the medical reports of recurrent vene-real disease) and comes to the pitiless conclusion: "Anyone puzzled by the way Hersh fell for the story of Laurence Cusack, a man passing him forged documents about Marilyn Monroe, has only to read this book to wonder what he would *not* fall for if it fit his purpose."

Another skeptical reviewer (Edward Jay Epstein in the *Los Angeles Times*) was equally dismissive of the "radical revision" of history which, in Hersh's version, now depicted President Kennedy as a sex maniac, marital cheat, biga-mist, speed freak, liar and corrupt politician...who employed in his covert service Mafia chiefs, panderers, Communist spies and political fixers...and engaged in stealing national elections, shaking down corporations for contri-butions, plotting assassinations, and in the Cuban missile crisis (wherein he was once inevitably portrayed as a cool and courageous spirit, even an heroic and honorable man) secretly caving in to Soviet conditions. This, according to our investigative and revisionist author, is all new and substantiated. Epstein dissents, and writes, "much of what is substantiated in his book is not new, and much of what is new, including his most sensational findings, cannot be sub-stantiated." As for the forgeries, Epstein gives Hersh credit for not including the fraudulent Cusack documentation in his book. But then he had no choice, given the massive pre-publication campaign of what I have called preventive debunking. And so, at bottom, it is an exercise in that brand of "creative journalism" which by its very nature cannot produce true and credible his-tory–and, in the end, the book turns out to be, alas, more about the deficiencies of investigative journalism than about the dark side of Kennedy's *Camelot*. (Edward Jay Epstein's review of the Hersh book, "Recovered Memories," in the Sunday Books section of the *Los Angeles Times*, 26 December 1997, p. 6.)

The whole game was neatly given away by a *Washington Post* columnist (or his headline writer at the *Herald-Tribune*) with a sly phrase in the caption–

KENNEDY'S PRIVATE LIFE?
IT'S ONLY AN ASTERISK

Here the sex and its salacity gets its singular star billing, and all the nod-and-wink innuendoes of our F***-L****r [four-letter] culture finally come of age, and into the big time. Concision is now the name of the game as in the new coinage (to which William Safire has already paid tribute) *the full Monty*. Read properly, asterisks have a fullness all of their own.[13]

In Britain the Hersh book was serialized before publication by the *Sunday Times* which can–as its (and my) readers well know–always be relied upon to find and feature the good bits. In the very first *Times* installment we were favored by a prominently shaded box, printed in bold face, and highlighting the celebrated bosom of the late Marilyn Monroe. Investigative reporters have long been suggesting, on the basis of no detectable tangible evidence, that the distraught and suicidal movie star had been having an affair with both the Kennedy brothers, President Jack and Attorney-General Bobby.* Here is how Hersh sets the atmosphere of such sexual encounters:

> Jack Kennedy's most famous affair was with Marilyn Monroe, the American film goddess who worked her way through husbands, lovers, pills, liquor and psychiatric hospitals until her death, apparently by accidental suicide, in August 1962....
> [She had] a lavish admiration for Jack Kennedy...[saying to her psychoanalyst] "he is the greatest and most powerful man in the world....This man is going to change our country. No child will go hungry, no person will sleep in the street and get his meals from garbage cans....No, I'm not talking utopia, that's an illusion. But he will transform America like Franklin Delano Roosevelt did in the Thirties."

These confidential quotes from the psychiatrist's couch lead directly to the scraps which Hersh obtained from "veteran Hollywood reporters" in the Beverly Hills Hotel. So do we link political ideology to sexual assignation:

> She said, "Once in a while I meet a nice guy, a really nice guy....And we have a few drinks and go to bed. Then I see his eyes glaze over and can see it going through his mind: O, my God. I'm going to f*** Marilyn Monroe–and he can't do it."

Then she started howling with misery over this. I just bent over double laughing. And she began pounding on me, "It's not funny."

---

*   The careful historians who argue that there is "no evidence" to be found include the two biographers: Donald Spoto, *Marilyn Monroe* (1993), and James W. Hilty, *Robert Kennedy: Brother Protector* (1997). Professor Wills points a finger at "Norman Mailer, who did so much to popularize the myth of Robert Kennedy's affair with Monroe," quoting Hilty (p. 553) to the effect that Mailer had "breezily told a TV interviewer that he included the allegations against Kennedy to please an editor who wanted to sell more books – 'I needed money very badly'."

The greed was contagious. The forger recast Monroe in a rôle where she also needed money very badly, and was supposed to have signed receipts for the cash when the Kennedys forked it over. A likely story.

Hersh seems to have got it right: not very funny indeed, in fact very sad. Associated with the *tristesse* classically connected with the f-word amd its aftermath. (*Sunday Times'* serialization of the Hersh book, 9 November 1997 (News Review), pp. 1-2.)

The trouble with investigative reporting, its "dark side" if you will, is whatever it investigates it is willfully prepared to believe the very worst. Normally professional reporting calls for "digging," getting at the facts, distrusting hokum and bunkum, making an accurate and coherent story of some newsworthy happening. What more can "investigativeness" add? A measure of more ruthless research, perhaps. Brow-beating and bullying sources who are not forthcoming; and then outraging editors and readers who are accustomed to a more agreeable tone of quiet objectivity. If there is sex it is likely to be of the tawdriest; if there is money involved we must expect greed beyond known limits of recorded corruption. When justice is seen not to have been done, journalism–stern, implacable–must rush to judgement.

Fair enough...so long as, in the final reckoning, the values of truth and reason prevail. Let's face it: the record of investigative reporting has too often been marred by a pattern of quasi-mendacity and willful self-deception which leave the newspaper culture wrestling with its conscience and always winning. *Our* story is *authentic* and *publishable* and indeed of *essential public interest*–because it *could* be true, *might* be true, *appears* to be true, is *almost* true. (These are the well-known slippery rungs of William James' "ladder of faith.") What's more, it is actually remembered by one or two characters who were said to be really there and duly confirmed by one or two others who were somewhere in the vicinity. If it is–or should it prove to be–sensational, or at least outrageous, and, even more, scandalous, bursting out of the conventional frame of previous stories and hence breaking a tired old taboo–then the will to believe grows until it crowds and displaces all normal common sense.

Among the true believers in the original sin of the Kennedys and total corruption of Camelot is Gore Vidal, a distant Kennedy relative and a famous misanthropic wit in his own right, who proceeded to pen a singular defense of Hersh and his findings in the pages of the *New Yorker*. With all the virginal innocence he could muster he asked: "why is there so much fury and fuss at Hersh's attempt to let daylight in on old, old black magic?" For Vidal it was unconscionable for the press to have criticized Hersh on the grounds that he had not "proved" anything. In Vidal's philosophy of history, most of it all scandal and skullduggery, "there really is no way for anyone ever to prove much of anything." In this light–so flattering to all unshaven suspects in the line-up–Hersh emerges as something of an heroic figure, a dragon-fighting St. George, tilting at monstrous evil, at –

the great disinformation apparatus put in place forty years ago [by the "thoroughly disreputable Joe Kennedy who bought his sons major political careers", a monster that even now continues to metastasize within academe and the media to such a degree that myth threatens to overthrow history. Spin is all. Spin of past as well as present.

If all is spin, where then was Vidal (and his ally Seymour Hersh) when the top was first twirled? Who excused them? Presumably we are all condemned to play out our small comic roles on the whirligig:

> Well, now we have the marvelous comedy of Hersh's book being published by Little, Brown which is owned by Time Warner, and reviewed negatively-nervously, nervously-negatively by *Time* (same ownership), while *Newsweek* (owned by the Washington Post Company and still, perhaps, influenced by Kennedy's old friend Ben Bradlee) denounces Hersh, while ABC (owned by Disney) prepares a TV documentary that is tied in with....Many years ago there used to be something called 'conflict of interest." No longer, I'm afraid. Today, we all bathe in the same river. It will be a relief when Bill Gates finally owns everything and there will be just one story.

The one story is, I am afraid, already the same story, as Vidal recycles quotes and anecdotes which he has told wittily many times before (and most recently, word-for-word, in his memoirs of 1996, *Palimpsest*). They all fit in with the "dark side of Camelot"–for "Hersh's case, slapdash as it often is, is essentially true, if not Truth." No proof is needed for charges of abysmal corruption, for "it is the way the world works." Evidently no proof or evidence of Truth is, alas, ever needed "in the tangled weave of human events." In a world of sinners it is quite enough to suspect, darkly, the worst. Lincoln had syphilis; Kennedy had Addison's disease (with venereal complications); Johnson blackmailed his way into the White House; Marilyn Monroe (not unlike Norman Mailer) needed money very badly. Where there is muck, there are muckrakers.

And (as in the bad Kennedy joke) where there is gore, there is Vidal. In one little passing aside Seymour Hersh's nose is badly bloodied in the *New Yorker*'s attempt at a face-saving operation. Hersh tells a flamboyant story of an insidious electoral plan "to run a Kennedy-Kennedy ticket in 1964." As his source, Hersh ascribes it to Gore Vidal who told it to him "in an interview." As Gore Vidal tells it, "actually it was Hersh who told me the story." What is the "essential Truth" of the tale? Who needs any "proof" as to who fabricated it first? Or who duped whom? Take your pick: it will be essentially true according to the counterfeiter's credo. No proof necessary.[14]

In the professional journals of media criticism I find the critics uncharacteristically at a loss for words to describe or characterize a best-selling work by a colleague who had enjoyed some reputation for investigative reportage. At best it is classified as an embarrassing work which attempts to give new impetus to what the *Columbia Journalism Review* terms "*gotcha*" journalism.*

---

*   "*Gotcha!*" is a tabloid coinage, most memorably used by the London tabloids during the Falklands War between Britain and Argentina (1982). In the full-page headline of the *Daily Mirror* when a Royal Navy submarine unceremoniously sank an Argentinian ship, the *Belgrano*, with all 500 hands aboard....*Gotcha!* the front page screamed and, alas, all readers got it.

At worst, despite its "creditable" effort to avoid fraudulent documents expressly counterfeited for the occasion, it represents yet another turning point in what the papers say. As a veteran Washington reporter (Jules Witcover, now of the *Baltimore Sun*) records,

> Ever since the political demise of Gary Hart ten years ago, when a photograph on the front page of the *National Enquirer* showed Donna Rice sitting on his lap on a pier in Bimini, the tabloid tail of American journalism has increasingly been wagging the mainstream dog. Once the supermarket gossip sheets expose other seamy scandals about national political figures, the major newspapers and newsmagazines feel obliged sooner or later to report them, if only to deplore the resort to sleaze. (Jules Witcover, "Unshining Moments," in the *Columbia Journalism Review*, January-February 1998, pp. 69-77.)

The sharpshooter's targeting of Camelot was a professional near-hit thing. Hersh has given us a wild ride and our newspaper culture wound up only with a brass ring, with the lesser evil of sleaze. Had the hoax come off we would have come away with a lie in the soul.

Martin Walser's "Catechism of Correctness"

Two additional examples, both from recent German politics, and they parallel in the heat and light they shed the previous illustrations from the Anglo-Saxon world of newspaper culture. For all press controversies over public scandals resemble each other: in their noise, excitement and other excesses; in their partisan (and partial) argumentation; in their compulsive readability. Beyond that, the German ingredients in cases of journalistic malpractice are mixed differently since such elements as "the breaking of taboos" or "political correctness" are necessarily related to a horrific Hitlerian past unshared by others.

Consequently the great polemical issues which have involved the editors in Bonn, Frankfurt and Munich in recent times appear to be light-years away from the turbulences which have hit the publicists in London or New York. I happen to have heard an eloquent German writer, the celebrated novelist Martin Walser, launch a furious attack on what he called the *Zeitgeist-Theater* of the German press in which histrionics were confounded with history. It was delivered in October 1994 in the medieval *Alte Aula* of the Heidelberg University which resounded with the echoes of what Karl Jaspers had said (in this very auditorium) about what Kant had warned about German guilt and Mme de Staël had truly observed in her travels in the *Allemagne* that used to be. But Walser did cause a topical storm by referring to the following two affairs in a Germany which, as he said, has always had "a certain difficulty in dealing with realities."

Philipp Jenninger sank without a trace in November 1988. Every newspaper pronounced on his sudden political lot; none that I have ever seen dealt with it adequately. As Walser remarked, "It was the fastest demise of any prominent figure in our public life since 1945." What had he done to deserve such a fate? *Spurlos versenkt* (as the communiqués used to say about ill-starred U-boats).

I met the man a number of times in the *Bundestag* in Bonn, and he was a decent, thoughtful if not very brilliant, Christian-Democratic member of Parliament, representing all the solid virtues of postwar German life; and they took him to the third highest post in the Republic, the Presidency of the *Bundestag*. On the 10th of November 1988 he presided at the session which commemorated, fifty years before, the *Kristallnacht*: that fearful first outburst of genocidal anti-Semitism which was to victimize the Jews in the Third Reich. He himself prepared a speech, and it was a good one; I saw him deliver it on TV and studied the text the next morning in the newspapers. What had gone wrong?

For the next day, after a stormy crisis in Bonn, he had already been removed, ignominiously. The chancellor had dropped him; his own party would not defend him; the Opposition had howled during the night for his blood; the leader of the German Jewish community had been shocked. One might have thought, if one didn't have confidence in one's own eyes and ears, that he must have delivered some outrageously unfeeling and insensitive speech, stirring up old traditional racial prejudices, and that his colleagues had dispensed swift justice lest the outside world, *das Ausland*, hears of it—and the foreign press gets to quote the juicy, bloody bits and thus to disgrace the new Germany after so many decades of good behavior. Had he?

Quite the contrary. I myself thought it the most anti-Nazi, even the most "anti-German" speech that I had ever heard in the years of the Bonn Republic. Jenninger was a grave and earnest man, and he wanted to say something chastening that had never been said before. He was well known as a friend of Israel, and was always leading parliamentary delegations to Jerusalem as a tireless proponent of "reconciliation." Now he had his singular chance to "make good." He wrote a text so strong, so full of radical and unprecedented criticism of "the people" who had rallied to Hitler and enjoyed the spoils of the *Führer's* early victories, so replete with quotations of the SS and Gestapo horrors—that he refrained from giving advance copies to the press or even showing it to his colleagues for "support" and "clearance." It was to be fresh, surprising, historic.

The Achilles-heel of his operation was that Philipp Jenninger was not a very good or experienced public speaker. Even if he were, his text required a subtle and eloquent actor, with a voice and eye-brows that could underline ironies and even a few hand-gestures that could indicate the dismay he was feeling at the appalling details he was citing. Incredible as it may seem—and even old Simon Wiesenthal, world Jewry's veteran campaigner against Hitlerism, was astonished as he (with the Israeli ambassador) tried, in vain, to lead a defense campaign—the whole thing was misunderstood. It was a tragedy of errors. When he argued that *das Volk,* the German people, had (alas) benefited from the Nazi aggrandizement, at home and abroad, they thought he was exulting in the popular support. When he quoted the horrific document of the concentration-camp *Kommandant's* ideological justification of the gas chambers, they missed the signal for the *Gänsefüßchen,* the quote-unquote, and got the worst impression.

A slow hum of disquiet filled the *Bundestag.* I saw my SPD-friend, Freimut Duve, whispering to his neighbors, getting up and angrily walking out. There was Heinz Galinski, the valorous but dour leader of the Jewish community, looking more stony-faced than ever. Row after row of CDU and SPD parliamentarians looked increasingly bewildered, as Jenninger bravely droned on, oblivious to the lurking danger: it was to be his last day in office.

Martin Walser calls it, some seven years after, a case of "lynch justice." The Israeli press considered it, with mild surprise, a very curious occurrence of German hysteria. The German newspapers were caught in their own stiff, unbending political correctness—if everybody thinks the man was saying it, he must be guilty of having said it—and missed out on the real story, the scandal behind the misfortune. As for the TV, for once the cameras were in place to play witness to the truth–for once, as the pioneering Edward R. Murrow liked to believe, one could "see it and hear it now."

The cameras were catching the news in real time. There were the usual difficulties of programming prime time and the pictures, when they came, were better than a thousand words—but, in this case, just as complicated. It was a sleepy public that saw and heard the farce in its parliament, the absurd theater that was being made of its tragic history. As Martin Walser put it, television commands power—but only over *die Schläfrigen,* the drowsy millions, half-asleep.

I was in Berlin at the time, and in various public discussions of the affair. I appeared to be in a minority of one. Yet one voice in the right place, I am convinced, would have deflected the course of events. The good man could have been saved by one parliamentary dissenter standing up–and/or one major newspaper urgently proposing–a Commission of Inquiry to look into the case. It would have calmed the hysteria over (as I was told) "what the *New York Times* would be reporting tomorrow morning." The *Times* surely would have gotten the story roughly right–not: "Bonn Outraged at 'Neo-Nazi' Speech in *Bundestag*/High Official Resigns"–if it hadn't been twisted by bent minds the evening before. The Commission would in due time have reported back to the *Bundestag* that there was, in point of hard fact, "no cause for alarm." And, perhaps, that if all schools and universities would be drawn into the discussion by having all students assigned to "*Read and Discuss*" the full text of the disputed Jenninger speech, something substantial would be contributed to democratic re-education at long last.

The second case concerns the best Easterner who never became President of the newly reunited German Republic. Chancellor Helmut Kohl favored, in his Western strength, an *"Ossie"* for the highest post in the land. It was to be a symbol of the reconciliation of the old ex-DDR with the fate of its absorption (voluntary, of course) into the BRD. Once again, since our German friends are not very good at this sort of thing, there was a catastrophic political failure; and this time our newspaper culture was not a helpless witness after the fact, but the active culprit in the nefarious deed.

The candidate's name was Steffen Heitmann, a reflective handsome man in his 40s who had been serving in the impressive government of Dr. Kurt Biedenkopf as the minister of justice in Saxony. In the years of the Communist regime he had functioned as a non-political lawyer, a decent man with a clean record. Nothing could have prepared him for his bouts with the press in a brawling new democracy. He was shrewd and intelligent, but did not know how to duck a question, give an ambiguous or non-committed answer, persist in saying what he (and not what the reporter) wanted to say, and all the other ploys in the repertoire of a professional politician. As a consequence, he was crucified. At the end of an unhappy season of awkward barnstorming, he withdrew—the press had shot him down, and pronounced him a dead duck.

Why? The ruthlessness which was on display in our newspaper culture in the Heitmann case went far beyond the call of duty: frank interrogation of a candidate about his views on the issues of the day. There were catch-questions galore, and no answer the man could give (apart from stale clichés that were not–not yet–in the new chap's rhetoric) could save him from embarrassment, suspicion, and worse. Martin Walser (in his prize-winning Heidelberg address, which was also published in *Der Spiegel* as part of its new muckraking) has a phrase for it: *"the catechism of correctness"* in which each query is put in such a ritualized form that any departure from the standard formula becomes blasphemous.

The question of women. In Germany, as well as elsewhere in the industrial West, there has been a tardy revision of the extreme feminist position on jobs and professional careers to consider the widespread "crisis in the family." Not only hard-pressed single mothers are having difficulties with parental duties. Steffen Heitmann was only pleading for some additional thought about the problem, of how to help women to cope, etc., when he was nailed–in a dozen interviews before a near-fatal one in the inquisitorial *Süddeutsche Zeitung* (Munich) which pounced upon him as an advocate of the pernicious old Teutonic doctrine of *"Kinder, Küche, Kirche."* No, he was not (as a Christian Democrat) against women bearing children; no, he was not against women cooking meals for their families; no, he was not against women attending religious services. But he was not–repeat not–saying that "a woman's place is in the home," in the kitchen cooking for the children, washing up for the whole family. Protest and deny as he would, he could not shake off the impression of male chauvinism, of *macho* neo-Nazi authoritarianism.

The question of the Hitlerian past. Heitmann's view, not very surprisingly for a politician in holding office in Germany (and not doing penance as a hair-shirted monk in Jerusalem) is that "we have to learn how to deal with this terrible history we have." How? By behaving normally, as other peoples and nations do. Is mass murder, then, a normal thing to be dealt with normally? No, the Nazi past is a horror that we must face up to. How would you *normally* deal with a million murders?... Between the normality of an adjective and an adverb, as well as a secret number of hidden assumptions, the candidacy was lost.

How would other men have handled it–say, the last President, the moralist Richard von Weizsäcker? or the present President, the wily Johannes Rau? With flying colors. With a bit of passionate sincerity, a touch of eloquence, a shade of humility; all amounting to–in Walser's phrase, adapting a saw of Hannah Arendt's–*die Banalität des Guten,* the banality of the good. If the press, in its penchant for investigative-inquisitorial ways and means, persists in its *"Tugend-Terror"* in the name of a republic of virtue, it is only banalities–well-meaning or ill-considered, as the case may be–that will survive the heat in the kitchen.

There is a dispiriting lesson in all this for that formidable figure in European letters, Martin Walser. He has been in his time a "tribune of the people," as is inevitable for your modern committed postwar German intellectual. He was once on the old Left, now on the new Right: then a separatist, today a national-patriot. He might well be headed for that "unpolitical" refuge that the young Thomas Mann sought as a private hiding-place: "Lock up your opinions deep within yourselves until they disappear" ("Schließ deine Meinungen fest in dich ein, bis sie verschwinden.") It won't be the first time that opinion perishes in a crudely and incorrigibly opinionated society. As Walser eloquently writes,

> Who are we really, we who want to be free?...Realities have always had a certain difficulty to be accepted in Germany....If we live in the past, then we are missing out on the present. And when we live in the present, what is missing is the past. We are never where we happen to be.[15]

Walser, the lonely critic and public dissenter, would appear to be as much of a victim as his two prime examples of "blasphemers" against a catechism of *"politische Korrektheit."* He is lost in a disoriented newspaper culture, addicted to regrettable malpractices and, especially in Germany, generally conducive to perennial identity crises. The psychic bouts run from a manic *"Who are we, really?"* to a piteous *"What shall ever become of us?"*

It is exceedingly rare that such incidents, involving in part willful misunderstandings and accidental misinterpretations, can get tested. The Jenninger text was subjected to an "ingenious experiment" in Berlin. An outstanding public figure, the late Ignatz Bubis (d. 1999), who was the vigorous leader of the small German Jewish community, assembled a group of his faithful and began reading a speech which he had handy. When he asked what his listeners had thought of the text (and its author), they heaped praise on both; for what they had unmistakably heard was indeed a cogent anti-Nazi analysis of Hitler's success in winning over public opinion in the Third Reich. What Bubis had been reading was the so-called controversial speech of the Bonn *Bundestag* ten years before: Jenninger's.. *Q.E.D.*

There is a bitterly ironic aftermath to this affair. In 1998 Martin Walser (who had dissected the Jenninger case so brilliantly) himself made a big speech in Germany which made headlines, local and worldwide. It was, in some ways, an attractive and thoughtful text–but it could be misinterpreted; and it was. In part, as I suggest, because of small defects in the prose and phraseology, aggravated by snippets as condensed by the press; in part because of the understandable ultra-sensitivities about any and all aspects of the Auschwitz theme. The Walser speech caused "a scandal." The foremost critic of Walser's words on the subject–holding them to be "regrettable... unfortunate... demagogic... untenable... inflammatory...," and, in the end, even pro-Nazi!–was the leader of German Jewry, Ignatz Bubis. Which may suggest, yet again, that arguments about the Holocaust in Germany (and not only there) are tinged with complex ambiguities and verbal behavior verging on the neurotic. How could it be otherwise?[16]

4

The New Shamanism

This leads me to underscore a tendency of our media in the contemporary political culture which combines the unfortunate predispositions which I have already put to the reader–(1) the exaggerated self-importance of some of our self-styled truth-tellers in the struggle for progress and enlightenment; and (2) the indefatigable oppositionism of an elite class educated either to forward-looking utopianism or to the habits of "debunking," exposing, unmasking the civilization which produced them and sustains them.

It may be hard for them to accept the bitter fact that their very civilization—faulty as it is—also contributes to their own disorientation and personal distortion. In order to communicate even the most dissident views, media-makers must necessarily operate within the cul-ture, the so-called "mass" or "popular culture"; and they take on the accents and stratagems of a communications world they would *ordinarily*–that is, if they were not part of it and profiting from it–criticize most mercilessly. Whom should it surprise that so corrupt a culture will produce hucksters of cultural dissent? Why should such an all-pervasive shabbiness not create shabby critics with threadbare characters?

In the New York of my own personal experience over the last three decades, there were three great cases which dominated the media; and they illustrate in their somewhat different ways what I have been trying to suggest about the communications culture. I refer to the two cases heard before the U.S. courts which involved the libel suits of General William Westmoreland against CBS-Television and General Ariel Sharon against *Time* magazine. The third matter was the formidable series of articles which the *New York Times* published about New York City's chief Medical Examiner, whose apparent misdemeanors (corrupt or careless or otherwise) in a dozen incidents of murder made, when I read about them each day, my hair stand on end. By comparison, the so-called Hitler diaries (the forger never got as far as Auschwitz, 1943) make anodyne reading.

The Sharon case was decided, with the Israeli general winning no libel damages, but enjoying a victory: *Time* in its extremist reporting about his

73

controversial role in Lebanon had been judged both inaccurate and negligent, as well as defamatory.

The Westmoreland trial was abrogated, with the defending lawyers of the TV media-stars still trying hard to prove that the general was actually involved in a *"conspiracy"* to deceive the president of the United States, his commander-in-chief. The general soon wearied of a courtroom battle in which the professional soldier was a rank hopeless amateur.

The matter of the unfortunate Dr. Gross, who allegedly made a disgraceful mess of a dozen autopsies (and thereby impeded the course of justice), led to inquiries, suspensions, million-dollar lawsuits, and profound doubts about the whole urban system of so-called law and order.

What all three cases have in common bears upon what I have been saying in trying to characterize the contemporary communications culture: that is the psychology of our leading Western publicists, the spirit of the public-spirited media, the ethos of our adversarial protagonists. In each case the media—a great daily newspaper, an acclaimed news-weekly, a much-honored TV-and-Radio Broadcasting System—claimed to be acting in the interests of truth, but with the arrogance of dogmatists who always claim to have a monopoly of it.

The evidence against Sharon was very hazy at best, and nonexistent (so far as the charge of being a revanchist-murderer was concerned) at worst.

The evidence against General Westmoreland as a "conspirator" was controversial, disputed, and easily susceptible to the interpretation that in the desperate conduct of a war like that in Viet Nam, or indeed *any* war, there are serious and honest differences of opinion about strategy, tactics, intelligence estimates, about what to do and how to do it. None of this needs to be ascribed to sinister intent, needs to be "criminalized" into motivations of treasonable conspiracy.

The evidence against Dr. Gross is lurid and chilling, but when the *New York Times* report-age was, in turn, looked into by reporters of a rival newspaper, the *New York Post*–and this is the latest style in our fashion of Investigative Reporting: investigating the investigators!–it emerged that a good many (who can say how many) of the charges were under a cloud, were loose hearsay, exaggerated misquotations, suspect recriminations by rival medical doctors, and the like.

There are two deviant cultural elements here.

1. The first is that at the edges of our Western cultural temperament there has always lurked a tendency towards conspiracy theories, and to the demonization of culprits. The Jacobins were certain that the King and his Queen were monsters who really deserved to lose their heads; historians take a more differentiated and sceptical view of this. Scholars have also rigorously qualified the extreme *pro-et-contra* views of Napoleon (as in Pieter Geyl's masterful history); and they have relativized the total guilt of the Kaiser in World War I or of the "Merchants of Death," the armament-dealers, in bringing

American troops to the France in 1917 to fight on the Western Front. The vast literature re-examining the mysterious aspects of the Kennedy assassination in Dallas speaks for itself.

This simple, primitive, and essentially mythological attitude towards historical causation has been moving again into the center of the Western mind. Immoderate passions rage, unreasonable convictions gain an upper hand. This process intensifies under the influence of the pressures for immediate and sensational effect which, to a lesser or greater extent, grips almost all of our media.

The *New York Times* just would not devote fifty columns of space to an investigation which reported *on-the-one-hand* and *on-the-other* and went on about how complex and morally ambivalent criminal police work can often be in the largest and most violent city in the world. They had to find a villain, a dyed-in-the-wool malefactor, a monster of iniquity. The TV reporters just couldn't produce a backward glance at the battle of Saigon, an unsensational documentary which didn't cry havoc; it might be too quiet, too boring, too lacking in punch. Prime time cries out for a sensation or a scoop, in this case a sinister criminal conspirator. What Tom Wolfe has called (and he knows, for he's practised it) the *biff!-boom!-bang!* style in journalism prevailed against all other considerations: especially those that might lead to a sense of the complexity of tragedies and the complications of human moti-vation.

More than that, the editors of *Time* exposed themselves as theologians of the printed word, as dogmatists of the dispatch, persuaded of a truth *a priori*– and if the evidence for conspiracy, murder, or being an accessory to the crime isn't in "*Appendix A*" or in "*Appendix B*" then it must be *somewhere,* probably in other secret places or among hiddenaway witnesses which involved or guilt-ridden officials are refusing to reveal. They *know* this, the truth, in advance—even if they don't (as yet) have the facts of the matter. This is pride, *hubris,* of Mephistophelian proportions.

What I have called deviant cultural twists–the distorted semi-intellectual conviction that the full truth is theirs for the asking, and that the ensuing revelation is of such evil that men and women will be stopped in their tracks– may well be what Lévy-Bruhl would consider examples of primitive, pre-logical thinking. They may well be deep human tendencies which thousands of years of progressive civilization have not been able to eliminate. But they are also, ironically enough, a product of our very sophisticated and literate culture.

The irony is that the men who have fallen under its spell are not the shamans, or the witchdoctors, or the demagogues, or the corrupt cynics from whom in the past we have such effusions. They are all educated and cultivated men, children of the Enlightenment and of public-spirited ideals. In their Western education they were exposed to the intellectual he-roes of a sceptical frame of mind: from Socrates to Galileo and Pierre Bayle, from Voltaire to Bertrand Russell. They were nurtured on the legal ideas of meticulous fairness, as developed in the Anglo-Saxon juridical tradition from Blackstone to Maitland, from Holmes to Brandeis to Cardozo. They have been immersed in the complexities and subtleties of modern literature from Flaubert and Stendhal to Proust and Camus, from Kafka to Bellow, from Manzoni to Silone, from Dostoevsky to Thomas Mann. But *here* there are no simple and easy human motivations; *here* there are no black-and-white villains or heroes. *Here* there are investigations into the news of life of the highest order.

We need not be so immodest as to think that we, in the world of the media and of periodical literature, writing and editing quickly for daily, weekly, and monthly deadlines, must aim so high. But there is surely a profound paradox lurking here, the very modern contradiction of the contemporary communications culture, produced as it is by publicists of the richest potential and regressing under the pressure of progress to poor and primitive forms of ritualis-tic noise, to incantations worthy of the darkest witchcraft, to electronic mumbo-jumbo.

I leave you with this paradox, and my own puzzlement. The only true flash of hot- and spot-news I have for you this morning is that we are having real troubles in our tribe. Perhaps I should have looked into the anthropology of it after all. "At this hour" (as the studiously vague phrase of *CNN* time-keeping has it), the shamans are amongst us.

Part 2

Sex and Other Ongoing Titillations

"Given the finite number of things that can be done between sexual partners of whatever kind, the length of time and the number of people that have been doing it all over the globe, and the persistent interest of human beings in exploring the subject, it can be safely assumed that absolute novelty is out of the question."
—Eric Hobsbawm *in* The Guardian *(1997)*

*"**Obscenity**:....indelicacy, bad taste, grossness, shamelessness...ribaldry, bawdiness, dirt, salaciousness,...pornography, double-entendre, prurience, voyeurism, immorality...wicked, naughty, piquant...carnality, lascivious,lubricity, whorishness...suggestive, randy, blue, scabrous, scatological... licentious,lecherous, priapic, debauched... rakish,wanton."*

*"**Profanity**:...indecency, immodesty, sex...coarseness, nastiness, bawdry...smut, filth, nasty, racy...unexpurgated, spicy, unbowdlerized, juicy...immoral...risqué, daring, scurrilous...foul-mouthed...swear-words, cuss-words, bad language, evil speaking...oaths, invective, abuse, curses...sluttishly, slatternly, slovenly...* bedraggled vocabulary, dissheveled style *(unkempt)."*
—*Roget's Thesaurus*
(1832; rev. ed. 1953, 1988)

"...Thus, if everything is interesting, everything is boring."
—Søren Kierkegaard *(1813-1855)*

5

The Ennui of Obscenity

Between Sexual Virility and Erotic Fatigue

The difference between the nineteenth and the twentieth centuries is that, in the former, the popular words of sex were secret and prohibitive and the rough-and-ready words of race were open and flagrant. In the latter, and especially in our own times, it is the other way round. Racialist terms are subjected to the controls of a code of political correctness and even Mark Twain can't get away with *coon,* even Leo Rosten can't get away with *kike.* But no obscenity in any of the European languages has not been having its regular flashes of public exposure. The discussion of sex in every kind of publication from how-to-do-it books to the newspaper accounts of racy divorce trials and even more lusty rape-and-murder cases is free and relatively uninhibited. Few long for the good old Puritanical days when it was necessary to fight through all the courts before prudish and uncultured judges in order to win the right to publish (and read) unexpurgated editions of James Joyce's *Ulysses* (a famous victory was won in New York in the 1930s) and D. H. Lawrence's *Lady Chatterley's Lover* (the landmark Penguin victory was won in London in the 1960s).

We have had in our time revolutionaries of every stripe and colour, and they have been mostly consigned to the "garbage can of history." Only the sexual revolution has triumphed. It seized power, and now rules in all the living rooms of the Western world where TV-talk shows can be seen offering "erotic advice" (with demonstrations) and Hollywood films are rarely without salty dialogue, boudoir nudity, and erogenous calisthenics.

Which leaves newspapers in a quandary. Their economic interests usually determine how much of the sexual revolution they can absorb in their pages. If they consider themselves to be "a family newspaper" it will be a minimum; if they feel themselves more and more "losing out" in the media war, they too will have to compete in the dissemination of bawdiness, titillating their readers (when they have time to read, away from the "potato couch"). The London tabloids have long featured what Fleet Street called "tits and bums" on their

Page Three. The American press will go to lengths to fill in on the "biological details" of Bobbittry, where the unfortunate Mr. Bobbitt had his penis cut off by Mrs. Bobbitt (the organ was later successfully sewn back on); and the TV "live" filming of the courtroom spectacular couldn't focus sharply enough on some of the surgical details.

Will it all last? Is it a "permanent" revolution? Already there are signs that a kind of erotic fatigue is setting in, and TV-moguls are alarmed at the evidence of boredom in the viewing surveys of their late-night porno film-fare.

True, there are considerable differences in usage when one considers factors like geography, history (or indeed cultural atmosphere) or eccentric editorial temperament. The obscenities which the flashy style of *Der Spiegel* (Hamburg) finds permissible, and even desirable, would never appear in the old-fashioned newspapers in Munich and Berlin; President Nixon's deleted expletives may be restored in newspapers in New York or Los Angeles but they remained absent and unaccounted for in the hundreds of publications in America's Bible Belt.

Finickiness on the subject differs in London even in papers of the same "quality." In the obituary notices (not infrequently masterly pieces of prose) no punches are pulled any more, ever since that radical *Times* piece of appreciation of the life of Randolph Churchill in which he was referred to, in a candor which shocked in its day, as "a drunkard" and "a hack journalist" (and the obit writer proceeded to adumbrate the connections between the demon drink and the wobbly prose).

In a recent obituary of Professor James Joll, a fine scholar and gentle teacher, it was not left to the simple and discreet last sentence of the *Daily Telegraph*'s notice: "He was unmarried." the *Times* went on:

> When Anthony Blunt was on the run from investigative journalists in 1979, it was Joll who sheltered him, not from any political sympathy but because he respected Blunt's great eminence as an art historian, and because they had been for years homosexuals at a time when to be an active male homosexual was a criminal offence: he had therefore had some degree of personal sympathy with him. (*Times*, 15 July 1994)

In the *Telegraph* "the Blunt connection" was mentioned but left shadowy and unexplained:

> Among Joll's circle was the historian Anthony Blunt who was unmasked as the "Fourth Man" in the Cambridge spy-ring (i.e., Burgess, Philby, and Maclean). Blunt sought refuge in Joll's house in west London, where he stayed for three days until discovered by the BBC.

No large conclusions, I am afraid, can be drawn from this comparative discretion: one paper is neither more "Tory" nor "prudish" than the other, and in other cases the boot would be on the other foot.

Still, a line has been crossed, and poring over a newspaper will remain a new experience for the squeamish, a rousing read for the ribald, an immodest challenge to writers and editors who have put away their blue pencils and now worry about getting the right number of asterisks or dashes in the story's f—— words (or f*** words, if you choose to be a tad more decorative). It remains to be seen whether the stimulation is greater with the printed word than the spoken word. Bad language, one suspects, is fouler when uttered...although readers are known to move their lips. Print journalism is under pressure to go further, to go "too far"; it is being sexually harassed both from the culture and from the competition. Will video push it to virility? The zeitgeist seems to be blessing progressive profanity.*

Whatever the range and depth of the reader-writer collusion which the f-word stratagem achieves in current journalism, it does not preclude a serious quality newspaper from taking the high moral ground whenever the nasty element of prurience turns up elsewhere, sometimes in the "low yellow press," occasionally even in the highbrow world of scholarly publications. A senior columnist on the *Sunday Telegraph* (which, as the attentive reader may have discerned, has pioneered innovative tactics for "outing" vulgarities in the public prints) thinks the new editions of the old classic encyclopaedias are going too far:

HOW THE MIGHTY HAVE FALLEN
Kenneth Rose says the Dictionary of National
Biography is Becoming Too Prurient[1]

Hardly a fault can be found in almost a hundred volumes since first publication in 1885. But in the more recent supplementary volumes some additional facts in a subject's career have been demanded by the *DNB* editors from their writers, including explicit data on "sexuality and marital relations." In the beginning–and, in the famous dating of the poet Philip Larkin, this was the 1963 (when "sexual intercourse was invented")–there was a certain discretion; to wit, the homosexuality of Somerset Maugham (who died in 1965) received no more than a glancing reference; and Rebecca West wrote of Noël Coward (who died in 1973): "There was impeccable dignity in his sexual life, which was reticent but untouched by pretence." Later–and Kenneth Rose waxes indignant as the texts move from the "prurient" to the "epicene," or vice versa–all the great and good who have earned entries in the *DNB* are stereotyped with a vengeance. Some show "signs of unabashed homosexuality,"

---

*   Since our ideal paper, as promised in our opening pages, will not be competing against a local channel with its soft-porn films, nor against transatlantic raunchy Ophra Williams-type libertinism, it will be quite free to make its own declaration of independence from the prevailing ideals of life, libido, and the pursuit of post-coital happiness.

others have "both male and female lovers" or are "rumored to be bi-sexual," and a few are said to have died of AIDS. The noble sentiment is worthy of publication on a Sunday (which used to be, in the British Isles at least, called "the Lord's Observance Day"):

> It is not edifying to see contributors to the *DNB* peering through bedroom keyholes as if they were tabloid reporters. So pervasive is this prurience that when recording that a man was unmarried, the contributor often feels obliged to add that he was nevertheless not a homosexual or that he enjoyed the company of women.

Mr. Rose is himself an unmarried journalist, and he should know by now that edification is not the name of the game among his colleagues (at least when it comes to what used to be known as private matters); titillation would be more like it, or even ribald realism. How far does one have to go to become *"too prurient"*?

In point of fact the Anglo-American literary critics, concentrating on avant-garde novels and new verse and not in the least deflected by the considerations which make for journalistic euphemism (i.e., the circulation of "family newspapers"), are quite happy with the progress being made. An American student cites with youthful satisfaction an Oxford study which registered confidently how far we have come:

> The word "fuck" is canonical now. The poem by Philip Larkin which most people find easiest to remember is the one that begins with a fine pun in it: "They fuck you up [our mum and dad]."

It only remains to explicate the hermeneutics of the fineness of the pun, to wit:

> The pun–that your parents both generate and ruin you–*is* fine, and it plays on one of the many properties that "fuck" and some other dirty words, have: Their common figurative meanings have very remote relations to their literal meanings. Heterogeneous ideas are yoked together through the pun.... Four-letter words (as the pun in "They fuck you up" makes clear) are not only sites of aggression, affiliation and disaffiliation, but also of ambiguity. Sometimes we can't even be sure what a particular dirty word means, how figuratively to construe it, whether it's a compliment or a slap: "She thinks he's the shit." Does *Fuck Yeah!*—the former title of a fanzine–connote a sex-positive attitude, or only a generic, joyful affirmation? (Robert Crawford, "Larkin's English," *Oxford Magazine* 23 (1987), pp. 3-4; Stephen Burt, "High Windows and Four-Letter Words," *Boston Review*, October-November 1996, pp. 18-19)

I leave our obscurantist literary critic here, almost choking on his own hang-ups, for the poet himself was closer to the journalistic mode than to deconstructionist theory. Here is Philip Larkin, in a letter to John Sparrow, the warden of All Souls, Oxford, unpretentiously (as was his wont) trying to explain the different forms his four-letter words could take and, in general, what he was up to, this side of disaffiliation and generic joy:

It can be meant to be shocking (we live in an odd era, when shocking language can be used, yet still shocks–it won't last); it can be the only accurate word (the others being gentilisms etc.); or it can be funny, in that silly traditional way such things are funny. (Andrew Motion, *Philip Larkin: A Writer's Life* [1993], p. 444.)

Or it can be obscene, in that silly traditional way (sometimes aggressive, sometimes ambiguous) such things are obscene. Even when they contain fine puns and sex-positive connotations. As I write, I note an item in the *Sunday Times* which reports from Sydney on the intensification of Australian republican sentiment. A new Sydney exhibition documents the mounting critique of the existing "Royal Connection" (i.e., the queen as head of state). "The exhibition, *Flagging Australia,* featured one entry with the slogan 'F*** Off Back to Fag Land.' Monarchists said it represented the worst aspects of an anti-British campaign." (*Sunday Times*, "Australian glitterati...," 16 November 1997, p. 21). What happens, then, to the achievements of canonical exegesis when distinctions have to be made among the endless f-word variants between figurative fancy and literal affiliation, from "*up*" and "*off*" to "*out*" and "*over*"? There are innumerable such additional entries in the exhaustive Random House dictionary on *The F Word* (1995), and they play fast and loose with any kind of canon.*

Low Notes in High C

There is, as the famous Australian syndrome in obscenity demonstrates, a point where the four-letter words lose their original function, become a kind of verbal goo, and for hardened ears almost lose their audibility. Similarly, in constant repetition with the printed word, the eye tends to become jaded to f-words and their related expletives; and alternative ways to achieve reader titillation are explored. The sexual suggestiveness becomes more allusive; art and fashion and other subjects as remote as real estate are dragged into it, so that the story can carry its punch without always be seen to be hitting below the belt.

A beautiful, successful young woman named Linda Evangelista ("aged 28, Supermodel and Catwalk Chameleon ... the woman who said she didn't get out of bed in the morning for less than $10,000 a day") is the subject of a new-fashioned "interview" invented by the London press, in which the reporter interviews himself and is thus free to touch upon all indiscretions. The reference was to Evangelista "striding down the catwalk in Milan, all shimmering curvaceousness"–

"Curvaceous? Isn't that the f-word in modeling?"

"Indeed it is. Fat, flesh...and the fashion media fires its most dreaded missile: the pregnancy rumour." (*Daily Telegraph*, 9 October 1994)

---

* See: *The F Word*, edited by Jesse Sheidlower (1995), *passim* in its 232 pages.

We have gone here from copulation to childbirth in a few seconds without dropping a stitch. The technique is to move from a lascivious implication almost absentmindedly to humdrum motherhood, or from lust to biology in one go. It can flit from art to music, hover above them fleetingly before it gets too serious, and then pass on, the quick climax having been achieved. No less earnest a writer than the music critic of the *Times* (London) gives us this vignette of the eponymous soprano in the première (in Protestant Glasgow!) of Donizetti's very Catholic opera on *Maria Stuarda:*

> And she acts the role with true regality...dignity...she lingers with such relish on the initial *"f"* of *"Figlia impura di Bolena"* that you feel she is about to loose off a string of old-fashioned Anglo-Saxon expletives rather than a tangy Italian insult....*Maria Stuarda* is a simple, earthy piece. (Rodney Milnes, in the *Times*, 11 October 1994)

If he meant the old Stuart war-cry, "F— Elizabeth!" (without launching the dreaded missile of a "pregnancy rumor"), then this is probably the deftest way of saying it. Readers may be willing to pay a bit more for royal expletives nicely covered up. Four-letter words have become a tease of the seven veils.

At this point I should clarify my argument to say that one cannot confidently assert any monocausal explanation for the proliferating patterns of profanity that I have been trying to document. Metaphysicians are wont to offer their philosophical theories, pertinent abstractions from Brooks Adams to Marshall McLuhan and Allan Bloom, from H. L. Mencken to Jacques Barzun and George Steiner—the degradation of democracy? The degeneration of language? The disappearance of "basics" or "family values"? The way the world ends, not with a bang but with a [expletive deleted] whimper?

One more mundane and, arguably, overriding consideration is central for any but the most saintly of newspaper editors and publishers (the "Press Barons" of notorious greed): it is, at all costs, to hold on to their readerships. *Too little* spice, and the paper loses circulation to the more outspoken competition–*too much,* and one risks offending what a loyal old-fashioned sector of the existing circulation finds intolerably offensive.

The substratum of attitudes which determine when, and how, what used to be called *"swear words"* or *"bad language"* can be safely used, or impudently suggested, range from the traditional censorial instincts of a Thomas Bowdler to the well-nigh full alphabetical exposure of the erstwhile unmentionables. The daring course of "going further and further" is, as we have seen, tarted up by a teasing manner, a kind of foreplayful titillation.

To be sure, one can find in outlying precincts simple stratagems of olden days which appear, even if only mere decades old, decidedly archaic. In the columns of the *Athens News* (editing affectingly in Anglo-American by, I imagine, provincial expatriates and old-time emigrants) I find a Reuters dispatch from New York which quotes the then still imprisoned former heavyweight champion of the world, Mike Tyson. Mike, superb boxer and convicted rapist, naturally continued to protest his innocence: "I'm not guilty! I don't beat on women! She never had no bruises!" (And perhaps the double negative was misunderstood by the judge as positive evidence, which would unfairly impose an additional handicap on thems-that-don't-speak-English-so-good.) But, about to be paroled, he also gave forth of this plangent cry: "I don't really have anybody I want to go to. I've been alone all my life and every time I did accept someone in my life, they've [expletive deleted] me." (*Athens News*, 19 October 1994)

It could be that the f-word (or the s-word?) was censored less in a spirit of prissiness than a passing political reminder of the obscenities that were once covered (and covered up) by this parenthetical interjection in the days of ex-President Richard Nixon. They were classically recorded on his "White House tapes" and popularized two previously "hard words." Who, but professional editors, ever "*deleted*"? And who amongst us uttered "*expletives*"? There are some who hold that the odoriferous phrase will–more than the most compre-hensive slew of a- to z-words of scatological misdemeanour–forever live in infamy.

A-Word to S-Word, and Their Synonyms

In the campaign for the 1994 national elections in Germany, much promi-nence was given to every word by one of the Green leaders who would cer-tainly be figuring in a new Bonn cabinet, if the left-wing parties would get a workable majority. He was Joseph Martin Fischer, a member of the Bundestag who had been the Greens' minister for the environment in Hesse, and was known flamboyantly all over the country as "Joschka" (he had a Hungarian mother). He slyly allowed only the *Frankfurter Allgemeine Zeitung* to refer to him formally and accurately ("as per *Taufschein* [birth certificate]") by his full Christian name. In return the *FAZ* hangs on his every word with similar accu-racy. And so on the 7th of October, when Joschka confessed that his popularity in the country was matched by his unpopularity in his own party he was quoted with the frankness that benefits this by-product of the '68 generation of revolutionary candor. The a-word gives nobody in Germany any trouble, least of all this conservative and most staid of Germany's leading dailies: "I have to live with the fact that 85 percent of the Greens think I am *ein Arschloch* [an asshole]" (*FAZ*, 7 October 1994). A few days later when the *New York Times* got around to interviewing "Joschka" Fischer, this bit of self-denigration–so characteristic of the outspokenness of the young radicals who grew up in what they fancied to be a "revolutionary struggle"–came out as: "I have to live with the fact that 85 percent of the Greens think I'm a jerk." (*NYT/IHT*, 14 October 1994)

The reasons why German journalism has this free and unencumbered ap-proach to the usage of obscenities which still trouble so many Anglo-Ameri-can post-Puritan consciences is, I am afraid, not a subject that can be gone into here. It is a long and complicated tale of what anthropologists would call "the culture of private parts," deriving on its nether side from the traditional paganism of a people that invented European nudism (and, even more than that, a naked form of social life stripped bare while cavorting, say, on the "Abyssinian" beaches of Kampen-on-Sylt). On its upper side it derives from a literary culture where the vulgarities in the table talk of Martin Luther and the lewd bits of dialogue in the plays of Goethe are permitted household words. Foreign visitors, with only a formal unpracticed knowledge of the German language, are inevitably shocked when the s-word (*Scheisse!*) crops up in normal, formal everyday discourse. And when they hear the so-called "*Götz*"-word often enough —they are driven (and it happened to me) to look up Goethe's play, *Götz von Berlichingen* (1773), to find, with a blush, in Act III, Scene xx, the medieval Knight's furious words of defiance, "*Leck' mich im Arsch!.*" I leave this to another place, and to those whom William Safire would call the *mavens* of comparative scatology. For now only an illustration of what distinguishes the approach of the otherwise prim-and-proper *Frankfurter Allgemeine Zeitung* from the stolid-and-staid *New York Times*.

German newspapers have a fool's freedom when it comes to obscenities in a foreign language, and their columns are peppered with earthy Anglicisms that never see the light of day in their American counterparts. Take the first novel by the young American writer, Robert O'Connor, which describes the military life–and its barracks-room language–of a U.S. Army battalion stationed in a Mannheim *Kaserne* in the 1980s. (Mannheim is only a few miles away from Frankfurt, and the *Frankfurter Allgemeine Zeitung* promptly reviewed the translation, entitled oddly *Krieg im Frieden*, "War in Peace.")

Avid for the military low-down, the local reviewer subjects the novel to a careful linguistic analysis which amounts, probably, to a rather original contribution to German literary criticism. It goes into italicized detail to explain why the author's sociology pushed him to divide his characters into two confrontational groups, the *M—f—ers* and the *M**f**ed*. The distinction is deemed to be an elaborate effort at creating "a closed system of coded communication (*ein geschlossenes System codierter Kommunikation*)" which, when decrypted, should go a long way towards clarifying the passive and the active elements of the illicit drug trade in the Mannheim area.

As I say, foreigners have it better when it comes to cracking the code of carnality.[2]

Whatever the compulsions may be that brought on such singular exhibition of liberal libertinage, the Teutonic vigor of unadulterated prose should not be allowed to put the pallid Anglo-Saxon practices in the shade. Some European literary publishers have been thinking of preparing new editions of certain modern classics in which the bowdlerized and self-censored versions of profanity and obscenity, in the original or in translation, are now re-touched up and properly restored. As I have been assured, the German texts of Hemingway and Mailer would, accordingly, be even "more authentic" than the American! This is pedantry pushed to no good purpose. I would hope that even the most rigorous of German scholars and *Zeitungs-wissenschaftler* (as they call their professors of journalism) would concede the modest adequacy–if not the strict necessity–of a few dashes here and a couple of asterisks there.

Brought up, as I was, on the unexpurgated texts of D. H. Lawrence and James Joyce, I at least deem the literary status quo roughly adequate: I have made my peace with compromises of our half-way house, and have retreated into a position of leaving well enough alone. Even the demands of archival excellence–which rationalize such moves to restore all the edited f-, a-, and s-words to their original earthiness–cannot, for the moment, persuade me otherwise. Perhaps one has grown accustomed to the passive role of complicity into which contemporary porno-prose has cast us all, lip-reading when we must, puzzling out missing letters when we can. Bawdry breeds concurrence.

We have for centuries gone along with Hamlet rudely consigning Ophelia to "a nunnery," although we suspect–some scholars claim that we know–that she understood it (and was commensurably hurt by the indignity) as a bordello. As for the current restoration of a modern writer's first intentions–before, that is, the self-censoring second thoughts set in–it is surely a very precarious enterprise in the history of prose. What has been deleted may have been too direct and unsubtle; what has been interlineated might be reconsidered to be first-best. Spelling things out is a must among orthographers (and spelling-bee prize-winners). It is not at all mandatory among professional writers trying to put meaningful and mature sentences together. Love, if it is not mere sex, also needs to have something left to the imagination.[3]

As my next, more topical illustration suggests. It appeared in the hapless *Washington Post*; and it was reprinted in several forlorn American newspapers (the world is too much with them, and a foul-mouthed world at that). It concerns yet another attempt of the Singapore officialdom to defend itself against the criticism in the U.S. press of its harsh police procedures. The regime ordered the caning an American youth for vandalism, and now the imprisoning of an American businessmen for abusive language. One would have thought language and its dirty words had long since lost their efficacy for criminal abuse and even insult; but, be that as it may, the Sino-Singaporean culture is evidently more sensitive. Here is His Excellency, S.R. Nathan, the ambassador of Singapore in Washington, trying to close the case by offering the verbal evidence in the arrest of the U.S. businessman, a Mr. Robert Freehill:

> Mr. Freehill was charged for assault and using abusive language. The article [in the *International Herald Tribune* for 19 Sept. 1994, reprinting the dispatch of the *New York Times* correspondent, Philip Shenon] did not include Mr. Freehill's actual words, "Why don't you teach this dog s— to park the car?" "F— you, f— you people are

always picking on us white men." "F—ing Singaporean Chinese Chink, bastard Chinese."⁴

The original story had only offered a touched-up account, "fit to print." It referred unspecifically to "using abusive language" and "yelling a racial epithet." If the Ambassador's correction to the documentary record (whatever the justice of the law which would have sentenced poor Leopold Bloom to a long term in the pen) is still deemed to be culpably incomplete—those in-fernal hyphens represent the modern form of Bowdlers-at-work — a current Japanese technique can be recommended: *Karaoke,* singing along. Even moving the lips silently will do to restore what has been lost by dastardly commission and omission.

In the serious, if not highbrow, newspapers where journalists have more column-space not merely for naughty words but also various bits of pertinent (or pretentious) cultural information, the a-word usages can be dressed up or even sublimated to inter-disciplinary heights. For example, in literary news emanating safely from abroad. A French art-historian composes what the publisher of the English translation calls "A Brief and Elegant History of Bottoms through the Ages." The reviewer in the *Times* writes that she is happier with Jean-Luc Hennig's original edition. For one thing, it is better illustrated (although one might have thought that Yoko Ono's pictorial study on the same subject would have sufficed to round out the subject). For another,

> Hennig's translators like the word 'buttocks' and use it just a little too much. It's an uglier word than the French *fesses*. Hennig seems to invest this part of the body with an intelligence and sensibility of its own: "Buttocks are always delighted when anyone falls back in ecstasy and surprise at the sight of them."⁵

This kind of posterior analytics, if successful, can lead to other brief but elegant histories of a number of other surprising parts of the body; but perhaps national-cultural differences will always determine what kind of illustrative (if any) material should be included. Recondite references to Renaissance paintings and to post-Praxiteles sculpture are clearly inadequate. The "rear view" is too foreshortened: "Hennig presupposes that his readers have a vastly erudite knowledge of art history. I studied for four years in a British art school, but he mentions pictures that I do not know."

Still, perhaps it is all for the best. The English reader is advised, in an unusual warning to "those of a squeamish disposition," not to read pages 149-152; those other readers whom the *Times* has sedulously accustomed to be non-squeamish about such things now know exactly where to go for the details of "the anatomical consequences of various anally-oriented tortures, including Edward II's execution."

Obviously the French have it better. Are they even burdened down with a word for *squeamish?* The English may well have to struggle to come up with a rhyme for bottoms or buttocks; even Cole Porter in Paris in the springtime worked hard to devise a "merry air" to go with a wagging "*derrière*." Some cultures get all the breaks.

I write before the end of the U.S. political campaign of the summer and autumn of the year 2000, and it is difficult to calculate how many new and ingenious tropes intruded themselves into the language of journalism which, like most branches of the entertainment industry, tries to avoid driving chronic repetitiveness too far. Reporters, paying close attention to the words slipshod politicians naively come to use, may every now and then come up with a scoop. The sound of an odd phrase or the buzz of a flight of fancy, not to mention a catastrophic slip of the tongue, can in the reverberations of our noisy media campaigns sway a million voters (or even a decisive thousand in a key electoral corner).

In the efforts of the vice president to distance himself somewhat from the Clinton-Lewinsky scandals, Al Gore suggested to Oprah Winfrey on her popular nationwide television show that he and his wife, Tipper, his "soulmate," had reacted with disbelief to the revelations about the White House affair. Ms. Winfrey asked pointedly: "Did you and Tipper talk about it over dinner and say, 'Can you believe…?'"

"I'm not giving you any exact quotes," Gore replied. "But you're in the ballpark."

To be in the *wrong* ballpark obviously constitutes the greatest disaster that ever could befall an American fan on a Wednesday baseball evening or a Saturday football afternoon. What game is on–and who's winning?–are lesser questions. To be "in the ballpark" means Oprah got it right, even if nobody can come up with the specifics of a quotable quote. The place was right. The address and zip code were correct. It was the right stadium.

The recognized status of the players is often crucial. To digress, I recall losing a libel suit in, of all places, Ireland over the meaning of being "an amateur" or "a professional." I had published in *Encounter* a polemical article by one of my assistant editors to the effect that a prominent Irish intellectual was so consistent in his activistic behavior (signing protest petitions, marching on week-end demonstrations, etc.) that, innocent idealist that he was, he had now "*lost his amateur status*." My argument, somewhat hair-splitting (and possibly pettifogging), was that to be "a professional" was not necessarily pejorative. But the final court decision was that, in the view of the opinions of everyday men and women, the popular distinction of status meant that…amateurs do it for love and fun, professionals do it for money. The libel was obvious, and the imputation of corruption had to be paid for.

I suspect that a similar semantic shading played a role in the notorious *Bush-speak* reference to the *New York Times* correspondent whose hostile dispatches the presidential candidate had reason to dislike. The remark was made in an aside to the vice presidential candidate Cheney at a campaign event when, not realizing a microphone was switched on, Governor Bush called the journalist (Adam Clymer, on the press bench up in front of them) "a major-league asshole" Would it have been more, or less, offensive if he is classified him contemptuously as a "minor leaguer"? Baseball has its passions and gradations; and it is important to get the stadium or the ballpark right (are the Brooklyn Dodgers still in Ebbets Field?) as well as not confounding the major and minor leagues. He might well have called Clymer, in a curt dismissal, a "minor league rookie."

The use of the a-word introduced a new and different note in the political metaphorics. Flights of fancy are one thing, filth is another. For some it was "profanity" that was raising its ugly head, for others it was "obscenity." Not since the hey-day of the Monica Lewinsky transcripts was one word–a "seven-letter swear word" (in the phrase of the *Daily News*)–subjected to such national debate. Even down to its spelling and its literal semi-pronounceable transcription (although on television it was consistently "bleeped out"). Even including the "human interest story" of whether the insulted correspondent would still turn up at the Bush-Cheney campaign stops. From Scranton, Pennsylvania, the *New York Post* reported–

> @#$ percent Times scribe
> doesn't miss a beat

In London the *Times* translated the Americanese into English and told its readers–

> 'MAJOR LEAGUE !$#&!'
> Adam Clymer has gained instant celebrity
> after being insulted by George W. Bush
> (the *Times*, 8 September 2000, p. 21)

The *Times* man was brave and valiant although he had to endure additional humiliations. The vice presidential candidate agreed with "his boss' barnyard assessment." Cheney was quoted as saying laconically, "he is [an a–h–], big time." Once again, would a disdainful reference to "small-time" have been worse?

Words, like the proverbial eggshells, have to be treaded on carefully. For months on end in the early stages of the Bush-Gore campaign for the U.S. presidency, something called *Bush-speak* was a big story, indeed a rare exercise in etymological scoops in the language of journalism. Here is a sampler of what the papers had to report on mangled syntax, bizarre phraseology, and other instances of what consultants in psycho-linguistics were quick to identify as "dyslexic."

"The errors you've heard Governor Bush make are consistent with dyslexia," Nancy LaFeyers, a Houston expert told Vanity Fair, referred to such Bushisms as "tacular" for "tactical nuclear" weapons and "we won't raise trade terriers," an apparent reference to either trade tariffs or trade barriers, or both....

In another passage, Bush notes that it takes a veteran 745 days on average to get a decision on a disability compensation appeal. "Nearly two years," Bush pointed out. It's actually 15 days more...

Those campaign lines came a few days later he explained his wife's absence by noting: "Laura sends my regards...."

Ears were being cupped around the country as reporters scoured their tapes to confirm yet another slip-up. Did Bush say that Al Gore would create "over 200,000 new or expanded Federal programs"? He meant 200. Did he say that the "*Federal* government ought to have maximum flexibility"? He meant that the flexibility should be with the various *states* that receive the money. And what was he on about when he pronounced that he had "ruled out no new Social Security taxes"? Of course he had meant that he had ruled out...new Social Security taxes. The *Washington Post*, covering the campaign in every little whistle-stop, picked up what used to be known in Mayor Fiorello LaGuardia's classic confession of errors as "*beauts*" (i.e., beautiful mistakes)–

Austin, Texas.— ...In Beaverton, Oregon, he said, "More and more of our imports come from overseas."

In Redwood City, California, he promised "a foreign-handed policy" when he meant "an even-handed foreign policy."

How serious were such "semantic gaffes"? Some journalists, not especially distinguished for the impeccable purity of their own prose, were alarmed that some voters found the phenomenon of not-speaking-English-so-good "endearing." They were reassured by other voters that all this was evidence that Mr. Bush had a shaky grasp of both the issues and the English language. Our press regularly turned to university experts who were quoted as worried about the correlation between grammatical sloppiness and misleading high-level policy inaccuracies: "for a President every word matters...." What they called "Bushisms" could endanger the national security. The daily story became one of "tangled talk" and "slips of the tongue" and "wild ad-libbing." Could one find a regular way to turn on microphones that were meant to be turned off?[6]

Observers of the newspaper culture have had differences over whether Governor Bush's printable difficulties were more–or less–meaningful than the journalistic crisis on how to spell the a-word and how to classify its misdemeanor. Was the delinquency "obscene" or "profane"...or what? How should the expletive be deleted? Continental-European papers translated freely, but in London the Anglo-Saxon editors had to explain the explanations: Should the a-word be prefixed by either *a* or *an*? Then, again, as one reporter wrote, "by a *******, I mean, of course, ass**** or, according to what paper you read, ***hole." The antediluvian hyphen (as in ***-****) didn't even have a look-in or a look-see.*

Still, the *Washington Post* went beyond the orthographic variations to venture a definition of the noun in question: "...a vulgar euphemism for a rectal aperture." For some journalists this sounded even more explicit. How to avoid misleading generalities which could usher in more anatomical complications?

An Associated Press dispatch was headlined:

BUSH USES PROFANITY ABOUT REPORTER

This touched off a round of theology. Profanity was taken to mean "...serving to debase or defile what is holy." Mark Steyn in the *Daily Telegraph*, among others, pointed out that "to the best of my knowledge, no major religion regards the rectal aperture as sacred."**

In full semantic flight from further linguistic embarrassments, the *New York Times* left it to Maureen Dowd to express in her op-ed column (6 September

---

*   The lexicographer, Jonathon Green, famously sensitive to the metaphysics of the hyphen and other punctuation marks, gives in his latest study "*look-in*" with, and "*looksee*" without....The a-word is, consistently, spelled as one word, unhyphenated. See Green, *The Cassell Dictionary of Slang* (1998), pp. 33, 746.

**   The *Daily Telegraph* man erred here. His theology is not wholly accurate, and misses out on several important complications. But I will refrain from going into the dubious subject of the physiology of sexual metaphors here raised by (1) the imputation of the non-sexuality of the a-word; and (2) the thesis of "non-sacred" areas of human intercourse.

I confess that I had trouble enough when I published in *Encounter* an adventurous article by John Sparrow (then the Warden of All Souls College in Oxford University). It argued (rather convincingly, I thought at the time) that "there was an undisclosed element in the case" which determined the outcome of the *Lady Chatterley's Lover trial* (London, 1962). It shed new light on Lawrence's notion of coital tenderness; also on his quasi-religious infatuation with the idea which derived from certain Indian myths and the special importance which mystical Hindu erotomanes had attached to the area around the abse of the spine. See: John Sparrow, "Regina v. Penguin Books Ltd.: An Undisclosed Element in the Case," *Encounter*, February 1962, pp. 35-43, and reprinted in Sparrow's *Controversial Essays* (1966)...and/or in Sparrow's *Independent Essays* (1963).

The Sparrow essay also deals with other themes touched on in these pages: from the idea of "the sacred" seeking the "redemption of four-letter words" (and Lawrence's hatred of the "dirty practice" of using asterisks). Almost alone in all the commentaries on the Lawrentian sexual creed, Sparrow ventures to discuss the relevance of "buggery" (and *penetratio per anum*) as well as the significance of what D.H. Lawrence called "the phallic hunting-out." Still, he was less interested in the language and, in general, "the validity of Lawrence's sexual doctrine" than in the critical demonstration of "the failure of the book as a work of art." This became plainer, after a rambunctious controversy, when Sparrow penned his "afterthoughts" (*Encounter*, June 1962, pp. 83-88).

2000, p. A27) the paper's dismay at what Mark Steyn had referred in the *Telegraph* to "the assholian status of Mr. Clymer." Ms. Dowd recorded:

> *Washington.*—Here at the New York Times, we were exceedingly dismayed at the news that George W. Bush had called our redoubtable reporter Adam Clymer "a major-league (expletive deleted)."

This sounded a shade light-hearted, and even more so was the memorandum that the *Times'* "estimable arbiter of language," a Mr. Al Siegal, had prepared for the *Times'* political editors on the occasion:

> Folks, if we have to refer to it again, let's call Bush's word a vulgarity, not an obscenity. It has nothing to do with sex. Nor is it profane, having nothing to do with religion or the deity.

Ms. Dowd was obviously also relieved that the matter didn't actually have to do with unprintable sex–what did she think the Kinsey Report had meant by all those studies of "anal eroticism"?–and she was pleased to register her most serious objection, to wit:

> The really troubling part of W.'s epithet was not the noun we are not allowed to print....No, the really troubling part about the epithet was the adjective we are allowed to print: "major league."

Drawing herself up to her full editorial height to deliver her three-line peroration on the matter at hand–and on the temper of American politics in the first campaign of the twenty-first-century–Maureen Dowd thundered for the *Times*: "Before W. makes any more snide cracks about the major leagues, he should remember he's in them." Now that was a stern editorial warning which was fit to print, in fact a ballpark kind of remark. But it led one English newspaper to put a summary of the whole story–from the elements of bias in journalistic reporting of political campaigns to the frivolous use of dashes, hyphens, and asterisks in the deleted expletives of the English language as she is spoke–under a banner full-page headline:

DUBYA'S ["W" as in George W.] EXPLETIVE EXPOSES
UNDELETED PREJUDICE IN MEDIA

It admitted its own prejudice, a contempt for the real-existing majority of U.S. newsmen who were recently polled, and it turned out that 92 percent had voted for Clinton-Gore. That, as their American correspondent put it, "does help to explain why their papers are the dullest and most unreadable in the English-speaking world, with a pronounced tendency towards conformity." Strange, these revolutionary English tones against their former colonials. They dream of joining in a new Boston Tea Party to subvert the

American journalistic establishment–"to hurl a glass of cie water in its face and give it the boot...."

"Calling 'em a ******* is an excellent start. Way to go, Dub!"[7]

A funny thing happened to the s-word on the way up from the latrine. Unlike its fellow-shockers (all derived from sex, anatomy, and the like), faecal references in contemporary journalism appear to be enjoying an expressiveness which is conspicuously inexplicit. I detect a certain olfactory reticence in the reporters and columnists who can be normally expected to be finicky linguists when it comes to recording the language of the streets, the conversation of raunchy writers, or the outrage of athletes in defeat (or in heated argument with an umpire or referee).

In the papers of this morning, as I write, I note a sports correspondent quoting one hero of the two-man rowing team awarded an Olympic gold medal in Atlanta about the achievement of his mate: he had been "******* brilliant." There were other reflections of this order, but recording at least one sufficed–together with "a sharp reminder to all broadcasters that athletes in the throes of exhaustion and high emotion are best left alone for a few moments until they have regained their breath." One British broadcaster was reluctant to wait so long and so his microphone caught the breathless remark which "must have been a linguistic first for afternoon family viewing on the BBC. We are unlikely to see that little exchange in the Olympic highlights" (Robert Hardman, "Olympic Family Need Contraception," *Daily Telegraph*, 31 July 1996, p. 36).

To *say* it and to *hear* it seems to be culturally easier than to *spell it out,* and one is grateful for the free-talking broadcasting techniques for this special kind of verisimilitude in reportage. It is a case of sight reinforcing sound. A TV newspaper critic appreciates the realism of a documentary film about an old Kazakhstan slave labor camp in which the prison wardens of LA-155 are called "barons" and "Each baron manages a gang, at the bottom of which are the ragged, randomly chosen 'shitbags–fit only for buggery and beatings.'"[8]

After tirelessly collecting bulging envelopes of cuttings marked s-words (incl. b-s), I have convinced myself that, despite all the tiresome trivialization and sheer schoolboy superfluity, press usages sometimes fulfill a truth-telling purpose and satisfy a legitimate curiosity, indeed my own conventional "need to know." It is an interesting question whether, for example, the specially invented languages for the handicapped (*viz.,* the deaf and the blind) include the obscene words and rude phrases without which many translated texts in Braille or in sign languages would be obscure. And so, as I say, I appreciate the curiosity of a *Sunday Times* reporter who was assigned to write the offbeat story of an Around-the-World-Race in which only handicapped sailors participated. (The point was to influence public opinion's prejudices against the disabled, and the jingling yachting motto was: "*Racing the Latitudes to Change Attitudes*.")Among the interviews with the virtually blind crewmen and the partially crippled skipper with a limbless first mate (other sailors had a variety of degenerative nerve diseases which robbed them of their old strength), there is this passage: "With Paul Hebblethwaite, a crewman who is profoundly deaf, she uses sign language most of the time. Davies, who is partially deaf, has her own jokes: she has taught the skipper the sign language for 'bullshit.'"[9] To a certain extent, quoting the expletive goes a long way to taking the curse off them. But in the case of the s-word there is an additional safety-catch in peri-phrastic profanity. By this I mean the extension of the effect of "dirty realism" by resorting to roundabout, if still pungent, references. Here is another *Sunday Times* report, this time from the re-unified Germany about the smoldering resentment, even after almost a decade of re-unification, between anti-Com-munist Westerners (*Wessies*) and ex-Communist Easterners (*Ossies*):

> "F*** the Wessies, we don't need them," said Michael, 18, from Malchow, near Lake Plau. Another youth chipped in: "I'll tell you a joke. When God created man he took clay for the Ossies. For the Wessies he reached into the toilet." (*Sunday Times*, "Envious East Vents Hate on Rich West Germans," 28 July 1996, p. 16)

This image, I would venture to say, is graphically adequate, if not very felicitous; but then it might lead to circumlocutions like "when the toilet outreach hit the fan."

This kind of toilet-trained vocabulary is especially developed in proper circles of big business counseling; for, as the *Financial Times* reports on one counselor's discovery: "You find them in all organizations–the passed over and the pissed off (Popos)....The Popo presents a great problem for the man-ager." The characters in question, so-called *Popos*, are frequently in late middle age, of limited education and qualifications, and are often soured and incom-petent. How can they be "downsized" and the company "right-sized"? Through early retirement? with redundancy slips? The writer in the *Financial Times* is not too specific but direct and forceful for all that "The Popo is clearly a problem. Organizations that have too many of them and do not deal with them soon become chronically constipated. A laxative management style is clearly a requisite if some organizations are to be healthy."[10] Scatology is obviously one of the required subjects in which you have expertise if your degree in business administration is to be worth its salt. Managers in corporate cultures quickly learn to be adept in translating f-words and s-words into pharma-medical equivalents. A "laxative management style" can work emetic wonders with synonyms.

Who, then, will be left to "*tell it like it is*"? Or, perhaps, *like it shouldn't be*. But, arguably, it was knowledgeable, if naughty, for a young newspaper critic to read the stern lesson to the editor of an ambitious new publication. The magazine was something glossy called *Frank* which promised to be "intelligent, irreverent, provocative, witty and non-patronising." (As which journal, old or new, doesn't aspire to be?) She deserved a scolding. In a critique by Thomas Sutcliffe in the *Independent*, Ms. Tina Gaudoin was subjected to an intelligent, irreverent (etc.) review; and the message was "Somebody should have told Gaudoin, incidentally, that her description of the magazine as a 'no bull-shit take on the way we live in the Nineties' is self-contradicting. Only bullshitters use the word bullshit."[11]

The last phrase may prove to be, I suspect, a suggestive form of scatological aphorism. If it catches on, then we will be richer by a half-dozen maxims, re-identifying all free spirits: by their words shall ye know them. Nobody but m*-f***ers use the m-f word; nobody but s—s call each other s***s. Etc. Similarly for all obscene epithets, easily reversed in a variety of *tu quoque*'s. This kind of repartee could be taken by future semanticists as the greatest invention since moist cleansing tissues. There was a time (and not so long ago) when the first part of the word was as taboo as the second. *Bull*, as other nouns of male animals (*buck, ram, cock, stallion*, etc.), was considered "indelicate" and, as we know from Mencken, *male cow* was recommended.[12]

The press usage of the s-word, especially in the English newspapers, becomes increasingly charmless unless very important persons have been reported to be exchanging obscene insults. Even then it takes on an anodyne boredom especially in view of the widespread acceptance of the fact that most competitive politicians and almost all rival authors think of all the others as "*s**ts*." Usually the remark merely denotes a literary indolence or a rhetorical poverty, for the English language is in fact rich and resourceful enough to be forthcoming with rather more original (and hence more forceful) terms of total contempt. In addition to which the scatological area, if recent evidence is not misleading, appears to be subjected to a remarkable sanitization, a cleanup which might mean the end of an immemorial expletive.

The Germans have long since taken the lead. Even the classical allusion to the Goethean *Götz*-word is in the early stages of detoxification. I note in a recent German weekly a full-page advertisement which provides some evidence that the s-word and all its correlatives will soon be transvalued. The picture which is supposed to be serving the Hakle Company for its toiletries is a striking photograph of a handsome young brunette, lowering from the backside an anonymous young man's Y-front shorts, and kneeling to kiss his pair of firm and youthful buttocks. The reader–and, presumably, the customers of Hakle's products–is enjoined for his part to reserve the whole area for signs of affection, to wit, "*Machen Sie Ihren Po zu Kusszone.*" (which might be coy baby talk for kissing a baby's bottom). Hakle's products include "dry and wet toilet tissues," and these as the manufacturers say in a nation-wide publicity campaign sell out of a corporate pride "*Ihre Po zu liebe*" (or: just for love of your fanny).[13] Vulgar? Tasteless? Or yet another courageous round of taboo-breaking? In German newspapers and periodicals, as we have had occasion to point out, most of what Anglo-Americans think of as obscenity has almost become standard demotic and legitimate headline fodder. Vulgarity has become the vulgate. An imprecation such as *Scheiss-Kerl!* is often employed as a term of endearment. Something similar is occurring in English usages.

For example, in the newspaper reportage about the death of Jeffrey Bernard–he was the widely read columnist of the *Spectator*, and the subject of Keith Waterhouse's hit play, *Jeffrey Bernard is Unwell* (1991), starring Peter O'Toole. Tributes were paid to him, warts and all. He was an obstreperous alcoholic and, altogether, a disagreeable fellow. As the Londoner's Diary in the *Evening Standard* reported, his good friend, the proprietor of *The Coach & Horses* (one of Bernard's regular Soho hang-outs) had said, "He was the nicest s**t I ever knew. I told him I was going to say that when he died."[14]

The Anglo-German difference I have already mentioned remains, mostly, of academic interest except in those unusual cases where we are confronted with the complexities of outsize German lives, in politics and sometimes in literature, which call for a sensitive awareness of just such shades of scabrous meaning. One such case is the life of Oskar Schindler who was made famous by Steven Spielberg's film *Schindler's List* (1995). This, in turn, was based on the best-selling account by Thomas Kenneally (*Schindler's Ark*, 1982) of "the louche Nazi war profiteer who became an unlikely hero."

It was indeed a heroic and heartening tale of the rescue of a thousand Jews from certain death in the gas chambers of the World War II Holocaust. Schindler cheated Auschwitz; and the survivors in Israel and elsewhere paid tribute to him, rewarded him, mourned him when he died in 1974. But his widow, Emilie, lived on; and it was well-known in informed journalistic circles that she never forgave him his vices although she shared the risks of outwitting the Nazis in that most singular rescue operation of those tragic years. For the wife, Emilie Schindler, her husband was a scoundrel: chronically disloyal, untrustworthy, a womanizer, a petty thief who stooped to squalid compromises with the Nazis.

On the occasion in October 1997 of the publication of Mrs. Schindler's own memoirs, entitled *Where Light and Shadow Meet*, Western newspapers sent correspondents down to Argentina (where she still lives in a bungalow built for her by B'nai Brith benefactors) to get the other side of the story. Charles Laurence, the *Daily Telegraph*'s correspondent in New York, reported from Buenos Aires that the ninety-year-old widow had watched with "acid wonder" the building of a myth "rooted, like so many, in a need to find something worthwhile in the worst of circumstances." The adventurous reality was that helpless, doomed Jews, forever to be known as *Schindlerjuden*, were in fact saved by a daredevil of a man of checkered human qualities. True, too, was the fact that decades after his death the embittered wife, a modest self-effacing woman, could not forgive the husband. As Laurence aptly remarks, "There is no doubt that Emilie is truly loved by Jews for what she did, but she seems unable to find redemption in that love."

How could one account for heroes with feet of clay? What was the word for double-edged characters who combined sterling virtues with tawdry vices? There may be a subtle word in Greek for it, but in German everyday speech I am used to hearing the scatological expletive which even has a shade of slight affection, even of rude respect, to it. Frau Schindler, a German-speaking Czech farmer's daughter who had married the man in 1928, used it. And the *Daily Telegraph* in a moving full-page feature published it: "'What did I think? I'll tell you', she says. *'Scheisskopf'* (s—head). But I was the idiot for falling in love with him.'" I find this an especially moving moment, strangely mixing all the erratic elements of profanity and prudery which we have been confronting in English-language journalism. A reporter and his editor made a rare, well-intentioned, and commendable effort to capture the note of an unusual human relationship. It serves to give a hero and a *Scheisskerl** an extra cubit of immortality.[15]

I should conclude this exposition of Anglo-German expletives on a positive note, with this commendable effort at honorable truth telling. Before, that is, doubts begin to gather that this could be yet another stratagem of titillation, seriously camouflaged for a moment and set apart from the usual buffoonery and hypocrisy which dominate the language of journalism in its low demotic mode.

A certain suspicion is in order. A few days later, in the same paper and from another one of its resident foreign correspondents, a dispatch alleged across a full-page banner headline that the FBI had "known in advance" of the Oklahoma bomb which devastated a Federal Building in Oklahoma City, killing 168 innocent victims and for which a young ex-soldier, Timothy McVeigh, has already been sentenced to death by jury trial. Apparently a former German Army officer named Andreas Strassmeier had something to do with the "plotting," and he had been involved (according to FBI wire-taps) in neo-Nazi activities in the U.S. Could it have been "a sting operation" that had gone horribly wrong? Was there a *provocateur* who had turned informant? Strassmeier was interviewed by a *Telegraph* correspondent in Washington; and although he denied that it was he who was the source of "a tip-off," he subsequently fled to Germany. The story requires a few good quotes for authenticity, and I will quote a passage from a transcript which was offered. It doesn't quite prove a point but it does illustrate the insurgence of bilingual profanity and the new

---

*   This must have been the original usage; and either it was mis-heard by the reporter or he touched it up a bit to give him an easy translation and a literal faecal equivalent. The *"s—head"* (s-—*sskopf*) usage doesn't exist in German. Such are the pitfalls of bi-lingual obscenity. A similar erratic playfulness led the novelist Joseph Heller, in his famous American novel of World War II, *Catch-22* (1961), to take a comparable linguistic liberty in calling his satire of an American officer, "Lieutenant Scheisskopf."

Anglo-German alternation of asterisks-and-dashes "for us" and *italics* "for them."

> "Of course the informant can't come forward. He's scared sh**less right now."
>
> "It seems to me as if you've got a problem, Andreas."
>
> "*Scheisse.*"[16]

It is several centuries since Gibbon famously took refuge in Latin footnotes for such indelicacies that he felt obliged to record in his great volumes of history. Modern languages nowadays are surely more accessible and reader-friendly, and can serve a variety of multi-cultural purposes.

I am not sure how far this linguistic drift can, or will, carry words of profanity and obscenity into calmer waters. These are ebbs and tides which are very complex. Can the s-word, monotonous and almost meaningless, stay afloat and be driven by other currents? A not unrelated sea-change is beginning to move the f-word–not exactly in the direction of s-word endearment but to a literary employment which is surprisingly (and even unrecognizably) non-profane. There are f-word usages which lay claim to being said just in innocent fun. They have a touch of humor, even if crudely put. For example, here is Peter Cook's widow, in a letter to a newspaper editor, protesting as "outrageous" an account of her dear husband's last hours. Evidently these were wrongly re-counted in a recent unauthorized biography, but she quotes one passage and gives it even wider currency–

> ."..an ambulance was called and Peter was lifted gently on to a stretcher. Peter gripped his neighbor's hand and breathed: 'Will I be OK, George? Will I be all right?'.....
>
> "George reassured him: 'You'll be fine, Peter. Everything is going to be just fine', he insisted.
>
> "'Oh, f***', replied Peter, his fate sealed. It was his last joke."[17]

If it was really a joke, it surely was not one of Cook's best. Wittier and more original last words have been recorded. But reserved for such and similar occasions–*i.e.*, for weddings as well as funerals, not to mention the birth of a child or a prize-award ceremony–the f-word may well be extending its shelf-life date by taking on a new note of freshness.

Of Ideology Scatology

The code of carnality depends, to be sure, on the central importance of the f-word in pornographic prose and obscene speech. In referring to German newspaper culture one should, more accurately, speak of the code of scatology. As I have suggested, the literary problem is not how differently and at what various tempos the code in our contemporary permissive enlightenment is being broken–but why in certain cultures, mainly the German, the code has been fractured centuries ago; and in the judgement of many anthropologists and historians (mostly foreigners, i.e., non-Germans) never properly existed before under an unbroken wholesome taboo. This is a thorny subject, and replete with rancorous argument, dubious research, wild overstatement, stereotypical prejudices, and other malodorous elements in what the Germans call in a problematical word: *Streitkultur*, a querulous culture, a culture of controversy and endless argument. It usually winds up in quarrelsome discourses about the concept of national character itself, its uses and abuses; and nothing has been added to that debate for at least a century or two. At least since David Hume, that eminently moderate Anglo-Saxon spirit, put the case so quietly, so undogmatically: "...Each nation has a peculiar set of manners, and some particular qualities are more frequently to be met with among one people than among their neighbors" (1748).[18] One liberal American scholar has written a masterly exposition of what he was convinced to be German national character, and although he tried to avoid the lingering Western mindset which relegates all Teutonic things into a course of evil which has periodically challenged the virtues of civilization as we know it, in the end he also reinforces the conceit of a "national character," which is taken to be singular and inexorable.

For this reason I am hesitant in unreservedly recommending Alan Dundes' work entitled *Life Is Like a Chicken Coop Ladder: A Study of German National Character through Folklore* (1989). It does, in its 150 quotation-studded pages, venture a trenchant and cogent explanation of everything from Luther and Goethe to Auschwitz, and thereby hangs its weakness. Nothing explains everything–not even five centuries of a cultural addiction to a fæcal-erotic habit which has, with remarkable compulsiveness, insinuated itself into songs, postcards, household toilets, and high literature as well as into the excremental parameters of great wars and genocidal tragedies. As Professor Dundes concludes,

> It is not I who is claiming that the German love of order may stem from a love of ordure–it is in the folklore. It is not I who am suggesting that the famous three *K*'s of the World War II slogan: *Kinder, Kirche, Küche* (children, church, kitchen) might be added a fourth: *Kaka* (*Kacke*) or *Kot*–it is in the folklore. It is the Germans themselves in their own folklore who have said all along that life is like a chickencoop ladder. And if the Germans are right, then they–and perhaps we–had better watch their step. (P. 153)

All is folklore–scatology is all.[19]

Avoiding the higher abstractions of sociology, anthropology, and anecdotal gossip frozen into folkloristic forms, I still find myself seeking a modest explanation of an item in my newspaper of this Sunday morning. It is the *Welt am Sonntag*, once published by Axel Springer in Hamburg (but now in Berlin). In a *Zitaten* column on its editorial page the paper quotes prominently "Sayings of the Week," among them from one disappointed German politician who was asked how it feels not to be sitting (as expected and predicted) as a member of the new German cabinet in the nation's new capital. He offered us this fragment of sound advice: "*Vielleicht ist es nötig, dass wir erst einmal alle Scheisse fressen.* (Maybe it's necessary for all of us first to eat shit.)" (*Welt am Sonntag,* 28 February 1999, p. 30). Analysts of the language have varied in taking such remarks, which anthologies have collected in the thousands, as literal or as metaphorical. Scatological excesses in the twentieth-century wars are alternately taken as barbaric eccentricities or as–in the sickening documentation of concentration-camp enormities–anal-erotic neuroses compulsively translated into regular governmental policy and systematic state violence.

No detail of what scholars call "*latrinalia*" escapes the scatological eye. What Professor Dundes calls an "infatuation with scatological illusions" (mostly in his reading in the Germanic culture) is only paralleled by his own infatutation with a prehensile thrust to assembling "countless proverbs, riddles, latrinalia verses, jokes, and folk poetry." He affects a rather reasonable stance in his concessions that *every* society imposes *some* kind of toilet training on its infants. He knows that millions of Americans may say "*shit,*" and (as is well known) Frenchmen say "*merde.*" But he still argues that "one does not find anything like the infinite [*sic*] variety of metaphorical anal expressions which can be shown to be traditional throughout Germany." He goes on about Luther's famed theological inspiration in the privy; he recalls Mozart's unseemly playfulness (dramatized for us in Peter Schaffer's *Amadeus*); he scours Hitler's table talk for evidence of a peculiar, a singular preoccupation with digestion, constipation, toilet paper, and fæcal uncleanliness (mostly associated, in the *Führer*'s obsession, with "dirty Jews"). Others, like Erich Fromm, thought of Hitler as "a clinical case of necrophilia." It is a short, unavoidable step to Auschwitz where hapless millions were put into the gas chamber–why should it have been "a shower room"?–to disguise their murderous end. The touch of hygiene is always relevant to scatology: as in "ethnic cleansing." The excuse of cleanliness-being-close-to-godliness was an obsessive delusion in the psychology of Holocaust perpetrators. Unclean peoples did not deserve hygienic privileges...until, in the final act, they headed "for the showers."

It is a deadly thesis. The nasty and rancorous quarrels about it have managed to be a well-kept secret. Otherwise the post-World War II re-education campaign–and the far more extensive half-century of German self-criticism and a whole nation's attempt to come to terms with its unfortunate past–would have been refocused from ideology to scatology, from collective neuroses about race and intolerance to individual psychoses about anality.

It might have been foreseen twenty years ago. In 1980 there was a meeting in Pittsburgh of the American Folklore Society, and the presidential address was to be given by Alan Dundes. He proceeded to try out a first sketch of his researches, even at the risk that it might be received (in the running gag of the day) as a *"turd de force."* A few well-informed souls who were German-born members of the society approached him…and draped Dundes' shoulders with toilet paper. There was, at the beginning, much laughter and high spiritedness. But when it came to "Auschwitz"–and so much intolerable documentation of how the prisoners, "these vermin," were humiliated, how the "final solution" consigned the scum-of-the-earth, unwashed, to the garbage-bin-of-history– there was an emotional impasse. Many academics became "violently angry"; others were speechless. Professor Dundes remained undaunted; he went on with what he himself calls his "excremental repetition."[20]

Over time a certain pedantry has developed on the subject, and in turn it serves to compound the singularity of the German obsession. I cannot imagine where elese one could have had the following debate on the scatological quotation which has figured so prominently in these pages. The argument involved the leading literary critic of Germany, Marcel Reich-Ranicki, and his differences with a young and attractive TV talk-show personality, named Sandra Maischberger. Sandra had challenged the old master on his Goethe-manship, and insisted that the notorious a-word in Goethe's play *Götz von Berlichingen* involved–I could not believe my ears that this was the point of issue, but it was!–*"Leck mich am Arsch"* or *"Leck mich im Arsch."* The literary scholar stood by *im*–the TV show-mistress countered (incorrectly) with *am*….One can't calculate how it divided nationwide TV audiences that both these estimable public personalities commanded. But when a national newspaper got it wrong, then it was obliged to print a stern correction from *"Prof. Dr. h.c. mult.* Marcel Reich-Ranicki" putting the classic usage absolutely right. He spelled it out. Tampering with the classics–not to mention a scatological icon–can be a very serious matter in Germany.[21]

I mention all this only in passing because my own exercise in comparative newspaper cultures cannot avoid certain intellectual controversies. Odorifer- ous as these arguments might be among academic readers whose perceptions of the big stories that make the newspaper headlines–or indeed the little items on the inside pages that can be taken to be so "revealing"–are derived from the higher regions of so-called cultural studies, given on hundreds of college courses on our American campuses. In the end we might be reduced to a tautol- ogy, saying in effect that the culture comes from…the culture. There are surely more agreeable, even more cogent, explanations of obscene extremism which are less elementary–less primordial, more contingent to our time and place– than the direct association with the human body's prime biological functions since time immemorial. One might ask: What was Neanderthal-speak like in the prehistoric Rhineland valleys? Did Neanderthal man also prefer the s- to the f-word, and pass on to his descendents (if any) the genetic elements of an excremental predisposition. These are not fanciful questions to any contem- porary moviegoer who knows how tortuous the passage from Hollywood's

Tarantino-like obscene dialogues is in the impossible transition into German.[22]

The persistence–if not dominance–of these traditional and perhaps even primitive excremental associations was underlined in the new century in the annual German competition for the ill-fame of the *Unwort des Jahres*, 2002. This is an "Orwellian" prize given to a cant word or phrase which has been newly coined, has invaded the language, and serves to elicit the contempt it deserves; for it functions to degrade humane values by dehumanizing speech and prose. The German language media give it, in an unusual burst of self-critical linguistics–usually (which means the rest-of-the-year) oblivious to the insipidity of every cliché, buzzword, and poor pun–prime time and page-one attention. Possibly it helps to salve their conscience for popularizing mindlessly all such shoddy lingo. Among the previous winners were:

1. *Gotteskrieger* (warriors of god, 1992)–which referred to the Allah-driven bombsters of Middle East terror. But everybody knows that God doesn't bless–any more–soldiers, warriors, or even crusaders, taking His name in vain. *Friedenskämpfer*, fighters-for-peace who convert swords into plowshares, are another matter.

2. *Collateral Damage* (1999). This Americanism was simply put into straightforward, if similarly grotesque, German translatese as *Kollateralschaden*–and it also tried to nullify or to counteract verbally the bloody mess that big bombs cause when they miss their target and hit nearby homes, schools, and hospitals. Although it was a rendering from *"the American"* (as the German literary reviewers insist on calling the English language as spoken and written in the U.S.) and the delinquent bombs (in Bosnia, in Afghanistan) were also American, it was curious that it did not have an anti-American tenor or echo. I suspect that it might have been because, in its nineteenth-century origins, this type of phrase was systematically borrowed by the U.S. Army's training corps from the much admired Prussian militarists: they specialized, in the tradition of Clausewitz, in making combat "a ballet of abstract categories," that is, by making war a discussable subject of study by coining abstractions to de-emotionalize the deadly mutual destruction of warring armies on the killing fields. I myself was, for a while, a trainee of the U.S. Engineer Corps, and I was fascinated to be informed that I was to learn all about the battlefield dangers of *"Anti-Personnel Mines."* Losing a leg became as "collateral" as breaking the leg of an office chair. Your gun or rifle became "a piece," and presumably pieces also killed personnel. Corpses figured in the body count, and added to the double-entry statistics.

3. *Ethnic Cleansing* (1992). The Balkan source here had been coined in Serbo-Croat (*"etnicko ciscenje,"* first used in 1991, quoted in July of that year in a London *Times* dispatch); but the German prize-winning *"ethnische Säuberung"* was in the Western tradition of circumlocutions for mass mur-

der. It derived from the unfortunate Serbian practice in the Yugoslav wars of the 1990s, and it was symbolized memorably by the massacres of Sbrenica (and elsewhere). All military establishments in history, or so I suspect, devise and employ especially denatured terms for summing up what their troops, in the end, had "cleaned up" in "mop-up operations." No dirty words to be used around here.

For this year (2002) the prize for mis-verbalization–for which they coined the unword *Unwort*–was given to a new governmental phrase minted by Berlin's "Special Commission on Mass Unemployment." Troubled by economic stagnation the experts had recommended an unusual course to every individual in the land: namely, to take new initiatives, to stake out on his (or her) own, to innovate and risk an enterprising business...as if they were all an *Ich, AG.* (Literally: *I, Inc.*–or one could translate this more loosely, less literally tas *Me, Me, & Co.*, or perhaps *Me, Myself & I, Partners.*) The moment it was announced a young German businesswoman, acting upon a creditable individual inspiration, applied for an exclusive copyright to the name and, if she is granted the "patent," she may collect royalties and amass a small fortune from the cliché's dissemination.

What in my context in this chapter is relevant and profoundly revealing is the runner-up entry, the phrase which *might* have made it. It would, as I sense, have renewed the redolent tradition dating from the medieval Götz von Berlichingen and the scatological obsession identified with his notorious quote. But it achieved only an "*also ran*" position. It was the phrase, a "hard word" rare and fancy and foreign-sounding, about the *cacophony* with which Chancellor Schroeder dismissed the irritating noise of opponents' propaganda on the eve of an imminent U.S. war against Iraq.

Many German commentators, classical élitists as they are, were enchanted at the possibility that "*ein schöner Gräzismus*," a pretty little derivation from the old Greek, might well have made it to first place. It had only one shortcoming. A substantial body of its supporters were under the mistaken impression that it was indeed a foreign word and of "fecal" origins. Cacophonony is certainly derived from the ancient Greek, denoting "ill-sounding" or "discordant" (*OED*, vol. I, p. 263), as opposed to the "harmonious" *euphony*. Thus scatology or "*Fäkalsprache*" has nothing to do with it.[23]

But in the German the disharmonious spelling is with two alarming *K*'s, *Kakophonie*; and it is too pungently close–by sheer linguistic accident–to the low and vulgar reference to *Kacke*. This was unfortuante for this would link Chancellor Schroeder's dismissal of dissenting voices in the *Bundestag* (and indeed in his Red-Green majority coalition) with excremental associations, with "*turds*" perhaps, or in more contemporary parlance, with *b—l–s—t*. The worthy philologists of the "*Unwort*" jury were not prepared to go so far afield. The k-word was discreetly left in the farmyard or (in Dundes' metaphor) the chicken coop. The jurors turned quickly to the economy, stupid, where egoism and rugged individualism were threatening to overwhelm us. The *homo oeconomicus*, according to the Berlin daily newspaper, *Der Tagesspiegel*, was being reduced by some monstrous new process which was spelled out in the fashionable mix called by the *"Denglish"*-speaking Germans as *"Ego-shaping.Persönlichkeits-Marketing.ein Unique-Selling-Point."*

The *Kakophonie* fans, evidently crestfallen when their favorite *Non-* or *Anti-Word* didn't win the support of the finicky philologists who ran the annual competition, had only brought it on themselves. They had been divided whether or not the word can (or cannot) be traced to vulgar defecatory contexts. One philologist, specializing in classical Greek, offered *kakoj* (meaning *"bad, evil"*) and asked whether there was a connection to *Kacke* ("dung"). A child psychologist was certain that the *K-k* word was a *Lallwort* or a *Lautgebärde* from the *Kindersprache*, that is to say, an infantile phonetic gesture, a possibly onomatopeic baby-sound from early toilet training. Lexicographers reported that it was apparently traceable back to the fifteenth-century's *Spät-Mittelhochdeutsch*.[25]

If this is too grim or recondite (or too humorless) for wider journalistic dissemination, we can turn for comic relief to its Yiddish history, also derived from late medieval Germanic usages, but with the characteristic extra-salty touch of the tribe's self-irony and mockery. Here is Leo Rosten defining *Alte Kocker*, the Yiddish vulgarism for a crotchety, fussy, ineffectual old man–and additional evidence for "ineradicable earthiness": "What kocker means I had rather not tell you in street argot, but kock means 'defecate'....My mother never let me use such a phrase, or employ such vulgarity." My *Cassell's New German Dictionary* (London, 1909; New York, 1939), perhaps similarly fettered by maternal restraint, gives *kacken* as "go to stool."[26]

Thus, Chancellor Gerhard Schroeder's major political campaign in the year 2002 against hostile "cacophony" was saved from going down in the history of language as a notorious example of anti-democratic dehumanization by its accidental phonetic resemblance to a fecal vulgarism. Had he been inspired to use the *Götz-Wort* (also a German *vulg.*, but made famous by Goethe), he might have given the scatological tagline an extra lease of life as a lewd insult. The chancellor used, as I say, a "hard word," rare and foreign-sounding; and, truly assessed, it attested to the decencies of his discourse.

Sometimes the true news story, deserving to earn an impressive headline, is the drama of the entry that almost won the first prize but didn't. The process of four-letterization, with its checkered choice of expletives, thrives also on dishonorable defeats. *Kakophonie* escaped being publicly disgraced, and "*Ich, A.G.*" took on the shameful burden of the year's anti-word.

Kakophonie should've won. In the cacophony of insults and *Schimpfwörter*, of putdowns and *Unwörter*, of political platitudes and what orwell once called smelly little orthodoxies–all obsessing right-thinking philologists and incorrigible scatologists–I surmise that it did. German cant is in bad odor.

The Snafu Known as Swag

A deceptive etymological reading of an ambivalent word can, in an embarrassing situation, serve to "clean up the act" and render a suspicious and suggestive phrase respectable. It might otherwise be taken to be coarse and inappropriate.

Take the post-Vietnam military term which emerged in the concentrated air bombing of Milosevic's Yugoslav regime in 1999: *SWAG*. It was of fairly recent coinage and was, in fact, previously uttered by General Westmoreland in some of his Saigon apologetics. Why didn't the U.S. bombing attacks destroy the enemy Viet forces? "SWAG," he said, and Saigon journalists smiled.

In effect SWAG took the place of the old *"guesstimate"* which had served very nicely in explaining unfortunate margins of error in previous aerial actions and other faulty wartime enterprises. Pinpoint targeting, after the damage was inspected, often turned out to be rather far from actual precision. When, in general, the scatological or generally profane dimension moved from army barracks slang to the normal vocabulary of high-level military briefings and official communiqués–in the f-word frowst (with related toxic fumes) which has descended on our language as she lives and breathes–then NATO experts in the war against Milosevic in Belgrade could emerge with the cynical, shoulder-shrugging *SWAG*, or *"scientific wild-ass guess."* This new bit of military parlance was percipiently first reported by John Harris in the *Washington Post*.

But the acronym did not spring spontaneously from the Kosovo hostilities where General Wesley Clark's B-52 aces flew to bomb Serbian Yugoslavia and sometimes hit Macedonia or Bulgaria or Chinese extraterritoriality. Their maps were not *so* accurate and up-to-date; their targeting was not nearly as pinprecise as promised. Politicians protested, and military men cursed. Editors of mainstream newspapers know full well that men at war need their obscenities as much as they need the reassurance of extra food rations (especially chocolate bars) or the mail-call consolations of letters from home. They feel even better when words get twisted conveniently, with one sort of tragic error being called *"friendly fire"* and another a *"wild-ass"* mistake....

According to the Safire column on Language in the *New York Times*, the U.S. Army's home page on the Internet actually lists *"swag"*–erratically in lower case, chides the *maven*–where it is defined simply as "a gross estimate or guess." But the Pentagon warns against using the term "when dealing with outsiders," presumably because of the civilians who might be vexed by the *"a,"* standing for the third word in the acronym. Happily enough, the *Times* columnist rushed to save the honor of the paper and its still authoritative neopuritanical stylebook.

First, an aside on the "a-word" and its standing in the community.

In its alphabetical glossary of editorial problems (from *"Achilles' heel"* to *"Zeitgeist"*), the *New York Times' Manual of Style and Usage* (1999) does not list *"ass."* Between *"as much as"* and *"assault weapons"* there is only *"assassins."* But then it doesn't list, even to interdict their publication in the paper, the f-word, the s-word, and the whole unhappy glossary of unmentionables. Under the general and very unspecific entry *"obscenity, vulgarity, profanity"* (pp. 240-242), it argues conventionally and a bit stuffily for "keeping the paper clean": in the nineteenth-century formula of its founder, Adolph S. Ochs, "in language that is parliamentary in good society." This nineteenth-century credo of the Ochs/Sulzberger family of founders still keeps it sensitive to what will "outrage readers" and predisposed to fit and seemly expressions. It does allow for "profanity in its milder forms"–a few *hells* and a *damn* or two–but reasserts its sedulous avoidance of "obscene words" and its proud century-old stand on maintaining its old and awesome "concern for the newspaper's character": "But if the writer perceives a compelling argument for an exception, a discussion with the department head is mandatory." Discussions there have been many; but no such "masthead editor" has within living memory shared any such compulsion.

It would be a rewarding task for some future historian of the *New York Times* to document such lexicographical confrontations of reporters and executives. For the time being we have the rare bits of evidence from *Times* staffers who have written (and published) their autobiographies.

One of the great by-lines of the 1970s and 1980s was John Corry, and he has told the story of the troubles he had getting into print any of half-a-dozen versions of his long and explicitly detailed account of the Masters & Johnson post-Kinsey research into the sexual behavior of his fellow Americans. As he writes in his memoir, "I had written the piece with great delicacy and tact, but unquestionably it was still about fucking...." The style-maven Theodore Bernstein was still an active senior editor on the paper and "he couldn't stand it." The story was passed to other editors, each of whom wanted some particular item deleted or altered. The Corry story shrank, expanded, and then shrank again; it moved from, and then returned to, the front page. The author was angry, upset, desperate, fit to be tied; and he concluded: "The narrow-minded old men who ran the *Times* were opposed to truth, justice, and beauty." Corry exaggerated. They only felt that certain expressions could never be used beautifully and couldn't ever sound true: so it was just literary justice to edit them out. In the final conflict of 1966, it came down to one last word: "It had been decided that my story could remain as it was except for one word. That was 'penis.' 'Vagina' was acceptable, but 'penis' had to be replace by 'male sex organ'...I could live with that."[27] For some it appeared to be a gentlemanly deference to the female of the species and was, possibly, the last courtly gesture in an old nineteenth-century institution. For others it was typical of a *macho*/shame culture, ill at ease in its masculinity and certainly ill-prepared for the feminism of the future. I suspect that there might have been veteran *Times* editors who could "live with" both versions of a political correctness which called for decent embarrassment and weak compromise. It was a language war that was being fought out in every newsroom, and it was to be–at least in this kind of contest between the p-word and the v-word–rather short-lived. Things were going to get much rougher, even at the *Times*.

It would be the more foolish part of naïveté to believe that the grim grayness of the *Times'* prose in all these matters is determined by consulting the alphabetized *do's* and *don'ts* of the house style-book. An old, cynical piece of newspaper lore of the *The Front Page* era ascribes all of a newspaper's sins of omission and commission to "the wife of the boss." But in the epoch of late finance capitalism it is often difficult in the corporate dispersal of media shares to pinpoint exactly where ultimate power lies. It might be somewhere between individual stockholders (who may not be able to get even a letter-to-the-editor into the paper) and a powerful chief executive officer (about to be summarily fired).

But not with "the good gray lady of Times Square." Ever since Julius Ochs (born in Fürth, Bavaria, also Henry Kissinger's birthplace a century later) established a family dynasty in the American newspaper world, those who carried forth the name and the bloodline (variously Ochs/Oakes/Dryfoos/Sulzberger) exercised, in the last analysis, power. Control, and the various types of personal influence–from hiring and firing of senior editors and/or columnists and what should (or may not) go on to the front page or into the "high society" chronicle–indicated confidently who is, more or less, "boss." Scholars have now researched a realistic history of "the private and powerful family behind the *New York Times*"; and now we know the kind of pressures which were periodically exercised in order to keep the "character" and the "standing" of the great newspaper which had emerged from the flimsy broadsheet (the *New York Times*, "with a quaint hyphen") that had been bought in 1896 and splendidly relaunched by Julius' son Adolph Simon Ochs. The family ownership, improbable as it may seem in the world of mergers and takeovers and mercantile failures, remained intact for over a century; and so did the tradition of having a *Machtwort*, uttering a powerful word from on high.

On our matter at hand–"the language of journalism" in a changing newspaper culture–family values prevailed over metropolitan and indeed cosmopolitan temptations. Here is an incident (or two) in the controversial 1970s involving "John" (Johnny Oakes, an Ochs/Sulzberger cousin who ran the editorial page) and "Punch" (Arthur Ochs Sulzberger, the publisher)—

> When John used the word *bullshit* in a column–a quote from one of his sources–Punch expressed "dismay and astonishment" and invoked the *New York Times* style-book, which forbade such language. "I don't like those kinds of words in the *New*

York Times," he said emphatically. John retaliated by sending him a copy of an item in the paper he found to be equally objectionable–a health column written by Jane Brody. The subject: vaginitis.*

Those kinds of words have been flourishing in postwar American society, coloring its politics, coarsening its social tone but, doubtless, enlivening its cultural communication. The childish Sulzberger/Ochs exchange of cuttings wherein my-expletives-are-larger-than-yours offered no mature solution to a serious professional problem of newspaper culture. Several of "those kinds of words" have indeed appeared in the columns of the *Times*, albeit by sheer unhappy accident. In general they are still not deemed to be fit to print, even in the medical-health columns. Even in Latin.[28]

I should note at this point at the expense of digressing yet again, that self-criticism has come relatively late in the history of the *New York Times*. For long decades it confounded its dignity with a stiff, unbending self-confidence. Critics have often teased the *Times'* editors about their paper's pseudo-infalli-bility as it blithely refused sharp letters of correction and never conceded even important errors or grievous misstatements. Irving Kristol in a trenchant essay in his journal the *Public Interest* (Winter 1967) acidly challenged the paper to shake off its bad habits which debilitated its general standards of journalistic integrity.

Many years later, under the innovative editorial regime of A.M. Rosenthal, a small department was introduced which drily called attention to the factual (and phraseological) slip-ups that had occurred in recent editions. It was an admirable step forward, and it sometimes registered (coolly, casually) even the most embarrassing of professional shortcomings (e.g., a so-called eyewitness report from a correspondent who, truth to tell, hadn't been anywhere near the action of the story).

But the *Times'* notorious sub-intellectual proclivities made over time the department into something of a superficial farce, as if the trivialization of erratic editorial ways would in its end-effect utterly disarm any unfriendly critic. One example.

There is a page of so-called news which the *Times*, in its journalistic wis-dom, persists in publishing; and it is almost always free of obvious mistakes…for the basic personal information is conventionally supplied by hordes of brides and bridegrooms (and their beaming families) directly to the paper's "Society" editor. In my short, rather stormy career as a foreign correspondent for the *Times* I once had a sharp exchange with one of the publishing seniors, the late Clifford Daniel whom I had known as a reporter abroad. (His marriage to Margaret Truman, the president's daughter, was indeed real news, and the

---

*   Susan Trifft and Alex Jones, *The Trust: The Private and Powerful Family Behind The New York Times* (1999), p. 527.

paper got their story impeccably right.) Daniel stood on his executive dignity against my imprecations against the newsworthiness of all those "nuptials" in the better churches and temples of midtown Manhattan (as well as certain exclusive sectors of Long Island and the New Jersey shore). I, for one, was weary under the information overload of where those lovely young ladies had gone to school and where all those handsome young men were going to work in Wall Street. I suggested that the *Times* could garner an additional source of much-needed income by ruthlessly spiking nuptial-news and allowing the snobbish, well-heeled East Coast in-laws to pay commercially for the announcements (in well-displayed boxes, oozing with *naches* or pride, as the case might be)–just as many European newspapers do in the event of birth, marriage, and death.

Needless to say, I lost the argument. The consequences were egregious. The straits, over time, became dire. Here is an example of what I mean, the *New York Times* dated 11 May 2000, and the *Columbia Journalism Review* gave it pride of place in its column ("*LOWER CASE*") devoted to quoting such absurdities:

Correction

A report last Sunday about the marriage of Nicole Judith Barth and Neal Andrew Thompson misstated the location of her mother and stepfather's current residence. They live together in Manhattan, not separately in Middlefield, Ohio, and Ridgewood, N.J.

The report also misstated the location of Ms.Barth's first encounter with Mr. Thompson. It was at the home of her mother and stepfather, then in Ridgewood, not at her stepmother's home in Paterson. In addition the report referred incorrectly to the Cape Cod home in which the proposal took place. It is owned by her mother and stepfather, not her stepmother.[29]

How did the paper manage to get it so wrong? Who was so fatuous as to want to get the Cape Cod property just right? Why should this concoction of irrelevant trivia have ever been published in the first place? To adjust it and give it finicky historical correctness is to defy even the forebearance of the gods.

With mounting regularity test-cases appear to be coming up to try the soul of the *Times'* editors. They wrestle with their consciences, and lo! the old Ochs spirit of the 1890s always emerges unscathed. Small scratches were inflicted during the coverage of the Monica Lewinsky/Linda Tripp cases. Like the *Washington Post* and especially the newsweeklies, *Time* and *Newsweek*, the *New York Times* was forced to recognize that the exact words that were used in Clinton's White House trysts could shed important light on the true nature of the sexual relationship about which the president seemed to be prevaricating and, thus, rendering himself impeachable. With some reluctance, especially in the mainstream press, the U.S. newspaper reader was offered a torrent of obscene expletives, few of which were deleted, all in "the public interest."

In December 1999 the matter of "the Columbine tapes"–first revealed by *Time* in an "exclusive" which seemed to get them even for the prize-winning scoops that *Newsweek* had had in the previous affairs–was an altogether different challenge. For one thing, the profanity involved could not be taken to be sexual or salacious. It was offensive slang but actually the *lingua franca* of streetwise American kids of all classes from coast to coast. It was rough and tough talk which might have some connection with aggression and vindictive mayhem.

In Columbine High School (Littleton, Colorado) two students brutally murdered 15 fellow-students and a teacher before killing themselves. What motivated the massacre? Why had they been driven to such an atrocity? The Denver police had accumulated a vast amount of evidence which had been treated as "confidential" for fear of re-opening old wounds in the community for whom the family tragedies were unbearable enough. Among the most re-vealing items–the basis for the *Time* scoop–were the so-called "Columbine tapes" (playing time: two hours) in which the two young killers filmed them-selves, trying out their weapons, explaining their strategy (the bombs didn't explode, and so they had fewer victims than originally planned), apologizing to their very nice parents (with a surprising Shakespeare quote: "Good wombs hath borne bad sons"), taking slugs of Jack Daniels whiskey before recom-mending to History about how it should record their dramatic act.

The vocabulary of the Columbine videotapes presented, in its obsessive use of four-letter words, the usual problem. The context of the foul language was, as I have indicated, not sex but murder; but evidently it was no less important for "understanding the news." One had to hear the seventeen-year-old killers talk about their young lives and how mounting rage against all and sundry had driven them to run amok. Only when the full evidence of the Columbine tragedy is made public can an informed judgment be made about how important the linguistic vileness was to the violence. Foul words do not necessarily presage foul deeds. Obviously other triggers had unleashed ag-gression: ill-digested bits of psychiatry, a scrap of yesterday's ideology ("we're going to kick-start a revolution"), images of Sunday theology and occult lore (they were to wear black trench-coats for, as they called it, "Judgement Day" after which they were destined to go "to a better place"); festering fragments of movies devoted to death *en masse*; etc. etc. In fact the two young men specifi-cally suggested the names of Hollywood directors who could make great cin-ema out of their story (Steven Spielberg, of *Schindler's List* fame; Quentin Tarantino, celebrated for his films of murder and massacre, and the sound-track to go with them).

The "exclusive" *Time* story broke on the third weekend of December 1999.[30]

In the next twenty-four hours all of the rest of the media reported the story with selected excerpts, with some adding (for obvious reasons) that the *Time* scoop was in violation of an agreement with the Sheriff's office to see the tapes "for background purposes only." The *New York Times*, trying to be demonstrably fair, also added a quote from *Time*, defending its honor, to the effect that no such agreement had been made.

In the *Time* story there were four-letter words galore, breaking ground with two banner headlines across two pages:

> "Tick, tick, tick…Haa! That f___ing shotgun is straight out of Doom."
> "I'm going to kill you all. You've been giving us s___ for years."

In the long account of the "culture of cruelty"–the secret videos which Eric Harris and Dylan Klebold recorded before the massacre, wherein the youthful killers revealed their hatreds and their lust for fame–the summary includes a dozen or more of presumably representative obscenities. It somehow betrayed the influence of the aforementioned Quentin Tarantino, that master of the obsessive expletive, and *Time* refers to the two young men as "natural born killers," the name of the Oliver Stone film which made Tarantino famous.

> "If you could see all the anger I've stored over the past f___ing years…."
> "If any of our parents had asked one question, we would've been f___ed…."
> "I will be armed to the f___ing teeth and I will shoot to kill…."
> "It f___ing sucks to do this to them…."

The usual f-dash-dash-dash style–three hyphens rather than underlined blankness–was adopted by many regional newspapers, including the local *Rocky Mountain News* in Denver. As for the *New York Times* it played the story as clean and straight as is its wont. It bore no grudge against *Time*'s "exclusive" and offered no comment on the magazine's defense that "the authorities had not insisted on any restrictions." Its *précis* of the pages was competent, even venturing to suggest with what "exquisite precision and detail" the arsenal of guns, bombs, and ammunition had been displayed on camera. It made no mention of the profanity on the tapes, and was exquisite in its avoidance of any specific reference to the innumerable obscenities.[31]

Abroad it was a fieldday for the English-language press; in London the *Daily Telegraph* used a dozen or so well-placed asterisks to cover the four-letter-word quotations in its story of "Hate and Fury Revealed in School Killers' Videos."[32]

What, then, of the strategy of dashes, asterisks, and the like? The *Times*' "*Manual*" rejects such "evasiveness and euphemism." These would be "a disservice to readers who need to understand issues." Which leaves us at the point some five hundred pages back–at the Brooklyn race riot when in the course of convulsive events, in a crisis of an alarmed public opinion, it became necessary (in order to render a-service-to-readers-who-need-to-understand-issues) to "pepper the paper" with newsworthy details that involved reporting unseemly words and phrases which, alas, already had disturbed and outraged.

Sometimes it is a matter of coarse slang, sometimes of racial slurs or explicit sexual crudities. In theory the *Times* has become "willin'," like Dickens' Barkis, but the wheels of its decision-making process sound rusty and slow moving when it comes to deciding whether or not to print "an extreme vulgarism."

> Only when its use will give the reader an essential insight into matters of great moment, an insight that cannot be otherwise conveyed. Such a case would almost certainly involve the use of the term by a figure of commanding influence or in that person's presence, in a situation likely to become momentous.

Presumably, this means that a little nobody, crying out in anguish or pain or hatred, in a war or revolution or in an ugly riot, will never make it. As far as the *Times* is concerned, he never has. Are quotable obscenities forever to be the exclusive preserve of power élites, credited only to figures of commanding influence in momentous situations? *Merde*, say I.

Still, the Pentagon's concept of SWAG did enshrine the vexatious *A* in the American vocabulary of war (did Clausewitz ever need Berlin slang to formulate his Prussian military doctrines?)...and it could possibly be causing a momentary (certainly not a momentous) measure of embarrassment to general officers and to other figures of commanding influence on the firing range. Its place in the columns of the *New York Times* came similarly under a shadow. But it soon turned out that the paper's published paragraphs on SWAG did *not* repeat *not* cross the line of family decencies. No less a *maven* than Safire told us to be "at ease," not to be stiff or uptight about it: "At ease: the attributive noun phrase *wild ass* is not a vulgarism. The juxtaposition of words (as adjective and noun) can be found five times in the King James version of the Bible." One of the five is, of course, the famous if odd analogy with donkeys in *Job 24:5*: "Behold, as wild asses in the desert, go they forth to their work..."[33]

But do donkeys–as well represented in high NATO circles as were desert pack-carriers in Job's world–have anything to do with it? This would seem to be a classic example of lexicographical laundering or (as Kenneth Burke might have said) *exorcism by misnomer*. Referring to *Job* (*24:5*) gave the old "guesstimates"–about how many bombs it would take to "degrade" the enemy, or how much "collateral damage" would be inflicted by putatively pinpoint bombing–a touch of traditional, dignified diligence. But actually "*wild ass*" is less Biblical and actually closer to Elmore Leonard's "*wild assholes*" who regularly figure as the sleazy protagonists in his shabby, irrational Miami underworld. On the one hand, the Book of Job respectably suggests a note of human or animal error in a workmanlike ethos. On the other, a word-trace leading to Elmore Leonard would suggest that our bombing scientists, not unlike our two-bit revolver-wielding gangsters, could use a bit of the "*kick-ass*" treatment (famously advocated by President George Bush).

"Wild-ass" is, indubitably, short for "wild ass-hole." Missing targets by a whole country and calling it *"collateral damage"* should not in all Biblical honor be attributed to King James' wild asses (revised in the *NIV* translation into the more modern "wild donkeys"). If I may, I call the reader's attention to the headline which Saul Bellow and Keith Botsford put on a small piece I once wrote for their little magazine on Elmore Leonard's whole genre of "tough guy" novels:

THE POETS LAUREATE OF WILD ASSHOLES WITH REVOLVERS[34]

Nobody has necessarily to win or lose in the etymological debate. The U.S. Army has its SWAG to put alongside its SNAFU. Both Army euphemisms mix modest self-criticism with a note of bellicose triumphalism. Operations successful, patients all dead. Even if merely fouled up, with scientific guesses turning out to be on the erratic side, situations are…you better believe it…normal. It's only routine to get some things wrong in a messy war. Yet…nevertheless…after all the chaos and foul-ups…we win anyway. The after-action moral of the story, signalled by such acronyms, is always reassuring: Victory will be ours even if situations get all fouled up, and guesses check out to be on the wild side. Most of the time. And the Pentagon gets its beribboned medals for valorous action.

The *New York Times* has, once again, decently averted the scatological danger. William Safire has had his little lexicographical joke, and SWAG gets added to his creditable reputation as a self-styled maven.*

Filling Out the Missing Details

The usage of "dirty realism" can be both systematic and haphazard. In the daily semantic opportunities enjoyed by the English press–in the serious American press, they only turn up once in a blue moon–the ration is certain to be fulfilled. But there are differences in the very same day's editions, depending on who is editing the particular page or section. I once asked a senior editor in Fleet Street how his publication decided which foul bits to publish and which to leave aside (*n.b.*, prudently for another day). He said, incredibly, that they had no stylebook of *do's* and *don't's*, but they proceeded to decide on the need for mentioning of the unmentionable whenever the delicate matter came up.** If true, then it would account for the conspicuous variations be-

---

*   Leo Rosten, the late *maven* on all things Yiddish, instructs us that it is pronounced to rhyme with "raven" (at least in the *shtetl* his family came from; mine said *my-vin*). But he himself spells it with an *i*. See Rosten, *The Joys of Yiddish* (1970), p. 226, *"mavin"*: "An expert…a really knowledgeable person….a connoisseur."

**   Conversation with Charles Moore (then editor of the *Sunday Telegraph*) in February 1995. Improvised decision-making tends to leniency, letting almost anything go through at the last minute before the presses roll. Editorial house-style guide-lines tilt toward stricter judgements, with time enough for the copy-editor's "subbing" to clean things up.

tween an s-word on one page or another, in a story in one broadsheet paper or the other.

Thus, in my Thursday's *Telegraph* (2 November 1995), a columnist comments on leniency for the accused before liberal judges, and quotes a critic: "Some little s*** is going to walk out of court with a slap on the back–'Please don't do it again.'" On another page an education reporter tells the story of the closing-down of a once-famous school in the East End of London and quotes a disgruntled teacher: "people say, 'This school is shit–look what's in the newspapers.'" imagine, as I say, that it is a sheer editorial accident that accounts for the orthographical difference. Perhaps an impersonal institution can better bear the brunt of a full-frontal four-letter attack; perhaps a poor little fellow in the courtroom should be given a slight benefit of the doubt (and the asterisks may go a small way to presume his innocence). In any case, it is not a fatal discrepancy, and journalistic factuality does not necessarily call for faecal consistency.

Nor does it call for being explicit when explicitness is taken to be all. the *Times* devoted substantial space to a trial over "racial discrimination" on the part of two black waitresses who had been serving tables at a charity dinner (500 men) which featured as "after-dinner entertainment" the stand-up comic Bernard Manning (see "*Comic Relief*," pp. 147*ff.* where we encounter his f-word antics again). The two young women charged that Manning had made "sexist and racist jokes" about them, and they had been left feeling "angry, hurt and degraded." They lost the court decision. The judge ruled that it was Manning that they should have sued, not the hotel.

Whatever the justice in the case, was it part of the newspaper's duty to report what it was that led the defendants to the embittered conclusion that "it is a white society at the end of the day"; and, more than that, to make credible the humiliation and bitterness? The *Times*' editors evidently thought better of it. Hooligans also read; bad words are contagious. Repetition spawns imitation just as, say, "ontogeny reproduces phylogeny."

On the same day the *Telegraph*'s fuller, franker report of the trial included one taunting reference, which was to their hair. Referring to their hair-braids, Manning had gibed, Lend us one. I need some new shoe laces for boots."A poor joke, but his own. The *Telegraph*'s report also added that he had been criticized "for using the word 'nigger' to the audience." In a busy day it was enough to be getting on with two flashes of diligent reporting, two blows in a single story for the cause of truth. Hopefully, the fuller, franker enlightenment is proceeding apace, making real progress.[35]

Private Parts, Public Lives

Like Arnold Wesker's *Chips* that go-with-everything, how can newspapers insinuate sex into all other themes on all other pages (barring, perhaps, the cross-word puzzle)? The lives of film stars are obvious; the conversations, free and easy, of pop and rock celebrities practically do it themselves; the offhand remarks of politicians are increasingly earthy; the trials of *les crimes passionnelles* cry out to be quoted. Beyond that, one's own off-color ingenuity can be sorely challenged. Can one get a sala-cious touch even into the columns about real-estate property? (Not impossible.) And can one find ways quickly to rewrite history by underscoring the rousing erotica? (Not *too* difficult, for even the ancient Romans, the medieval Popes, and the modern Empire-builders had their little reportable sins.)

And so here are, to chose only a few current samples, the circuitous ways with which one of the great "quality" newspapers of Fleet Street, Conrad Black's *Daily* and *Sunday Telegraph* manages to fulfill its daily pensum of "the color blue," heading off the incursions of Rupert Murdoch's *Times* in the ruinous circulation-war of the two British Press Lords (neither of whom happens to be British).

The paper assigns its Housing correspondent to do a story about so-called "property snobbery." He is a clever, well-connected and knowledgeable fellow, name of Hugh Massing-berd (author of a grand book on the *Great Houses of England and Wales* and who also doubles for a while as the paper's peppery television critic). The theme is an attractive one. It suits him especially, for he has long since been convinced that the "would-be grand people have distorted the real meaning of property titles with the pompous names"; and it suits the paper as well, which is true-blood Tory at least in its traditional persuasion that a man's home is his castle even if he doesn't happen to own one. Massingberd sniffs nosily at the so-called "manor houses" which advertise themselves as mansions, or villas, or country houses, or *gent's res.*; and he disposes of all these vulgarities—but not before getting in the one obligatory bawdy blip: "The trouble is that the more pompous words have taken on pejorative connotations. 'Why are you so interested in my *arse?*' I recall, blushingly, one country-house owner asking me when I inquired about his family seat." (*Daily Telegraph*, 8 October 1994).

Still blushing, he continues his "country-house crawling" in the piece of the next week in which he discovers "An Estate of Grace," namely, that the great English country house–the paradisical vision represented by Evelyn Waugh's *Brideshead* ("and even P.G. Wodehouse's *Blanding's Castle*")–is not at all an extinguished illusion but is enjoying a new "Golden Age." The reader will not only appreciate this bit of good news about their flourishing heritage (not all the Lords and Ladies have opened their houses to the public and withdrawn into a castle corner!)–he will also enjoy this cheek-flushing tidbit, amidst the Palladian splendour of Adam and Chippendale, the Duchess of Devonshire's Chatsworth and Lord Rothschild's Waddledon:

In this and several other cases, one can be confident that they have never looked better. It was fascinating, for the purposes of my researches, to see what are known in the trade as "the private parts."

"Would you like to see my 'private parts,' eh, what?" as the late Duke of Marlborough used to chortle." (*Daily Telegraph*, 15 October 1994)

Once the a-word gets to be part of the real estate will the next-door neighbours be far behind? What comes next, *eh, what* indeed? We just can't wait for the coming attractions.

For now it may suffice to upgrade the f-word (and all its variants) into first class, to think of it as the liberated literary language, even as a form of poetry. Reviewing a movie entitled *Poetic Justice* (in which a character, a Los Angeles black hairdresser, writes poems that Maya Angelou, President Clinton's favorite poetess, composed for her), the *Telegraph* film critic notes that it has some of the "gutsy energy" of "African-American *culcha*" in its "*gangsta*" mood. As for the dialogue, it is "authentically *street*," and we are assured that those in the know "will know how it goes": "you try to turn the f- and mother-f-words into as many different parts of speech as possible in the same sentence. This is itself a kind of poetry" (*Daily Telegraph*, 14 April 1995).

One statistic may be pertinent here. It emerged in the St. Louis courtroom which heard, sympathetically, the case of a dismissed high schoolteacher who had been allowing, and indeed encouraging, her students to include profanity in their "creative writing assignments." She wanted them to learn "to write naturally." The Missouri schoolboard had determined, not without alarm, that in its educational district "the students uttered a profanity every 12 seconds on average"; and consequently there was more than enough "naturalness" in the school's communication. In this spirit the most inspiring text for the creative writers would have been the Booker Prize-winning novel of James Kelman who had included in his several hundred pages several thousand natural expletives, breaking all previous records for profanity per printed page.[36]

Alphabet Soup

Interviews with salty characters in every walk of life (from high finance to low underworld figures) offer a standard opportunity for peppery language, and one obscenity per profile has become well nigh obligatory. Score a bull's-eye for Ms. Katharine Campbell, talking to a tycoon for the *Financial Times* (18 July 1994): "A suave and successful old Etonian, the chief executive of Mount Charlotte Investments...hates 'pretentiousness and bullshit'...and is a bit of a puzzle to his stuffier rivals." Similarly, according to another London interviewer, a hard-pressed Anita Roddick who runs the *Body Shop* empire with a thousand cosmetics outlets throughout the world (all sup-posedly green and ecological, if you don't believe the debunking of the investigative reporters), gives forth with equal vividness. The quotation was indirect and hence a shade more modest; somebody else said she said it. Thus, one former associate reports that she is unpredictable in her dealings with the staff, opinionated and highly emotional at board meetings: "If she liked something, she would jump up and down and scream and clap her hands. But if she didn't she would dismiss it as f-ing boring" (Megan Tresidder, in the *Daily Telegraph*, 14 October 1994). This orthography is rare, and it is one of the few instances in my collection. It could be a space-saver, with only one hyphen serving for the standard three, and so economizing a centimeter or two of valuable column space; or, alternatively, the dynamic Ms. Roddick could be guilty of slurring her expletives so they come out plosively foreshortened like, say, *phtt!*

In any case, the story's standard condiment has been added, and nothing more salty is needed. The former associate did go on—but by then the family newspaper has regained its formal composure and no four-letter words need to be dredged up to spice the remark (even if it were, probably, possibly, said): "When you work for Anita, your job is to follow behind the elephants and scoop up the dung." Had he said "s-t"? Expletive deleted?

They order these things differently in different cultures, in, say, the quality press of the U.S. and, astonishingly, of Germany.

Here is the new and young editor of the editorial page of the *New York Times* wrestling with the problem of what he calls "pollution along the Superhighway." He is evidently shocked by the intrusion into the international computer network—so rapturously hailed as a true revolution in cultural communications by vice president Al Gore—of undesirable language. The 25 million people, who are tied into the Internet for electronic (e-mail) group discussions, computer billboards, and for the communal warmth of a "virtual neighbor-hood," are increasingly being molested by what Mr. Brent Staples calls "porcine manners." "Beastly things" are being transmitted: "disparaging remarks" about former lovers or marriage partners; verbal venom and defamations; pseudonymous libel and slander; and many other awful things which are throwing a shadow over the high liberal hopes for "cultural innovation" via the Information Superhighway. The *New York Times* editor measures his words when he goes specific and cites one case where the transmitted comment of an *Internet* woman communicator "denigrated the man's sex appeal. The man's remarks were profoundly grotesque and anatomically specific, in line with what one finds on bathroom walls in bus terminals" (*IHT*, 14 October 1994).

This is perhaps as tasteful as you can get on the subject being dealt with, namely, obscene graffiti in toilet urinals. It spreads an old-fashioned and very decent linen doily over a multitude of sins, all naked and uncovered in the vocabulary of a- and f- and c- and p-words. A whole alphabet soup of the missing words can be easily identified and filled in, with asterisks or hyphens of your choice. But temptation raises not its semantic head. the *New York Times* will not be moved.

Nor, under the circumstances, would the comparable journals in Britain: the *Guardian*, the *Independent*, the *Times*, the *Telegraph*.

But in Germany one distinguished paper would, in all likelihood, have interested itself in the problem and would have thought bravery the better part of valor, rushing into print with exact details as a matter, to be sure, of complete historical and cultural record (see the review of an American novel in the *FAZ* which I cited above). Puzzling euphemisms and inscrutable acronyms are tricky to deal with in a language not your own. The s-word becomes the *M*-word in French; the f-word turns out to be a v-word in German. Spanish confuses questions by standing the q-mark on its head.

Mr. Bloomberg's "$!*@&"

Cash flow and bottom-line profits, those hard pecuniary factors in the communication industry's finances, are cautionary and, except for an occasional sensational breakthrough to an audience's gross tastes, they induce a hesitant conservatism in the expansion of the vulgate. What would be gained at the one permissive end (a sold-out box-office; a sneaking liberal sense of added freedom) would be lost at the other (protests, boycotts, circulation losses). "*We are a family newspaper*" is the refrain of Western press moguls, and they contend that if they were ever tempted to move to complete liberation they would be on self-destruct. Middle-class families have been known to cancel subscriptions; and the youthful offspring haven't, in the general functional illiteracy, compensated by sprinting off to buy copies for themselves. Going over the "blue" line is indeed an economic risk; using "foul language" in a context of a circulation war is like calling in "friendly fire" and willingly agreeing to take casualties.

There is yet another cultural contradiction that works from within to frustrate the best-laid plans of liberalizing editors, employed by enlightened publishers, all ashamed to look like prudes in a dynamic age of free-for-all permissiveness. It is the lurking fear of a legal backlash in a time when private ultra-sensitivity has led to an unprecedented public litigiousness. Caution has become laced with cowardice as the dangers of disastrous lawsuits loom, far beyond the traditional pitfalls of libel and slander.* Truth telling was in the

---

*   I once lost a law-suit for "libel" in which an *Encounter* intellectual had called another intellectual a follower of a distinguished Italian political philosopher. Conor Cruise O'Brien won the case, for a local light-skinned jury (in Belfast) would be unconvinced that to be dubbed "a Machiavellian" would be for an honest-to-goodness Irishman anything less than a swarthy insult, a demeaning "furrin'" sneer....Later we became friends, and O'Brien a valued contributor to the magazine. He now considered the old insult to be a badge of honor: the famous sixteenth-century Florentine had been a great man; to have read him and learned from him was a compliment. He was re-evaluated (as was Edmund Burke, and O'Brien did send me a copy of his new biography, *The Great Melody*, 1994). But we never talked about returning the damages he had once been awarded.

past an exoneration for hurtful reportage. To call a man a swindler or a woman a whore was legitimate and protected–when in point of demonstrable fact he was indeed a shady character and she had been regularly seen to be working the streets. New interpretations make this less than certain. Lurid and quite unconvincing pieces of evidence which were summoned for proof may have been obtained in violation of a man's or a woman's inalienable right to inviolable privacy, and thus were to be deemed legally inadmissible.

Recently a prominent Wall Street information firm issued a warning to all traders on the stock exchanges to mind their p's and q's (and even to dot their *i*'s and cross their *t*'s) if they could be misconstrued as suggesting **** or —. The company, an indefatigable news-gatherer which had become indispensable to Wall Street, could not, and would not, transmit judgements on "shady" or "suspect" stocks and bonds and especially on the hustlers, shysters, or bulls*******s who were peddling them. Nor would they include rude derogatory slurs on old and new companies who were led by "corporate raiders" or "merger magnates" or "asset strippers," et al.

But *how* far is *too* far? Capitalism is beginning to catch up on the perils that have plagued culture for a century or more. Mr. Michael Bloomberg of Bloomberg Investment Services (a billion-dollar agency for all bankers and financiers) warned that there are built-in loss-making reprisals. Indeed the Dow Jones Company disseminated the beckoning dangers in the columns of the newspaper it owns, the eminent *Wall Street Journal* (which has rules of its own, not necessarily Mr. Bloomberg's, as to the lengths one can go). The first victim was a David Halpert who had been sitting in front of his Bloomberg computer screen ("as he always does"), typing out some thoughts about a stock sale. When he tried to send the message to a Wall Street colleague it was blocked.

> A note from Bloomberg popped up on his screen, explaining that a variation on a certain four-letter word he had used to stress that the offering was overpriced, was "inappropriate in the context of business correspondence."
> "I was commenting in colorful language on a particularly heinously overvalued equity deal," says the fund manager, a principal at Zesiger Capital Group in New York. "And I found myself unable to express the full horror that the pricing of the transaction would have justified."[37]

The *Wall Street Journal* signaled the resistance and the outrage of traders at being censored by printing in its front-page headline the old keyboard symbol for foul-mouthed curses under taboo–$!*@&–which alone could express "the full horror." (In well-known masterpieces of modern literature the "full horror" needed no illicit mechanical help, as in Conrad's tale of horror, *Heart of Darkness.*) The danger could be ever so great, as when overpriced stocks and overvalued bonds were to be downloaded on to naïve and helpless buyers. Alas, they would have to make their decisions without the benefit of the full linguistic powers of advisers who needed obscenities to characterize adequately the obscenity of a horrific unprofitable deal.

The Bloomberg desktops were systematically ruthless. Indecorous language was promptly erased. Racist, profane, or otherwise offensive words were blocked from the terminals, and the subscribers ($1,225 per month per terminal) were admonished that "the cowboy atmosphere that used to be part of newsrooms and brokerage firms is no longer possible in this day and age." Harrassment suits were a constant risk. The *Wall Street Journal*–which prided itself on "using dashes in words in certain circumstances"*–reported (in almost unexpurgated fashion) the revolt against the counter-revolution subverting the linguistic freedom of this-day-and-age. Others may have memorialized the "dirty realism" of James Joyce's Bloomsday…a far cry from Bloomberg's neo-Bowdlerization.

> But incensed traders view the company's pop-up reprimands as the electronic equivalent of having their mouths washed out with soap. As soon as they discovered it, some users began testing the software for dirty words that could still be sent through. They then taunted Bloomberg's computer Help Desk with messages containing the missed terms. Traders reported that words that had worked before their morning meetings–like an expletive that rhymes with "rock chucker"–were blocked by lunchtime.

It would be a lumbering, cumbersome counter-offensive if for every black-and-blue casualty a pig-Latin rhyming substitute would have to be found in order to express an authentic early-morning Wall Street emotion. Devious minds devoted their energies–presumably still keeping their eyes on the statistics showing the fall of the yen or of the *euro* and the rise of the dollar on the Frankfurt *Börse*–to testing the four-letter diligence of the new code. One trader tried congratulating an old partner (aged thirty-one) as an "old f—t." The message was blocked, and the screen announced:

> COMPLIANCE ALERT. The following word is considered to be inappropriate in the context of business correspondence.

And arrows pointed to the offending term.

Mr. Blooomberg himself was personally on the alert, but not infallibly so. He missed the latest turn on the word "*shag*," but the *Wall Street Journal* reporter forgave him because she thought the word was only a "Briticism," or

---

*   What of the other circumstances? The *Washington Post*'s style-book instructs its staff to avoid generally not only obscene, profane and blasphemous expressions but dashes as well. [Expletive] is recommended (and it was used famously when the *Post* reporters had their Nixon-tape scoops). Brackets can also be used for Bowdlerized words: "*They're all [messed] up,*" *he said.* But, "when in doubt, consult the managing editor or the executive editor." They may not be infallible, but they are marginally more permissive than Mr. Bloomberg. See Thomas W. Lippman's handbook entitled *Washington Post Desk-Book on Style* (2nd ed., 1989), pp. 170-171.

perhaps it was mistaken by the software chip or disc for "carpet stocks," whereas an even "more obscure British term w—ker" passed through: with a hyphen too many, if *wanker* is to be meant, and it presumably is, for it is said to refer to "one who performs a certain type of self-satisfaction." Embarrassing obscenities are hard to sp—l right.

Millionaires joined in this form of high-spirited fun in a good cause–"free speech," after all–as if they were not grown men who came to be seriously rich. They discovered gleefully that the computer did not completely recognize compound words that had been hyphenated, nor could it quickly spot the missing vowels in dirty words that had been asterisked. Foreign traders drew on their cultural reserves by turning to their first native loves, namely Russian or Indonesian expletives or whatever. One New York-based bond salesman was reported to have been delighted that in dealing with a European colleague the Spanish word for "prostitute" simply "sailed through."

The altercation seemed to be developing into another one of those "culture wars" that has so devastated the scene of late. Communiqués flew fast and furiously: "Bloomberg didn't notify the customers that it was installing the new software." Which made it, or him, the aggressor in the war, or at least a peacetime delinquent in Unfair Trade practices. "Mr. Bloomberg says Bloomberg isn't willing to take it off even if they [the customers] request it." Which meant that he was undemocratic, authoritarian, and hubris-driven.

"I know of no legal obligation that we have to carry profanity," says Mr. Bloomberg, speaking from a cell phone in Australia. "Bloomberg does not want to help behavior that is racist, antireligion, that kind of stuff'…Mr. Bloomberg acknowledges that the system is imperfect, citing a harmless phrase like "a chink in the armor" that would be blocked.…if you can't use one word, use another. For goodness' sake, how stupid are these people?"

The *Journal* had the last word by noting drily that the word "*stupid*" still goes through. We might have been compelled to use "the *I.Q.*-challenged."

Abroad this whole affair was taken–stupidly, if I may–to be yet another outburst of historical American puritanism…and not a contemporary cultural crisis of public discourse in populistic media-inspired societies, a widespread *malaise* which involves as well all major European languages. The *Süddeutsche Zeitung* was quick to sound the alarm. That distinguished Munich newspaper puzzled over the Bloomberg story on its front page, and was astonished that some of their German industrial giants could not be handled on the New York exchanges because Mr. Bloomberg's desk-top machines hated the acronym by which their corporate structures were known, *viz.* FAG/AG. "*Fag*," as their editors knew, was lewd American lingo for a homosexual–a *Tunte*, as they explained to their readers. But why cause a little crisis in German finance capitalism because of the eccentricities of one man's literary index? They prepared their Bavarian readers for the worst that was still to come. If Bloomberg has his way, *prick* or *cock* could no longer be used to suggest "thorny" or "firearm," for that's not their true blue denotation. They shed a tear for the business prose which could no longer report on "pricking the conscience of bankers" or ribbing executives for "going off at halfcock" in a crisis. The editorial was full of familiar *Weltschmerz*. Even if recourse were had to agreeable foreign-language synonyms, and they were in most cases more mellifluous than English "four-letter words," there was the matter of "a grave capitulation to the totalitarian spirit." *Die Kapitulation vor dem Totalitären* is always presented with the velvet gloves of good intentions.

They reminded us of Orwell's *1984*. They pointed a finger at "Uncle Sigmund's obsessions," and the roots of our neuroses about *puta* and *coglione*. They took a dark Spenglerian view of the future: Today *Bloomberg*, tomorrow *T-Online*, and soon the whole *Internet*! They were full of nostalgia for the bad old days when Count Metternich's Habsburg censorship had to work so hard ungluing each individual letter to catch dangerous and distasteful ideas and expressions.

In our own time things have almost progressed to utter simplicity. A tiny little Compuserver, equipped with the proper algorithms, can stop in a minisecond the unworthy and the undesirable....globe-wise. *Allons, enfants*–let's get to hack in the politically correct program with the appropriate virus.[38]

6

"O Propheta"

The Last Refuge

One cannot always rely on the spontaneous cracks which were recorded on the day before; often enough they are dredged out of quips in history and folklore: "It was, so I have always understood, the Mayor of Blackburn who, on taking office, pledged himself to lean neither to partiality on the one hand nor to impartiality on the other" (Christopher Fildes, in the *Daily Telegraph*, 4 November 1995).

This is the way the piece opens, and the rest of it–about how "some of this even-handed approach has rubbed off on the prime minister"–was less noteworthy, certainly less quotable.

Newspaper editors and their staff are, in my own view, well advised to plunder history and biography for witty loot, a convenient and inexpensive method of getting a few lines of humor and even wisdom into their pages.

I note in a London newspaper yet another welcome feature on that unforgettably clever woman, Margot Asquith, the famed wife of the English prime minister, Herbert Asquith; and it serves to remind us of her memorable crack in 10 Downing Street when Lloyd George had successfully schemed to replace her husband in 1916: "Lloyd George cannot see a belt without hitting below it."[2]

Sometimes surreptitiously, sometimes with flagrant relevance, skilful journalists can plunder the past for publication in the morning's paper. The racy stories range from the annals of the ancient Greeks and Romans to the sexual habits of tribal Africa (Zulu lore is a favorite), from the private lives of a half-dozen Royal houses in the chronicles of Europe's monarchies to the true story of what happened on the frontier in America's winning of the West (what ever did go on in those li'l Ole Opry Houses?). What these mostly lack is an authentic soundtrack. The stories can titillate but only language, flaunting bad words and sinful expletives, serves as the icing on the cake. Accordingly I open this section with an example of how one English newspaper tells an old anecdote and gets in a c-word verbatim (just for the historical record, you know).

The Saturday edition of the *Telegraph*, rich and bulky enough to fill the day's leisure hours, features "The Saturday Profile"; and this time it was a study of old-fashioned English eccentricity in a present-day Tory politician who happened to be a blue-blood ("great grandson of a cabinet minister, grandson of Sir Winston Churchill and son of another minister") and who reveled in the foibles of his class. He was Nicholas Soames, himself a minister in John Major's Conservative government (1992-1997). And it could hardly have been an accident that his portrait was being sketched by a skilful female journalist, Ms. Alice Thomson. She is good at catching his jolly buffoonery, and wicked in pointing out that as minister of food when the BSE scandal ("mad cow's disease") was disastrously shaping up he didn't like to turn to experts, was suspicious of long and hard words (*N.B.* "BSE" stands for *bovine spongiform encephalopathy*), and had failed his schoolboy examination in elementary biology. In the latest Parliamentary crisis (did he at the Defense Ministry help to cover up the use of pesticides on the Gulf War?), he "looked like an overweight prep-schoolboy hauled before his headmaster to explain who had stolen the ice cream from the cook's freezer."

Still, she liked him, down to the last pinstripe in his blue-serge suits, rounded to the obesity of his persistent gluttony. "He is," Ms. Thomson writes, "loyal to a fault in an age when a loyal politician is an oxymoron, and he shows real bravery in refusing to pander to the dictates of the age of synthetic soundbites and spin doctors. What you see–and there is a lot of it–is what you get." All in all he proves that there is still a place for "a man with the style and manners of another generation in today's politics."

The man has class, in the various senses of the word. Whether it is his gentlemanly behavior (he apologized to Princess Diana for calling her a "paranoiac" after her bad behavior towards his close friend the Prince of Wales)–or his aristocratic habits (he is "a high pheasant man" and brings "the aura of the grouse moor to Number Ten"), Soames is an impressive and indeed unique product of Olde England and its particular social structure.

For which Ms. Alice Thomson has just the right and revealing story to explain what makes the man tick, as he divides the world into heroes and villains, into decent chaps and bounders, all the while thinking of politics as a great team-game in which it doesn't matter who scores....Is it the family inheritance out of an ancient haunted house?

> But he has also inherited the black dog depression that haunts many of his clan and his sensitive brown eyes, buried in his jowly face, often look haunted. He still rings his brother every day, and always followed the advice that people say his father gave him, "You have got neither money nor brains. You must get your cock in the till." (Indeed he married a Weatherall, Jardines money, and then a Smith, banking money.)

For the sociology of manners and money, in the class structure of love and marriage, you can turn, if you will, to something like Marxism for a sort of explanation. A racy anecdote, with a raunchy remark, will tell it better, if only you dare break the house-style of a family newspaper. It could be a cliffhanger of a till-filler.[3]

The dare, in this kind of journalistic derring-do, carries little enough risk with it. A few readers may be mildly offended; even fewer subscriptions will be cancelled. The context has a protective patina of the past. The topical source is not a present embarrassment, a vulgarity in a happening of the day before, but something blue (and something old) put into the historical present. If this is considered somewhat of a turning point, it reinforces my surmise that history will provide a valuable resource for the increasingly pallid porn of our banal back-street sex merchants. Profanities will be more and more authenticated by tradition and, better still, by the record of the conversations of mankind in an unbowdlerized past. As in the good obscene advice quoted reverently by Father or Grandfather Soames (or any of the ancestral kith and kin) to an aspiring scion seeking the opportunities of a lifetime, what can be placed in the by-gone past serves to legitimate present-day profanities.

History may indeed prove to be the last refuge of porno-journalism. If the past is a foreign country, you might well be able to get away with anything there. In the here-and-now the lurid-cum-lewd reportage of sexy crimes of passion—a standard ingredient in our daily newspaper fare (with sauce in the tabloids, and what passes for sociology in the quality broad-sheets)—may jade and fall out of favor. The scandals of public life, entailing the same over-familiar incursions into privacy by bugs, tapes, and voyeuristic long-distance lenses, can begin to bore; and the new, younger genera-tions will surely not be titillated by the once-daring semi-euphemisms that once amused their more conventional fathers and mothers. The type of stories I have been assembling here will increasingly lose force, point, relevance and, accordingly, the capacity to attract readers in circulation wars.

What alternatives remain for the editor with a touch for the salacious as a kind of an economy of scarcity threatens material shortages? My surmise: his cultivated sub-editors will be turning to the sub-cultures of the past, finding stories for the morning paper in the blue stories of sex and scandal of by-gone days.

The history of nineteenth-century Africa provides rich pickings, and it is already yielding ribald exotica on the frontiers of the bawdy. As among the Zulus, in various features about Paramount Chief Shaka's nineteenth-century royal excesses in the tribal court; and in similar researches into the practice of female circumcision; the by-ways of co-habitation in harems of old Zanzibar; the anthropological details of such tribal cannibalism that can be taken to be reliably double-checked non-fiction; the private life of the pygmies; the adventures and shortcomings (both illustrated in loving color) of native childbirth techniques, etc. etc.

Less colorful and more intellectual are the explorations into high-cultural episodes of Western civilization, ranging from homosexuality in ancient Greece and pederasty in imperial Rome to Boccaccian feature stories (shedding light on the dark Middle Ages) and Rabelaisian footnotes to the Renaissance (especially the checkered history of the popes in the Vatican).

The *Guardian*, for example, to enliven a grey wintry Wednesday morning in November moved backward only to the eighteenth century and took up, on some improvised occasion, the life and work of Edward Gibbon. It was, oddly enough, said to be merely the 257th anniversary year of his birth (and that had actually taken place in April, six months earlier); but the piece captured our attention immediately by describing the great historian's appearance as "ugly, clumsy, corpulent, grotesque, disgusting."[4] This sounded promising, and before the promise was fulfilled we were given, as one could only expect from the *Guardian*'s intellectual fastidiousness, a few bibliographical references: the Penguin edition of the classic *Decline and Fall of the Roman Empire* costs £75 for three volumes, as against £50 for the six volumes in the Everyman Library.

Now for some saucy investigative reporting into Gibbonology. What about those famous filthy footnotes?

They are in full in both editions but, alas, "all licentious passages are left in the decent obscurity of a learned language." The learned language in question is merely Latin, and presumably most *Guardian* readers have dabbled enough in ancient classics to puzzle out the purple passages of prurience. It was decent of the paper's Gibbonologist to give us at least one example: "*O propheta, certe penis tuus coelum versus erectus est.*" Here was a Gibbon for Latin lovers; and, still, it was discreet for readers in a multi-cultural society (which Great Britain has become since Gibbon's day) not to have been offered a translation but a modest explication: "The great English historian is referring to the fact that Mahomet surpassed all men in conjugal vigor." The explicitness of a p-word in this delicate connection could have verged on blasphemy, risking possibly a Rushdie-like *fatwa;* and I am not sure that the *Guardian* didn't go on to make itself an accomplice to sacrilege by further quoting Gibbon, at his most disdainful, on "the spread of Islam": "the first and most arduous conquests of Mahomet were those of his wife, his servant, his pupil, and his friend." The *fatwa* against Salman Rushdie for similar impieties is still in force; but I suppose that a newspaper of quality must remain undaunted and face even the rude impurities of the past with fearless candor.

The past does not merely present rich veins to be mined when an extra bit of coal is needed to keep a story warm; it does additional duty by debunking the private lives of history's great men and, indeed, exposing the dark nature of whole historic eras.

SADISTIC SECRETS
OF VICTORIA'S PM

Victorianism looks a little different in the eyes of *Sunday Times* readers when they learn, in a belated news story (based on a biographer's new research), that Lord Melbourne, Queen Victoria's first prime minister and friend, beat his wife and mistresses and took an unhealthy sexual interest in whipping children. We already know that it was a not infrequent Victorian practice for leading figures such as William Gladstone, the famous Liberal leader, to "mortify the flesh" during bouts of sexual guilt. Melbourne, who was Whig prime minister between 1834 and 1841, "was, in modern terms, a sadist and a child abuser."

> Melbourne encouraged friends and relatives to leave their children with him so that he could "educate" them. Letters from such children [where they have been stored under embargo since Melbourne's death in 1848] are full of references to beatings. One recalled as an adult how Melbourne asked her, "Well, Cocky, does it smart still?"[5]

The "dark pattern" is eagerly discerned by revisionist historians and racy journalists who go on to provide a quick, if long-distance, psychoanalysis–in Melbourne's case, of sexual pathology which included flagellation and the like (he also collected French erotica).

Would Queen Victoria have been amused? Not all is lost. An Oxford historian saves a bit of the era's reputation by insisting that she would not have put up with such nonsense; but, still, "she would not have been that shocked....She was a very strong-minded woman."

And that is what our newspapers can also do by telling all–build a young strong-minded generation of men and women who cannot be *that* shocked by anything.

The dual function of the technique I have been describing which gives break-points to newspapers in the media contest between printed prose and moving pictures is, I am told, sometimes known in the trade as "the double whammy." In the first place it serves to give the reader additional reassurance that the printed word is the older, sounder, more reliable, more civilized method of communication. In addition to this literary-driven reinforcement of a traditional sense of superiority, it functions inexhaustibly as a resource for off-color titillation. Even Shakespeare can, on occasion, prove useful, quite beyond the conventional stories about the Bard's sly usages of what in his Elizabethan day was saucy or wicked. If television goes in for exploiting classical literature, then newspaper reviewers will find good hunting in the lesser prey, say in the actor that plays the leading role, in his histrionic life and its private peculiarities.

A performer named David Harewood was the first black actor to play Othello at Lawrence Olivier's National Theater (which in its earliest days featured Olivier's brilliant black-face performance*). Harewood was, in my view, no

---

*   Putting on black-face for any purpose is now *infra dig.* An Associated Press news-agency story recently reported (*IHT*, 12 October 1998, p. 3) that "New York's police commissioner fired an officer for riding on a parade float whose participants mocked black people...." People on the float which had moved through a predominantly white community in the borough of Queens "wore blackface and Afro-style wigs and threw watermelon and fried chicken..."

Paul Robeson, whom I had seen in the role in Princeton, N.J., long ago; still, he had been praised and "toured half the known world in this acclaimed production." The BBC (and some of its equivalents in the U.S. and Europe) broadcast a "video diary" of Harewood's theatrical tour around the world. Ah, what exotic opportunities for footage, what glimpses of oriental nightlife and strange enraptured audiences! But, never fear, the reporter's pen is mighty in its way. As Stephen Pile concisely observed in the *Telegraph*, keeping close tabs on the player not the play:

> In Japan, he said, Tokyo "certainly beats Hammersmith," ordered a gin-and-tonic through room service and announced: "I haven't felt horny yet." That said, he moved on to Korea, about which he divulged not a single detail except that "it's a s***hole." Mr. Harewood added: "I could do with a shag."
>   Faced with the awesome illuminations of the Hong Kong nightscape, he said: "What the f*** can you say about that? Well, f*** it, really"….Then it was on to the "Great Wall of f***ing China."[6]

So does London keep up the maintenance of its highest Stratford-on-Avon standards. In New York the critic would have been risking charges of political incorrectness and worse. Who in midtown Manhattan would have dared writing about a black Othello: "He could have been any yob with employment he did not relish"?

Yob? "A mean fellow, a hooligan, a slob; *derog.*" (*Slang Dictionary*). It is, to be sure, mostly *Brit*. An Americanism like *boy* (*derog*: ex-slavery) would have been worse. I confess that I once accidentally caused an embarrassing incident (and minor scuffle) in a City University auditorium when, unfamiliar with her new ultra-sensitivities, I returned to my *alma mater* to give a lecture. I had–accidentally, thoughtlessly–used the deprecating phrase "*new boy*," referring to myself as a newcomer to the halls of academe. I was misheard or misunderstood. Obscenities are always in the air these days. How to clean them up a bit? How to avoid them when in speech one can't possibly pronounce an asterisk?

The dalliance with profanities in foreign languages, in a tongue not one's own, has its virtues and vices. Only a very few can feign outrage. Even the editorial danger of making a little error in the Latin, or whatever the camouflage is, often is of only slight passing embarrassment, for the publication of a correction, possibly with an accurate translation, adds credibility to one's score. This should not be taken as deliberate acts of cynicism. The true cause of sexual liberation (and the appropriate sound-track which is supposed to accompany it) is surely bigger than all of us; and I have known journalists who enjoyed their breakthrough at the outset of a racy career and they are still taking advantage of their openings at their farewells. Here is Adam Nicolson writing his last column for the *Sunday Telegraph*, "Farewell, angry reader," and reviewing some of the highlights of his ferocious years as a *provocateur* (a man of Left-liberal sentiments pronouncing on all things, not excluding priapism, for a family Tory paper): "I wrote a column a few weeks ago which claimed that there was no English equivalent of an Italian proverb which I translated as: 'An erect member has no conscience.'" He received a flurry of angry letters, mostly from women, and one of them pointed out that "I led a pitiably sheltered life and did I not know the well-known English saying 'A standing ***** hath no scruples'? I didn't, but I treasure the saying now and I particularly like the 'hath.'" This columnist, with his scruples and his conscience, will be sorely missed. He can quote old Italian proverbs, and is prepared to accept English-language versions thereof. It may not exactly be news, but this kind of thing is known to sell papers.[7]

Porno-Ploys and Crackable Codes

In this game of pseudo-shy suggestiveness, of transparent dissimulation, the Americans play a little rougher. On the one hand, William Safire, syndicated in the *New York Times* and innumerable other newspapers, will recommend in his "Language" column the thirteen fascinating pages in the new first volume of the *Random House Dictionary of Slang* explicating the f-word which, he wanly admits, has never ever appeared in any of the newspapers he writes for. This ploy is reminiscent of the schoolboy practice of passing along sexy novels with the smutty passages accurately indicated by bookmarkers. And, in point of fact, I immediately went to the library and photocopied Safire's esteemed f-word entry in its entirety.*

On the other hand, Dave Barry, also a syndicated Knight-Ridder columnist, will move rudely forward to the frontiers of family-newspaper decency, and try the comic turn of titillating transparency. This is also a schoolboy prank in the evasion of teachers' taboos and other grown-up prohibitions–communicating obliquely in the boy's own favorite language, namely "Pig-Latin."

Barry is a humorist (and at his best is very funny indeed); and he was upset at the reaction he had from reporting that an animal in a Denmark "zoo" had died from stress brought on by hearing opera-singers rehearse. He had concluded that "opera is probably fatal and should be banned, just like heroin or aspirin bottles with lids that can actually be opened." Firmly disagreeing, a dissenting opera director in a local American theater thereupon invited Dave to play a small role in Puccini's *Gianni Schicchi*. He was cast to be a non-singing character, in fact an early victim in the plot's intrigue, a "corpse" who just has to lie on stage without visibly or audibly moving. This exceeded the good Dave Barry's powers. He developed "overpowering urges to swallow, twitch, scratch, burp, emit vapors and—above all—lick your lips."

The whole operatic affair was a fiasco. Musically ill-informed as he was, he had made egregious errors about Mozart operas, and in one vitriolic–and foul-

---

*   *The Random House Historical Dictionary of American Slang* (ed. J.E. Lighter, 1994), vol. I, pp. 831-841.

mouthed–letter which he quotes (*IHT*, 18-19 February 1995) he was told off in no uncertain terms: "*Cosi Fan Tutte* is Italian not Spanish, you sock plucker. Duck shoe." As he was frank enough to admit in the same column, he sincerely apologized when all the rude exchanges were over to all the opera fans he had offended. With only one proviso: "Except for the gas poles who wrote the nasty letters."

Readers doubtless will be amused in the best traditions of Barry zaniness. Semanticists among them, registering the f- and c- and a-words in code, using a cryptography halfway between a fiddle and a diddle, will be reminded that the bawdy tradition of Cockney back-rhyme still lives. Straightforward, vulgar, and unadorned, it would have been unprintable, if not unspeakable. If it had been obscure and indecipherable it might have caused umbrage–for a vaguely suspected misdemeanor, camouflaging a premeditated lapse, can be worse than an open and obvious sin. But the dissembling was a transparently comic and easy turn, and thus anodyne.

Some think that lewdness, as in a translucent Marlene Dietrich gown, can take on a certain innocence if it is rigged out in see-through raiment. So are we teased along in a literary war to make the world safe for obscenity.

A*c*c*o*m*p*l*i*c*e*s, or: Participatory Obscenity

One further suggestion as to the possible magnetic hold which obscenity in its properly bowdlerized form is having on the reportage in our newspaper culture.

There used to be a popular food powder for making "Aunt Jemima's Pancakes," and it was advertised as simplicity itself for even duffers in the kitchen. Its rival product began outselling it. Its ad (and the instruction was repeated on the label of every packet) was: "Just add an egg." The Aunt Jemima people had to remove the eggish ingredients in their powder, and also advise cooks and customers "likewise" to contribute the last additive themselves. For the lesson was that housewives, or anybody else puttering about in the kitchen, did not want the full, real, easy thing to cook or fry; they wanted to do a little something themselves. Adding an egg was not too much; in fact just right. What was incomplete was better. The act of personal addition, helping things along a bit, is appealing, marketable, complicitous.

Just so, as I suggest, in the case of four-letter words. The abbreviated f-signal (or p- or a-) is clue enough. The reader will add his own egg, counting out the missing letters which should jibe with the indicated asterisks or hyphens, and then whispering silently the com-plete imprecation, with something of the satisfaction of finishing off the morning's cross-word or, indeed, the egg-rich pancake on the breakfast table. We are into the act, have been made partners or, as the case may be, accomplices.

In any case the reader is richer for some of the detail which would ordinarily get lost in even the most serious newspaper stories. For example, the racism which is said to be rampant in the Labour Party, a political movement famous for its devotion to universal brotherhood and camaraderie (as distinct from the vicious unenlightenment in the rest of the political spectrum). The *Sunday Times* reported (19 March 1995) over the by-line of its special correspondent, Rajeev Syal, who is presumably sensitive about such things:

ASIAN LABOUR MEMBERS
SUFFER PARTY RACISM

The account was distasteful enough. Drunken socialist colleagues in Southampton snarled at a long-serving Labour Party councillor, Paramit Singh Bahia—"Your lot are not that welcome here." Bahia went on to participate in the meeting by discussing the ideas of Mahatma Gandhi but with interruptions, as recorded by the *Times*, full of "racist insults, offensive comments, and prejudice."

Time was when that would have been it. The strong headline had been justified...a significant, albeit disagreeable, incident, as accurately—if not completely—reported. But the cur-rent stylebook of journalism permits, nay requires, something to be added to the who-what-when-why ingredients of the earthy story. Men of ideological good will were rendering mere lip service to professed ideals—and shouldn't we be told without further ado what the unfortunate lip disservice actually was? An additional paragraph completes the ac-counts: "Bahia, who has represented the party on local authorities for 14 years, was discussing Mahatma Gandhi with some other party activists. 'F****** Gandhi used to drink his own p***,' he was told by Peter Jenks, chairman of Southampton's race committee." It is time for the phenomenon—a formula for the vice that dares not speak all its syllables—to be given a name: and it is not unconnected with the Aunt Jemima stratagem of personal complicity. I call it participatory obscenity. It offers a sense of secret, silent achievement; an unnoticed taboo breaking in the utmost privacy of your reading chair; a touch of real-existing involvement in the raw openness of life where otherwise there would be only a dry semantic correctness or a repressive propriety. It is a safe and handy *D.I.Y.* form of "[expletive restored]."

One proviso should be noted. In the event that the grossness is relatively unfamiliar—this can occur when expletives are uttered abroad or in the boondocks, always-backward pockets of cultural ignorance–the stylebook allows the omission of asterisks. Thus when in the same number of the *Sunday Times* (19 March 1995), a dispatch reported on the strenuous ef-forts to "adapt"–*aka* to tone down–in New York for ABC Television the "excesses" of Ms. Joanne Lumley (untouched in the BBC's English broadcast), the London reader itched with curiosity as to what the Americans found to be "offending the sensibilities of the mass market." The original hit comedy series (called *"Absolutely Fabulous"*) had Ms. Lumley smoking, taking drugs, swilling champagne, drink-driving and otherwise exhibiting outrageous habits ... like swearing. Some of all this had to go: the cocaine snorting; the dangling cigarette; most of the swear words with "sexual references."

This American bowdlerization, be it recorded, occurred only over the angry objections of the British. The *mores* of American television executives were criticized as being "anti-bloody everything.... Basically, they are anti-life." Yet one item was overlooked in the general cleanup: "However, Lumley's shrieks of 'bollocks' were allowed: the censors did not know what they meant." For my own readers who may be in doubt as to my own loyalty to the principle of participa-tory democracy, I hasten to add in the broad spirit of freedom-of-information that "*bollocks*" is not included in my edition (1933; repr. 1941) of the complete *Oxford English Dictionary*–the gap occurs on p. 974, col. 1, of vol. I, for those who collect such items.

Nor is it in the *Shorter Oxford* (repr. 1974, with corrections)–the gap occurring at p. 213, col. 3, in vol. I.

The Oxford lexicographers proved to be helpful only in R.W. Burchfield's *Supplement* of 1972 where we are offered succinctly: *bollock. pl.* The testicles. In addition to the first appearance of a nautical meaning ("blocks fastened to the top-sail"), there is also a *low slang* listing denoting a *mess*, or *muddle*, or *nonsense* as in "*a load of bollocks.*"

Other dictionaries of slang which I have consulted, in order to illuminate this apparent issue of cultural divergence in otherwise peaceful transatlantic relations, do not add much of significance. Oxford's *Dictionary of Modern Slang** (1972) does some additional catching-up, but we learn only that the word which didn't register in Manhattan on American puritanical ears came from the late Old English for testicle, *bealluc,* and is "related to ball, *noun,* spherical object."

I note also that historians have located eighteenth- and nineteenth-century sources for the usage and how writers felt then that it was alright "now...and without blushing" to toss about certain words. As in these lines of 1786:

> "*Prick, cunt, and bollocks
> in convulsions hurl'd.*"

The convulsiveness persisted for centuries, and has taken on peculiar forms in the orthographic practice of modern journalism.

Sometimes these spasms in the whole process of finding the right words (or recognizable elements thereof) to transmit "all the news fit to print," seem to have developed an autonomy, a self-starting bowdlerizing vigor of their own. A four-letter word runs away with it-self, trailing clouds of asterisks.

Literary gossipers, especially, like to squeeze some extra sauciness out of a routine item by dressing up a slightly off-color remark as if it were a daring bit

---

* *Oxford Dictionary of Modern Slang* (1972, Penguin ed.), p. 23.

of bawdry. Here is Peterborough in the *Daily Telegraph* (25 March 1995) reporting some doings at the London home of Harold and Lady Antonia Pinter. There were "extraordinary scenes." Before the "imposing entrance" a parcel van parked and tried to deliver three large packages. It was mid-afternoon, and the van-man was whistling a tune. And what was the reception at the grand home of the playwright and his historian wife, "champions of the world's poor and oppressed"? The unfortunate man was told imperiously by Lady Antonia, "clearly not quite herself," to go away: they just didn't accept deliveries in the afternoon.

Well, the tidbit didn't quite amount to the betrayal of the revolution and of the interests of the proletariat by the imperial Pinters, otherwise impeccable progressives. However, the delivery man kept on trying, re-ringing the door-bell, and only getting the door opened again and shut in his face. The gossip columnist of the *Telegraph* couldn't resist the temptation to record what could only amount to the true voice of the people. Said the man in the street bit-terly: "I'm just trying to do my job and then I have to deal with stuck up old t***s like that. Unbelievable." Unbelievable is only why any variety of a t-word needs to be camouflaged in this way. Unless I missed a lewd variant when I tried to fill in all possibilities that would fit, the scurity lay not in what had been said but only in the manner of its transcription. Asterisks come to have their own immodest suggestiveness, and here they tart up a slightly naughty epi-thet as if it were the curse itself.

A newspaper obviously needs to fulfill its quota of carnality for the day, and on some clear and cloudless afternoons when there hasn't been a sign of sex on the ticker tape, one has to resort to taking targets of opportunity. But beyond such opportunism in the news rooms there is, obviously, the larger factor of our newspaper culture in the contemporary world–it enjoys the candor of the "sexual revolution" but at the same time enjoins the wearing of an editorial mask of modesty and restraint in the name of old "family values." This ambivalence in no way hinders the single-minded pursuit of the lubricious in our pub-lishing community. The motives, to be sure, vary. They run from the low greed to maintain a competitive position among the profit-makers to the high idealism of professional writers who are in tune also to the new literary spirit of *"dirty realism."** They are dedicated to "getting it right," even if we have to be seduced into salacity.

Over and beyond that, there is abroad in the land, in all corners of our Western societies, a general aggressiveness which carries forward our lust for the licentious. It has less to do with words, at least in their style, spelling, and insinuations than with a kind of verbal onslaught which verges on sexual harassment.

---

*   On the literary spirit of "dirty realism" and "the higher journalism," see Professor Malcolm Bradbury's article (on Bill Buford, then editor of *Granta*, who is credited with coining the phrase) in: *The Independent* (London, 27 March 1995, p. 20).

One example. Here is the newsstory as published in the *Times* (London, 14 March 1995), and its headline indicates that it will be exposing the "rough" and "raunchy" flipside of a screen legend.

> An outrageous tale of violence, voyeurism, and bad language explodes into Britain's bookshops next week, and sensitive souls are bracing themselves for protest. A woman is brutalised, taped having sexual intercourse, and bullied into talking dirty to a group of whooping young men.

The actress in question was Elizabeth Taylor, then young, with an English demureness and indeed prudishness. The book in question is a new biography, "a gory tome," which gives us the fruit of the biographer's researches into at least one decisive moment in the life of a celebrated inter-national movie star.

> Her on-screen innocence was seen as a challenge by the vultures who lurked around her. At a Beverly Hills birthday party attended by Dean Martin, Jerry Lewis, Gene Kelly, "the boys" tried to bully her into swearing.
> Say "f***," they insisted. She declined. "Say sexual intercourse," they tried, hoping to lure her into the unmentionable, "say copulation." But despite these cun-ning circumlocutions the group failed to make her compromise her purity.

Several years later, as the *Times* oddly put it, "she did that herself"; she finally came to participate by entering into her first, short-lived, and unhappy marriage. After that, we are reassured, "she was soon cursing like a trooper," which may suggest the literary advantages of loveless matrimony, more than even Jane Austen ever suspected.

All's well that ends well. "The prude" was now becoming famous for her "blue jokes and erotic limericks." The good news—and the moral of the story this morning—is that

> a first doomed marriage dragged her out of a bourgeois lethargy into a craving for the rough language, rough sex and rough treatment that she was to demand from all her subsequent men, as a foil to the claustrophobia of stardom.

We should have it so good. Prudish we are not, and demure we may not be, but still we will be dragged out of our own various lethargies, whooping farewell to cunning circumlocu-tions, going on to blue erotica, and finally escaping the claustrophobic stardom of an asterisk-studded vocabulary. Mean-while, down at the raunch, they are awaiting the arrival of a new wagontrain of unmentionables.

This kind of coyness has its variations, and in the U.S. journalism a shade more simple-minded than among the Britons who, as in their complex cross-word puzzle competitions, tend to allusiveness and ambiguity. Thus, in a long dispatch from Melbourne in the *New York Times*, the correspondent goes on at lengthy detail about the troubles of the American tennis star, Andre Agassi, who happened to injure himself on checking into his hotel for the Australian Open. He missed a step and smacked the top of his knee into the staircase's iron railing. Well, we want to know more, don't we? If a bad call on the tennis court induces all manner of profanities echoing in the stadium, would a howl of pain among tendons and nerves go unreported? The *New York Times*, as always, goes as far as it permits itself to go and notes: "After shouting, by his own account, a four-letter word, Agassi waited for the sharp pain in the knee to subside" (*NY Times/IHT*, 16 Jan. 1996, p. 19). It would have been an unusual discretion not to have specified in his own account which four-letter word he had shouted; protest against blind umpires is one thing, a cry of agony is quite another. But there it is, one of a possible half-dozen each filling the acoustics, and the reader slows down a bit to figure out the possible expostulation. Clearly, the conventional use of dashes or asterisks, hanging on to a dangling participle, speeds up reading habits and keeps literacy moving apace.

This kind of gamesmanship becomes (I am forced to repeat the pun) a sort of foreplayfulness, formally controlled to maximalize mutual writer-reader participation. The *Times*, on its front page, tries a bit of thunder against the unsportsmanlike emotions that have been artificially aroused by "pun-crazy headline writers" in the Fleet Street tabloid press, all busily crafting "inky shrieks of abuse." BRING ON THE GERMANS! shrieked one paper's headline; and the *Times* cited another: SEND THE FOKKERS PACKING!

Not to lose the effect of the wordplay, the *Times'* commentator concludes with the crack from the England captain, Tony Adams, when asked by the German correspondent for *Bild*, one of a staff of eight (8) journalists sent to cover the championships, "Do you have a word for Germany? "'I have two words,' snapped Adams, joking." Once again, readers pursed their lips, and silently went through the motions of mouthing the appropriate blunt phrase (clues were generously given in the text above). Once again the law of participatory obscenity had obtained, this time so innocently that there was no need to take caution, no safe-sex aid (asterisks, dashes, dots) in sight.[8]

When exactly, and where–in the post-Gutenberg era of printing and publishing–the typographical device of masking the curse words began is a history that remains to be written. Anthropologists as well as theologians have always argued that our words for ultimate good and evil–for God and the Devil, for what mankind has held in awe and reverence, or in fear and trembling–have tended toward the ineffable and the unspeakable. But how did an old sense of sacred and, especially, a new temptation to cross the line into a demonic profanity come about? In the beginning the context was theological, as in literal cursing and swearing. In the end, it was sexological, as in the f-word culture. How it all came to be translated into typographical strategies is undocumented.

In my own collection the example of a writer taking evasive action–and tactfully deleting the expletive poised on his lips–is scarcely a century old. One example. The English writers Anthony Trollope and Wilkie Collins were friends, and they often exchanged letters about their works in cordial as well as caustic terms. Trollope once said he could never lose the taste of the construction in Collins' novels. Collins, after reading Trollope's *Autobiography* in 1883, told a friend: "The early part of it is very interesting but when he comes to his own opinions on his own books—let that dash express my sentiments." Ah, if we could only decipher that elongated Victorian dash![9]

Steiner and Burgess on "Love"

In all of this, my critique of expletives in the press, and the deletion of same (or their circumlocution), has nothing to do with the traditions of puritan discretion or indeed the controversies over censorship and self-censorship. Offensive words do not necessarily offend me, and I am not usually frightened by the breaking of taboos. My modest concern is for the state of the language, its qualities and corruptions, its splendors and miseries. I follow here those acute students of words and meanings, Anthony Burgess and George Steiner.*

Steiner's famous essay on "Night Words"–which suggested, perhaps a shade too grimly, that bawdiness was not the most effective way for approaching human intimacy–was a polemic I published in *Encounter* some thirty-five years ago in what appears now to be a spirit of forlorn dissent. We had been castigating the absurd Cromwellian interference by the present-day Lord Chamberlain's blue-pencilling (one of those century-old and very peculiar English habits); and we had provided witnesses to the court on behalf of the Penguin edition of *Lady Chatterley's Lover.* A Labour intellectual, Roy Jenkins, outlined in our pages the legislative measures which would make for a new permissive era; and within a few years Cabinet Minister Jenkins' libertarianism had become law. Suddenly we had a sense that we had gone far enough, perhaps too far. I myself declined to testify on behalf of the "artistic merits" of Hubert Selby's violent novel *Last Exit to Brooklyn* (although my English co-editor, Professor Frank Kermode, did). The predicament was troubling. Would, in the old dilemma, liberty be confounded with license? We were surfing high on the first wave of permissiveness. These were the years when Maurice Girodias in Paris was breaking through with his Olympia Press titles, when Henry Miller's "Left Bank" books of the 1920s had a public resurgence, when William Burroughs' *Naked Lunch* was *le dernier cri,* and publicists like Mary

---

*   Anthony Burgess, *A Mouthful of Air* (1992), p. 261. George Steiner, "Night Words: High Pornography & Human Privacy," *Encounter* (October 1965), pp. 14-19.
        See also E.J. Mishan's formidable study in irony, "Making the World Safe for Pornography," in *Encounter* (March 1972), pp. 9-30, reprinted in his book of the same title (1973), ch. IV.

McCarthy and Wayland Young were pleading for total four-letter frankness. As Steiner wrote,

> the present danger to the freedom of literature and to the inward freedom of our society is not censorship or verbal reticence. The danger lies in the facile contempt which the erotic novelist exhibits for his readers, for his personages, for the language. Our dreams are marketed wholesale.
>
> Because there were words it did not use, situations it did not represent graphically, because it demanded from the reader not obeisance but live echo, much of Western poetry and fiction has been a school to the imagination, an exercise in making one's awareness more exact, more humane. My true quarrel with so-called high pornography and the *genre* it embodies is not that so much of the so-called stuff should be boring and abjectly written. It is that these books leave a man less free, less himself, than they found him; that they leave language poorer, less endowed with a capacity for fresh discrimination and excitement. It is not a new freedom that they bring but a new servitude.

Burgess, also a modernist and a devoted explicator of James Joyce, has written in a similar spirit:

> With the lifting of the ban on D.H. Lawrence's *Lady Chatterley's Lover* in 1960, the word [i.e., fuck] was admissible in print, but the Laurentian use of the term—in the context of sexual tenderness—wholly inappropriate—tended to prevail. The novels of Ms. Jackie Collins are rich in invitations like "Baby, let's fuck," but the term refers solely to the act of penetration. "Let's make love," though apparently evasive and vague, is probably more fitting for the total activity of arousal, penetration, orgasm, affectionate convalescence.

The trouble with this constructive coinage, as with all utopian proposals, is two-fold, involving not only the subversion of the past but the over-estimation of the radical future. For one thing, love enlarged will have to dispense with the whole history of *l'amour et l'occident* (which was the title of Denis de Rougemont's classic documentation of love in the Western world). The gamut of "romantic emotions" from the longing of the Provençal troubadours to the glistening "crystallization" of Stendhal will have to go by the board. Even some sweet jokes will be lost, as when a couple of dashing characters, in an Evelyn Waugh novel, meet and flirt and then withdraw to a corner table near the bar "*making love madly*" (as Waugh, in the idiom of the day, describes their intimate chatter and exchange of lustful glances).

For another, the larger difficulty is not in the problem of the past, revising soft love to include hard sex, but in the future which, if we have anything to go by (and the records of human experience are there to help), will produce patterns of semantic behavior not unlike the troubles we've seen. "Love" may well become yet another four-letter word in the new dispensation. ("*Luv,*" used aggressively, has always had an offensive connotation.) In the present and future culture of indiscriminate sexiness which already has addicted our press to a first law of titillation, a kind of journalistic foreplay, the newly refurbished

L-word will emerge as L— (or, perhaps, L***). The passionate puzzle of an irrepressible obscenity remains. Read my lips.

7

Chaucer and a Choice of Taboo Words

Inveterate readers, conditioned by journalistic habits, develop an irrepressible curiosity, especially about people-in-the-news in history. How did they
speak? How would they look and sound if one could press them in the course
of an interview? Would they get irritated or cross at close, if not impudent,
questioning? What boisterous and indeed bawdy words did they use? Why
did some expletives stubbornly persist in the language throughout centuries
and others fall into desuetude?

These are the standard rhetorical questions of etymologists, philologists,
and other students of language, faced with the thorny problems of popular
speech and demotic style in olden times when taboo-words were rather more
prohibitive than they are in our own permissive journalistic days.

Our own inquiry can, I think, be deepened by the long perspective of historians of the English language as they record the patterns of profanity when
what was blunt and rude, or daring and shocking, was colored by rather different cultural forces and institutional safeguards. As one scholar of the fifteenth
century has written (and his concern is not prurient nor his purposes trivial):

> When Chaucer wrote "pisse" would his audience have been shocked or titillated? or
> would they have considered the word innocent enough? Was it in fact a neutral term?
> Or was it the kind of locution, albeit reprehensible, that one would expect from the
> Wife of Bath, rather than the pompous, Latinate "purgacioun of uryne" which she uses
> at one point?[1]

It was a century not unlike our own in which there were discernible shifts in
the attitudes of English speakers and writers towards taboo words; and the
etymologist argues that Chaucer himself may well have been responsible for
an emergent acceptance of such words in polite literature. For one modern
grammarian "*pisse*" has lost its comic or its shock effect and "is no longer of
use to a writer who wants to make us laugh or gasp." In current up-to-the-
minute usage–say, in the "dirty realism" of Hollywood film dialogue (Tarantino,
et al.)–the repetitive "*piss off*" has completely displaced more colorful, if not

less peremptory slang commands such as *"Scram!...23-skidoo!...Beat it!...Get lost!."* Contemporary commentators reckon such changes in terms of a decade's verbal fashions. The philologists and etymologists, armed with a little more knowledge, calculate in centuries.

> The change in the fifteenth century was slow, and it is of course, still in progress. Terms, blunt or clinical, for copulation, excretion, and the middle anatomical parts are still not acceptable [Professor Thomas Ross was writing in 1984] in all situations. Many English and American families do not speak of bellies or belches but employ euphemisms like "tum(my)" and "burp" or avoid mentioning such things altogether.

There is, then, a line which can take the reader of Chaucer and the two great poems that are nearly contemporaneous, *Piers Plowman* and *Sir Gawain and the Green Knight*, to the journalistic texts which we have been glossing in these chapters. And there are more connections in the "Additional Manuscripts" of the British Library wherein a whole history of "primness" and deleted expletives can be detected. Scribes of the day felt free to gloss Latin names for parts of the body and for excretion; but they felt some delicacy about certain words that pertain to lechery and fornication.

We are told that the commonest English word for the sex act was once *"swyve."* How blithely does it adorn one's page today when, for one reason or another (mainly the triumphalism of the alternative f-word), it has not the vaguest lewd connotation! Still, it did not occur at all in some expected quarters; but then again, nor did *"fukke(n)."* As for some of the others – the a-word, the c-word, the s-word – certain eternal stratagems of evasion and ambiguity can be easily spotted in texts which wanted to go a little further and ran up against the familiar question of *how*-far-is-going-*too*-far? Thus, when *arse* can mean either buttocks or the anus, Chaucer felt free to play to confound theology and anatomy; thus, it was something to kiss (in humiliation) and it was the part of Satan in which villainous friars dwell. Other writers dared to add a crude bit more, a farmyard naturalism where variants of *"beschittin"* occur. As for *ars lyke* it is still considered distasteful and is, roughly, taboo today.

Some old words remain rude, some have coarseness thrust upon them. As with (as it is technically called) the increasing "perjoration" in the fourteenth and fifteenth century of *baud/bawde* where it moves from a relatively innocent sense (i.e., a low-life person) to the sinful organized community of pimps and whores. There are other items in the vocabulary which one old-fashioned medieval scholar refers to as having "the boisterous men's room tone." The c-word is not mentioned in Chaucer who mentions the female pudendum only under the guise of euphemisms (mostly French: *bele chose*). I was slightly disappointed when I learned that the spectacular reference to "The *Wowing* of the King" signified his *wooing*. (*Wow*-words had to wait for their own time to come.) But one can feel at home among wordsmiths who say *fylth of the nose* and thus avoid *snot,* and who use the Chaucerian pun on a farthing's worth and thus get around *fart*. (Five centuries later *Old Fart* is the accepted and publishable young athlete's word for an aged contemptible commissioner of sport.) The over-usage of the s-word was obviated by *muck*, a milder term which referred primarily to animal excrement, thus keeping barnyard words down on the farm. Euphemisms of a more abstract denatured kind were unavoidable, especially for the genitals, male and female, where "*Thyng*" was the common substitute. The Latin term (*penis*) was not in common English (or Scottish) use. Having a bit of fun with the language was often a sly way out, and for "the privates" and for the cloacal *privy* we find the delightful variations of *gumphus* and even *catacumba* which surely must have drawn a laugh in Chaucer's day. What remains is merely to note that "*turd*" was used freely although sensitive critics seem to think that Chaucer found it "a disgusting term." It must have had a lingering taboo, and *merda* came to its rescue and relief. *Merdula* is the diminutive that was available in case a *turdyll* came along.*

All in all, in the theological age the naked facts of life–especially of biology and anatomy–translated themselves into a diction of recognizable form and style; but one always had to reckon with the fact that not a low secular four-letter but a high theological three-letter word, was the operative expletive: *sin*. The *sinner* (or "fornicatrix") was on the receiving end of the worst slurs. Pejorative names for sex and lust, vice and corruption, could grievously put him or her in harm's way. The rest could be consigned to Latin, as in "*Clunigitant homines; sed crisantur mulieres; opus venerum consummare*" (men move their buttocks; women wag; to consummate the act of love).

Half a millennium of human experience and cultural conflict was to pass before this maxim of the fifteenth century could be freely translated. It is now available in art and literature, in the cinema and other soft-porn versions of drama and erotic documentation. Its full extension to the modern information media, especially the world of the print press, is still problematical and these chapters aim to illuminate the process. Chaucer would, among others, appreciate that something old was dying, something new was being born. In his century he found words and phrases to make a rich record of life and language. In our century even the most serious of our newspapers of record leave much about the way we live and speak unrecorded. We often have need of the poets to provide us with the glosses, to sketch in and fill out what is missing in the blanks.

---

*   I have been following here the scholarly comments of Professor Thomas Ross in "Taboo-Words in Fifteenth-Century English," in *Fifteenth-Century Studies* (ed. Yeager, 1984), pp. 137-160, especially his annotations of fifteenth-century vocabulary. See also Thomas Ross, *Chaucer's Bawdy* (1972). As he notes,

> "The scribes sometimes refuse to gloss certain Latin words in English, perhaps indicating their sense of decorum or shame....[T]hey are inconsistent in this practice, since the same Latin words are occasionally given perfectly English translations."

Almost like life among the dear old scribes of Times Square!

In this manner, do writers who may have published their best work before the fashionableness of profanity (and its legal rights as well!) had set in, get the advantage of an up-to-date modernity put to their credit. If they ever emerge again into the limelight of fast-breaking news–for one reason or another: a belated blow from a censor somewhere; a discovery of a lost manuscript or a hidden cache of candid letters; some revelations in a quarrelsome family litigation–they surely deserve being presented with their best foot forward as a reminder of their once-liberating avant-garde stance. Accordingly, some half-century after his untimely death in New York and thousands of *Under Milkwood* performances replete with the purest Welsh lyricism, Dylan Thomas, many long years gone, makes headlines again. The poet's previously unknown letters are newsworthy in 1999.

LAST DAYS OF DYLAN THOMAS REVEALED

His famous widow Caitlin, whose loving memoirs colored the memory of the brilliant poet, is now quoted, rushing into the Manhattan hospital and asking: *"Is the bloody man dead yet?"* But his latest biographer (Andrew Sinclair), whose new material is so audacious, gives us rather more than Caitlin's *"bloody"* (long since domesticated after Shaw's Eliza Doolittle kept hurling it at us in prose and song). Dylan in New York had been famously fraternizing with the illustrious literati of the day, including the playwright Tennessee Williams. Of the major work of Tennessee Williams (*A Streetcar Named Desire*)–as the *Sunday Times* makes sure that we learn–Dylan Thomas always referred to it as "A Truck called F***." This little rhyme, best quoted as a couplet, or even as a one-line *haiku*, may endear the Welsh poet to ever more millions.[1]

8

Strong Odors, Blurred Pictures

For a beleaguered press, chronically handicapped by self-censorship on delicate matters, the need still persists to counterattack and attempt to reverse the TV advantage of "revealing pictures" developed under the documentary auspices of anthropology, sexology, and even strictly biological science. If a first break-through film is sensational (as was Desmond Morris' series on *The Human Animal* a decade earlier), then the follow-up series are perforce quieter and more routine; and they elicit critiques in a lower key. Television came up with yet another exploration of sex (Channel 4, London, 16 November 1998), entitled *"Anatomy of Desire,"* offering information that viewers may never have known before. How many sperm does a man produce? Twelve million of them in an hour. Which prompted the thought in one newspaper reviewer that this could be the reason for "men spending most of their day feverishly think-ing of ways to expel these burdensome 12 millions from their body." This dovetailed with another statistic offered by a scientist in his university labora-tory: that men tend to have more sexual fantasies than women: "roughly twice as many per day as women."

The fascination of facts on the subject, if facts they be (and no matter how questionable and dubious the Kinseyesque inquiries appear to be), is obvious. The press' way to hit back is to challenge in this skeptical spirit the nature of the research–and, more invidiously, just how did these experts get into sexual academic research? Estimable professors all, such as the anthropologist from Rutgers (who told us how small a sperm is); the psychologist from the Univer-sity of Texas (who counted the erotic fantasy production rate); an ethologist from Vienna (who calculated the factors of ovulation, sweat, and aroma in ingenious experiments with vaginal mucous). Distrust oozing out of the para-graphs, Joe Joseph asked in the *Times*: where did all these sexologists come from?

but if you watch television regularly and see how many sex-related documentaries there are now, and how many sex experts can be summoned to shed light on our sexual behavior, you'd know that there must be more people involved in academic sex research than there are accountants. Only it's a lot more fun than accountancy, because much of the job involves thinking up improbable research projects using government money. Do Dutch taxpayers know that they may have paid for Ellen Laan, a psychologist at the University of Amsterdam, to monitor young women as they watched porno movies with a probe inserted into the vagina?[1]

There is, to be sure, not only the sexual element which plays a role in the media's competitive exploitation of our political attention and personal interest.. There is also, of course, what used to be called *news* by the newspapers but has become, in the dominance of television, "flashes" and intrusive programme-interrupting "sound bites." Almost all of the news in the morning paper has been broadcast, even if only in bits and pictorial pieces, during programmes of the evening before. The camera is faster, if not perhaps mightier, than the pen. Even the speedy word-processor takes time to reach the final print-out in the first edition of your local paper, mailed or delivered by hand or picked up at (if your neighborhood is so lucky) the nearby newsstand or kiosk.

Having said that, one must concede that the newspaper campaign against television's taking of certain liberties is anything but relentless. The box is too popular with the masses, and even with the educated élite, to be constantly going on with high and mighty put-downs. The coyness of reviewers to which I have referred offers one way out; they make light of the "smut" they would ordinarily revile, and even offer a sample or two. A headline over seven columns in the *Times* sums up its TV-commentator's views on a show which he judged to be "rude, very rude."

Ooooh, they are awful, but I like them[2]

It is, to be sure, a professional pose, but under the circumstances the coy attitudes–"twee" is what the English say–begin to harden in a form of gamesmanship, wherein the wordsmiths try to make up for the natural media advantages of their rivals who feel free to play with suggestive pictures and risqué innuendo. Pondering on the problem of how to deal with a BBC2 program entitled *Third Rock from the Sun* (1996) which was, after all, "quite funny, if you're in the right, rather adolescent mood," Matthew Bond writes (again, in the *Times*):

> I could fall back on the asterisk, perhaps even making it doubly difficult by not giving you the first and last letters. But no, having tried it with a couple of last night's lines the page would end up looking like a Join the Dots competition. Who wants to watch a programme called *Third **** from the ***** anyway?
> Or I could just resort to that old standby and solemnly tell you that much of the material therein was not suitable for repetition in a family newspaper.... Funny, though, wasn't it?

But, when all is said and done, all this fun and games always finishes up frustratingly with a kind of *grammaticus interruptus*; and, in this case, we are offered "three shuddering ********" with only this slim clue: "eight letters and no, it doesn't begin with '*o*'. " What began on the screen as sexual acrobatics winds up on the page as double acrostics. Yet, in the end, the word always seems to survive; prose, however compromised, has the last say.

There are dramatic moments when the newspaper gets its own back, when print reporters take their revenge on their colleagues in the TV-studio—where the picture is proverbially better than a thousand words, but *not* if what it shows is misleading and the spoken commentary, up-and-under, is simply and crassly wrong. One such moment occurred during the excited week in Washington when a small plane tragically crashed–by accident? On purpose?–On to the White House lawn. (President Clinton was not at home.)

A few days later Washington firetrucks rushed again to the White House because of a report that someone smelled smoke. But there was no fire, just a short circuit in a light fixture. Denying that anything at all had burned, the White House press secretary, Ms. Dee Dee Myers, not especially noted for her verbal felicity, said undiplomatically, "There was only a strong odor."

What led the newspapers of America, and possibly in the rest of the world, to put the false alarm on their front pages? Simply because the nosy editors had another "smelly" story about unfortunate goings-on in the Clinton White House? Hardly. Mainly, I suspect, because of their main competitor in the field of news, the CNN–famous for its scoops in wars and riots and natural disasters–had televised "the fire" *live* around the world. As it transpired, a CNN camera team just happened to be present at the White House (for a meeting on the Haiti crisis).*

Was there a moral to the story? That the *Times* "prints all the news fit to print" but you can't always believe what you see on CNN? That pictures in "living color" can be deceptive? And that in the beginning, and in the end, there is *the word*, accurate, meaningful, reasonable, trustworthy? They would say that, wouldn't they?

In point of fact the distrust between the printed word and the modern picture is deep-seated; and it goes back at least to the last century when our contemporary concept of newspaper journalism was shaped by speedy presses and fast photographic plates. What came out of the linotypes of Mergenthaler had its rival in the shadowy daguerrotypes of Daguerre. The coming of the movie-house newsreel only sharpened the rivalry and class struggle. Whom would you trust for your information about what is happening in the world? — The typeset Reuters dispatches or Charles Pathé's flickering film?

---

*   The captious story on the front-page of the *International Herald-Tribune* (17-18 September 1994), was credited to the AP, AFP, and "combined dispatches," which sounds a little like "ganging up" on their *CNN* rivals.

And indeed it was Pathé, with his Gallic rooster crowing to newsreel audiences in all of the Western cinemas, who put the mark of Cain on his own ambitions. Film, as he said prophetically (almost a century ago), was "the theater, the school, and the newspaper of tomorrow." And so it has come to pass. But in the beginning was a fault, a hoax, a deception, almost an original sin. The first newsreels were not real but *enactments*. We know now that Pathé's report on the frightening and disastrous tidal wave in Martinique was shot in suburban Paris against painted canvas backdrops...splashed with buckets of water.[3]

After such knowledge, what forgiveness for the purveyors of pictures? The *BBC* stages its scenes of natural sex, with a cast of professional actors and handy mechanics for the special effects. CNN sends forth TV images of fires in Washington or bombs in Damascus, and there is no guarantee for the truth of what you are seeing. If there is only "a strong odor"—and there are not yet "*smellies*" as in Aldous Huxley's notorious vision of the camera's futuristic capabilities—then don't trust the TV's nose for truth. Your favorite morning newspaper–slower but more thoughtful, *unlive* and not in "*real time*" but with its two eyes wide open–can get it right, can get the real picture in focus. A fixture or two may burn again, and another light can go out. It may be nothing darker or more sinister than that, for news.

Marshall McLuhan, for whom (famously) the medium was the message, might have gone on to surmise that the camera begets the news. Its fast lens will always come up with a story–"because it's there"–not *it,* the story, but it, *the camera.* Light and conveniently transportable the camcorder and its TV-eye can more often than not be myopic, astigmatic, almost blind to the true big picture out there. Like Jean Cocteau's surrealist mirror, it should reflect a little more before sending forth its images.

I have often used the word *scandal* or *scandalizing* in the context of an outing of an obscene phrase in the public prints. For my part, it is, I confess, more often than not a loose usage, for the strict meaning which would include elements of surprise and outrage, offensiveness and anger, obeys the conventional rule of semantic fatigue. Never since the historic outbursts on BBC television of Messrs. Tynan and Worsthorne–whom I have portrayed in the first volume as "the Godfathers of the f-word"–has the public embarrassment been of such pristine purity: authentic, widespread, and short-lived.

The deep and irrepressible four-letterization of our language and culture has moved into a higher phase. Profane spirits rushed to imitate and confirm the new liberty–liberties, if one counted all the cuss-words separately that rushed out of the trenches into open advance. Hasty consequences were made good, and neither of the two London pioneers suffered serious setbacks in their flourishing careers.

Still, we cannot be getting on without our taboos, and other shady demotics were conscripted to do obscene duties. They served to revive the old sense of propriety as to what one might or might not say when expletives become tempting.

In the White House scandal of a president's dalliance with a young Washington interne, the proliferation of published profanities (I have documented a choice selection in another chapter) exhausted itself, and has left few traces. Only a handful of unintentional obscenities remained, as when foreign diplomats committed an unusual number of faux pas (in Berlin where President Clinton was welcomed with a box of Cuban cigars in the original humidor, or in London where he happened to be seated next to a young person who was a Monica Lewinsky lookalike). Otherwise the whole episode which was at its worst in the 1990s–perhaps on the occasion of the Starr Report and its innumerable Internet copies, or the day of the leakage of the Linda Tripp telephone tapes–did embarrass, offend, outrage millions, but seemed to be filed and forgotten or, probably, repressed. There were a number of sly references to the whole wretched affair but who can extract titillation from the passing philological reference (even with a-wink-and-a-nudge) to "It-all-depends-what-you-meant by *is*" (the President's famous grammatical evasion of the imputation of sexual foreplay). Or from the philosophical title of a new Philip Roth novel (2000) which was entitled *The Human Stain* and was taken by almost every reader to be a wicked reference to Monica's soiled blue dress.

It fell to the improbable scatological cliché–"*crap*"–to have a moment of linguistic glory and to suggest that the deployment of an inappropriate word could have devastating costs and consequences in a society where alertness to aural nuances is still present.

The story is, I think, well worth retelling, although it is still only a yellowing cutting and has not made it into the history books. As the *Times* reported (on 28 April 1991), "Gerald Ratner, head of the jewelry store chain that bears his name, yesterday tried to dismiss his admission of selling 'total crap' as a tongue-in-cheek joke that had backfired." The forty-one-year-old multi-millionaire had been speaking about satisfying the public demand for shoddy or "tacky" low-quality goods. He confessed that it had been "in the worst possible taste" to peddle a Ratners imitation antique book (with curled-up corners and fake dust). Ratners could sell this (and rings, pearls, brooches, and the like) at a seductively low price because all the goods that the profitable chain store ever offered were…"total crap."

The public response to this "gaffe" was as if he had told Queen Elizabeth (II, or even I) where to stuff her glittering crown. Ratners staff was demoralized. Hostile publicity ensued. Sales fell off drastically. Attempts to employ damage control appeared only to deteriorate the situation.

> His wife Moira, arriving in a chauffeur-driven Bentley, visited the office wearing a pair of gold earrings and a gold chain that she said were from a Ratners store. She said: "Ratners jewelry is not crap, it's very good. I wear it all the time."

And they, up to this fatal point, had been making profits all the time. In 1990 the balance sheets of the Ratner chain (which included *H. Samuel* and *Watches of Switzerland*) amounted to £112 million. Now the business was going down the drain; Gerald Ratner's explanation that his now legendary gaffe had just been a joke rallied for a day or so the share prices on the stock market. His position could not be held, and he had to resign. the *Times* reported that "the company's image was so tarnished that it eventually renamed itself Signet."

All due to the little four-letter word *crap*? Would it have been better, or worse, if he had said *s—t*? or any of the other four-letter word combinations to which any speaker of the English language is heir? Etymologists on the scene insist on the importance of the scatology in the incident. The usage of, say, *Scheisse* in a similar incident of undermining (or "insulting") commercial confidence...surely no one's moral sensibilities....would, in Germany, in a peculiar demotic culture which has become inured to, and in the end welcomed, excremental phraseology, surely have gone unnoticed. In the English context a faecal complication can lead to unforeseen disasters. (For a while, Mr. Ratner wound up in jail.) My explanation can only be tentative.

It is probably significant that the official and historical turning point of colloquial obscenity should be an English usage of an Americanism which gained currency in the turbulent 1960s. Then–and forever more (one imagines)–everything is a *copout* if you say it's a cop-out.

Eric Partridge, limited as he was to the usages in his own "culture," gives an early "to cop out" usage in a South African Boer war context, meaning *"to die"* or perhaps to be killed. American philologists, like J.E. Lighter, trace "cop-out" from Duke Ellington to James Baldwin (without suggesting, invidiously, that it emerged as a black, or Negro, colloquialism). Ellington's "cop-out" was dated from a piece in *Music is My Mistress* (1956). Baldwin's *Another Country* (1961) suggests–under the dictionary entry ("A person who evades an issue, reneges on a commitment": *"Now, come on, baby, don't try to cop out that way."* Thus, there are acceptable as well as unacceptable ways of copping out and presumably some commitments are legitimate and others so illegitimate that not to renege them would be the very worst way of copping out. Individual evasions in the 1960s-1970s involved whole wars (Vietnam) and the traditional patriotic loyalties to nations and home lands. *Copping-out* was signaled by burning the national flag (usually the star-spangled banner), leaving one's native shores (for Canada, Sweden, and other places that offered asylum), hailing the enemy forces as heroic, and the like. Thus, in undeniably wide American circles, *cop-out* was taken to be an admirable act of civil disobedience. (Even a President–Bill Clinton, as an Oxford expatriate–got away with it.) In the light of all this one can only conclude that a personal choice or an individual decision–ranging from fighting in a war and referring to an obscenity in print by using sort of discreet punctuation marks or orthographical tricks–can be classified, arguably, as convincing and definitive, even if it ends an argument ad hominem. In point of fact it has no special force of logic, apart from its colloquial strength. Its demotic energy–from *b—s—* to *m—f—*, from *"p—s off!"* to *"it's a cop-out!"*–adds a certain spurious persuasiveness to the put-down as if it were, technically, the final term of an unassailable syllogism.

In any event, it is not–standing alone, all by itself, in the *Guardian*'s decision to out all obscenities, without fear or figleaf–a cut-and-dry case. *Copping out* can also be used derisively and it has disorienting echoes from the contempt for *drop-outs* and the ambivalent feelings about *copping a plea*. Although I have myself cast an ironic eye at the history of the asterisk in the transcription of words under a traditional taboo, I find the *Guardian*'s one-liner proscribing asterisks (or dots or dashes) unnecessarily peremptory. Without offering a larger argument–and not trendy sloganeering–about the role of profanity in a free-for-all culture, its charge of *copout* is itself…a *cop-out*.

Perhaps a "stylebook" and its necessarily flippant guidelines, devised for hasty consultation under deadline pressures, is not the sort of text with which one could enter into arguments that have been in embarrassed disputation for as long as one could remember. Still, sententiousness is always suspect. In a newsworthy world where reporters and their editors have to deal with rumors and alarums at a decent distance, the very sight of some fixed rules and confident recommendations appears to be welcome, even more so when it is thought to be a professional necessity. Any editorial respite from chronic uncertainties and the pitfalls of error does a newspaper good. What such *Guardian* corrections or clarifications do for the newspaper reader is another story. Here is the *Guardian*'s stylebook guide to the use of *swearwords* (again, no hyphen, as if they were intended to be swallowed at one gulp):

> swearwords
>   We are more liberal than any other newspaper, using words such as cunt and fuck that most of our competitors would not use, even in direct quotes.
>   The editor's guidelines are straightforward.
>   First, remember the reader, and respect demands that we should not casually use words that are likely to offend.
>   Second, use such words only when absolutely necessary to the facts of a piece, or to portray a character in an article; there is almost never a case in which we need to use a swearword outside direct quotes.
>   Third, the stronger the swearword, the harder we ought to think about using it.

And after so much harder thinking we are still getting thousands of *"such words"* in our morning's *Guardian*, uncasual in their offensiveness, all *"absolutely necessary,"* and multiplying all the time. Most are indeed *"straightforward,"* as the editor's guidelines prescribe. An increasing few will, if the Normans have their way, be transformed by *homo ludens*, or by the paper's grim spirit of fun-and-games. (Some may suspect this to be only a new way of "copping-out," if not of recidivist bowdlerizing.) Vowels can be added, consonants be subtracted. Future *Guardian* guidelines may well instruct us, with an old-style wink-and-nudge, to *pick* your swearwords–then *count* them–and then *sit* tight. (Prizes can be offered to readers who are quickest to spot the p-, c-, and s-words therein boldly smuggled. *Hint*: Subtract one vowel, add two consonants. *Remember*: it's so easy to be naughty.)

As we modestly predicted in our previous volume only several years ago, the old ordure will be giving way to the new. Ambitious newspapers trying to ride the wave of the future–surfing the new technologies as well as the seasonable life-style fashions–can achieve a limited success by accommodating themselves to what is apparently inevitable. The vocabulary of four-letterization appears to many mainstream newspaper editors to be as unavoidable as publishing large garishly colored photographs or having an Internet website of their own. A great many readers will somehow miss the dimension of profanity in their papers when all around them it is popularly used and apparently "absolutely necessary." They are beginning to be convinced that it is not only entertaining–and I, for one, confess to being so entertained–but also obligatory if one wants to guard, or protect, or even extend, the enlightenment which recognizes no cultural taboos.

It is not, of course, an English-language phenomenon. The new ordure is international, if not global. On the old European continent two of its major cultures have been learning to live with Gallic *merde* (and, in the famous locution of General de Gaulle, *chien-lit* [dog-shit]) and its associated Habsburg *Scheisshäuser'l* (outhouse). If there will be, as was prophesized long ago in Aldous Huxley's *Brave New World* (1932), a sensory expansion into "smellies" our newspaper culture will shortly be taking on an olfactory challenge.

Newspaper reading is an ocular phenomenon and, to a lesser degree, a matter of holding and touching ink-smeared pieces of paper. Contemporary "performance artists," occupying a goodly portion of the available space in our galleries and modern museums, have already pioneered the way forward with sound, with variegated bits of noise, highlighting the classical *objet*: a man in repose, a woman in pain, a room full of people, a house on a quiet street, a still life trying to come alive….With the recent notoriety of Tracey Emin's *Bed* (2000)–an installation which features the unmade bed with stains and other tell-tale wrinkles of recent coital calisthenics–there was a detectable olfactory breakthrough.

The art of language, or the language of art, will surely influence "the language of journalism." The *avant-garde* will seize the opportunity. The *Guardian*'s rich reserves of obscenities can be amalgamated with the new fashionable turns to multi-sensuality, where sight and sound join touch and smell (taste is waiting somewhere in the wings). Now is the time for total communication with no nuances left out. Familiar pictures as well as old stories will, as in digital remastering, come out sharper and clearer than ever before. The thousands of bits of effing profanity, the innumerable items of post-coital evidence or of life's own detritus, will merge in new pride and significance from under the antiquated régime of repressive taboos. Elephantine dung...casual lover's semen...the innards of animals...all will be helping to give a new redolent dimension to felt aesthetic experiences. This will save the imminent avalanche of four-letterization from wasting itself in the trivial pursuit of Tarantino coefficients. Just as color-film is thought to have saved black-and-white pictures, so may the *graffiti* on a thousand toilet doors come into their own if the aroma of the classical Paris *pissoir* (and its nearby *chien-lit*) and the romantic rural outhouse (at the end of the garden) can be skillfully wafted on.

The writings on the wall were, to be sure, always in the semi-public domain. But our present-day obsessions with bodily functions as a semantic source for all basic expressiveness will be bringing–when our noses are no longer protected (by "good taste"?) from the natural realism of our life processes–a whole range of (swear)-words out into the open. All that is missing, at this stage, is the old authentic odoriferousness, some sort of combination with the old pungency.

It shouldn't be hard to duplicate. What we might expect, given a little bit of luck, is what P.G. Wodehouse, who had a fine nose for the unusual, once suspiciously referred to the "acrid smell of burned poetry." He may have almost gotten it right.

The olfactory element can enhance the sound or general sense of words...but in several and contradictory ways. For prophets of *dystopia*–Aldous Huxley, George Orwell, Ray Bradbury, et al.–it accentuates the negative. In the dark vision of an illiberal future every social tendency, and indeed each elementary human instinct, can be manipulated to serve the imminent cultural enslavement. Huxley's "feelies" and *soma*--derived "smellies" were devised to add to the illicit pleasure of being helpless in an odious totalitarian civilization. Nothing human is foreign to the ways and means of domination and subjection.

On the other hand, the sense of smell–from fashionable aromatherapy to a visionary experience of a total art and culture–can accentuate the positive. It was a distinctive mark of the European avant-garde to attempt to incorporate into its highest aspirations for the grand future of all the fine arts this sense of smell–an aroma which signaled the involvement of the nose and its nostrils, so close to the ear and the eye and tip of the tongue. The so-called Seven Arts needed the additional complement of the Five Senses if ever the perfect achievement of what Richard Wagner (and, thereafter, many others) called the *Gesamtkunstwerk* was to be realized in its totality.

In musical composition, for example, the work of Alexander Scriabin (1872-1915) included an ambitious effort to mix into sonatas and symphonies, composed according to a nineteenth-century theory of *synesthesia*, not only colors but smells. As one music historian has written: by adding "smell machines and color keyboards" Scriabin was "hoping to present almost every type of musical timbre imaginable, a quasi-comprehensive but non-theatrical spectacle of sensations." Out of a dazzling mulitplicity would emerge a cosmic unity. Scriabin's *Poem of Fire* was very Promethean, altogether cosmic.

But, as I suspect, buried in his manuscripts and unfinished scores is the secret of how it was to be done. He had been turning for help to his friend, Alexander Mozer, a professor of electrical engineering, who perhaps was a bit far away from Scriabin's original "theosophical" inspirations which he first had during his mystical experiences en route in the U.S., during his tour of 1906-7.

Adding the suggestion of color to sound was relatively easy, if one had access to the "mystic chord" which was to be "played pianissimo by the winds and tremolo strings over a hushed bass-drum and timpani...." Could the "primitive" machine of Professor Mozer achieve similar sensations? Our historian writes drily: "Attempts to include this facet of the score in performance have been rare."

But surely the usual ways of olfactory accompaniment could be improved upon–impregnating paper or spraying the scent, passing out breath-sweeteners or infiltrating incense-burners, keeping toilet waters or smelling salts at hand or attaching lavender sachets to the seats in the concert hall. The sultry imagination of the orgasmic adventurers–from D.H. Lawrence to Tracey Emin–could go on from there.

And it need not be, as in Scriabin's case it was, associated with mystical purposes nor with what a music critic (Michael Kennedy) has called his "obsession with extra-musical ideas." Not every aesthete can be easily persuaded that he is hearing colors and smelling sounds. All is totality, in "a supreme esctatic mystery," accompanying a final cataclysm.

Thus, the sense of smells is, among sensitive spirits who create with words and sounds, a vague and tempting resource to heighten the impact of all communication, especially the message of art, even though the olfactory element has no precise vocabulary of its own. Hence, it is multifaceted and indeed can conveniently mean all things to all sniffers and snorters. Smells may be taken as whiffs of evil; but it is no accident that a rank whiff from a witches' brew can be said to "smell to heaven" (which cannot obviously be the same as a "hellish stink"). Poets have recorded the difficulties involved in associating words with aromas; and these may explain the late emergence of–as I have suggested–the modest proposal, inspired by the *Guardian*'s adventurousness, of the coupling of obscenities with reeking fragrances. Odorlessness was a flagrant cop-out for cowardly taboo-molesters like Andres Serrano (working with urine in *Piss Christ*) and Ofili (plastering with dung), both in a religious context which smudged a Christian cross and a Holy Mary...without having the courage of their convictions.

Still and all, one need not go so far as to invoke the extremes of ultimate things in order to have your favorite newspaper (or, in time, your reliable

Internet website) smelling appropriately, just as it should. I think of the lines by Gerard Manley Hopkins –

> *Generations have trod, have trod, have trod;*
> *And all is seared with trade; bleared, smeared with toil;*
> *And wears man's smudge and shares man's smell....*

Other poets have detected the hint of an erogenous element–profane prose had not yet been outed–without which (to steal a phrase from Shelley) –

> *...this world would smell like what it is–a tomb.*

No, there is a pungent promise of life–Hopkins' thought of it as "God's Grandeur"–in the association of smudge and smell. If obscenities in the four-letterization of our whole culture can be heard and seen, they could also be sniffed and scented.

Our modest proposal was to have our favorite newspaper (or indeed your reliable Internet website) smelling appropriately as it should. Given the popularity of profanity in California, it could be that someone in Silicon Valley may well be already working on it.[4]

9

Obsessions with the S-Word

The proliferation of profanity in the public prints, as well as on television and in the cinema, is in part method and in part mindless imitation in accordance with the compulsions of fashion and keeping up with the noisy neighbors. What is said in the movies gets reproduced, mostly without benefit of bleeps, on TV screens. Documentaries–which might in the past have cut the rougher frames in the reels-and-reels of street-talk they filmed before editing the montage of the final version–now bask in the reputation of the *verismo* of the hand-held camera and the all-attentive microphone. Even the book-reviewers on otherwise staid and highbrow literary pages go out of their way to spot (and quote) the good bits in long and rambling novels.

For example, there must have been a dozen important themes to be considered in Timothy Mo's fifth novel, *Brownout on Breadfruit Boulevard* (1995), an ambitious, if bleak, appraisal of life in the Philippine islands, issued under his own publishing imprint. But the reviewer in the *Times* (London) affected a distaste of one literary element and gave us enough of the pungencies to get wind of a style which had to deal with corruption and coprophilia. The opening gambit is to quote the very first sentence as evidence of: "the unsavory in full pursuit of the indecent": "When the shower of shit, which he welcomed, spattered over his chest and belly Professor Pfeidwengeler was thinking of his worst enemy, Dr. Ruth Neumark." The *Times*' reviewer goes on from there to reassure us the quote is not at all taken out of context since "Defecation does seem to be the motif of the book. Faecal imagery bobs up and down in the pages; at the end poor Pfeidwengeler is blown up by a grenade while in a toilet cubicle" (the *Times*, 20 April 1995). In the end the reviewer hastens to mention what Timothy Mo has called his own publishing house, Paddleless Ltd, remarking, "the name that Mo has chosen for his own imprint, "Paddleless," must surely allude to shit creek." As the faecal imagery bobs up and down in the pages of the *Times* (which was once so prim and proper that it called the Nazi *Führer* "Mr. Hitler"), the question of who is more obsessed with the unsavories is a close-run thing. Or it could be that scatology is infectious.

The non-committal term "four-letterization" has cropped up occasionally, and it should have served to underscore a large movement from the specific salacity to more general semantic levels. But, betraying its origins, it tends often to return to the scene of the crime. A slight twist and a curving turn...and the euphemism boomerangs. A prominent daily radio critic, Ms. Gillian Reynolds, is here reviewing an embittered and angry Anglo-American documentary drama on the tenth Chinese anniversary of the Tianamen Square massacre. As she writes, "We were warned before transmission on Friday night that there would be strong language to match the characters' strong emotions." This, she admitted, kept her "tuned"...and then, at a high point in the protest demonstration in the Square: "it happened about three-quarters of the way through, when a soldier four-lettered the young woman worker for being on the demo, and she replied in similar vein." Ms. Reynolds' judgement was that "it neither wounded really nor was it shocking." This could be. But perhaps it was because the London filmmaker hadn't got the Chinese ideographs right, and the "*four-lettering*" which went on between the militant Red Guard and the protesting Peking proletarian amounted in the original tally only to two pictures or maybe three signs. Needless to say, in Chinese the f-word equivalent, those fateful four characters, are necessarily different, nonetheless shockingly real in their own cultural context.[1]

A newspaper of quality is only doing its newsgathering duty by keeping us informed so unblushingly. But there is so much more that we need to know; and, fortunately, the *Times*' theater critics have an equally sharp nose and eye for the new ways in which we speak and write and emote on the stage.

At the National Theatre it has become not in the least unusual to hear four-letter words, as the *Times* reports (12 April 1995)–"but you still don't expect them to come thudding from the mouths of characters in 2,500-year-old plays." But thudding they come, earning the headline

Classics Up-to-date turn the Air Blue...
Translations into the Language of the Streets give New Life

Thus, in Gilbert Murray's famous translation of *The Trojan Women* by Euripides, Cassandra gives her view of the Greeks as: "One love, one woman's beauty, o'er the track of hunted Helen, made their myriads fall." At the Olivier Theater's recent production Benedict Nightingale heard: "For one woman's sake, one f***, they hunted Helen, squandered a million lives." This daring and inspired turn-of-phrase on the part of the translator (Kenneth McLeish) is, in the judgment of the *Times* man, helping to bring "a new boldness and, at times, brilliance to Greek drama."

Equally bold is the epithet "*Bastard!*" that Orestes hurls at Menelaus; and the real autochthonous New York "*Wow!*" with which Ion greets evidence of his divine origins. Brilliant is the blue air in which the Troll King in *Peer Gynt* boasts that "our cows shit cakes and our bulls piss wine," after which Peer describes an Arab dancer as "a tasty bit of meat, that girlie."

The *Times* offers an invaluable compendium of the fruits of its investigative cultural journalism, all in support of its pathbreaking conclusion: "Can a translation actually be better than the original? Sometimes." Candidates for the better prizes are the following:

1. Trevor Griffith's version, in Chekhov's *Cherry Orchard*, of Firs' riposte to a fellow-servant. Instead of "Eh, you're daft" —

   "Up yours, butterballs!"

2. Kenneth McLeish's colloquial rendering of Orestes' question which Gilbert Murray puts as "Prithee, what man of all the King trusted of old is this broken thing?"

   "Who's this old relic, whose side is he on?"

3. Jeremy Sams (also the translator of Molière and Racine) who courageously substituted in Chekhov's *Platonov* whatever it was that a 19th-century gentlewoman had originally said to the financier —

   ."... Put your chickenshit offer where the monkey puts his nuts."

4. Michael Meyer who spruced up his published version of Strindberg's *Dance of Death* for a new London production by revising an old-fashioned reference to manure with a more forthright description of a character as

   ."..a barrow-load of shit."

5. Last but not least, the late Robert Bolt's peppering up his text for Molière's *George Dandin* with phrases like –

   ."..go ape-shit...jealous old git...threw a wobbly...silly sod...gave me a bullocking...."

The thoughtful, if puzzled, critic of the *Times* puts the problem as he sees it: "Does the gain in immediacy and, presumably, relevance justify the loss of period decorum?" And Nightingale's decisive answer is: "It is a good question."

Presumably the bad question would have been: Does the gain in accessible argot, consisting mainly of broken bits of tired profanity, justify the cheap and vulgar betrayal of a prose master's personal style?

Equally bad and awkward would be the query to the Editors on the part of not only old relics: Why are you telling us all this? After all, searching for the good bits all by ourselves is half the fun. You're spoiling the sport.[2]

10

The Case of the Missing F**r-L****r Word

April is (as the poet has it) "the cruellest month." The first week of this April in 1995 was an especially trying time for the *Standard*, that scrappy, intelligent and often courageous London daily newspaper. Among its distinctions was its pioneering efforts—after the court's 1960s decision in favor of D.H. Lawrence's *Lady Chatterley's Lover* in all its pristine impurities—to keep the liberated language salty and realistic.

Lawrence's venture into sexual discourse had been justified on grounds of its "literary merit." The prose of daily journalism was far removed from those heights. Still, the *Standard*–under its celebrated editors, Charles Wintour and (subsequently) Stewart Steven, both of whom I knew and worked with personally—was, with the ruses and stratagems which we have already documented, persistent in trying to break down the traditional barriers be-tween what was considered proper and its over-the-line counterpart, impropriety.

Among its other distinctions was its devotion to "culture," that is, high culture, specifically or the metropolitan stages of London. Its annual awards for the best theater productions and performances is a highlight of the season. In that cruel April I have referred to, there developed a curious conflict of interest, a contradiction between distinctions, a cultural clash between bad lan-guage and good art.

Let the *Standard* tell the story in its own words. On Monday, the 3rd of April (1995), its front-page headline ran:

FOUR-LETTER DIATRIBE
STUNS AT STAGE AWARDS

What had happened was that, at the ceremony of the Laurence Olivier awards, the master of ceremonies, a comedian named Tony Slattery (famous only for the crack, "Slattery will get you nowhere.") launched, according to the *Standard*'s "Arts Correspondent," "a crude and abusive attack on theater critics–including the *Evening Standard*'s Nicholas de Jongh and Milton Shulman." The report went on:

> The audience was reduced to silence, discomfort and nervous laughter as Slattery delivered a stream of insults intended to be tongue-in-cheek, but falling decidedly flat.
> In a bizarre joke...he used a four-letter word to describe de Jongh....This dia-tribe, delivered at break-neck speed, had some of the audience laughing, while others felt uncomfortable at his use of language.

Well, what *had* he said? The *Standard* was never famous for feeling uncomfortable at any use of language–after all (as we were always reminded), Shakespeare had his own moments of bawdy genius–and its writ-ers were never reduced to silence. This time it was evidently having a case of nerves. Some of their own chaps were involved. As in the old days of so-called yellow journalism (for which Upton Sinclair used to award his "Brass Checks") when the front-office of the editors and publishers controlled whether the reporter could "name names" in his story, and they picked and chose among friends and enemies, a curious reader was plunged into darkness. We were supposed to be outraged, but were not given the details of the scandalous offense. No asterisks, not even a hyphenated suggestion.

Suspicions and surmises swim around in an alphabet-soup of a-, c-, f-, and p-words, each having their proper fit (and partisans thereof). What could it have been? There were only limited possibilities. What was it in point of fact? The news was not fit to print—or at least in the newspaper whose protagonists were involved. Why were they all beating about the b**h?

The next day, Tuesday, the *Times* saw an opportunity to defend its own in another way. It offered its critic, Benedict Nightingale (who had also been "insulted" on that stunning evening), space to sing his own song about critical standards in a chirpy kind of way. He wrote of a recent London production (which, as it happens, did not win an award):

> Stay away if you cannot cope with the sight of a junkie scrabbling through his excrement in search of the opium suppositories he has inadvertently shed. Stay away, too, if you have problems with four-letter words, for the characters casually gorge on them.... There is, after all, a certain grim comedy in seeing a battered woman turn on her would-be rescuer as an interfering **** and give him a pasting. (*Times*, 4 April 1995)

In not giving us even an initial hint of the grim joke, the *Times* was almost paralleling the decline in standards of candor which was suddenly setting in. The day was saved when, as I have suggested before, journalism on the distaff side came to the rescue of the old familiar outspokenness.

As it happened there had been another "cultural highlight" over the dramatic April weekend. The novelist Martin Amis, newly come into a fortune when his New York agent landed him a million-dollar contract for a few new books, was giving a party. Among those attending was that ill-starred author of *The Satanic Verses* (1989), Salman Rushdie, who aroused the ire of the Iranian ayatollahs and had a *fatwa,* a sentence of death, hurled at his head. He had come out of hiding for an evening, and he was seen dancing with that dark beauty, Nigella Lawson, daughter of the former chancellor of the exchequer in the Thatcher cabinet (and also, as Nigel Lawson, a former editor of the *Spectator*). For some odd reason Ms. Lawson, who seemed to be luring the endangered Rushdie into frivolous risks, aroused in turn the ire of the tabloid press. None of the reporters of the gazettes had been there. Ms. Lawson, as a columnist of the *Times*, was a specially invited guest. And she was furious. Unlike the discreet melodies of Mr. Nightingale, she was going to tell it like it was. The headline in the august *Times* newspaper was:

SO SORRY YOU
WEREN'T INVITED
Only the wallflowers got excited
about my dance with Rushdie

(*Times*, 4 April 1995)

She went on, quite oblivious (which she never was in her flirtatious Oxford days) to the element of erotic challenge which her own handsome self had introduced into the affair:

Why is there so much hatred towards Salman Rushdie? In anyone's scheme of things, going out to a party and getting on down is not a particularly heinous activity. What do people want? For him to stay locked up out of sight?...

Of course not all the attacks were due to covert racism or copy-hungry opportunism. Some were fired simply by resent-ment. Those who were, as the parlance has it, NFI (Not F****** Invited, should you need a translation) went in for the kill.

The day, as I say, was saved, and the *Standard* recovered its poise and made up for lost time. In the Wednesday edition the *Standard*'s columnist, Peter McKay, was found dancing with the wolves. No vile epithet could be associated with their own, but Nigella was only "my old colleague." She could be served up naked, and then gallantly acquitted for indecent exposure. Here is McKay's parlance (and in his haste he doesn't even reproduce the unspelled seven-letter word quite right, giving more away with his suffix than is standard)–

"Why must (the press) be so nasty?" laments my old colleague Nigella Law-son in the *Times*, deploring those who sniped at Salman Rushdie for dancing with her at Martin Amis's party. She supplies the answer. They were NFI–"Not F***ing Invited." How very true. These back-biting press harpies will never get a jig with Salman, who knows a proper journalist when he sees one. (*Standard*, 5 April 1995)

And where were the proper journalists in the *Standard*'s own Slattery number? Their readers were left in silence, and had to jig to their own tune.

Except for Milton Shulman, the *Standard*'s most famous by-line and who as a long-time theater critic had also come in for dirt in the scandalizing "four-letter diatribe." He said sweetly that "it was flattering to be included in the denunciation." He opined understandingly that frustrated people in the theater could become "bellicose." He wrote with all humility that the obscene insult–"*What a prat!*"–troubled him a little, and he looked the expression up: "My dictionary defines a prat as a fool. He could be right about that." My own *Oxford Dictionary of Modern Slang* defines it a bit differently (p. 177): "*prat*...the backside, a buttock...pratfall: to fall on the buttocks." So would it have been entirely appropriate to deal with the a-word or indeed *A***-h**e*? What has come over our tongue-tied friends on the free-speech front?

On the same day, with Milton Shulman's self-effacing innocuities, the *Standard* indicated that it was recovering its old form by publishing in its glossy Friday magazine section a not irrelevant article about what actors do when they make "tricky public appearances," some being "noisy and demonstrative." One incident is recorded. A rambunctious man of the thea-ter is asked in a pub an "unwise, disturbing question," and this gets "the response so favoured by the publican Norman Balon, 'F*** off.'"[1] At last we are back to our starting positions in the post-*Chatterley* era.

But the Slattery incident remains semantically unresolved. Here the *Guardian*, that old stalwart of liberalism and progress, came to the rescue with one of its characteristic excur-sions into the parts of speech that the other newspapers don't dare to reach. In a blue week of dilatory irrelevancies with not a true hint of the word-of-Slattery which was beginning to rival the historic *mot de Cambronne* (in my dictionary: *Merde!*), the *Guardian* exposed the c-word without benefit of asterisks or dashes in a profile of "slippery slappery Tony Fat-tery." In reality he was "an artist, tortured and creative." It is not true that he is "oleaginous." He was just standing up for "all the other artists who care about their craft at *Sunday*'s Olivier awards by telling the press a few home truths": "*Such as?* One critic, he said, was 'barking mad', another 'boss-eyed,' while a third was a 'cunt'" (the *Guardian*, 4 April 1995). But, you may well ask (and put paid to this whole story), *who* was *which?* Don't wait for answer. Be grateful with what you've got. The old ordure passeth, and giveth way to the new.

11

Asterisks: From Byron to Madonna

I have on various previous occasions referred to the high-minded rational-izations which first accompanied the modernist breakthrough of puritan lan-guage taboos. They persist; but the intellectual or ideological pretenses are wearing thin. In our present-day context of journalistic practice in the main-stream English-language press the lofty excuses and hidden rationales–rang-ing from psychotherapy (certain-words-will-make-you-free) to theology (saving-your-soul or some other conventionally unreachable parts)–are cur-rently not very high in credible, serious intent.

A reporter in New York, at a loss for a good anecdote in his Saturday col-umn, recalled an old story of Mayor Ed Koch in the days when he was first turned out of office. A hostile voter exulted by shouting at him in a Manhattan street, "You were a lousy mayor!" Freed from the shackles of office, Ed Koch yelled back a…"two-word obscenity."

As it is now told (although the vocabulary is mainstream high-brow and not the usual Koch demotic), the ex-mayor especially explained: "I felt cleansed and redeemed." There was no hint of a clue to either of the "two words" in question, for all their hygienic and redemptive virtues. It could be political restraint, for "Big Ed" does still have a lingering reputation; it could be fear of appearing to be "anti-Semitic" (or anti-black) with an attendant backlash by the Jewish (or the Harlem) lobby in the Big Apple…so sensi-tive to anything that might bring a co-religionist (or a local ethnic voter) into disrepute.

There were no such editorial qualms in another story in the same newspaper on the same day (10 February 2001), reporting on the plight of one young star of the "show-biz culture" which, as is well known, thrives on the profanity that is still, self-servingly, considered taboo-breaking. The police authorities had been investigating a twenty-eight-year-old American who "appeared to con-sume Ecstasy pills" and to be encouraging the largely teenage audiences on his concert tour "to take drugs." In fact the prospective charge included the star's swallowing "s—" on stage as well as inciting more than 15,000 fans to do likewise, that is, to proceed to swallow MDMA (Ecstasy), an illegal class-A drug.

Eminem, the name of the controversial American pop rapper star, didn't take the suspicions lightly. In the true spirit of rapping he had been hitting back eloquently, and told the crowd:

> My friend Xibit gave me some Es and I say pop the pill. I told you that yous[e] were a bunch of f***ing drug addicts. I hope these Es are good s***–if they're not, you'll all be carrying my sorry ass home tonight.
>
> In the house are some good-ass Manchester drugs–make some f***ing noise for good-ass Manchester drugs.

What was the quality of the pills he had recommended popping, and what the alcoholic strength of the vodka with which he had threatened to "drink himself to death"? In one show this threat was playfully accompanied by a pretense of executing himself in an electric chair, all the while brandishing a blood-red chainsaw.

Journalistic critics might well ask about the stylistic guidelines were which had been proscribing the quotation of one single word (or, perhaps, two) in our favorite newspapers? We are, after all, well into the fifth or sixth decade of pop culture and we surely cannot trust any fan under the age of sixty not to have experienced the whole gamut of obscenities, from salty GI "*scuttlebutt*" to the latest "*gangsta rap*," liberating or cleansing as the lingo may be. Would even the little old lady of Peoria have escaped noting that our culture's taboo on curses and coarse language had long since disappeared from anybody's scene? A modicum of robust lingo was on everybody's agenda. Nowadays it was all a fixed pre-arranged gig, even something of a rambunctious ritual. Free speech was liberated–and as one of its stalwart apologists explained, "But nobody was doing nothing or saying anything, or that…like, you know what I mean,…that they really sort of meant it." The stars on the stage appeared mean and ornery: sometimes romantically dangerous, sometimes madly destructive. The teenage fans in the hall or stadium roared their shock or approval which came in the din to the same thing. The plainclothes police in the back made notes for a possible inquiry or investigation. The next day's newspaper reports gave space, except for a few missing vowels and consonants, to a good selection of all the expletives one could take in a cursory early-morning reading. The asterisks still did yeoman service.

They still do.[1]

The asterisk's long journey from punctuation to profanity has tempted many etymologists. Eric Partridge* makes a stab at it in an obscure, almost cryptic entry entry entitled "*eight eyes, I will knock out two of your.*" The great

---

*Eric Partridge, *Dictionary of Historical Slang* (1961; Penguin ed. 1972), p. 295.

British lexicographer notes that in addition to the six of a well-known Billigsgate fishwives' enumeration of eighteenth-century catchphrases, there are also "the two bubbles, the belly probably implying the navel, 'two pope's eyes' (? anal and urinal orifices), and 'a *** eye' (? what)." These were the usual hieroglyphics of a persistent philologist who was driven to follow up every clue, no matter how problematical. Partridge concludes: "by the 'pope's eyes' is perhaps meant rump and anus, while by the asterisks is almost certainly understood the sexual aperture." If this is so, then the substitution of asterisks for the alphabetical omissions only compounded the obscenity, making dirty words even dirtier.

What an irony for the cleanup brigade! A little star in the beginning had a high symbolic significance in religious ritual; and it took on, inevitably, a lower significance with sexual or other references still under taboo. The censors and other guardians of linguistic decencies saw only the protective virtues of the discreet omission, and were blind to the vices of its shady meanings. So it came to be reproduced in our contemporary newspaper culture, as so many pages of my book suggest, tens of thousands of times in order to help keep the language clean. The asterisk was the guardian of conventional decencies, the safeguard for the primness of semantic propriety, the defender of the fastness of so-called family values. Little did anyone suspect that the enemy was already within the gates. This may, I suspect, have something to do with the gross failures these simpleminded editing techniques have registered on their record. The historic process of four-letterization has gone forward, and the sly little tricks of orthography and alphabetical cover-up have not proved very helpful. Down with the ill-starred asterisk!

For the time being it has been serving well enough on certain occasions which call for discretion or a complex kind of intimate hesitancy to express an untoward relationship. President Clinton lost a number of loyal advisors during his two terms in the White House; and only a few remained mum and others seemed to be rather tongue-tied. In a report of a lecture in the University of Pittsburgh by one former White House spokesman who had served three embarrassing years, it was recorded: "When asked how he felt about leaving the White House after three years, he jumped in the air, spread his arms wide and shouted 'Free at last!'" This was Mike McCurry who still thought of his old boss as "enormously gifted" and as a "richly qualified leader" but who was, alas, "exasperatingly stupid in his personal life." Some other critics of the former president would not want in this simple compartmentalizing way to separate public qualifications and private behavior. High political office can be taken to call for enormously gifted personal self-control–that is, the man is not supposed to live like an abbott in a monastery but he should not, upon his vows, be smuggling nuns into the chapel at midnight. And among the other rich qualifications is, or should be, a certain cheerful spirit of resignation when it comes to the self-denial which deprives him of the normal lustfulness of still virile years. (After all, two terms of high office amount–maximum!–to eight years, and this is not an eternity.)

In any case Mike McCurry was convinced (at the time) that "history would never forget the Monica Lewinsky case." This particular presidency would "always be marred–stained–by the episode." The "stain," especially after the widely read Philip Roth novel *The Human Stain* (2000), was one of the short-hand metaphors used to refer to the whole historic, and increasingly unmentionable, affair. Another, as I suggest, was *asterisk*. Like stain (*"Out, damned spot!"*) it has reverberating echoes in our literary culture. As Mike McCurry said in Pittsburgh, "I think there will be an asterisk next to his name in the record books."[2]

In world athletics, and especially in American baseball, the multipurpose asterisk is taking on a new outdoor life in a clean-living career as a simple footnote. It serves to qualify, make fair corrections, put things belatedly right. It would be foolish, I admit, to look behind the hidden curtain of every asterisk for lurking villainous meanings. They can crop up quite innocently, without any covert suggestiveness. But the odd power that resides in the little star cannot be denied; and it will out.

Not that our sports writers are, even at their best, particularly interested in historico-semantico-orthographic aspects of the language which they use so robustly. But they are reliable guides to changing slang and modish twists of phraseology. Some grammarians think that they are the greatest single influence on journalistic stylebooks and hence to what does (or does not) get into the paper (and how it is spelled). In the American press–unlike in the London dailies–obscenities are relatively rare; and even the ingenious English euphemisms are seldom imported. Asterisks, perhaps more than dots, dashes, and hyphens, have (as we have seen) had a soiled reputation in recent decades, when they were diligently covering up for the salty obscenities which newspaper editors felt that their readers needed to have in their daily diet of space. But U.S. sports are, on the whole, a world series unto themselves. Otherwise a word like "asterisk" might well not have such an easy entrance into American usages.

Here is an Associated Press reporter (writing from Milwaukee, 22 September 1998), leading off a story on the homerun rivalry between Mark McGwire and Sammy Sosa which dominated the season. McGwire had already hit No. 65–five more than the record that Babe Ruth of the New York Yankees set when I was a lad in the Bronx cheering him on–but No. 66 was taken away by an umpire's controversial ruling. A fan in the grandstands had caught the ball (he was subsequently ejected from the stadium and fined $518 for "trespassing"). Was he, as he insisted, doubled over a chain-link fence behind the railing? Or in front of it (as the umpire ruled)? TV replays were indecisive and ineffective. So the AP story's lead from Milwaukee was "Mark McGwire's home run total might need an asterisk, after all."

It has now become, for another example, part of the standard punctuation and the slang (as in "she was finally asterisked") of the historians of the Olympic games. They are reluctant to rewrite history, and hold fast in their stodgy way to the original official accounts. But they are increasingly pressed to find a small casual tactic in order to revise some famous victories and thus to correct erratic entries in the world record books. Scandals which began as press sensations of a failed "doping test" or some other illicit behavior or–mainly money-taking, especially in the old days of "amateurs" and "professionals" in various sports–often persisted to throw a shadow over famous athletic achievements and gold-medal awards. Substantial rewriting seemed to be called for; but truth-telling historiography, although it also had classical Greek origins, is not usually included in the Olympian ideal. Still and all, sports writers have more and more been calling for modest attempts to set the record straight. One journalist on the *International Herald-Tribune* (the thoughtful Christopher Clarey) called attention to the consequences of "letting the record of the past stand essentially untouched." True, the case of Jim Thorpe, that unforgettable American-Indian athlete, is an exception. In 1912 his gold medals were "stripped" because he had played professional baseball. They were restored in 1982. Clarey wrote vigorously on behalf of "a new course." He regretted that "it has been left to outsiders to suggest the asterisks." An asterisked footnote would give proper due to all the "victims of drugging," by which he meant the whole host of athletes who had come second or third in competitions which were captured by champions who had the illicit advantage of performance-enhancing steroids (and the like). It was, as I say, a new upstanding role for a punctuation mark which had been doing mainly latrine duties for a century or so. The full paragraph of its outdoor outing is worth quoting:

Medal redistribution strikes me as an attractive but potentially troublesome idea: If an athlete who, for example, finished fourth was not tested for drugs at the 1976 Olympics, is it fair to give that person a medal? But at the very least, there should be an asterisk by the name of the medal-winning offender and a brief explanation of how he or she was discredited.

Double justice can now be seen to be done–to athletes who "also ran" and who were in effect cheated of their proper awards. And (in a smaller way) there was a rehabilitation of a little diacritical remark whose moral function would have been appreciated by, say, Herodotus of Halicarnassus (now the Turko-Anatolian city of "Bodrum"). Even the daily newspaper hints at the long perspective: "It is a Herculean task [facing up fully to the issues of drug-taking in sporting competition], but then isn't Greek lore at the core of the Games?"[3]

It is allusively appropriate to note here that more on the strange significance of all these matters can be found in Anthony Grafton's "curious history" of *The Footnote* (1997). It is a brilliant guide to what he calls "the luxuriant thickets of annotation"–including even "a set of four layers" (i.e., footnotes to footnotes to footnotes to footnotes). But he is curiously insensitive to the motif of the asterisk, except as a tiny typographical decoration.

Still, the use of "*to asterisk*" as a verb suggesting a revised historical justice would fit in to his stirring scheme of things. Here is the Footnote's combat record on two fronts:

> Only the use of footnotes and the research techniques associated with them makes it possible to resist the efforts of modern governments, tyrannical and democratic alike, to conceal the compromises they have made, the deaths they have caused, the tortures they or their allies have inflicted.

And again, on the second front:

> Only the use of footnotes enables historians to make their texts not monologues but conversations, in which modern scholars, their predecessors, and their subjects all take part.[4]

Thus, the ideology of the Footnote in Professor Grafton's interpretation is virtuously militant: it resists government-fostered lies and builds up the *espirit de corps* of the partisans of truth.

But sometimes, as in all ideologies, the style and the language it regularly employs undermine its own effectiveness. Asterisks are the exception, being abstract and singular. But hundreds of op. cit.'s in the scholar's wearisome apparatus can induce mental paralysis. Numbered footnotes listed consecutively into the hundreds make for a soporific indifference. Grafton is enchanted by the confession of Harry Belafonte and the pop singer's path to an intellectual education: "I discovered that at the end of some sentences there was a number, and if you looked at the foot of the page the reference was to what it was all about–what source [the author] gleaned his information from." So far, so good. But I suspect that in thousands of other cases the hundreds of op. cit.'s and the innumerable ibid.'s were more of a hindrance than a help towards critical intellectuality.

Even Harry Belafonte had a narrow escape. He developed a taste for reading footnotes, and a hunger for bibliography. Once, as he recalls, he went into a Chicago library, and demanded of the librarian: "Just give me everything you got by Ibid." When she informed him that there was no such writer, he called her a racist. "I said, 'Are you trying to keep me in darkness?' And I walked out of there angry."

At least if he had demanded everything in the library by and about Asterisk, he might have gotten an armful of thoughtful and witty French comics.[5]

So far as I am aware, the history of the asterisk is as yet unwritten. Most grammars are intended as they are for the young in schools, "kids" who are just learning the formal rules of literary composition; and they prudently ignore the shady private life of promiscuous punctuation marks. A knowledgeable historian could clarify for us the important turning point in our inquiry into the language of journalism...namely, when and how the modern usage of the saucy a*****sk emerged.

In the standard works I find only conventional (if fascinating) accounts of the emergence of an "art of punctuation." The mainstream story is how the post-medieval printing technology stabilized a system of symbols which, of course, included dots and dashes and the slow acceptance of literary rules for the use of the asterisk and the commata as well as parentheses and crotchets, apostrophes and quotation marks. Still missing are the signs in extraordinary extreme situations for wayward theological messages (*viz.*, the name of the true, or the false, god) and, closer to our problem, for sinful lapses and shameful human tendencies which need to be repressed, censored, or omitted in acceptable discourse. Asterisks–and hyphens–were still waiting in the wings.

I have consulted here M.B. Parkes' "introduction to the history of punctuation in the West," entitled chirpily *Pause and Effect* (1993). It is a scholarly work, and lavishly illustrated (to pinpoint the exact début of the *punctus interrogativus*, and other valuable signals on the printed page). It breathes the humanist reasonableness of Renaissance spirits. He quotes to good effect the credo of John Locke who had devoted himself to "Reason" by which he understood connections between ideas. Locke saw Knowledge as "the Perception of the Connection and Agreement, or Disagreement and Repugnancy, of any of our Ideas." Consequently, our language has to be intelligible to others in order to communicate our perceptions sharply; and he argued for propriety in language, and for common usage. One passage (from his famous *Essay*, 1690) rings out over the centuries:

> Men's Intentions in speaking are, or at least should be, to be understood; which cannot be without frequent Explanations, Demands, and other the like incommodious Interruptions, where Men do not follow the common use. Propriety of Speech is that which gives our Thoughts entrance in other Men's Minds with the greatest Ease and Advantage: and therefore deserves some part of our Care and Study.

For our own part, "care and study" have been devoted to the "Incommodious Interruptions where Men do not follow the common use." It is surely one of the great ironies of our civilization that the use of punctuation marks was invented to encourage attempts to reflect the phenomena of spoken discourse; and, in its current modern phase, it serves–at least, with asterisks plus dots and dashes–to cover for dark improprieties in the language.[6]

Somewhere in the early nineteenth century, I suspect, such punctuation ceased to be merely a convenient masking of the real name of a scandalizing man (or a scarlet woman) in some delicate public affair. It went on from its discreet function of "not naming names," of evading the outing of the perpetrators of embarrassing conduct–to a blatant covering-up of the name of the transgression which the transgressor, to the irreparable injury of public morals, had committed.

Some words were deemed acceptable, just. *Homosexuality* could be openly referred to, even *sodomy*; but *b-gg-ry* was out. Letters and other documentary evidence which were to be exhibited in court cases were appropriately edited (or, in the case of Byron's famous Diary, burnt beforehand). General histories of censorship—and the personal idiosyncratic excess of the censors themselves—are profusely available. But not enough attention has been paid to the telltale trail of the blue-pencil markings—and how the signs of an honorable (and even, in places, sacred) little star became the asterisk of a thousand lewd references. It made the unmentionable—well, mentionable...(sort of). The acceptance of suggestive synonyms was tantamount to an evasion of well-known sexual and scatological taboos.

What a fall was there! As a superb irony would have it, the asterisk—from the Greek diminutive, *asterikos* (little star), and the late Latin *asertiscus*—had, very early on, a religious and even a sacramental function. In the Eastern Christian Church it denoted a star-shaped instrument which was "placed above the chalice and paten [used by Shakespeare: a sacred silver dish holding the bread in the Eucharist] to prevent the veil from touching the elements (1708)."[7]

In his *Cambridge Encyclopedia of the English Language* (1995), David Crystal reminds us that asterisked (or starred) forms have a place in a philologist's glossary, and they refer generally to a usage that is not acceptable or not grammatical (* *do had gone*). Or they indicate a form for which there is no written evidence (Indo-European * *penkwe*, "five"). This is a far cry, for example, from one vivid contribution to the vast Lord Byron critical-bio-graphical literature—G. Wilson Knight's erudite study of *Lord Byron's Marriage* (1957) which was tantalizing subtitled *"The Evidence of Asterisks."* What new or reinterpreted evidence the author had to offer was mostly concerned with the asterisks that decorated the letters, diaries, and other handwritten literature of hundreds of protagonists in the various Byronic scandals. Who precisely were the players—and how culpably were they involved—in the lurid incidents of adultery, homosexuality, and incest which have preoccupied literary researchers and readers for a century? As Byron himself put it –

> And if our quarrels should rip up old stories,
> And help them with a lie or two additional,
> I'm not to blame, as you well know, no more is
> Anyone else...
> And science profits by this resurrection;
> Dead scandals form good subjects for dissection.
>
> (*Don Juan*, Canto I, 31)

In one mystifying aspect of an unexplained incident, did the suspect four asterisks [****] camouflage a reference to a mistress in Venice, to a young male lover in Cambridge, or to incest with half-sister Augusta? Or was there an even darker secret coupling Lady Byron to an unimaginable intrigue of unmentionable delicacy? We are grateful for every bit of help that the philologists provide. A single asterisk for an excised name may puzzle or mystify; but four (4) can reveal one or the other of the various "Mary's" involved.

The asterisk is in its modern history scandalous, tragic, ill-starred. Our encyclopedist, David Crystal, coolly notes that "the asterisk is conventionally used to symbolize this kind of deviant information," and, accordingly, the deviance makes for a "strange" use of language. Dr. Crystal effectively covers his back for any surprising contemporary incursions by adding, in Orwellian fashion: "Deviance, it seems, is Normal. Strangeness is Familiarity. And familiarity as everyone knows, breeds content."

These may be poor bits of word-play, but quite acceptable in a scholarly and encyclopedic context where language is routinely subjected to lifeless autopsy.[8]

Still, the asterisk is not now usually employed to "protect" identities of protagonists who may have transgressed...but to sidestep the shocking name of the transgression itself. Gibbon, among others, used Latin as a learned evasion. But for a century now of "mass communications" our newspaper editors were faced with, among other instances of word-control (by authors, lawyers, judges), the linguistic insurgence of the vernacular, of the demotic, of streetwise four-letter patois.

Except, possibly, for a bit of inspired Byronic punning there were very few problems with words in dealing with whatever incursions Lord Byron had made into the moral-sexual code of his day. The imputation of "incest" could only technically be levelled in connection with the poet's half-sister, Augusta.

On the other hand, in the case of Jacqueline Du Pré, which I take up in another part of the present volume, it was not her desperate conduct in the family circle that was destined to be bowdlerized but the profane expletive with which she dared to give her sex cry its demotic name. There is an interesting difference. I offer at this point the contrast to the Byronism of Kenneth Tynan who, as my readers may recall, emerged in my previous, first volume, as one of the century's "Godfathers of the F-Word." He once wrote half-apologetically to his wife about an adulterous affair with a young English actress he was hiring for the National Theater: "I just had to fuck her." No asterisk in sight–what's more, no sign of delicacy in his wife's official edition of his letters in which this is publicized. All this transpired in a time when it was fashionable to let all things hang out...even by a thread. Asterisks would have proved sturdier.[9]

Here is G. Wilson Knight trying to unravel "The Evidence of Asterisks," writing about "the mysterious troubles adumbrated by the asterisks of Byron's 1813-1814 Journal, or the heavy rows of asterisks in his letter to Moore of 10 February 1814." Knight records his dogged efforts to decipher and to decode as if he were working on the Cretan *Linear B* or pharaonic Egyptian hiero-glyphics–"Asterisks play a large part in our study. We run up against them continually...at the more important parts." He is thinking generically about obscenity evasion; for *dots* and *dashes* also play a role in the masking of evidence. Sifting through the archives of Thomas Moore and John Cam Hobhouse, of Sir Harold Nicolson and Lord Holland, he records what he calls "this shattering comment" (p. 222): "Something of this sort, certainly, unless, as Lord Holland told me, he tried to—her." Again, in a letter to Lady Byron (of 9 July 1816), he runs across this intriguing remark: "Your feelings I perfectly understand. I will even whisper to you I approve... ...[sic]. But you must remember that your position is very extraordinary." The insight of G. Wilson Knight's asterisk-trained eyes is not to be denied; as he observes (p. 98), with sly under-statement: "the dots of the text may be significant."

Possible significances be damned–back to our asterisks! For as Thomas Campbell (a popular poet of the day, one of Byron's critics and accusers) put it, we are dealing with "*aspersions*" that amount to what he could call at that time "*crimes inflicted on (our) delicacy.*" In a private letter to his sister (of 27 May 1830), Campbell was, as Knight says, "too outspoken for print." But also in the lone copy of the missing original that has come down to us, too outspoken for the calligraphy in a handwritten manuscript! As Campbell confesses in a transcribed, hopelessly bowdlerized copy of his letter, complete with the best of a half-dozen spaced-out asterisks, suggesting unimaginable secrets–

> The defense of Lady B. was a bold step on my part; and I do most gladly rejoice that I meet with your approbation. If all the world were of a different opinion, I should still feel and think that I had done the right thing, and the best thing for the cause of truth and humanity; and that right and the best thing was only to be done with bold and blunt earnestness....
>
> I do assure you that I am not affecting indifference, but really *feel* entire indiffer-ence about the opinion of the worst half of the world. The abuse of part of the press I take rather as a compliment. What I now have to say, I don't give you in absolute confidence; but as it *will* be out one day, I give it to repeat with discretion.

*   *   *   *   *   *

(p. 229-30)

The human capacity for this kind of discretion often tries to balance "abso-lute confidence" with "bold and blunt earnestness." It is arguable. The various virtues of prudence, loyalty, candor, and truthfulness are notoriously frail and short-lived. Invincible, I am afraid, are the asterisks pertaining thereto. The nineteenth-century prediction that "it *will* be out one day" was a worthy pre-sentiment for one concerned with the cause of truth and humanity; but history has a way of keeping its little secrets. We still don't know...

The original manuscript, and one lone copy, of Lord Byron's famous un-published *Memoirs*–he had written them only for posthumous publication–

was famously destroyed, put into the fire. Among the arsonists were: friends, relatives, publishers. It was on Monday, May 17, 1824, three days after the news of Byron's death in Missolonghi had been received. The asterisks ever since have been standing stalwart guard over the evidence in the ashes.

I intend no pun at all when I report that the asterisk in the latest phases of pop culture has begun to have terminal trouble with the stars.

Show business has always thrived on the common touch, and incremental vulgarity is deemed to have brought both popularity and profit. Whole genres in very recent rock-and-roll music have been devoted to the fast flow of obscenities—so much so that high-powered conclaves have been held with pop groups and their recording companies to "self-regulate" a lascivious lyricism which has been running amok. Newspaper stories about what the excess has amounted to—and what "progress" has been made in the cleaning-up of dirty talk or the strict rationing of the number of lewd lyrics per concert—are necessarily as restrained as the momentary mood. Privately the interviews, even with famous performers with their chat, laundered by attentive sub-editors, reveal the full force of foul fulmination; and it cannot help but spill over to the public performance.

The media have worked hard to keep up. Readers and TV-viewers want to consume the highlights; young pop-fan enthusiasts want to relive their ecstatic pleasures in the entranced audience. And so our newspapers, more and more, are beginning to cater to them and not to the more conventional tastes of the straight families of mainstream society. A pop performer like Madonna talks as she pleases in private, and in playing to vast audiences feels free to put her mouth where her money is. This evening (I write in Berlin, in June 2001), was the last of Madonna's local concerts in the sold-out Max Schmeling Halle, and it brought the total tickets sold for four shows to over a hundred thousand.

What she actually said on stage to these masses is not easily "edited out." Too many heard it; and she's too big a name to be messed around with. I can sympathize with the *Times* editors' reluctance to "*go all the way*" when they feel in their hearts that this might be "*too far.*" What their correspondent Kathleen Wyatt in point of fact reported on the occasion of Madonna's opening concert of this long-awaited tour (she had taken time off to get married and have a baby in wedlock) is, perhaps, in the newspaper's archives.

Ms. Kathleen Wyatt evidently did not need any editing or rewriting. She was alert to every sound and movement as Madonna, the "dominatrix diva...rose up through the stage in a black kimono with 26 ft-long sleeves...," intent on "ravishing a stadium full of fans," and timing her change to "*pimp chic.*" This had something to do with her wearing a fur coat and fedora, as near-naked dancers sprang out of trapdoors and crawled across the floor...and (lest I forget) as levers and pulleys reshaped the stage for each new routine.

These items may be of small interest to the historians of show-biz technology. But from the point of view of the language of journalism, a flawless newspaper of record has its correspondent registering every significant detail of an historic news event:

"Her first words to the audience were 'f*** you m*****f******...."

If she went on her "global tour" greeting audiences in five continents with the same salutation (the missing hyphen in m-f is silent), it might prove to be a winning contribution to the sense of identity and solidarity of pop culture fans in the new era of globalization. If she gets as far as China and maybe North Korea, don't worry: the f-word can even be sung to the tune of the *Internationale*. Whether asterisks, all by themselves, are capable of suggesting a standing ovation is another matter.[10]

12

Who's Afraid of the Big, Bad F-Word?

Numbers obviously play a role: but it is not merely a matter of mathematics. Counting the number of profane expletives may teeter on the verge of an additional indecency. Quantity, as in the old dialectical saw, gives way to quality; and the echoing loudness of the sound–especially when it becomes a roar in a football stadium, packed with foul-mouthed fans–can become an acoustical factor whatever the original mass intention. Dirty words come in all shapes and sizes, and sometimes in very clean disguises. Accordingly, the Russian football team named *Fakel Voronezh* has been impelled to change its name–this is the year 2002, month of February–because (as the newspaper report had it): "because the first word sounds like 'f*** all,' thus leading to potential misunderstandings during international matches when fans burst into their chant of 'Fakel! Fakel! Fakel!'..." The Russian club director explained that when they went to the U.S.A., they had "problems." Fakel which in Russian means "torch" (Fackel in German) has been replaced by "the prosaic FC." The German club in Köln (Cologne) uses a shortened version of Fussball-Club-Köln–"FCK"–which looks like an anagram that in London's French Connection affair caused many more such "problems." At the moment in the European chaos, between a Russian chant which is misheard in a stadium roar and a German alphabetical ambiguity, the process of four-letterization is caught up in a confusion confounded.

Qualifiers can do the f-word a power of good, diverting attention from the simplest of vulgarities to the rather more complex longer words, with other elongated, dark associations. The M-F-variation highlighted the year 2002's "World Economic Forum," held in New York's Waldorf Astoria Hotel. A pop star named Bono, an Irish lead singer for the U-2 group, called for a great new Marshall Plan on behalf of poverty stricken Africa, and he tried his best to arouse the assembled billionaires of the globalization klondike to action. He called them "corporate mother-fuckers"; but at this late stage of the vernacular breakthrough, nobody batted an eyelash or blushed an earlobe. Bono went on to discuss the implications of his remarks with President Bush's Treasury Secretary, the worthy Paul O'Neill, and then to solidify his militant global front against the M-F-hordes, chatting up the UN's Kofi Annan and the South African clergyman, Bishop Desmond Tutu.

What is proverbial for the good and the great in the powerful economic counsels of the globe is surely old routine for the nameless Anglo-American servants, trying to cope with the political crises caused by their superiors in the ministries of world politics. Here is a bit of British dialogue, spoken in unmistaakable English by Sir Richard Mottram, when he was entangled in a political embarrassment in Whitehall which called for one or two humiliating resignations. I quote from a story in the Daily Telegraph (25 February 2002, p. 6) although the asterisks in their star-studded fullness proliferated throughout the London press:

> According to Mr. Sixsmith's account in the Sunday Times, Sir Richard told a fellow civil servant: "We're all f*****. I'm f*****, you're f*****, the whole department's f*****. It's been the biggest cock-up and we are all completely f*****."

Since the source was not classically unimpeachable–it was a former journalist's account of what he had heard, or had been told–the number of expletives which were said to have been said might be impugned. If the passage–which one paper dubbed "the sub-text to the unflappable language of Whitehall"–stands the test of time and rigorous double-checking, it can serve for our purposes as a prime official example of what I have called serial scurrility.[1]

In this hurly-burly what used to be an ongoing titillation becomes a matter of routine, something indeed of a mindless obsession. There is an element of serial scurrility but also of a kind of compulsive-repetitive disorder. Here is the whole of another news item in the London newspaper of some journalistic distinction, the Independent, and one is left wondering whether at the end of a long history of taboo words we will be winding up with just another source of boilerplate:

> A viewer wrote with a complaint to a TV company in Minneapolis. Back came several emails from a member of staff, including "You suck big time, Mr. Jerk Bob…f***head," "Yeah, well watch out…you are my number one ***hole!" "Have a f***ed-up day, s**thead," "I think you are a mean motherf***er who deserves to die." That nice Ms. Moerke of customer services is helping police inquiries.

Not really a bit of news; nor actually a coherent item which meets the minimum standards of accuracy and context. But it does manage to fill some white space; and it does appear to be sort of interesting. Nothing to be afraid of there.[2]

The profanization of the language of journalism, as we have been documenting and analyzing it–mainly in the areas of politics, literature, and the media–would not nearly be so serious a phenomenon if it had not had a larger, an all-embracing growth potential. I am not merely thinking of such significant areas, yet to be explored, as science and the relaxed talk of the natural scientists in private discourse, seized up personal hope and professional despair.

Formal concepts and informal conversations, even among Nobel-prize-winners, are clearly subject to semantic fashions. At the Princeton Institute of Advanced Studies, as I was once told by the director, the physicist J. Robert Oppenheimer, enthusiasm for scientific achievement (and especially the happy surprise of a breakthrough to an original solution) was expressed in his lifetime in various and different ways. He heard Albert Einstein scratch his chalk across the Institute's blackboard to a new formula–and then be appplauded by his scientific peers with loud shouts of *"Q.E.D.!".."Correct!," "Perfect!," "Logical!"* and the like.

The next generation chose different words of praise. After another Einstein-like breakthrough by Paul Dirac the noisy approbation of the Institute's enthusiasts ran rather to the aesthetic side, and his Nobel solution was acclaimed as *"Beautiful!"* and *"Enchanting!"*

The point of his recollection was the changing styles of recognition in the scientific community. *"Nowadays,"* said Dr. Oppenheimer (and he was speaking about the 1960s), "when a particularly ingenious solution to an old troublesome problem is demonstrated convincingly on the Princeton blackboard, the question is whether it is '*mad*' or '*outlandish*' enough. And I have heard the youthful enthusiasts crying out '*Crazy!*'..Two or three decades on, it might well be only a casual *"Cool"*...

These shifting patterns of positive expletives are reproduced–one suspects, but I have no evidence for this–by similar fashions in negative scurrilities which reveal that the scientific community is not, as is sometimes naively thought, singlemindedly devoted to the objective or disinterested search for truth. The intrusive, qualifying factors range from personal envy and professional jealousy to political prejudices and a few other private idiosyncrasies. What must have been the obscenities that were hurled across Europe's borders in the stormy era of Newton and Boyle, of Leibniz and Harvey? Only the most publishable of insults have characterized the modern squabbles over, say, Werner Heisenberg (and his disputed services to Hitler's Nazi régime); over Edward Teller (often called "Dr. Strangelove" to his face for his Cold War views against Soviet Communism); over the Editor of the *Bulletin of Atomic Scientists*, Leo Szilard (newly converted to pacifism and conscientious objection); indeed over J. Robert Oppenheimer (for his embarrassing fibs about the "Manhattan Project" and mixed ideological loyalties in Los Alamos), etc., etc.

I wonder: Are there certain professional communities which enjoy a special semantic immunity? If there are, as Lord (C.P.) Snow famously argued, "Two Cultures," which have turned out to be different in style and temperament and verbal resources–then the phenomenon of "four-letterization" might well be stopping short at the doors of our laboratories, where no curses are allowed. How robust is the demotic which scientists, in professional or private discourse, employ? Who called Albert Einstein "a dirty —" ? What "——ing ideologies" were responsible for "*******-up" the nuclear research program and landing President Kennedy's Pentagon with a dire Missile Gap? There are times when our scientists can talk "beautiful" or "crazy"…and times, doubtless, when more energetic bits of strong language are called for.

There is some body of evidence in the borderline disciplines which cannot find safety for themselves in protected areas of abstract language or mathematical symbols, as do nuclear physicists or molecular biologists (among others). Softer specialties like, for instance, child education or pediatrics are more vulnerable, that is, subject to the vagaries of street language and its printability. A heated vocabulary is more likely to flourish when one has to deal with temper tantrums than with cold fission. One example, and it may suffice to indicate what I mean.

Sociologists have to study new family structures; and psychologists have to deal with the related difficulties of single mothers trying to maintain a measure of old-fashioned control of their children. Our newspapers are, accordingly, full of "*Mummy Columnists*," offering their readers good and sound advice based on the latest scientific evidence. How much is science and how much is journalism? Won't a kind of Gresham's Law see to it that the good (say, the abstract-libertarian doctrines *in re* child behavior of John Dewey, Dr. Spock, Jean Piaget, et al.) is driven out by the bad (short punchy pieces, rich in anecdotes and poor in prose)?

Here is a woman's columnist in London, writing on a "Parents" page in the *Daily Telegraph* and reporting in her "Mummy Diaries" on how to negotiate "the maze of modern motherhood." The problem is child behavior on long holidays, especially extended plane trips, where one mother's three children were beyond the sheer ear-splitting noise of what she called "the old Sony Walkman syndrome." As she notes, "The children are thrilled with video screens on the seat backs, allowing them to watch unsuitable movies for hours on end." They all change planes for a last hop, and once more "the children are again very satisfied with the in-flight arrangement."

I spare my reader all the instructive details of dealing with small empirical matters such as cramping pains, toiletries, dehydration, and the like. The full case history might get boring, and the current editorial stratagem of mainstream Anglo-American journalism is to work in something titillating to maintain reader interest. But how does profanity get into it, at three thousand feet? The unsuitable films are taking their toll at that altitude. Ms. Rachel Johnson, trapped in "the maze of modern motherhood," writes in her "Mummy Diary": "They particularly enjoy giving each other advance notice over every smutty scene [the children had already seen the *Austin Powers* film three times]." The smutty bits are the funny bits for the kids, as mummy "swooned dysenterically" and tried to bury herself in a book:

> But it is too late. I had forgotten the punchline of the scene....Soon my infidel children's shrieks of "Fook Mi!" and "Fook Yoo!" are soon penetrating the cabin, and I am returning toxic looks with my most charming, kids-say-the-funniest-things type smile.

And this is the way four-letterization came into the maze of motherhood, strapped into cabin-class seats; on the last leg of a long flight home to London from darkest Africa.[3]

This may be taken to be a trivial bit of child psychiatry and a merely amusing example of obscenities penetrating babytalk under the noses of the pediatricians. Such incidents are surely not to be compared to Princeton blackboard meetings of physicists and mathematicians; nor to the chat in the labs of the Salk Institute or Watson's Cold Spring Harbor establishment. Still, it might be the children who will be leading us in the other direction.... Yet another new generation, brought up in a "scientific atmosphere," may well be seeing to it that "the culture of profanity" shapes the family and its homely discourse with the usual unintended consequences. New Newtons in London will be acclaimed with "*Wow*'s" and up-and-coming Einsteins in Berlin with "*Mensch, geil!*" As for American researchers there can be a revival of "*swell!*" or "*right on!*," in any case jubilant exchanges of "high-fives."

Meanwhile, at this point of time, I am persuaded of the following differentiation. Where anecdotal evidence is acceptable and even necessary, where quotation marks are the clinical instruments of investigation, then the language of social scientists (be they historians or sociologists or literary critics) will tend to be closer to the actual speech of common man. Where the science is embedded in logic and abstract formulae (physics, chemistry, genetics) and its requirements of hard replicable evidence, then the language will be capable of resisting fashion and verbal fancies, of withstanding the demotic urges to gain popularity or notoriety by breaking taboos. The linguistic conservatism of such scientists may be deemed old-fashioned, but it is the fashion of tradition and (if you will) of a classical chic.

There may be deep cultural lessons to be learned here: how one can be innovative, make progress, and yet be of a quasi-cosmic cleanness.

13

Tiger, the *Times* and a Dreaded
Black Asterisk

Historical accounts are beginning to be written about asterisks, and not merely in the context of scholarly footnoting (as Professor Anthony Grafton has admirably done).* The asterisk has an in-built starring quality, and has figured radiantly in old-time religious literature as well as in our nether regions of obscenity and its conscience-stricken camouflage. It is marginally ahead of its competitors. These are staid and blank punctuating marks of conventional practice–I refer to the small (formerly known as the "two-em") *hyphen* and the somewhat longer *dash* (still known in German for its putative thoughtfulness, i.e., it is called a *Gedankenstrich*)–both clearly runners-up in their usage in the language of journalism for purposes of disguise and dissembling. I have already argued that the asterisk is versatile, functioning effectively as both emblem and metaphor, to cover as lazy cusswords or to wound as sharp irony. Professor Grafton reminds us that it was already employed in devious and evasive ways by the "amiably vicious wits" in the Scriblerus Club of eighteenth-century London; and it served well in the polemics raging around the so-called *Battle of the Books*. No one less than Jonathan Swift, elegant swordsman that he was, used the asterisk as a rapier. As the historian of the footnote records: "Swift showed that he knew the minutiae of philological technique when he left gaps in his own text, filling them with asterisks and describing them, in the margins, as 'hiatus in MS'"(Grafton, *Footnote*, p. 113).[1]

The asterisk has, of course, retained some of its traditional functions on the printed page, mostly in books, as an alternative to a footnote number, mixing with tiny pointy daggers and discreet crosses…or in an old-fashioned comic strip with its occasional blankety-blank expostulations, mingling here with the likes of ampersands and exclamation points (#!&-@!). It has had its period of full employment in the late twentieth-century polemics about racism and the deleted e*x*p*l*e*t*i*v*e*s which, according to the latest rules of po-

---

* See Anthony Grafton, *The Footnote*: A Curious History* (1997).

litical correctness, should be edited or omittted or, even better, printed untouched (at long last!) by prudish qualms. Given more playtime when obscenities
have become (*gulp!*) altogether acceptable and are spelled out full-frontal-wise,
the asterisks take to having brief casual affairs in varying circumstances; but like
all casual or brief encounters, they don't mean so much. In my London club I have
earned an asterisk beside my name in the official book of Garrick membership
by moving to (and/or living in) New York or Berlin or wherever, and thus
switching to a special status as a so-called supernumerary* (*sic*).

In the case of Tiger Woods, the black reigning champion and three-time
winner at the Augusta National Golf Club, the various militant Women's Movements have had high hopes of enlisting the man to their own cause. (He has
quietly declined arguing that he disapproves of "discrimination" but he also
believes that private organizations should be entitled to make their own rules.)
The *New York Times* has been leading the cry for a boycott on the part of all right-
thinking players coming to compete in the upcoming Masters tournament (men
only). The *Times'* editorial writers are trying to convince all and sundry in "America's
All-Male Golf Society" that "discrimination isn't good for the golfing business."
The gender bar is not exactly humiliating and oppressive since the best of the
women golfers do have their own lucrative circuit of clubs and competitions
(in which they emerge as well-paid masters or, er…mistresses).

The vocabulary of the journalistic reportage is not usually as problematic
as this; but there was at this writing some semantic storm building up when,
and if, the Rev. Jesse Jackson, the outspoken civil rights campaigner, brought
protesters to the Augusta (in the Deep South's Georgia) tournament gates.
Pungent one-liners would be inscribed on their placards, and rousing slogans
were to be chanted. There might even have been some *contretemps* of record-
able interest in the history of politics, passion, and punctuation.

The *Times*, well-informed as it is, may well know something secret or occult
when it darkly hints, "The absence of golf's best player would put a dreaded
asterisk by the name of next year's winner."[2] *A dreaded asterisk?* What dread-
fulness is this which escaped even Byron and his relentless rearcher? Our little
asterisks are fallen from the stellar heights of a pious millennium, from hand-
tinted pre-Gutenberg denotation and divine allusiveness to low, lewd and
shameful evasiveness. More than that: even when exhausted by the f*o*u*r-
letter innuendoes of the modern sexual revolution, they may well have some
reserves left in them yet. Champions must perform correctly; or winners can be
declared losers. Names marked with an asterisk may be destined for fateful
things, for special treatment (as ticked). We have been w*rn*d.

The press controversy was, in the main, long, indecisive, and tiresome; but
on the surface, as well as in odd hiding places between the lines, there were a
few noteworthy elements. Tiger Woods' behavior throughout was deemed, in
most of the media, unexceptionable. He was–following on from the bullying
of the Augusta bigwigs (especially the chairman in Atlanta named Hootie

Johnson in Atlanta)–being subjected to the professional lobbyist's pressure of Ms. Martha Burk, the influential head of the National Council of Women's Organizations. Hootie was a sexist, and Tiger was a pussycat...and, as she added, with menace, he would have been a caddy on the golf course–not an honored player–if others had been so kittenish....She didn't go nearly so far as Harry Belafonte did when he called Secretary of State Colin Powell an Uncle Tom with a "house nigger's" access to the slaveholder's big white house. A whitey must be more careful.

The counter-argument was not exactly a stabbing philosophical insight into the ambiguities of good and evil when existential pressures force a moral choice–and yet Tiger made his point, not without a certain homely charm. "Hootie is right," he said, "and Martha is right. That's the problem." As for their tactical differences Tiger stood by his guns or, rather, golf clubs. Again, his final reply in the altercation wasn't exactly in the lofty, noble tones of John Stuart Mill's *On Liberty*, but it had its own simple dignity: "I certainly understand her opinion. I don't agree with it, but I respect it. I wish and hope she will feel the same way about my opinion."[3]

He refrained from debater's details which gave the whole controversy an unreal pacific atmosphere as if only neutralistic non-combatants were involved. Journalists on the sidelines pointed out discreetly that although women were not admitted as "members," they had played more than a thousand rounds of golf last year (2001) on the Masters links; it wasn't as if females when spotted on the greensward were in danger of being tarred and feathered at the nearest hole. As for the old-time "Negro" issue which did not come up directly, we gathered that black members have been admitted to the Augusta club since 1990, and in 1975 Lee Elder was the first black to play the Masters.

In an uncharacteristic reversal of roles, where male journalists were now polemically and irascibly their old selves, women columnists turned up as moderating elements, even in the *Washington Post* which felt it had good reason to lose its temper with its ally and rival, the *New York Times*. It published, after one ferocious critique of the *Times'* editorial position, a mild and eminently reasonable piece by Anne Applebaum. (The *Post*'s man in Paris, Managing Editor David Ignatius, promptly rushed to reprint it in the *Herald-Tribune* although this would inevitably be taken to be an unfriendly act.) Ms. Applebaum expressed surprise that U.S. women were teeing up for "the wrong cause":

> Leaving aside all the world's more obvious afflictions–crime, poverty, terrorism–it does seem there are also a few more significant women's issues that a group such as Martha Burk's National Council of Women's Organizations could profitably interest itself in (and a newspaper could sensibly campaign upon) other than the admission of a handful of millionaire women to a men's golf club....
>
> The systematic rape of Iraqi women comes to mind, for example, as well as female circumcision [by] genital mutilation....The situation of Afghan women, still illiterate and lacking health care.[4]

There is nothing wrong with Ms. Applebaum's "alternative" agenda; but she misunderstands the real nature of the quarrel if she thinks it was merely about "membership of an archaic club whose members pay up to $50,000 a year in dues, just to have the privilege of hitting a small white ball across a manicured green lawn."

Many argumentative columnists who were veterans of such "racial" controversies since the days of Martin Luther King were notably hesitant to join in the excited debate. This remained the case even when the white mainstream press, heavyweights like the *Washington Post* and the *New York Times*, which are usually the very models of liberal humanity, began to fall out loudly amongst themselves. For example, John Leo in *U.S. News and World Report* (and syndicated coast-to-coast in a hundred local newspapers) confessed that he had avoided writing about "the great golf flap at Augusta" because it had seemed "so trivial and idiotic." He couldn't take it seriously as did some others, those "professionals of protest," as an allegation of grave civil rights violation. As he saw it, the feminists were fighting to force admission of "a few hyper-rich women into a hyper-rich private club." How could this be reasonably equated with a 400-year oppression of a people who had been bought in Africa and sold in America as chattel slaves? The language of this kind of dissenting journalism, avoiding all the resonant tones of political correctness, has a welcome bit of a common populistic touch:

> Augusta is not resisting [John Leo writes]…out of sexism, but because the members want to smoke cigars together, tell dirty jokes, discuss prostate problems and scratch themselves in odd places without glancing around first. It's ordinary male behavior in a male setting, now defined as a worrisome social problem.[5]

On the evidence which one could gather in their respective newspapers– the news-items were spare, discreet, and tantalizing–the altercation which I have mentioned between the *Times* and the *Post* came to a boiling point in October 2002; and it would have earned only a technical footnote, and mainly because it would have affected the old "Paris *Trib*," now flourishing as the *International Herald Tribune*. The *IHT* was newly advertised as "the first global newspaper," and it was co-owned by the two papers and their publishers' offspring: the Meyer and Graham family on one side, the Ochs family and the Sulzbergers on the other.

Why they didn't get along, and when the bitterness began–and indeed how it influenced or distorted the editing of the estimable *International Herald Tribune*–will, in good time, emerge. For now we merely know that the *Times* made the *Post* a buyout offer which would have put New York completely in charge. The *Post* refused to surrender its 50 percent—and, eager to escape from the "corporate difficulties" with which New York was irritating its Washington partners of a half-century's co-ownership, the *Post*'s counter-offer (in the "exact same" amount) was made and just as promptly turned down. The divorce trial continued until a truce and secret agreement was reached before an imminent trade war developed: the *New York Times* had threatened to pull out and start a rival "global" newspaper in Paris.

The *Washington Post*'s side of the story was put in a long, revealing article.[6] It offered some graphic additional details of the New York paper's long-planned effort "to seize total control of the *IHT*...," all of which amounted to a picture of rapacious empire-building, given the successful business strategy of recent years which resulted in the *Times* Company earning $3.1 billion last year and, in January, a 45 percent increase in fourth-quarter profit. The *Washington Post* had "reluctantly" sold out to the Times for $65 million dollars.

Certain efforts at "compromise" proved to be futile, and the given reasons for the failure have something to do with the Tiger Woods story as we have been reconstructing it.

> The *Post* said the *Times* threatened to starve the *IHT* if the *Post* refused to sell; the *Times* offered the *Post* a 10 percent ownership in the *IHT*, which the *Post* refused. the *Times* also offered to print some *Post* stories in a wholly *Times*-owned *IHT*, which the *Post* deemed journalistically unacceptable because *Post* stories would have been handled by editors from a rival–the *Times*–rather than neutral *IHT* editors.

One wouldn't have thought that such unclean customs–rival editors handling each other's stories–had been going on in Paris for decades (and it had made only for a livelier paper). What practices are held to be "journalistically acceptable," or not, seems to be confined in this war of media giants to the most trivial matters of editorial pride and bureaucratic vanity. But these grew to be nasty issues of spite and sabotage (and even, as we are seeing, "racial conflict"). For instance, "the *Times* wouldn't force its correspondents to file on time for the *IHT*'s deadlines...." So long as New York, in another time zone, gets the breaking story...and the European readership of the *Herald-Trib* be damned. Is this considered in Times Square to be "journalistically acceptable"?

I mention all this in this place because, as it appears, it also invokes the golfing champion Tiger Woods–whose mixed race genetics make him sometimes a black, sometimes a brown (there are no "yellows" nor "*high-yallers*" around any more). Once in a while he appears (in his own coinage) as "a *Cablinasian*"...since his genetical mix includes *Ca*ucasian-*Bl*ack-*In*dian-*As*ian, his mother being Chinese and Thai. In any case he found himself between two titanic thunderers in the middle of a *melée* on "racial issues."

What the man from the *Washington Post* contributed to the "raging debate" was an unprecedented note of rancor–in part explicable because of his radical disagreement with the *New York Times* on the issue in question, in part also due to the organizational tension and hard feelings which prevailed between the *Post* and the *Times*. Some other hidden factor could be surmised, but there was no obvious evidence for it–at least for the vast readership that were not privy to the personal (and personnel) details–until (at least for me) the *On-Line* services reprinted Michael Wilbon's *Post* article for the Internet users with a photograph of the author over his by-line.

The picture of the proud author constituted some kind of clue. But does it really make any difference what he looked like? Is one falling into a physiognomic approach to the problems of prose? If his nose was long could the battle be put down to an intra-Semitic feud between the Meyers and the Ochses? If he were black (as he was) would the debate amount to an internal faction-fight among Black Power partisans who were now well placed enough in the white executive world to command space for their special ethno-tactical interests? I am merely asking…and indeed summing up the questionable views on all sides of a thorny, undeniably "racial" controversy.

Michael Wilbon had read all those "diatribes criticizing Woods," and added one of his own. Why is Tiger Woods supposed to be the moral caretaker of women's golf in America? This thesis of the *New York Times*–whose editorial-page chairman was also a senior black journalist (who probably authored, or co-authored, the original leading article)–infuriated the *Post* man. Throwing caution to the winds (and the old injunction in the press world against "dog-eating-dog"), Wilbon wrote:

> I read an article in Monday's editions of the *New York Times* that suggested that Tiger should boycott the Masters, the most prestigious tournament in the world…so that he could send the message that discrimination isn't good for the sport.
>
> Oh, is that right? I'll bet that the editorial pages of the *Times* never said Jack Nicklaus should have boycotted the Masters because Augusta National didn't have any black members.

And why Tiger? Why not a dozen of his fellow players (all white)? And why not some of the famous South African players (Ernie Els, Gary Player) who came to fame and fortune during the old conscience-stricken apartheid days? And why not call on the moguls of great white American institutions like the major television networks which owns the TV rights (CBS) not to have anything to do with Augusta? "Why Tiger…? Because Tiger is black."* This was so illogical as to verge on incoherence; but most furious arguments are unreasonable; still, one can understand the emotions of one black writer getting mad at

---

*   Another black columnist, Ms. E.R. Shipp (in the *New York Daily News*, "Tiger is taking too much heat," 3 December), arguing that the discrimination issue is a battle that honest white liberals should be leading, put the point more lyrically:
      "…Tiger shouldn't have to tote their barge and lift their bale."
      Such singable *Show Boat* tag lines popped up regularly, as if Tiger Woods was filling in for the late Paul Robeson…not unlike in the famous L.A. murder trial (for the murder of his beautiful blond wife!), in which O.J. Simpson was cast in the role of Othello, with plenty of Shakespearean quotations thrown in for good measure. On this, see my pages in Volume One on the journalistic language in the Simpson trial, and (in the same volume) on the Broadway musical *Show Boat* and Robeson's textual revisions.

another black writer for "picking on" his hero by unsuccessfully "fingering" him to fight in the frontline trenches.

> Tiger, the *Times* suggests, needs to have a social conscience, but other golfers–read, white golfers–do not. The men who run broadcast networks do not. I didn't realize that of 248 golfers who made money on the PGA this year, only one 26-year-old black golfer is supposed to have a social conscience, and everyone else gets a pass. The *Times* ought to write an editorial explaining why that's so.

Of course, the *Times* wouldn't write any such a thing, nor would it cease to insist that a black champion should feel honor-bound to lead the way to progress and enlightenment.

Wilbon knows–and this is his real, underlying grievance–that in the liberal (black as well as white) world there has been a "desperate search to find a clear and unwavering voice on social issues"…and so "we've rushed to anoint Tiger Woods." His father, Earl Woods, was partly to blame for he launched his son on to the world as a moral force who would "one day" be "as important as Gandhi."

This, for Wilbon and other alert militants, was "insane." In the struggle to achieve momentous human ideals, a brown-tinted professional golfer was deemed something less than the heroical figure History was calling for. The well-known precepts of a black sociology and a black social science, taking their controversial place in programs of Black Cultural Studies, taught differently. In the first place, Tiger "grew up middle class in Southern California and wanted for virtually nothing." (Only the poor and downtrodden, scarred by deprivation, can lead us.) Secondly, "his parents gave him everything so how could he possibly have a fully developed social conscience and know how to express it on the world stage?" (Arthur Ashe was different, Mohammed Ali [Cassius Clay] was different; and so were, possibly, Hannibal, Spartacus, Nat Turner, and Martin Luther King, among others.)

We have run into this complex prejudice before. But it is very rare that it is so openly expressed in the mainstream American press. The supreme charge of a militant's inadequacy–and his (or her) impending failure–is for a black not to be black enough.

Sometimes it is the chromatic quality of the color itself. I remember as a boy in New York being caught up in the crusade to rescue a victimized young Alabama Negro named Angelo Herndon from Southern lynch justice. "*Free Angelo Herndon!*" was the lapel button I wore. When he was in fact freed, and took the train northwards to Penn Station in order to join in the joyous liberation celebrations, the Left's welcoming committee was visibly disappointed when Herndon alighted; as one militant whispered, crestfallen, "He isn't black enough!…" Angelo and perhaps all of the famed "Scottsboro Boys" of the 1930s were too light-skinned to fit into the militant-ideological preconceptions of the black struggle. Their face should have been their scar, their badge of sufferance.

Sometimes it is life's naked experience that needs to be *just right*: so as to entitle one to be a messiah, or to lead a crusade, or to wave a flag on the barricades; or whatever the challenging utopian task calls for. Obviously Tiger Woods can't sport the C.V. to make him eligible for such heroics and ultimate martyrdom.

> Tiger [Michael Wilbon writes] didn't grow up in the shadow of Jim Crow "whites only" signs in the South, or on the wrong side of the tracks....He has no legitimate reason, not yet anyway, to wake up every morning in a rage over the injustices he has faced because he hasn't faced many, if any. He'll get there, I suspect, in time. But damn if he should be pushed there by the *New York Times*.

According to the black canon of ethnic correctness, protagonists of the good old cause need to accumulate brownie points to establish eligibility and entitlement. Like some Siegfried, they have to pass the test of fire before, like some Launcelot, they can win in the ordeal of battle. True liberators have to come in the right size, shape and color. To come with the recommendation of the newspaper competition is not just right on. Still, the *Post* was not advocating a fanatical party line, with fixed and total prescriptions; it was only having an argument among former friends and current enemies. As Wilbon generously concluded: "If Woods wanted to boycott the Masters, I would applaud him. But for the old grey lady *Times* to suggest he should, while making no such demands on anybody else is too arrogant and too transparent for me."[7]

The editors of the *New York Times*, having won a historic media victory by ejecting the *Washington Post* from its editorial share in the Paris *Herald-Tribune*, found the occasion timely for an act of generosity of its own. It had suppressed any note of dissent and disagreement within the paper itself in the face of *Times'* heretical views on the stormy Augusta issues; and now it was big enough to say they were sorry, if only in twisted and tortured prose. After all, this is a haughty newspaper which took some fifty years to introduce a little nook in the corner of a page which would concede that it was fallible–admitting little errors of slipshod typography, erratic population statistics, misspelled politicians' middle initials, etc., and thereby chronicling their correction. The self-critical story was published on page A17 on 7 December 2002, a day of unfortunate associations, and it had a note of "infamy" about it.

2 REJECTED SPORTS COLUMNS
TO BE PRINTED BY THE TIMES

By Felicity Barringer

Howell Raines, executive editor of the *New York Times*, said yesterday that revised versions of two sports columns rejected by editors two weeks ago would be published tomorrow.

This was a deathly confession, and the words were (as in Trotsky's image in his obituary of Lenin), "like giant rocks falling into the sea." The *Times* editors had been guilty of the mortal sin of censorship (even if it was only or merely self-censorship). The self-styled Jeffersonian defender of the Freedom of the Press had suppressed the freedom to disagree, had repressed its own reporters from publishing differing opinions. "Say it ain't so, Mr. Ochs!..." echoed the cry in Times Square.

Howell Raines proceeded to rationalize the "rejection."

> He added that the editors' [i.e., the edition of the *New York Times*] original objections were based not on the opinions stated in the columns but on separate concerns: one column, by Dave Anderson, about the Augusta National golf Club's refusal to admit women, gave the appearance of unnecessary intramural squabbling with the newspaper's editorial board; the second by Harvey Araton, which also dealt with the Augusta issue, presented problems of structure and tone.

Unnecessary intramural squabbling, the appearance of. How feeble and weak-kneed can you get? After all, it was only a game, fellas, hitting a tiny ball into a little hole! As for presenting *problems of structure and tone*, it could only have been worse, more disgracefully formulated, if they had sub- or copy-edited *infrastructure* into the tone of the story. This had become the distinctive style of the *Times* prose: platitude, with attitude.

"We have invited Harvey and Dave to resubmit the columns," they now genially promised after critics both inside and outside Times Square had become loud and bitter. A Harvard academic who was a specialist in newspaper journalism found the *Times'* exercise in censorship "appalling"–because, in a series of clichés worthy of the *Times* itself, "the message it was sending" (namely, the columns were stopped because the point of view they took) was "a very damaging perception for the *New York Times* to allow."

The *Times* editors did try their hackneyed best to disallow it. Mr. Raines insisted that he "had absolutely no problems" with the "opinions that Dave expressed." But did that mean that he now agreed with the views he had prevented from being published in the paper? It all depended on what he actually meant by *absolutely*. As to the matter of Harvey's deleted column, the point at issue was not Tiger Woods and the Augusta Club's record of discrimination but, believe it or not, some other raging debate on the future of some phenomenon called "*Women's Softball*" and its dubious future as an Olympic sport. Harvey Araton had apparently gone too far by drawing a parallel between it, "*Women's Softball*," and the golf controversy. This was inadmissible. Golf, after all, as is very well known, is very much a hardball game.

By this time, the *Times* was becoming a figure of fun. A critic for the online magazine *Slate* pronounced that "by almost any measure the paper's coverage of Augusta has shifted from overdrive to overkill." A tabulation in *USA Today* established that (as of 3 December) the *Times* had published thirty-three articles–without counting the belated and "revised" columns of Dave and Harvey–on the dispute since July.

The most deleterious effect of this neurotic over-emphasis on an "important story" of their own fabrication–"Augusta is a great story; it's one of the great sociological sports stories we've ever had"–is that all other American papers have to devote valuable space to stories of their own, following the line of the St. Vitus dancers on the *Times*. It proudly recorded that among major newspapers, hopping along in its trail, "the *Los Angeles Times* had written 27 pieces, *USA Today* 24, and the *Washington Post* 22."

The *New York Times* story on that 7th of December, a day that has a chance to live on in obloquy, is arguably one of the most dispiriting pieces that the paper has ever passed on to its long suffering readership. If this paltry self-serving substitute for an apology is the best they could do on a story concerning themselves, knowing all that is to be known about what happened and why, what must we make of thousands of other published stories which purport to be competent and coherent reports by honest and intelligent writers on life and politics, science and (yes!) sociology, and all the rest of the world's work? Should not each of them have a little italicized warning that what follows may be fit to print–but, more important than that, it has been passed-for-publication-by-The-Editors…who are obliged to veto anything that appears to suggest Intramural Squabbling and to present problems of Structure and Tone?

The *Times'* problem could have been easily and honorably resolved by the simple and conventional Voltairean tag adopted by hundreds of Western newspapers and magazines which flourish without egregious self-censorship, namely: *The Views of our Writers do not necessarily represent the Views of the Editors or the Publishers*. Period.

The tenuous explanation offered by Howell Raines, the executive editor (what ever happened to Press Row's old proud title of editor-in-chief?) reads: "The ideas that we are raising questions that others are not bothering to ask seems to me to be one of the things a newspaper does." The self-critical idea that he has been providing misleading answers to badly phrased questions, and arbitrarily tampering with the responses, does not pass his mind. If this is one of the things a great and illustrious newspaper is caught doing then it could be in danger of losing much of its ill-deserved reputation. One sentence stands out in Ms. Felicity Barringer's report; trying to sum up the reaction of the journalists on the *Times* staff: "A lot of people in the newsroom feel that this has been an embarrassing episode." If so, it has been an *embarras de richesses*, or rather a richness of embarrassments.

The half-literate explanation offered by Gerald M. Boyd, the *Times'* managing editor, is equally embarrassing. He is defending the cutting of material which would be "out of step with the *Times'* practice of keeping its news columns from responding to the newspaper's editorials." He said that he was afraid that such responses would make the paper appear "parochial and self-absorbed." Such invincible editorial vanity–how utterly objective and cosmopolitan we are, speaking with a single voice!–is not afraid of the charges of self-censorship. He calls it "editing the paper." He feels that this was his "primary responsibility." He thought that "if content is, in our view, not ready to be published, it is our responsibility as editors, to get it ready to be published."

Ready? what means *ready*? This formula would not pass muster in an elementary journalism class. To get a story ready to be published can mean anything from preparing the edited text, dotting the *i*'s and crossing the *t*'s, so that a printer (if such still exist) can easily read it…to scrapping the whole story because you hate it and so judge it in its present form "*not ready*" for publication. The latter has been the century-old rationale of all narrow-minded censors who were out to kill disagreeable news and dangerous thoughts. It constitutes a form of editorial cleansing. Firing the writer, or even purging them, is another.

It was hard accurately to predict, some months before the Masters Golf championship in Augusta, Georgia, what would be happening in that "cruellest month" of April. Sportsmen can change their tactics; editors may revise the thrust of their leading articles. Even agitators, as in Brecht's pacifist phrase, can call for a demonstration…and nobody turns up. No one really knows how a "gender issue" of the Woman's movement, confounded with the "racial" cause of the Black struggle, could actually "play out." Events are uncertain, and even more so are the categories on the scorecard, when everything–e.g., "gender…race…black," for starters–is subject to the vagaries of interpretation.

Given these vague and manipulable elements any outcome was imaginable. A political hole-in-one, the surprise shot on any playable course, is always a possibility…as is the open question whether the *New York Times*, somewhat battered and a little bit contrite, would be withdrawing its cryptic reference to a presumably new champion whose name was to be nicked by "*a dreaded asterisk*."

As we have seen, the asterisk is known to have had, in its long, playful and checkered history, certain magical and mystical properties.

When the actual tournament began, after so many months of what can only be called *agitprop* on the part of the *New York Times* (and its favored agitator or propagandist of the day, Ms. Martha Burk), the championship play for the Masters title in 2003 was something of an anti-climax. Tiger Woods played the first round very badly, and almost "missed out" to enable him to play on. No reporter, or at least in the Atlanta accounts I saw, went so far as to suggest that the previous excitements had "rattled" him. Good thing, too, for in the next round he was in such good form that he almost broke the course record. Nevertheless he did not (in the *Times*' journalese of the day) "*three-peat*," and it fell to other competitors to finish with top scores. Had the *Times* won "a sort of victory"? It had started a small war, and on agitated days it sounded as if the prospect of violence on the front lines was imminent. Selena Roberts (in the

Times, for 9 April 2003, p. 85) reported that "leaping the fence can result in having your ankles gnawed like a hambone…." She went on to indulge yet again in her paper's usual exaggerations about "Augusta's power" which, incredibly, "decided which ism–racism or sexism–is tolerable on the local and national level." Woe betide those among "mighty Martha Burk's band of freedom fighters" to get on the wrong side of "Hootie and his inner circle of octogenarians." As Selena Roberts concluded, with a kind of Clausewitzian finality, "to stay in power is to remain on the right side of the fence that is marked by a Members Only sign. Stray, and hear a voice from the clubhouse shout, 'Release the Hounds.'" Not a leg was bitten, nobody was mangled. The *Times* reporters, "embedded" with the professional golfing élite (all men, almost all white), wrote fairly about the winners and losers…in "just a game," albeit a lucrative one.

Others were, in the end reckoning, less impartial, and rather more complete in their assessment of the campaign in all of its ramifications. A federal appeals court had upheld the local sheriff's decision "to only allow" the protest demonstration a half-mile from the club's front gate.* (The American Civil Liberties Union lawyer objected that "the right to free speech doesn't mean much if you can't communicate with folks you are trying to communicate with.") According to *USA Today*, Ms. Burk's "mass protest" had attracted some 40 supporters, and they were outnumbered by more than two to one by the attendant police. According to a Canadian paper (the *National Post*), Ms. Burk's protest had attracted two dozen supporters, and thus was outnumbered by five-to-one by the reporters and cameramen present. Yet another statistic; Burk supporters were outnumbered two-to-one by the number of stories the *New York Times* had published on "the allegedly raging furor"…and perilously close to being outnumbered by the holes on the golf links. These little pin-pricks may have drawm no blood; but it was Mark Steyn, that irrepressible Canadian polemicist (for mainly British publications: *Telegraph, Spectator*), who attempted the unkindest cut of all. He had counted in all ninety stories which the *New York Times* had published on Tiger Woods, Martha Burk, and the crusade for a famous victory on behalf of a good cause. And he asked,

---

* Evidently the old-fashioned sporting credo, penned by the legendary golf champion from Atlanta, Bobby Jones, helped to define (and decide) the issue as to how close noisy free speech demonstrators can get to the action. Jones had written, and it is printed on the back of every Masters Badge given to the fans who follow the tournament on the club's greens:

  "It is appropriate for spectators to applaud successful strokes in proportion to difficulty, but excess demonstrations by a player or partisans are not proper because of the possible effect upon other competitors."

  The vintage prose cadence of this injunction sat heavily in the columns of the *Times* now so committed to quick, light, and short sentences.

The *Times'* carpet bombing of Augusta has proved a pathetic bunker-bust. This is supposed to be the most influential newspaper in America, the one whose front-page all but dictates the agenda of the network [TV] news-shows. And its most fiercely sustained campaign can't fill a single school bus?

Who will be proposing next to put that "sinister little asterisk" (whatever it may signify) beside the mast-head logo of the *New York Times**?[8]

14

Morphing the A-Word

To be sure, what I have referred to as an emblematical alternative is related, in its way, to the disguises of punctuation masking taboo words. But the hieroglyphic squiggles remain, a distinct rival to the invention of synonyms vainly invested with sly contraband. The English, more in fun than in bawdry (if the two modes are not mutually exclusive), press their language to extremes in order to get some element of ribaldry into discourse which has lost its traditional guidelines, *viz.* "*bonk*" and "*shag*" which represent only the more recent serviceable coinages.

The English facility in their own language for flippancy or superciliousness is well known; and, to be sure, it is not confined to the written word and the newspaper culture. It would take us too far afield to take up here the verbal trickery of the Cockney skill at "back-rhyming" or the secretive *argot* of the kind which Anthony Burgess perfected for *A Clockwork Orange* (1962). These ingenious literary inventions, as far as I can detect, do not directly influence the language of journalism. Still, one recent newspaper story appears to break new ground, and hints at a new route which rude slang might take in its efforts to transcend self-censorship while still maintaining what we recognize as the shock of the blue. (For Cockney back-rhyming see: Crystal, *The English Language*, pp. 182, 395.)

Apparently the habit of medical notes being used to incorporate abusive acronyms is widespread among doctors. A London "doctors' defense body" warned general practitioners about making flippant comments about patients, usually disguised as acronyms. Generations of family doctors, reports the *Independent* (trying hard to be fair about it), have eased the stresses of the job, and shared a joke among colleagues, by summing up their more demanding patients in colorful abbreviations.

But: times have changed. Patients now have the right to see their doctors' notes. Some of the standard references will surely win no friends in court. Among the derogations being warned against: "…SIG (*'Stupid Ignorant Git'*)….WOT (*'Waste of Time'*)..TATT (*'Tired All the Time'*)…."Etc.

The advisor for the Medical Defence Union (*MDU*, or *"Messy Doctors' Unwords"*) raised the specter of "malpractice" in our flourishing "compensation culture." He argued,

> The derogatory comments are historical anachronisms and we have advised doctors for many years not to use them. They are something which raise a laugh but when you are standing in court with the injured patient opposite you, it is not so funny.

More than that, there are unfortunate medical complications when a casual reminder in the confidential notebook that the-patient-is-daffy (*PID*) can be misunderstood as Pelvic Inflammatory Disease (a sexually transmitted infection) or Prolapsed Intravertebral Disc (a painful back problem).

The story in the *Independent* was written by the "Health Editor"; had it been assigned to the "Language Editor" we might have had several richer examples of acronyms touching on more intimate diagnoses: *viz.*, *BMH* ("Bonking Might Help") or, alternatively, *STCA* ("Shagging Threatens Cardiac Arrest").

The dilemma is cruel enough to be called, as the objectionable phrase goes, obscene. Acronyms are too private, and lack the verbal power to break (or seem to be breaking) taboos. Synonyms are too anodyne, and prove to be limp and impotent for the *macho* task at hand. The complexities are compounded by the misinterpretations that inevitably hound transatlantic usages; and they make for Anglo-American confusions which, as a side effect, bewilder the rest of the English-speaking world.

In a recent column in an American news-weekly a writer cogitated on the troublesome thesis that "what counts as cursing changes from era to era"–and she went on to report (25 September 2001), "That's why Americans took their kids to a movie called 'Austin Powers: The Spy Who Shagged Me' while the British were slightly breathless at the marquee use of a verb that, in their country, is a vulgar term for sexual congress." The blankety-blank solution has been with us a long time, perhaps as long as Mergenthaler's invention of a linotype machine which was subject to good-looking typographical errors. "*Etaoin Shrdlu*" turned out to be a lusty, high-spirited fellow who made a fair contribution in his day to gross impudicity. *Newsweek*'s recent headline, *In Defense of *S##@ &$ percent#* is as good a version as any (although in France a çedilla, and in Spain an upside-down question-mark, are peppery additions). But the linotypist's lasting contribution is evidently not tipped for (except for me) a popular revival.

Ms. Anne Quindlen, a former op-ed columnist at the *New York Times* turned novelist (and now a contributing editor to *Newsweek*), is a post-Mergenthaler type. What she hears rather than what she reads is cause for alarm. She listens to the talk of "potty-mouthed American children" and is upset at the ubiquity of "the ultimate swear word," used indiscriminately and incessantly as a verb, adverb, and "even a participle." In some obvious distress she puts the meaningful question, "What does it mean when a word doesn't mean what it meant anymore?" With some solace she records that the *New Yorker*–unlike the *Times*–spelled out (in full) what George W. Bush said about a hostile *Times* reporter.

There was a brief nationwide discussion about what exactly was scandalizing about calling a Washington critic "*a major-league a—h—e*" (wiseacres thought that a "*minor* league classification" might have been permissible). It seemed to foreign observers to be rather old stuff. One Berlin reporter cracked that the sixteenth-century German controversy over the *Götz-von-Berlichingen-*-*-Wort*–"morphed," as we would say, from *Arschloch*–had finally reached the Alamo. The Texan president-to-be was reported by the *New York Times*–says Quindlen, "taxing the reader's imagination even more"–as "expletive deleted." the *New Yorker*'s editor, David Remnick, seemed evidently to be proud that he had that week won the obscenity stakes, and for good reason. As he argued–and apparently convinced Ms. Quindlen, and that made him two-up among the national weeklies: "So long as we're not using or quoting such a word mindlessly, it seems patronizing to me to invent euphemisms or insert dashes. The readers are grown-ups. They've heard these things before." It is strange logic to argue that because "we" have heard obscenities before, we should now be subjected to reading them all the time or, at least, on every inappropriate grown-up occasion.

There is no other course open to us than to be patient with the recommendations for our newspaper culture from those two great established forces that shape the usages in our mainstream language.

The pragmatic initiatives of journalists, enlightened or cynical as they may be, will continue to come up with catchphrases and demotic derring-do that will amuse, inform, and maintain minimum attention spans among the millions who still persist in reading a printed page.

The more abstract guidelines of the linguists, philologists, and other academic language experts will be reinforcing one or the other warring camps, inescapably engaged in the argument for and against conservative traditionalism...or for and against innovative breakthroughs.

Occasionally an eccentric poet may prove to be helpful. (My readers will have noted the subtle, if also devious, insights of Robert Graves. Idiosyncratic thinkers–from McLuhan to Baudrillard–pondering the metaphysics of cultural communication and the written word, can be relied upon to be fitfully illuminating. I also think of those irrepressible Italian intellectuals, Umberto Eco and Roberto Calasso. The latter, in one of his recent books (*The Ruin of Kasch*, 1994), crowded with suggestive obscurities and mental acrobatics, meditates on an ancestral credo to the effect that "*If one consecrates, it is in order to desecrate better.*"

To what extent does the whole phenomenon of "four-letterization," the contemporary devotion to obscenity and pornography, represent a civilized tension between an old desecration and a new consecratio that is, between the humane limits of the sacred and the subversive, of the banal and the profound? Calasso writes, as he peers back at us from his seer's vantage-point in the future:

> *Ahnungslos*, "omenless": this wonderful German word describes the condition in which the West now finds itself, after millennia of tortuous history. To be born "omenless," unshadowed by guilt or grace, is our original modern *status*, the unexpected demand that we rid ourselves of the world–a demand lurking behind every shop counter, laboratory table, professor's desk, cash register....In those days, the world weighed horribly on everyone; everything had too much meaning; every twig contained too much power. An ineffable dream began to take shape: that the most beautiful thing was to lighten one's load, to cast off the world. To do this, one had to concentrate the sacred into one victim–and kill it. Afterward, there was nothing to do but return to intoxicating banality, which was at last profane.

Whatever this, in the last analysis (if ever we come to it), may mean, we can be sure that ironies and paradoxes will abound, and we will be continually surprised by new turns which promise a kind of solution to the great cultural complex of a disoriented language trying to find its way.

The path ahead may well be too simple and obvious to be easily found out.[1]

15

Terms of Endearment and Agreement

In the writing of the obituaries of famous American jazz figures there seems to be a special entitlement. No tribute would be complete if it did not recapture the flavor of the old jive talk with a touch of dirty realism. It is surely not enough to report (at least for "Whiteys") just a word or two: "Tony Williams, who has died aged 51, was one of the greatest drummers in the history of jazz; his revolutionary approach to time-keeping and the drummer's role had a profound and lasting effect." The *Daily Telegraph* goes on properly to quote the finest compliment a drummer had ever received: "Miles Davis spoke for many when he hailed his new percussionist [for his celebrated Miles Davis Quintet] as 'one of the baddest m*****-f*****s ever to play a set of drums'" ("Tony Williams," obituary in the *Daily Telegraph*, 1 March 1997, p. 17).

Not all the stories in that morning's paper were able to feature the day's quota of obscenities with such star-like clarity. Ms. Sue Mott struggled in her long "Saturday Interview" with the chief executive of the Football Association; and after four long columns of forceful questioning she allows him to emerge as a former bank-teller who no longer lives in an ivory-tower and whose rough diplomacy recently headed off a clash with a famous football star who might have, as she tells it, shouted "You're a bag of ****." Is it important to know what the expletive was? Two obvious fillers ("s—t," "s—m") do fit, but there may be several others, and Sue Mott has been clever enough to keep us guessing. ("Sue Mott Interview," *Daily Telegraph*, 1 March 1997, p. 18.)

There were one or two other saucy items in the paper's daily allocation, but since the one was not published in anything approaching full-frontal phallic plainness and the other was not a four-letter word, I will leave them for another time and place.

The times are long since gone the various games in a "sporting culture" could be categorized, if the sociological impulse be so strong, by social class—"upper class" in tennis (in the days of ritzy Forest Hills and old-style Wimbledon), "working class" in soccer (and nothing but Cockney was heard in London on the days of the big matches). By now the obscenities are democratically distributed among all players and followers, and there are few, if any, differences between the curses of English rugby rowdies and the expletives of the embittered Thames regatta enthusiasts taking tea at Henley. Here is the dainty Sue Mott, again, of the *Telegraph* trying to rehabilitate a handsome young cricketer who has been getting into trouble. As he tells Miss Mott:

> Last year I had a shocking six months. I think I just forgot how to score runs. I was trying but the runs just dried up. In the end, the chief coach, Bob Simpson, called me into his office and said, "What the eff are you doing?" Only not that politely.
> He didn't know what the eff he was doing. But perhaps he does now.[1]

The difficulty over the years is to keep the reader on the run, persistently guessing; and the verbal variety of an athlete's conversation helps a little to keep the so-called "in-depth" interviews various and undulating. Occasionally the journalist is driven to take recourse to what must be called f-f-f-flirtatiously toying with the f-word until she gets the original note she wants–say, with an old-fashioned macho star who has moved up a class and apologizes profusely to the good lady for his lapse into coarse language, or with a grand managerial personality who wouldn't be caught dead saying a dirty word in the presence of a woman.

Typical of the former is Mick Channon, once an idol of English soccer fans but who turned his back on the game and went up-market into horseracing and became a successful trainer. His odd theory was that he always starts with a raw product, "a lump of horsemeat," and then with time and sensitive training the athlete in him brings out the athlete in his racehorses. It was an eccentric theory, and it came to him in a flash one fine day, when the gallop of a talented filly had been "cocked up," and he blamed the jockey:

> I blamed the feller working the front…I said, "What the **** happened there?"…He said, "It wasn't me guv'nor. It was 'er." All of a sudden I thought: "Christ!" It's something you can't explain.
> He paused. "Oh, you'd better take the effs out," he added politely.

But Sue Mott knew her man, and she in turn added realistically, perceptively, "But you cannot entirely take the effs out of Channon. They act as spontaneous punctuation, entirely unobjectionable, just like their owner."

The interview was thus studded with good sports-page stories, all spontaneously and precisely punctuated. One memorable goal in Mick's football career was recalled with all the bitterness of the old shameful occasion when the goalie had inexplicably allowed the ball simply to go through his legs; it had been a shocking defeat and everybody in the dressing room was crestfallen: "'Sorry lads,' the goalie said. 'I should've kept my legs shut.' I looked at him. 'No, you shouldn't. Your ******** mother should have,' I said." This story can play and play, and I have even heard American versions of the hapless major-league short-stop who made a similar error. Ms. Mott has her booty and allows Channon to add his hopeless, useless editorial aside: "You'd better take the effs out again, by the way." Fat chance. The columnist's style-book ration is three, and what's on third only makes it home on the last paragraph, where the aging athlete is mourning the loss of joy and carefree pleasures in yesteryear's game: "Remember the time the Scots dismantled the crossbar at Wembley. But what ******* 'arm did it do? Nobody died…', he said with a roguish grin. Was it such a bad thing?" No, presumably it wasn't, and with a vixenish punch-line, she adds, "And, I know. Take the effs out." Did she? She didn't. A quote is a quote.

Don King, the celebrated boxing impresario, gave her a harder time. He was no man for dressing-room expletives. He has mixed and mingled with all the heavyweight champions of the world, made millionaires of most of them, collected a fortune for himself, and attributed all of his success as the greatest promoter of all time–after a short jail sentence (in 1966) for manslaughter–to divine guidance (and, on occasion, intervention from above). "My protection, my salvation, my shield of righteousness is all set with the Lord." The skeptical big-time reporter doesn't believe a word of it. "It is possibly," she surmises, "the greatest negotiating tactic there is. Passing the buck to God."

No, the scandalizing, black boxing promoter, a giant of a man, maintains an unshakeable faith in God (and in himself), and writhe as she will the pretty, long-haired interviewer doesn't get a rise out of him. She blames it all on literacy, even on culture. It affects even his physique with its "vast pin-striped suit and the seen-a-ghost hair-style that rises like a rocket exhaust from his scalp." His whole style is alien to her spirit that has proved so superior to all the rookies and veterans whose lovely quotes have graced her notebook for years.* "He is inviolate, impervious and all those other long words that he

---

*   The weak responsiveness to rude or coarse language, whether calculated or casual, is usually in strong contrast to a robust ethical attitude in social affairs. Obscenities (verbal) are free and flavorsome, if taken in decently small doses. Obscenities (political) are an abomination, *viz.* war, torture, child labor, wife-battering, etc. In her angry polemic against women fighting in the box ring (*viz.*, Laili Ali, daughter of Muhammad Ali, who in October 1999 won her first match), Sue Mott's piece is four-letter free in a closely-argued column which indicts "the whole thing" as a "money-making gimmick for gawping vampires who like to suck the last drop of blood out of celebrity." She writes ("Legend and Honour," *Telegraph*, 25 October 1999):

"…What we are dealing with here is obscenity. A mild obscenity, but obscenity none the less….There will be those who depart from the spectacle with the knowledge that society sanctions the splattering of a woman's nose all over her face….As if there isn't sickeningly enough of that in the world already."

It is an old story of all-power-to-the-metaphors. Historians report that the imprecation *bloody* (after the Stuart regicide of 1649) was for long centuries far more horrific than the original blood-spilling. A passing event (tragic, singular) blemishes the color of a word; the stain remains.

learned to weald [*sic*] like clubs during his prison term, famously pouring over Shakespeare and Aristotle and Nietzsche and Schopenhauer." No four-letter words hanging around here; only (famously) an obit for "*G-d*" who passed away recently. But he is still one letter short for the purpose. Sue Mott didn't like any of it, not a bit; and over half-a-page, eight columns wide, there was not a glimpse of an asterisk and its usual camouflage. A sure way to lose readers, even in a family newspaper.[2]

16

The Mergenthaler Option

The technique of orthographic camouflage has, as I have had occasion to suggest before, the hidden invitation to participate in mouthing, silently or in a whisper *sotto voce*, various choice items in off-color language. But the level of challenge becomes intensified when the words are so disguised that both the opening and the final letter are omitted and consequently a certain shady amount of mental guesswork has to be involved. As in a rather more sophisticated crossword puzzle, the missing entry ("across" or "down") has to be decided upon without a direct or obvious clue.

It is still very elementary double-crostics, especially for those newspaper readers who know, from contemporary literature or from the boys-on-the-street-corner, the basic vocabulary. Here is Oliver Pritchett, the humorist son of that most fastidious of English stylists, V.S. Pritchett, replying in his weekly column to correspondents who had been challenging him on the question of the modern acceptability of "swearing." They keep on asking: "How much bad language is required?" The younger Pritchett goes off on a cultivated tangent which takes him from *Hamlet* to A.E. Housman's *A Shropshire Lad* (it pays to have a father who is a learned literary critic), but not before he gets a rough remark off his chest: "I am sorry to say that most of these letters miss the ******* point. I will try to explain" (*Sunday Telegraph*, 16 June 1996, Oliver Pritchett, "Leonardo da Vinci was a lad," p. 31). Whatever the point was, or the persuasiveness of the explanation, I suspect that getting the word right, seven letters, horizontal (although "vertical" might have been a shade more original), wouldn't have added a jot to the Pritchett argument. The asterisks only add décor, the expletive merely touches up the color; swearing has precious little to do with it.

Arguments dressed up in this manner often have a pretense to being rudely convincing. In a conversation with Sir Bobby Charlton about the qualities of various teams in the European football competition, a newspaper correspondent records and then submits, "'I tell you something,' he said, 'your lot are absolute ****.' It was hard to disagree." Since the reader is not quite certain what his *lot* is–or is *full of*, or disgracefully represents–it is, as I imagine, equally hard for him not to disagree.[1]

In the last two usages profane journalese, hiding behind a handful of asterisks, veers between a pithy irrelevancy and a diffuse contentiousness.

I recall an early modern version of the conventional discretion, dating at least back to the early uses of the typewriter and its standard keyboard. These were the days of the curiously jumbled linotype errors in newspapers which emerged as some cryptic city-room character known as "*Etaoin Shrdlu.*" And in the popular comics of my New York boyhood–the strips were syndicated in the *Daily News* and *Daily Mirror* and the *New York Post* and *World-Telegram*– prohibited cuss-words which some character would be permitted to utter in his "balloons" of conversation, and they were disguised properly in the house style. This was an amalgam of random keyboard symbols. I noted the other day that this is still a usable convention, for the Pinocchio-like character in the syndicated comic strip entitled "*Wizard of Id*" finds himself in difficulties in a stable and expostulates: "This @*!!!#! horse won't show me his teeth!"[2] The cartoonist at least, unlike the journalists, are offering us some variety and elusive complexity. (I suspect this does not include any of the *chic* adjectives but could merely be the "G*d-d****d" word.)

In the present-day quest for an immoral equivalent of profanity and obscenity–just in case the f-word fatigue sets in or, perhaps, a neo-puritanical backlash and cleanup threatens–there is always fall-back position well-inked during the Mergenthaler yesteryears. Like "*Etaolin Shrdlu*" the sensitive keyboard of the linotype machine almost automatically produced a hot-lead conglomerate of signs and symbols which can be usefully revived and re-enlisted in domesticated service.

My generation first encountered the emblem in the U.S. comic strips of the 1920s, some seventy or eighty years ago; and, as I say, it served to keep swear words of one kind or another out of the sight of children and other vulnerable readers. No alphabetical clues were given; and the arithmetical number of exotic signs that occurred in the arrangement were (unlike precise hyphens and asterisks) irrelevant to what was being self-censored and disguised. I imagine that at the time the comic strip characters could have gone in for "*Crikey!*" or "*Goddammit!*" or even the equally quasi-blasphemous "*Jeepers-creepers!*" Nowadays, yesterday's children are still being kept a modest distance away from the more profane expletives in the vocabulary of expostulation. But, then, these have the easier opportunity to solve the puzzle (as I have already suggested) by divining the forbidden words with a little bit of lip-reading.

English tabloids have already staked their claims to the new-old cliché by taking up the Mergenthaler option. The *Daily Mirror*, reporting on a scandalous courtroom scene in which a philandering husband was getting a divorce from his wife and in a fit of macho temper shouted at her (as the banner headline had it): "*I COULD HAVE ANYONE, YOU UGLY @!*!*" In the text the report quoted it as "you ****," so the *Mirror* had the best of both orthographic worlds.[3]

If one adds a few ampersands, question marks, @ signs, and any other available abstractions or abbreviations on the Anglo-American keyboard, then there is a rich reserve for any ribald situation. At the moment the results appear to be rather meager, as in the repetition of the exclamation point above, and the recurring sterling signs below. the *Standard*'s attempt to do a TV-review of "really horny programs" which turned out to be "much too raunchy" was, alas, unprintably difficult to unravel: "The film's literary tone: 'Give me a ££*@'...'I want to @£& percent you in the @@££." There is more of this kind of cryptic shenanigans among the film's "frigid" and "priapic" characters, until the reviewer, a Mr. Victor Lewis-Smith (whose free-speaking TV notices have just been anthologized by a London publisher), confesses that "I began losing my grip on the plot" when one hero commanded a heroine to "grasp your @@ percent percent and put it around my *@@£..." For the rest Mr. Lewis-Smith took the trouble to note "the heavy breathing and the grunting," and then proceed to climb the heights of philosophical equanimity for which his journalism has become famous:

> I mused on the way technology is always immediately used to promulgate filth, from satellite TV and the Internet, to camcorders and Polaroids....
> The moral of this review is that pornography is no good unless you buy a pornograph to play it on.

To which Outraged Reader might say, "Blankety-blank off, Vic, punning will get you percent@$&! nowhere."[4]

By comparison with what can be in store for us in the event that the cryptograms of the obsolete Mergenthaler linotype machine do actually come into fashion again, the current standard mode is simple and unproblematical. When tennis star Andre Agassi gets ejected from a Grand Slam tournament for using "foul language" he is quoted as saying,

> It was tough for me to gather any thoughts and I just sat there. Then I said "get the f*** out of my face" because I couldn't even begin to grasp the ignorance, the unprofessionalism and lack of consideration. That decision was wrong on every level.[5]

And when on the eve of a grand tour of the U.S.A. the British pop star of the *Oasis* group, Liam Gallagher, missed the plane–he walked out, quit, all the time fulminating against the "f***ing Yanks"–one newspaper was relieved to be able to report it in a full-page story in eminently straight prose. It confined the foul language of other *Oasis* group-members (especially brother Noel Gallagher) to a separate, slim box offering "exact transcript" excerpts. It used, by my count, some twenty-two asterisks shared out to a half-dozen f- and s-words. Not an ampersand or exclamation point, a dollar sign or an exclamation point or even a hyphen in sight. Still, as I suspect, the Mergenthaler option looms.[6]

I suspect that the news has not quite gotten around about the agility of "asterisks," and how nimble they are for such mental-sexual calisthenics. In some quarters there appears to be a culture lag, and the fault is surely not in the stars. For example, in the unworldly atmosphere of the editorial chambers of the *Osservatore Romano*, published by the Catholic Church in Vatican City. I am instructed that three asterisks at the bottom of the column means that the article above is from the office of the Vatican's secretary of state, and–probably–enjoys direct Papal approval. In the unlikely event that the asterisks might be misunderstood, given the present Pope's deep moral interest in controversial sexual issues, Vatican journalists can always have recourse to other, less ambivalent ways of suggesting sound theology. Latin would do.[7]

17

A Matter of Illegitimacy

On those occasions when a prominent public figure–say, a high elected official, or a celebrated sportsman–slips into rude speech, the uncensored obscenity becomes fashionable for a season and enjoys the popular repetitive-ness that "*expletive deleted*" had in the immediate aftermath of Richard Nixon's "Watergate" scandal. Two examples:

A rugby captain lost his temper with the game's commissioners who, in their multitude, had been governing the sport badly–he called them "57 old farts." Thereafter the word was "*in.*" Its popularity became slightly embarrass-ing when Will Carling, the rugby star in question, turned out to be a current lover of the Princess of Wales whose language problems were of a different order.

Again, when in the spring of 1995, the British prime minister referred, in a momentary loss of his vaunted cool, to his opponents in the Tory party and in fact in his own Cabinet as "*bastards,*" the word replaced in every British newspaper–and even in polite London society–the usual circumlocutions for scheming or otherwise untrustworthy colleagues. One "bastard," the Minister for Wales, John Redwood (who mounted an unsuccessful campaign to dis-place the Tory chief, John Major), was removed in a Cabinet reshuffle; but was his young successor William Hague any more reliable? The rumors were flying fast. One Major loyalist defended the new man by referring to his friendship with Sir Leon Brittan, the British commissioner for Europe, explaining "and Sir Leon would never keep up with a bastard." The appellation had lost for a day its cussedness, and had become a political category, a colorful place in the parliamentary spectrum.

"Bastardy" was less a matter of illegitimacy, for all had a right to be as right wing as their convictions or ambitions took them. Surely no factions in a functioning democracy were less or more "natural" than any of the others. The youthful Hague had mixed with some of the prime minister's enemies, and his promotion from the lowly status of a back-bench M.P. to a Cabinet post came as something of a surprise; or was it? The *Standard*'s political pundit argued:

"Far from being a sop for the bastards, his promotion comes as a fresh blow to the already battered morale of the Tory Right" (the *Standard*, 12 July 1995). Pundits became smitten with the *B*-word; bastardy had become legitimized. "Old farts" were still under a shadow.

It was only in the vaunted spirit of English fairness for the leader of the British Labour Party to have his turn with a truculent expletive. Tony Blair had been having a difficult time of it with some Scottish journalists on a recent political tour, and in an irritated outburst blurted out, "Who are these unreconstructed wankers?" The *Times*' correspondent in Edinburgh, in a coy aside, wrote in his account of the incident ("Mind Your Language, Mr. Blair," 12 December 1996):

> When John Major uttered his famous eight-letter expletive to describe the right-wingers in his Cabinet, his stock in the country rose enormously. "Bastards" has a satisfactory ring to it. People knew what he meant and probably agreed with him. It certainly showed that he was human after all. Whether "wankers" will do the same for Tony Blair is more doubtful: indeed I'm not certain whether the Editor of the *Times* will permit its use in these columns at all. It's not really a *nice* word, is it? It has a sneering quality more suitable on the football terraces than on the lips of an Opposition leader.

So far from objecting to publishing a rather unfamiliar and even obscure bit of obscenity the Editor must have welcomed an opportunity to help fulfill his ration of profanity for the day with the benefit of full orthographic candor. "To be honest," as the author (Magnus Linklater) wrote me in a personal letter, "I didn't think that the Editor of the *Times* would shrink from using the *W*—word, since many worse things have appeared in his columns."[1] Better things have also appeared, and there was indeed a literary fall-back position in that the standard dictionaries of slang offer additional meanings as utterly respectable as "an objectionable person...contemptible, incompetent, pretentious, or ostentatious" whose habit of *wanking on* refers to his "complaining or whingeing." Not at all an unusual perception of hostile journalists among irritable politicians in a free-talking democracy. Still, let's face it, it was a Philip Roth/*Portnoy* kind of word and its primary definition (as the *Oxford Dictionary of Modern Slang* records it) is "*l.* A (male) masturbator."* If the rude expletive does have a sneering quality "more suitable on the football terraces," the leader of the Labour Party can console himself with the knowledge that there's where the votes are, and the latest score from the opinion polls had shown him to be some twenty points ahead.

When a highly moral institution like the *Guardian*–that successor paper to the old revered *Manchester Guardian*–searches its soul on the subject of publishing obscenities, and finds it relatively spotless, it assumes the editorial

---

*   *Oxford Dictionary of Modern Slang*, p. 280. Jonathon Green, *Slang Down the Ages*, pp. 119, 134.

right to preach unto the others. It recently found an urgent sermon to be read to popular journalism when one of the sleaziest of the British tabloids, the *Daily Star*, published a headline which read–

YOU'VE GOT SOME RIGHT W*****S OUT THERE

Properly transliterated and interpreted in depth this could bode ill for a mass newspaper culture which is arguably slipping out of touch with its millions of readers. As a *Guardian* commentator wrote:

> Now there are two reasonable approaches a newspaper can adopt to this word: either to print it, on the grounds that it is part of everyday speech; or to avoid it, on the grounds that its readers will find it offensive. The *Star*, bafflingly, opts to get the worst of both possible worlds, by printing it prominently for no good reason, but still censoring it.

Thus commanding the high ground of profane rectitude the *Guardian*'s columnist announced that "the time has come for the chattering classes to stop banging on about the evils of the tabloids, and to start feeling sorry about them." The *Guardian* presumably gets the best of both possible words: censoring nothing, and publishing all offensive words for the very good reason that they are part of our everyday speech and that their straight-shooting readers have a right to know and have all things under the sun spelled out for them. The tabloids don't even show any of the courage of the convictions they used to have. They always used to be able (and this was the strength of "the popular press") to address readers simply and directly.[2]

18

The Guard that Failed

One American reviewer of my first volume on *Newspaper Culture* suggested that I "reach more deeply into the tangled chicken-egg relationship between manners and public discourse"; and he voiced his suspicion that "there is more to it than the personality-led cause-and-effect." More, that is to say, to the emergence of obscenity as a ubiquitous pidgin in conventional communication. More to it than, presumably, the literary obsessions of a powerful novelist (D.H. Lawrence) or the sex-ridden vaudeville of an imaginative man of the theater (Kenneth Tynan).

Doubtless. In the first place, the English tongue has been graced by dozens of "personalities" who, from a variety of motives both high and low, set out to liberate the language from its enslavement to a tradition of euphemism and taboo. All taken together they did "make history" and in the only way that history can be made–by individuals, by "personalities" driven to make their mark. But, secondly, all the individual impulses had to express themselves within (as even Marx never tired of insisting) a framework of larger social and cultural forces which, at once, facilitated their impact and were, in turn, shaped by their vitality and excess. Each of their lives–writers and poets, journalists and other professional phrase-makers–intertwined and "tangled" the unique elements of their own personal biography with the cultural opportunities which the larger society offered as a provocation and challenge.[1]

I do not mean to impinge on problems so difficult as the philosophy of history and its possible explanations of the "deeper causes." But surely the linguistic qualities of our newspaper culture have something to do, in the beginning, with small journalistic coinages (often only irresponsible wordplay); and–sometimes before the end–also with overarching quasi-intellectual attitudes about "the whole world" (what-it-all-means, and where-it's-all-going). Thus, D.H. Lawrence was singular in his devotion to the f-word as a verbal liberator in a faithless, frustrated world from whose neuroses not he nor even Dr. Freud or Professor Jung could promise a life-saving escape. As for Kenneth Tynan, he was a stage-struck young man "who would be king," and in the theatricalities of his life and career left a notable, if ephemeral, mark. Both were lone twentieth-century creatures, left to their own devices. But even "outsiders," as I say, were sustained and propelled by oceanic forces of a new, a modern mass culture. A small English-language Penguin paperback, pocketed by millions, could (and did) reach half the reading world. The lights of Broadway put a pun on "Calcutta" onto the stage of historic happenings and changed the legitimate frontiers of popular entertainment forever.

The documentation of this radical phenomenon in our contemporary culture can, as is my wont, be illustrated by cohering fragments of a choice newspaper. For the *Guardian* has been in the enlightened vanguard of the four-letter movement; and, as it happens, the appropriate evidence is in three cuttings on a single day in April of the year 2001.

The center field of our journalistic rationalization is filled by a conventional middlebrow lament about how the widespread usage of "poor English" simply murders clear-thinking; and prominent among the culprits are academics, politicians and journalists themselves. Most of it we have heard before, but the dirge is largely true, even if unoriginal. The *Guardian*'s contributor is a Labour member of Parliament and an editor of an estimable scholarly periodical, the *Political Quarterly*, and he seems to have been freshly shocked by the obscurantism of English prose as employed in the social sciences. Tony Wright gives an example (and he could have found worse): "It is possible to offer a discussion of the 'Pacific Asian model' in terms which gesture to an ideal-typical political-economic configuration, related to social-institutional structures, and associated cultural forms." The dismay at academics who write inscrutably "more and more about less and less" is widely shared, as is the despair that a "mutilated language" cuts scholarship off from the public arena. The general situation is only exacerbated by a fast-talking political class whose "verbless vacuities" constitute a robotic repetition of words and phrases that have long lost any connection with cogent meanings. M.P. Wright is so distraught as almost to lose his way by invoking the "progressive" spirit of George Orwell and, before him, the Julien Benda of *trahison des clercs*. He trumpets his outraged intellectual disdain of what he refers to as "the stale tea leaves that block up the drain, preventing any fresh thoughts or arguments getting through." The sub-editors of the *Guardian*, reading Tony's copy, might well have asked what those thoughts and arguments were doing in the drain anyway? (Perhaps they weren't so fresh after all....)

No such indictment can be complete without a stab at the latest phenomenon of "*spin*" as it covers up the rawness of old manipulative propaganda techniques. Our media class, in becoming the accomplice of the political class, serves only to help close down "serious political argument" (of which nobody, as I write, has yet given a sign). Still, the disaster–as I trust we know (from my own previous pages)–is persuasive enough. "News is routinely spun, by journalists as much as by politicians (and often in collusion). Stories are no longer expected to be true, even by those who write them. Speculation and suggestion is all. What matters is what sells." Too true; and one tries to suppress the suspicion that it was such spin that even managed to sell this particular article. But Tony Wright candidly admits that he has been engaged in biting the hands "that have kept me moderately well fed for most of my life." The world may be going to the dogs, but our kennels are still well stocked.

No matter. The middle-field case against the Establishment–academic abdication, political suffocation, and journalistic collaboration–has been officially made to rationalize the *Guardian*'s moral stance, also its intellectual position, and finally its linguistic stylebook prescriptions. Still, something more–another one of those arguments, stuck in a blocked drain–is needed before we can instigate the free uninterrupted flow of progressive language. Ideology, not to mention a utopian vision, requires quasi-metaphysical heights, and the onward drive of *Guardian*-style four-letterization needs to have a more high-brow super-structure, rising into a more rarified atmosphere.

On the page previous (*Guardian*, 6 April 2001, p. 7), Ms. Polly Toynbee does just this, true to the radical tradition of the old Mancunian liberalism and, indeed, of her grandfather, Arnold Toynbee, of taking long views and hinting at eternal verities. Her portentous doom-laden judgement of the contemporary crisis is an extra-large attitude worthy of an Oswald Spengler or any other German purveyor of an overarching *Weltanschauung*:

> *WHIMPERING NATION*
> *We see every mishap as a portent of doom.*
> *The message we are sending out is that we are*
> *as sick as our cows.*

Taking the temperature of a whole society or civilization is the regular editorial task of a newspaper culture that aspires to capture minds and hearts. In the case of Britain it usually comes up with a diagnosis of a country on the verge of a nervous breakdown: its stiff upper lip is wobbling, and hysteria is in the air. The symptoms are not unexpected. A national nervous reflex–or an involuntary panic spasm–that greets every event…disastrous diseases on the farms; carnage on the rails as locomotives smash each other up; traffic paralysis as airports strike and motorway bridges collapse; a new wave of tuberculosis stalking the schoolhouse corridors; and now half of Beachy Head has fallen into the sea; and the like. "Any minor setback sets off a *crise de nerfs*, a fit of the vapors turning any mishap into a crisis"–and turning any crisis back into a national neurosis in which "twitchy sensation" takes over from reason.

Where no reason is, harsh vituperative words can take over. The *Guardian*'s e-mail includes one letter catchlined "*Eat shit, euro-scum*"–but why is this classified as "*unprintable*" when it is not only clinically necessary to the diagnosis as well as…being already, obviously, in print? In any case, there are "cultural" differences in the vocabulary of a political depression, in the language of the free fall into melancholia, in the expression of paroxysms of panic. The transatlantic critique, as it reaches Polly Toynbee, is remarkable for its unproblematic printability. The *Guardian* would, rest assured, have been prepared to go–and rather often enough actually does–with more extreme and profane formulations of *Weltschmerz*. Curious, how these Americans are constrained, for once, to keep it clean:

"Lady, you are a moron…
"Your whole infrastructure is decaying around you. Your crime is higher than ours. Your football hooligans are the recognized gold standard, the most loutish yobs this side of the Taliban. The British have lost their collective wits. Your whole country ground to a halt because a bubble-headed ditz of a princess committed involuntary suicide in a careening automobile with a man who was not her husband. Your tree and bunny huggers are out of control and Luddism is running riot. Until foot and mouth your national priority seemed to be banning of fox hunting….You get the idea?"

The idea to be gotten becomes at this point basically unacceptable, for it is beginning to run counter to the party-political commitment of the newspaper's New Labour enthusiasm. Only a few years ago–a brief moment in the long-term development of societies–it would have been a thoroughly accurate indictment of the System that was condemning itself to decline and (hopefully) fall. Now in the fourth year of Prime Minister Tony Blair's New Labour régime, it cannot, must not, should not be true. The people are now in power. We should be defensists, not defeatists. The current crisis is not one of our making, but of *theirs*, the old Tories, the *ancien régime*.

It is a familiar dilemma when one wants desperately to hail a new society and see off, at long last, an old, decrepit, and hateful one. The difficulties of the present are taken to be only the heritage of the past; they are transitional and not endemic; Five-Year Plans always have glitches in the first four. In the Marxian framework our coming to power is always darkly overshadowed by the sickly bourgeois inheritance of "late capitalism"–the work of reform, not to mention revolution, is unexpectedly more complex than one thought. Why, then, when things are essentially becoming so good, are we feeling so bad? For Ms. Toynbee, "this has been the most golden economic moment in living memory….At last, serious money is there on the table for health, education, and transport." And yet, and yet–whence all the gloom and doom? How could a new dawn be possibly confounded with an old twilight? Well, weathermen (and -women) can't be implicitly trusted, especially when metereology tends to speak in social and political metaphorics. Or indeed in other bromidic or platitudinous formulas. As Ms. Toynbee asks, on the verge of hesitation and even confusion:

this is a fertile time to believe superstitiously that nothing makes any difference, nothing works. Things fall apart….
But does the center hold?"

When journalism arrives at this Yeatsian cliché for the thousandth time, there is no longer any room for sober analysis; the vague and diffuse fancies of ideology have become all. Surely sinister forces are at work. The enemy is nefarious. As Ms. Toynbee puts it,

> The Tory party may be in unelectable decay, but in its death throes its inordinately powerful press still has the capacity to poison the national air. If it can't win, it can still spoil, sour and frighten. By any objective measure, things are getting better, with more money in almost every pocket, including benefits and pensions. This has been the most golden moment…. [etc. etc.]

Is this a viable way "to fill a political void that has turned us into a nation of hysterics"? Could be. (I write in May 2001, in the midst of the recent British electoral campaign.) What will hold? Who will fall apart?

I have touched upon two standard modes in the language of journalism, as reflected in one day's edition of the *Guardian*. A middlebrow approach in one feature story debunks the culture of communication as readers and writers wallow in meaninglessness. Then followed a highbrow exercise which added the images of reform and counter-revolution as old societies teeter on the verge of catastrophe and hysteria. All good things come in three's, and there is just room for the *Guardian*'s lowbrow attempt to give voice on this frivolous Friday to "Comment & Analysis" of an especially meaningful sort.

In Matthew Norman's *Diary* the stabbing insights of the day range from gossip and innuendo to arch-irony and near-libel. In these days the antics of the Royal Family have been providing easy targets, especially the japes of the younger members; and the youngest son of Queen Elizabeth II appears to be, at the moment, the most vulnerable of all. If Lords will–soon–no longer be called Lords (or Earls, or Barons), what will we be calling Princes? Well, the *Guardian* made one of its famous errors by referring to Prince Edward as a Count, mistakenly; and its Diarist hastened to add his own sense of distress to the correction. As M. Norman writes, "It's all well and good being marauding republicans, but we must never be sloppy about titles. We also wish to make it clear that this reference to Edward as a 'count' was not a cunning taster for a new [form of] cartoon, Added Vowels." We know the old form in which by simply adding a dash, or a dot, or an asterisk you can just say anything about anybody. We have registered as many as we could comfortably endure under the already quoted s-, p- , and c-words.

Here is a new twist. Add a vowel, and then when you get around to substracting it, *hey presto*! the scathing truth is out…wild, abusive, obscene, revolutionary. It's almost a genuine life-style! A full monty hit from a marauding republican! (For the enemy is a c(o)unt.) Get it? A bull's-eye strike where more ambitious attempts to subvert the monarchy–as well as to protect and advance the ideas and ideals of the *avant-garde*–were seen to have faltered. Who is there to say, then, that the guard had failed? Adding and subtracting a vowel is worth a boulevard full of barricades, built to batter down rickety, outdated institutions. Our cause will be finally saved if we ever find a way of doing something constructive with…added consonants. It will come.[2]

Each of these points of departure has necessarily played a role in the four-letterization process which has been transforming our newspaper culture.

1. On the highbrow level there is the drive, well-documented in all histories of revolutionary movements, to hurl new words–and sometimes even the beguiling prospect of new, more beneficent languages into the struggle to change things "fundamentally." In the European seventeenth- and eighteenth-century the English Diggers and Levellers and then the French Jacobins flaunted previously unspeakable phrases about everybody's equality and a pursuit of happiness for all. In the late twentieth century this became for rowdier revolutionary spirits "F- the System!" and "Burn Baby Burn!"…and its sequel: "Fry every last M—f— of 'em!" in order to fulfill long-repressed hopes and lusts. Many such spokesmen (like Sartre) led sects in an effort to purge the old, reactionary language and try to replace it with something purified and profound. This would excuse or rationalize a troublesome period of obscenities serving as a felicitous transition. If Schiller's *Sturm und Drang* revolt demanded a high-falutin' diction on behalf of noble and romantic ideals, the '68ers of the Student Revolt sensed that real radical change needed the shock therapy of lewd expletives. The coarse curses would signal the rough end of the old world.

It is an open question whether the *Guardian* would be content to break–and be seen to be breaking–all conceivable taboos in the profane liberation of everyday speech, that is, would they be prepared to move from Ideology to Utopia? All words are–must be, should be–free and unfettered; but is slouching toward obscenity the chief end of man? Who among even this distinguished newspaper's most faithful readers could willingly accept the task of wading through the thousands of f-, s-, c- and p-words–possibly for the rest of the century (at this moment still ninety-nine years)–if a few wizened old subeditors were not still around to edit an acceptable and tolerable daily ration of profanities?

2. The middlebrow point of departure leads forward into specific complaints and then on to certain predictable reforms; and it is, thus, a quasi-conservative and ameliorative force which explodes in anger at the Academy and even at the whole Establishment. But, at bottom, it only wants to make things "better" and "cleaner." Expletives have, when you stop to think about it, only a limited purpose and serviceability. What's the point of fulminating "*Damn the Political Quarterly!*"? Still, for the time being, "Down with the rest of blue-pencil censorship! Screw the effete pack of namby-pamby editors and publishers! They're all full of s**t!"

3. On the lowbrow level, uncomplicated by these kind of cultural considerations which inevitably trouble the radical reformers who feel called upon to

make the word live, to make the message come alive for the benefit of weeping humanity. In this general and diffuse spirit of swear-word protest the process of four-letterization gets its strongest support, indeed its mass base…and the mindless flow of obscenities at home and abroad surge into the language as she is spoke and writ. Even clever-by-half intellectuals can find a comfortable place here, putting in and taking away vowels and consonants like scrabble pieces, playing with asterisks and hyphens in a tense and sometimes tantalizing game of semantic dominoes. The *Guardian* Diarists, like Matthew Norman, busy themselves by devising ways of outing obscenities without the cover-up of fig-leaves, by adding and subtracting vowels–and, sometimes in a burst of inspiration, consonants–in order to emerge with a pimply-faced schoolboy triumphalism, flashing…you-know-what.

I offer this old "triad" of high-, middle-, and lowbrow inclinations as an intellectual context for the *Guardian*'s remarkable surge into first-place among the world's mainstream newspapers (at least in the usages of obscenity) for two reasons.

First, the *Guardian* editors over the years that they have been assaulting all available totems and taboos seem to have been emotionally hesitant and/or morally reluctant to rise to the occasion of their unique avant-garde status. As one of the younger generation of editors on the paper put it, "I think it's a privilege to work on a paper which has the liberal values and readership to permit publication of the strongest of swear words, a privilege that we should guard by not abusing it…using swearwords only when absolutely necessary."

Secondly, to set them off from their other mainstream colleagues (say, on the *Daily Telegraph* and the *Times* in London or the *Washington Post*) who have shared the built-in hesitancies on the subject of swear-words–not only with respect to the total theory of profanity going proudly public but also the aversion in practice to spell things out to the last dot.

Here is a recent story in the *Telegraph* (one which, I surmise, the *Guardian* in its style-book virtue would have found shaming and disgraceful to have published). It was about a beautiful model now stalking the catwalks of *haute couture* as a "paragon of icy glamor." Evidently Ms. Helena Christiansen was remiss at observing the pieties of genteel–and "Christian"–language. The reporter relished everything about the story, from the "ironies" of her name to the news that she was getting some emotions "off her chest" (photograph of plunging neckline, attached) to the additional headlined hints that she was finally getting around to "blowing her top." In any case, it was "refreshing to learn that she swears like a navvy with a stubbed toe."[3]

Titillation loves company. It was the competitive *Sunday Times* that had first tried to thaw the icy side of this hot number. She was, to begin with, only going in for a routine exercise of public relations on behalf of wild life and animal conservation (in this case, the hard-pressed orangutans). The *Sunday Times* story, as printed, was mildly skeptical. Ms. Christiansen was furious. Her environmental agenda was not to be patronized. It was cheap (and worse) to make jokes about her breasts, or how money-making she was, or that her husband's name was Norman. She promptly wrote a letter to the editor which expressed her outrage. The *Sunday Times* judged it (or so the original author of the offending article said) unfit to print. As the *Telegraph* revealed, in a speedy burst of investigative journalism,

> Before the letter appeared, I'm told [Peterborough reporting on the Op-Ed page], something like eight instances of the F-word, four of the T-word, and one of the B-word had to be removed.…'I saw the original, and it *was* a little bit fruity in the hallowed pages of the *Sunday Times*.'"

Go figure the names of the sinful fruits, without confounding apples and oranges. Happier are the gardeners over at the *Guardian*'s patch where no hallow obtains.

"In the past year [1998]," wrote the *Guardian*'s Ombudsman (locally called the Readers' Editor), "the *Guardian* has used more four-letter words than any other 'quality' newspaper on earth." Whether this is confirmed by a final entry in the *Guinness Book of Records* deponent knoweth not; but it is unlikely that other quality newspapers somewhere on the same planet would be rushing to challenge its entitlement to the golden expletive. The *Guardian*'s ombudsman, Ian Mayes by name, even if he doesn't seem to be very enthused about the high-cultural quality of the achievement, is a truthful and independent fellow; as he wrote in a piece which the *Guardian* was proud to reprint in its book of confessions:

> Not to beat about the bush, there have been more than 400 pieces in the Guardian since October 10 last year in which the words fuck or fucking appeared at least once (even more, no doubt, in the couple of days since I wrote this)–and that is eliminating any references to the play, Shopping and Fucking. In the same period there were 28 references to cunt in the Guardian. Our nearest rival was the Independent, almost 100 items behind us in its use of fuck or fucking and offering only nine pieces in which the word cunt occurred (the Times and the Telegraph, by comparison, are expletive-free zones).[4]

At least one *Guardian* reader's objection is given a fair play. His point about gross language, even when slightly camouflaged by asterisks, was well made: "Every reader merely substitutes the correct letters and the offensiveness of the sentence remains intact. It seems coy to suppose otherwise and insert the asterisks." The editorial lesson the paper and its special advisor drew from this conflict was unexpected, and must have surprised readers who were accusing the paper for not recognizing its partial responsibility for coarsening the printed language. The *Guardian* proceeded forthwith to remove, not the usage of the gross vulgarities but…the asterisks which had ineffectively disguised them. Ian Mayes recommended that "probably" they should be abandoned altogether. Impressed by this confession of quasi-certainty the editor, thereupon, wrote in the official style book of rules and recommendations: "Finally, never use asterisks, which are just a copout." The editor here is relentlessly correct: *cop-out* without a hyphen, please. Certain things are unforgiveable.[5]

There is, thus, in the language of journalism something which can be called the mathematics of profanity; and it was indeed a breakthrough of almost Euclidean proportions. Previously one used, and subsequently referred to (angrily for many, prideful for the few), a single obscenity no matter how obsessive the repetitiveness. As we have seen, the *Guardian* in England was in the 1990s the first to tabulate anuual usages of the f-word and the reckoning was broadened liberally to include related expletives. Nowadays, a certain *ennui* has begun to infuse the reporting of what off-color words were said by whom and to whom (and how often). Then the tired news items of yesterday became the still-saucy stories of what is still in store for the viewer or reader over a long glorious weekend of media fare. Like in the fanciful René Clair film, it happened tomorrow. This adds an extra interest to the pornographic play stations, and one can check whether the prediction or prognosis has been correct or not. In the week before Christmas in the year of Our Lord 2002 a columnist in the *Sunday Times* ventured to suggest, running his calculator in heated overtime with the preview tapes, that "we can expect the F-word nearly 200 times and more that 40 even cruder words on Channel 4 on Christmas Day." A Swiftian letter to the editor, dripping with irony and just in time to help revise the Channel's salacious strategy, made a few ingenious offerings–provided the TV programmers observed the 9 P.M. watershed (i.e., "not in front of the children"): "Why do none of the major broadcasters use the words in their program trailers; or advertisers in the commercials or the government in promotional material?" The watchword could be: "After all, we're all obscene now...." And so: "How about the BBC's 'Have I Got News for You'–it's really f****** funny; the Home Office with 'Don't Drink and Drive–you know it makes f****** sense; or Orange with 'The Future's f****** brighter.'"[6] Actually, the speculation about the once and future obscenities was quite supererogatory. The promised profanities were not new and up-to-the-minute, but old, familiar and actually pre-programmed. Accordingly, one reviewer noted the TV Channels' well-known proclivity for "alternative" holiday fare, and gave his readers a fair summary of what the viewers may have given a miss. Almost all alert London newspapers–once known as the Fleet Street press, from "the Street of Shame" which then housed their midtown editorial offices–seized upon the cost-free opportunity to offer their readers a belated Christmas treat; but I intended to leave the gory details buried in a backnote, but they do belong here.

The reviewer was Simon Hoggart, in the *Spectator*, 28 December 2002, pp. 44-45. The program was entitled *Offensive*, as if it were a warning to the squeamish, and Hoggart wrote:

Channel 4 like an alternative Christmas, and this year they gave us *Offensive*....This celebrated the records Peter Cook and Dudley Moore made in their personae as a pair of foul-mouthed losers. The Yuletide welkin rang to cries of "So ths f***ing c*** comes up to me and says, 'You f***ing c***!' 'Who you calling a f***ing c***?'..." and so on. Various comedians were shown reduced to fits of insane laughter by these drolleries.

In the unexceptionable interests of complete journalistic documentation Hoggart went on–and we, in his trail–to report that the commentary "in a hushed and reverential voice" tried to persuade you that "you are in the presence of the defining comic geniuses of the age." The voice then proceeded to introduce yet another comic turn which deserved to be remembered:

"The worst job I ever had was retrieving lobsters from Jayne Mansfield's bum"–accompanied by shots of Jayne Mansfield, followed by a tankful of lobsters, a demented piece of literal-minded editing–you might find this, if I may say so without sounding prudish and repressed, even funnier than the 'so this f***ing c***' routine.

Our four-letterized culture may have its offensive moments but it never stints at offering us a real democratic choice. Like Henry Ford in Dearborn, Michigan, you can have any color you want, so long as it's blue.

19

The Desperate Search for "the Good Bits"

As I have suggested, one of the most compelling factors in the changing language to be found in our newspaper culture is the professional competition with the dominant and more successful TV media which specialize in fast, sharp, moving images and quick "sound bites" to match. In addition, there are the pressures to be "in" and "with it," and these come fresh every season from an artistic avant-garde addicted to revelling in adventures on the periphery of taste and taboo, of obscurity and pornography, of deviance and eccentricity.

In motion pictures (and frequently on theatrical stages and in museums) you can *see* it; in newspapers and magazines you can only read about it, albeit with the help of an occasionally daring illustration. The basic free-for-all involves conflicts of passion and outrage, of ambition and greed (for it also deals with millions of investors' money); the climax may well be, as the pessimistic media-sociologists predict, the death of the written word, the end of books, the coming of a total illiteracy. I suspect we will have time enough to wait and see. There are signs that exciting images can produce optical fatigue. There are indications that prose can do "the dirty job" better and more lastingly than pictures. There may be a surprising turning point, possibly even (after the late Thomas Kuhn) a paradigmatic change of climate.

But for now, journalism tends increasingly to emulate what is happening in the world of soap operas, news flashes, kitchen sink melodramas, blue movies, sex shop specialties, locker room kiss sessions, video nasties, full-frontal nudie mags, and assorted other sensations which may, in their own good time, demand from the constant reader a somewhat longer attention-span than the techniques of instant titillation.

Readers of a newspaper have come to know how writers have to talk (quite apart from the books they publish which may go forever unopened). Here is an interview with an American playwright, David Beaird, in a British newspaper:

> I set myself to write the best play I could and to discover my true voice. Most of me is a producer-director-con artist who talks too much and clowns around. The real me is

the guy who sits there suffering from growing up an alcoholic child, sexually abused. When I write at my best, it's like I'm orgasming or vomiting. (The *Standard*, 14 July 1994)

Only a few readers will want this cleaned up: surely not the post-coital melancholy, not the emetic inspiration.

Nor would more than a few ask for any more in this illustrated scoop of a flagrant case of censorship. The *Sun* in London compared the few numbers of the magazine *Elle* which had featured a beautiful dark-skinned model sunning herself.

A U.S. magazine was branded prudish yesterday for covering up model Naomi Campbell's boobs with a fake bikini. Identical shots of the 23-year-old British beauty relaxing on a sun-lounger appeared in the European and American editions of top fashion glossy *Elle*.

But while the issue on sale here showed Naomi naked (*top picture*), the U.S. photo included a skimpy bikini painted on to hide the catwalk's nipples (*above*). (The *Sun*, 29 July 1994)

A *Sun* editor, true to Jeffersonian ideals of a free press, remarked that "This is one of the strangest censorship jobs I've seen." And what his *Sun* readers got to see (*top picture* and *above*) were the two "super-revealing" blown-up photographs, taking up in colour most of the page, with a snippety G-string of an explanatory story below.

No matter what information gets shaken up in the editorial offices of our newspapers, more often than not it comes out with the same kaleidoscopic scatter; only the angles and the colouring are a shade different. In a long biographical story on the actor Marlon Brando we can learn, by-the-by, that he was married three times; was bisexual; named his son Christian (not after the famous role of Fletcher Christian that he had played in *Mutiny on the Bounty* but after his French homosexual lover Christian Marquand); and that, incidentally, on the set of the film version of *From Here to Eternity* Montgomery Clift "had fallen in love" with Brando, and then with Frank Sinatra, "unrequited of course" (*Daily Mail*, 29 July 1994).

Film news is sex news, and literature is not far behind. When it was finally discovered who really wrote that "shocking best-seller," Pauline Reage's *The Story of O* (Paris, 1954)–it was not, as long rumored, André Malraux or Raymond Queaneau, but the Légion d'Honneur's Madame Dominique Aury–this bit of a fact about a long-since forgotten novel served usefully, stirred a little and shaken well, as a sensational cocktail for a London newspaper which suspected all along the pornographic truth about those French novels. The four-column headline was:

THEY SAID NO WOMAN COULD EVER HAVE WRITTEN
A BOOK AS SHOCKINGLY EROTIC AS THIS.

THEY'VE BEEN PROVED WRONG.
(*Daily Mail*, 29 July 1994)

Two small photographs graced the story: a demure portrait of Madame Aury; and a snapshot of the somewhat lustful Gallic face of Jean Paulhan, the famous Paris critic. He had written the rapturous foreword, for he was Madame Aury's lover to whom–as he insisted–she had to read the good bits while in bed.

If any gifted journalist is ever tempted to indulge in any of this–and there are the varieties of soft porn, hard porn, or (as in most of the above) corn porn– let him answer the call by doing an honest day's work and accepting the higher challenge. Felix Salten (of *Bambi* fame) did it by writing that classic of pornography, "*Josephine Mutzenbacher*" (in 1910). Vladimir Nabokov did it by fantasizing a novel about a nymphet called *Lolita*. Edward Fuchs dealt with his temptations by compiling erotica into exhaustive many-volumed sexual encyclopaedias.

Dirt should not be wasted on newspapers; pornography is too valuable to be left to mere journalism. As for the sex simulators in Hollywood–and in TV-film studios the world over which have "morning setting-up exercises" for nude lovers on their mattresses–the real thing is just too good to need imitation.

Sporting Language

The outcry against certain words of rudeness or obscenity are subject to what can be called unequal laws of commotion, and accordingly vary from case to case. The worst verbal offense in British sport, for example, is generally termed as "bringing the sport into disrepute." Expletives even under the breath brought fines on the head of John McEnroe at Wimbledon, and Wembley referees have been known to lip-read the bad language of angry soccer players and to send the villains off. What they say in their expostulations is not usually re-ported in the press, for fear of compounding the offense and bringing journalism as well into disrepute. Thus, bad language on the playing field remains unexplored–although it is child's play to imagine what many, if not all, of the incriminating phrases might have been. This goes, to be sure, only for the hard words. The soft words also cause a commotion but are printable, even in family newspapers.

The reluctance to publish may, in a few cases, reflect a personal ethical sensitivity to the broadcasting for an even larger audience the illiberal grunts of the hooligan mob in the grandstands. The dilemma deepens–what details can be printed? How explicit should one get?–when the athletes themselves are involved. In the Football Championships (held in England in June 1996) the rivalries among even the European participants induced language on the playing fields which the newspaper reports would have one believe were not unlike those in uncivilized battlefield hostilities.

How far indeed can comparison go between war and athletics? It is here in this interface where one remarks, while viewing the splendors and miseries of journalism in the era of globalized wars and commercialized athletics, that the line is thin.

There may be some who still hold sporting activities to be a moral substitute for militarism; but there are as many (or as few) who think that sports writers, with their flair for victory and defeat, their penchant for fame, glory, and the bitter dregs of loss and despair, can succeed where war correspondents and combat reporters usually fall short. To be sure, we are not judging a classic account of a baseball thriller (even when penned by the likes of a Bernard Malamud) with the standards of a Leo Tolstoy. But even some moral elements–although far from the lofty religiosity of a pious pacifism–are coming more and more into it, as fun and games degenerate into hooliganism and stadia of mass violence.

Here is one journalist's journey into what he calls "a vortex of savage soccer hooliganism" and, as a matter of fact, to a sporting scene which the *Washington Post* headlines as a "war zone" and even "Vietnam" (to which subject the *Post* has a special relationship). Its man in San Salvador, curious about the riotous tensions which featured in a recent international match between the United States team and El Salvador, noted that the local fans and their Cuscatlan Stadium have been collectively dubbed *"Vietnam"*–"a folklorish moniker that reflects their battlefield brand of rooting." *

Neither he nor the reader need to be held up by description of the twelve-year civil war which ended in the UN peace accords of 1992, nor with "the culture of violence and lawlessness" which still persists in the country (Serge F. Kovalevski, "Soccer's 'Vietnam'...Fans Create a War Zone," *Washington Post/IHT*, 14 October 1997, p. 20). The game is enough, the game is all–Napoleonic and Caesaresque in its triumphalism, Bonapartist and Carthaginian in its defeatism. As the *Post*'s dispatch records:

> There has been the sacrificial throwing of animals, mostly chickens, cats and iguanas, both dead and alive. There are the occasional showers of urine, fecal matter and pica-pica, a plant dust that causes itching and irritation of the skin.
> Goals are sometimes celebrated with gunshots. Firecrackers, rocks and other projectiles routinely erupt. A referee was left staggering after he was belted in the head with a bottle at the end of a recent World Cup qualifying match.
> Welcome to "Vietnam."

---

*   Evidently the closer to the real Vietnam the more realistic it becomes. An Associated Press dispatch from Jakarta in this same month (October 1997) reported:
"Police with gas masks and automatic weapons were needed to restore order as 130,000 fans lit fires in the stadium and forced the soccer final at the Southeast Asia Games to be halted at halftime....State-owned television, which was broadcasting the game live, changed to other programing soon after trouble began."
("Jakarta Soccer Final Halted," IHT, 20 October 1997, p. 16.)

Other writers, other metaphors. Flavius Josephus might have introduced a note of tragic Judaism, Livy a sense of Mediterranean empires in decline. The *Washington Post*'s reporter thinks appropriately of "the dirty little war" to which the paper has a special affinity, having won all press prizes for its exposure and left a powerful president staggering. Can it be "only a game"? Well, *ce n'est pas la guerre;* but kicking a ball around can also be hell (and can be so recorded).

Just on the eve of the new millennium there was a notable backward glance by one *New York Times* sports correspondent which might still augur a new note in the journalism of sporting events and the presentation of star athletes, from home and abroad. The old era was too long ago to prompt a reminiscence or a retrospective nostalgia, but as Christopher Clarey wrote,

> In the early years of this century, sportswriters did not bother interviewing athletes after games or events. They watched; they took notes; they wrote. And why not? Did reviewers need to talk to tenors after the opera finished? ('So, Luciano, is it my imagination or is your range slipping?') Were they obliged to talk to the actors after the theater? ("Did you feel you conveyed pathos better tonight or last night, Luciano?").

Still, a new style had to set in because of the necessity of providing a measure of entertainment through the printed word...since everyone already knew the final score and other athletic results from TV. One had to offer a bit of the background (the notoriously "unfocused" style of an unhappy coach which explained a team's losing streak). The reader came to expect a *soupçon* of the gossip (why the long-time champion is no longer "well motivated"), and a couple of attention-grabbing quotes ("oh yes, the quotes," sighs Clarey affectingly). Thus fortified, printed prose had a chance of competing with real-time pictorial excitement. Readers need to have something more and rather different than the TV interview of a Maurice Greene who has just broken the world record at 100 meters.

> How many times have we seen a microphone and a question thrust in a champion's face in the moments immediately following victory? Winning a race is hard enough. Giving a decent answer while desperately trying to catch your breath is arguably more difficult still. But, this being the electronic age, athletes feel obliged to oblige insetad of saying the logical thing: "Are (gasp) you (gasp) nuts (gasp)? Can't (gasp) you (gasp) see (gasp) I'm (gasp) in (gasp) oxygen (gasp) debt (gasp)?"

In an ideal journalistic world the athlete on the spot, when he has caught his breath, composes himself and confronts a relaxed and civilized reporter, with a lined notebook and a fountain pen. The record-breaker is, by turns, funny or impressive or (gasp) just sheer quotable–even if you may be presenting the hero in the next morning's paper as a comical, laughable foreigner or a pretentious little California kid trying to sound grown-up. In the weeks after the Clarey confessional, deep into the U.S. tennis open at Flushing Meadows, I seemed to detect the slightly new note with losing foreigners (they sounded even more outlandish) and triumphant local talents (who were a shade more impressive and literate). Here is one of each, from Cedric Pioline and Venus Williams:

> Pioline described his winning tactics this way: "I tried to come in, go to the net, come in and put the pressure on his shoulders, don't let him play his game what he likes to play, and it worked. I was like smelling which side he was going to make the passing shot on." (Robin Finn, in the *New York Times*)

> "We always thought we would–that's what we were practicing for," Venus said when asked if she used to dream about playing Serena for a Grand Slam title. "We had an aim and a goal. It was a given." (Rachel Alexander in the *Washington Post*)

Now, more and more, our correspondents can all be relied upon to smell out a given.[1]

One suspects now that the genie is out of the bottle, the search for the good quote–pithy, revealing, amusing, and (above all) space filling–will go on and on. Perhaps a stabilizing point of no return–and, hopefully, of no further progress–can be reached somewhere along the line between superfluity and inanity. Here is Robin Finn, the tennis correspondent of the *New York Times*, reporting on the U.S. Open (1999), when Goran Ivanisevic was tipped as a hopeful and was quoted to this effect:

> "You cannot ever predict who's going to win any Grand Slam," Ivanisevic declared Wednesday....
> "Anything is possible," said Ivanisevic, who has never won a slam.

With press-stopping quotes like these, who ever needs to conduct actual interviews?[2]

When the opportunity arises, even if rarely, then the horns of the dilemma for sensitive, public-spirited newspaper editors are easily averted.

Report the obscene word, or the vile gesture, of the player who was sent off by the outraged referee–or fined by the national sports association (for bringing, as they say, "the game into disrepute"), and roundly reproved by all the sports columnists on the morning after–then you risk disseminating and indeed popularizing that particular bit of nastiness. Discreetly avoid any specific reference to what, as a matter of newsworthy fact, was said or done on the playing field and you fail in professional duty "to tell it like it was." For all your squeamishness, you will probably be stimulating lurid guesswork as to the imagined nature of the shocking incident. Still, every now and then an international event provides a perfect way out.

Foreign athletes usually lose their temper in their own, their native tongues. The insult is, in its way, only self-serving; the man loses control, and his temper as well, and just lets off steam. But his obscene Neapolitan hand gesture or his German *schweinerisches Wort* scarcely registers on the Russian or Hungarian match referee in the noisy London stadium. In Wimbledon or Flushing Meadows Anglo-Saxon tennis referees can catch out American stars (John McEnroe, Andre Agassi, et al.), mumbling their swear words audibly on the No. 1 court–but who spots and translates the Slavic outbursts of temperamental expletives (Goran Ivanovic, Andrej Kafelnikov) in the adjacent contests? Sports writers who can afford to exhibit their literacy to their educated mainstream readers can put together a fairly good and unusual story of the grotesque Babylonian linguistics which usually ensue. One example.

In April of 1999 the formidable footballers of Real Madrid only managed a 1-1 draw with Salamanca, one of the bottom clubs of the Spanish soccer league. The English coach of Real Madrid exploded. He called his own players "*cabrones*." It is unlikely that John Toshack only knew the literal meaning of "*cabrones*," namely *goats*. London reporters took the trouble to consult the Spanish Royal Academy dictionary and learned that *cabron* not only means a male goat, but also refers to someone whose wife has committed adultery, or is a ruffian. Other dictionaries offered references to louts or hooligans. So far, not much reason for a vendetta or a duel at the break of dawn. But was he using the word, as a Madrid newspaper surmised, with a special twist of "English humor"? Was he making fun of his lads…or going in for serious slurs? This would in effect suggest something between the f- and the c-word, and fury raged on all sides.

The remark dominated the European media. All eleven "*cabrones*" on the Madrid first team were loud in their protests. How much of a semantic expert was the voluble Yugoslav international, Predrag Mijatovic? His soothing, mediating remarks–in Spanish? in English? or in his own native Serbo-Croat?– managed to appease the explosive temperaments. He is quoted as saying that, "It would have been better to have used a word that does not have various interpretations." What sage advice! With such wisdom many bitter courtroom trials could have been averted, even great and bloody ethnic wars.[3]

Sports are very far from being the moral equivalent of war, or a harmless substitute for emotional excess. Friedrich Engels even thought that the sports fanaticism (and its associated gambling habits) among the English working class which he had observed in Manchester might obviate any natural turn of the masses to Marxian socialism. A century later all such heavy nineteenth-century German theories were proving awry. As the London *Times* wrote in its front-page commentary on the eve of a decisive England *vs.* Germany soccer match (June 1996), which Germany won: "Clausewitz was wrong: it's not war that is the continuation of politics by other means. It is football that is the continuation of war by other means."[3] In a match between France and Bulgaria which took place in Newcastle the correspondent of the *International Herald*

Tribune wrote of the crisis caused by "a mean and unapologetic foul" committed by a French player against a Bulgarian opponent. In ensuing incidents the referees had to separate the combatants, especially Marcel Desailly (who was born in Ghana and normally plays for Milan) and Hristo Stoichkov (the World Cup's leading scorer who plays for Parma).

Desailly accused Stoichkov of "making racist comments," first in Spanish, and then in Italian. Stoichkov defended his language: "'It's normal,' said Stoichkov. 'It happens all over the pitch. If you took a microphone around the pitch for every player, they'd all be saying things like that.'"[5] Like *what?* Is it important, or useful, or necessary to go into any detail? The worst among readers will have their store of expletives topped up, if any are lacking; the best, however, may have their sensitivities reinforced as to what a civilized fan of the game should decently avoid. I wonder whether any sports-page reader spent more than the half-minute I myself devoted as to what the cuss-words (in Spanish and Italian, yet!) might have been. If they had seen the light of day, or the sound of a TV recording, something would have to be done about it. After all, we all aspire to be gentlemen of sport.

Disciplinary action was taken against Mickey Duff, an English boxer, who had "brought the sport into disrepute" for calling the super-middleweight champion, Chris Eubank, "*scum*" and "*the lowest of the low.*"[6]

One would have thought that, on the scale of the hard words of the hard porn that are in general circulation, this would be small peanuts.

A linesman at a tennis tournament is insulted by: "*You must be blind!*"

A footballer objects to a yellow (or red) card from the referee: "*Got eyes in the back of your bloody head, eh?*"

These and other unconscionable outbursts are promptly disciplined by the moguls who run the industry of professional sports. The language has to be kept clean, but no such strict and total vigilance is seen to be kept in the recurring scandals of bribery and corruption, drugs and doping, and the like. In an official inquiry of the Premier League (soccer's world-famous first division) it confirmed "a cult of dishonesty" in the finanical affairs of English football. Whereupon the London sportswriters waxed indignant–with the optimists referring to the misbehavior as a "*cult*" which, presumably, is easier to clean up and get rid of than (in the phrase of the pessimists) "a *culture* of dishonesty."

In any case, fraud and corruption seem to be rampant in the much-loved "national game," and the cry went up to "punish those who have been damned."[7]

The puritanism is, not for the first time in the history of strangely held beliefs, selective, intermittent, and is a dismal mélange of public propriety and private hypocrisy.

There is a parallelism in the world of politics where bad language in Parliament includes calling a political opponent "*a liar*"–later to be amended, under the Speaker's reproof, to "being economical with the truth" or some such euphemism. In one recent imbroglio in the House of Commons involving John Major and Tony Blair, the then pime minister cast imper-missible aspersions on the future Prime Minister's I.Q. by referring to him as "*a dimwit.*" The conventions of sanctioned language are arbitrary and, varying as they do from context to context, remain subject to the laws of unequal commotion.

The general pattern of inconsistencies are shaped by many factors, not merely the tactical hesitations which inevitably accompany a whole cultural movement's progress towards permissiveness and indiscretion. Not least among the other variables is a favoritism which exempts certain figures, and even institutions, from a possible embarrassment in the face of a traditional public opinion which still cares for its older, conventional proprieties. These privileged exemptions are more common in an older society such as the British which in any case has proved to be more subject to the scandalizing transcription of some outrageous remark. In sports there has been, as I have already indicated, a problem with obscene expostulations; and in certain games–tense contests among competitive rivals in soccer, where class factors (i.e., the largely "working-class" composition of both teams and fans) mix in–naturally rude language colors the game on the playing field and on the terraces. But what of golf? How about tennis?

It was extremely difficult, nay virtually impossible, to find out what young Timothy Henman, the new star of the British Davis Cup team, had actually said, least of all in the story below the headline:

CURSING HENMAN KEEPS US IN
WITH A SHOUT

What *had* he shouted? It was during the decisive English tennis match in Kiev against the Ukraine where his victory kept his team in the competition. Forthcoming were the usually pithy sports commentators not: "His tetchy mood was audible and between sets he received a warning from the umpire for giving a frank assessment of his own performance in unusually coarse language." Young Timothy was only twenty and was the most promising star in the English game since Fred Perry a half-century ago. There is an understandable reluctance to soil the reputation of a popular folk figure, a culture hero, as if he were just another Liverpool lout or Cockney brawler.[8]

At least in the case of Nick Faldo, Britain's most celebrated golfer, newspaper readers were informed about the general category of coarse language involved in the next day's regrettable incident. The *Daily Telegraph*'s story reported that Faldo had "stormed off the 18th hole" (on the links at Loch Lomond) and "unleashed a volley of abuse." This was, as always, said to be "a testing time for golf's reputation"; and that means, in plain English, minding your language, especially on the greens near the clubhouse: "One elderly spectator said: 'I have been coming to golf tournaments for more than 50 years and I have never heard anything like it. Every word started with 'F.' It was absolutely disgusting.'" The story did all it properly could to reduce the offense, referring to it by indirection, suggesting a rather improbable sequence of alliteration, resorting to circumlocutions like "castigation...a terrible dressing down...a tirade of boorish behavior." Still, the large truth, if not all the facts, had to be told: namely, that "many fear that Faldo's vulgar behavior"–others were worse! for such vulgarities were "thought only to be the preserve of a boorish element among freeway crowds"–would "do little to help the game's tarnished image."

Faldo himself sought to make amends after the outburst. He signed an autograph for a young boy as he made his way back. Decent behavior, at long last, befitting the game of gentlemen.[9]

In that very same week one *bête noir* of the *Telegraph* editors–it happened to be Steven Spielberg, a star player in another section of the paper–was given due credit for his obscene outburst during the course of active duty. Obviously he was not entitled to native privileged exemptions–perhaps because he was a foreign billionaire, perhaps because he was "a little Jewish boy" (in the Shylock tradition, which would "explain" his riches). His image was freely available for tarnishing. And so the anecdote emerges naked and explicit. It concerns his estranged wife. When she finally divorced him she received $100 million in the settlement. But for now they were still seeing each other, and one day she was visiting the Spielberg set where he was filming *Close Encounters*: "He confided to his producer, 'I wish she hadn't come. She keeps crying, and I keep wanting to say, 'Don't you understand, I'm f—ing my movie.'" It was an encounter too close by far. And to appease his newspaper critic's sense of fairness he had to raise the question whether Spielberg had meant by the obviously ironical expletive that he was pouring his passion into his art. If so, "the best that can be said is that it's hard to spot." Hard was unfortunate; spot was a disaster. Never was an f-word so unconvincing.

Its most famous usages–and I have cited some: from Tynan, Worsthorne, Hemingway, Whitney Houston, etc.–rarely have this kind of copulative reference. It might be a hateful school-system (Crosland)–it might be a disappointed star player who has flubbed his chance to score, or a strained relationship among friends (Martin Amis)–but, unlike D.H. Lawrence, intercourse was very far from their minds. Being out-of-sorts was more like it, and the f-word serves to take revenge on a disagreeable state of affairs. By not quoting "obscenities" explicitly the journalist using the -f--word maintains an atmosphere of sexual taboo and doesn't disclose that the rude remark was just a lazy mindless filler for diffuse anger, for contempt, or disapproval, and the like.[10]

Tom Jones and the Language Police

Do they order these things better in a foreign language? A few remarks on what (and how) the papers are saying in Germany.

The alacrity of the adoption by mainstream German journalism, from the *Frankfurter Allgemeine Zeitung* to *Der Spiegel*, of American-style speech and porno prose candor, should not disguise the conservatism of its formal linguistic establishment. The *FAZ* feels free, on its highbrow literary pages, to use the f-word (i.e., *"ficken"*) a dozen times in a short review, albeit questioning the new conventions among young writers everywhere to "let it all hang out." *Der Spiegel* considers the old indigenous profanity flaccid and useless in its weekly stories; but the imported Anglo-American usages, in proper unitalicized spelling, appear to be *chic*, expressive, and in some ways even shocking. Thus, an interview with the international Welsh pop star of three decades, Tom Jones, has the following exchange (in German, if that's what it is):

> SPIEGEL: Just recently your young fans met you at the biggest English Underground Festival, with a banner upon which, 'Tom! Fucking! Jones!' was written. Does something like that make you happy?
>
> JONES: I figured, "Fucking," what a nice middle name. Plus written with exclamation points. That's powerful. Tom! Fucking! Jones! *

(Der Spiegel, no. 2/9 January 1995)

Here we encounter one more multilingual complication. There is, usually, a conversational discrepancy in linguistic usage where the prose we speak is, in some contexts, more daring (in others, less) than the prose we write. There are also a whole variety of sub-cultural lags, where books can print what newspapers have to bowdlerize and the rules for public discourse (in a meeting hall, in a theater) can diverge widely. In Germany, whatever the latiditudinous range of profanity in talk and in print there is, as one recent case has dramatically highlighted, a legal lag. Jurisprudence has not quite caught up with the culture of obscenities. Thus, a famous editor of a popular weekly has taken to the German courts to obtain "damages" from a satirical review that had been poking f-word fun at him and, accordingly, "embarrassing" him, "sullying" his reputation, and otherwise harming his good name and repute.

Hellmut Markwort had led a fairly successful advertising campaign for his expanding news-magazine, *Focus* (the main weekly competitor of *Der Spiegel*, a kind of "Munich *Newsweek*" to the "Hamburg *Time*"). The main thrust of the message was that *Focus* was offering concise objective reports whereas the competition was long-winded, partisan, and altogether less readable and reliable. The slogan, repeated a thousand times in Television Sound-bites, was (and Markwort himself barked it out) *"Fakten! Fakten! Fakten!"* They were

---

*   "SPIEGEL: Vor kurzem haben Ihre jungen Fans Sie auf dem grössten englischen Underground-Festival mit einem Transparent begrüsst, auf dem stand 'Tom! Fucking! Jones!' Freut Sie so etwas?
     JONES: Ich dachte mir: 'Fucking', was für ein schöner zweiter Vorname. Noch dazu mit Ausrufezeichen. Das hat Kraft. Tom! Fucking! Jones!"

committed to offer only *facts*. Whereupon the satirists of *Titanic* did a series of cartoons where the great factual journalist was promising only: "*Ficken, Ficken, Ficken.*" Markwort sued. The f-word, published without hyphens or asterisks as a hard fact of life and libel, became an explicit blue code word for the unfortunate *Focus* editor. In the first trial he was awarded only part of the 60,000 DM his lawyers were demanding. In a second appeal, which involves other publications which had reprinted the *Titanic* caricature, the sum of *Schmerzensgeld* has been exponentially increased. But how will the judges in the higher Berlin court react when they, like everybody else in the *Republik*, find themselves to be readers–and writers?—in a libertarian *Kultur* of *Obszönitäten?*[11]

Nevertheless, as I say, the established conventions reveal the same persistently old-fashioned resistance to new words and/or breakthrough usages that have characterized the twentieth-century work of English and American lexicographers. The latest revision of eight volumes of the *Duden* were republished in 1996, and they indicate that the editors of this standard handbook have been prim and reluctantly cautious in going along with what the language is already featuring in novels, films, newspaper and magazine reportage. Among the taboos–and some newspapers ran a whole list of omissions under the rubric, *Pfui!* (i.e., our *phooey!*)–are: *Männerliebe* (male love); *Missionarstellung* (missionary position); *kesse Vater* (a "masculine" lesbian). One critic objected to the absence of the English word "lover" on the presumption that the foreign word was sexier than the native "*Liebhaber.*" Still, there was joy among the avant-garde in the inclusion, at long last, of such worthy erotica as "one-night stand" (which comes out to a cumbersome "*flüchtiges sexuelles Abenteuer für eine Nacht,*" losing its camouflage in being so explicit); "blind date"; as well as those old standbys of German coitus, "*ficken...vögeln...bumsen.*"

What alarmed some is the suspicion that not all was done in the true lexicographical spirit, slow-moving that it may well be. For example, the word "sauna" was omitted in its denotation as, on occasion, a sexual establishment–due to protest of the organized Association-of-Sauna-Owners, Inc. The word "*Französin*" was also not to be found in its eight revised volumes, for there was a delicate diplomatic-political aspect to the imputation that practitioners of oral sex were French females. The Germans are still trying hard to be loyal to the spirit of the Paris-Bonn reconciliation, dramatically initiated a generation ago by General de Gaulle and Dr. Konrad Adenauer.

One last gnawing doubt, and here too there is the parallel with dictionary-makers in the Anglo-Saxon world. Does inclusion in the *Duden* register merely the recognition that the word is increasingly, or generally, used? Or does it imply–over and above the conventional little flagging about its being *vulg.*– a certain approval, at least a positive tolerance? If dictionaries still have a traditional authority, is there not a danger of creeping authoritarianism? One newspaper critic referred to lexicographers as *"Sprach-polizisten,"* and every small sign of a new police state in the offing causes local alarm. The Germans have their sensitivities, and they go beyond mere semantics.[11]

A final word on my opening quotations from *Roget's Thesaurus* (1832-1988), giving kaleidoscopic definitions of "Obscenity" and "Profanity." In over a century-and-a-half of groping in the darkness the two terms have almost become interchangeable in meaning, usage, and synonymous off-color innuendo. Still, I want to recall a landmark American court case in which a Federal Supreme Court, with that brilliant jurist Jerome K. Frank presiding, pronounced a profound and possibly disagreeable distinction. Mr. Justice Frank threw out the prosecuting attorney's case against several literary texts that had come before him on the grounds that they were, as charged, "obscene and pornographic." He ruled that this was an untenable contradiction in terms. For what was *pornographic* would, in its lustful manner, stimulate to sexual activity–and what was *obscene* would, in its distasteful way, discourage and dissuade. A book could not be both at once. This, for a time, was the ruling legal reading of the matter.*

Something of the same distinction, defined to strengthen a libertarian loophole, was made by U.S. judges in the various notorious trials of Lenny Bruce. Accused of foul and offensive language, the comedian won some, lost some; and in one (1962) the court argued that–

> "Sex" and "obscenity" are not synonymous....The use of blasphemy, foul or coarse language, and vulgar behavior does not in and of itself constitute obscenity....An evaluation must be made as to whether the performance as a whole had as its dominant theme an appeal to prurient interest...[or] the degree of sincerity of purpose evident in it, whether it has artistic merit. If the performance is merely disgusting or revolting it cannot be obscene, because obscenity contemplates the arousal of sexual desires.

No matter that this contradicts Judge Frank who cut the distinction the other way (it is pornography which arouses, whereas obscenity disgusts). American judges were groping in their enlightened, well-meaning way towards a recognition that bad language can also mean well. Bad words can be enlisted for good causes: "A performance cannot be considered utterly without redeeming social importance if it has literary, artistic or aesthetic merit, or if it contains ideas, regardless of whether they are unorthodox, controversial or hateful." The defendant was found not guilty of the offense charged: "a misdemeanor," to wit, violating Section 311.6 of the Penal Code of the State of California. This was in March 1962.[12]

---

*   See the decision rendered by Hon. John H. Woolsey on December 6, 1933, United States District Court, in: Southern District of New York, United States of America vs. One Book Called "Ulysses," Random House, Inc., A-110-59. The judge remarked in the case against James Joyce's *Ulysses*, ."..In many places it is somewhat emetic, nowhere does it tend to be aphrodisiac." See also Jerome K. Frank, *Law and the Modern Mind* (1930).

Several years later, after Bruce's fifth arrest in Los Angeles, making it a grand nation-wide total of nineteen arrests, a decision by the Illinois State Supreme Court rejected an appeal in Chicago and unanimously upheld a verdict of guilty. At the same time the U.S. Supreme Court happened to rule that a film that had been charged as obscene was *not* obscene since it was deemed to have "social importance" (22 June 1964). Because of the Washington ruling, the Illinois court dropped its affirmation of Lenny Bruce's guilt. The logic of the higher court was not completely persuasive but it was compelling in its argument that "the obscene portions of the material must be balanced against its affirmative values to determine which predominates." Well, then, how tip the scales of the balance?

The high federal judges affirmed the right of Lenny Bruce or any other citizen to "satirize society's attitudes on contemporary issues." (Or on any other? What about the jokes about the crucifixion of Jesus which were a staple of Bruce's monologues?) He also had the right to express his ideas, "however bizarre." (However blasphemous? Bruce would hurl curses at any church, religion, or piety.) But they would not support the Chicago court in its argument that "material, no matter how objectionable the method of its presentation, was constitutionally privileged unless it was utterly without redeeming social importance."

The loose use of the concept of redemption–and the vagueness of what is socially important (what is not?)–left the argument thin and fuzzy. It didn't get any stronger with weak repetitions. "Material having *any* social importance is constitutionally protected."

Still, Lenny Bruce brought out the best in American Jeffersonianism, and the Supreme Court hesitated only a moment and went on from there in the spirit of Voltaire–

> While we would not have thought that constitutional guarantees necessitate the subjection of society to the gradual deterioration of its moral fabric which this type of presentation promotes, we must concede that some of the topics commented on by the defendants are of social importance.

If only the man had been ingenious enough to think up more unsocial or anti-social questions! If only he could work out material whose unimportance could deceive those black-robed pillars of the establishment! He could have been permanently busted, and in the end emerge as a true and complete martyr to the faith that always burns underground. But no, he had to go and try to win arguments with old men in Washington who liked to think that a four-letter word like *"free"*–as in being free and constitutionally protected by human rights and civil liberties–was preferable to Bruce's show-stoppers. Thus, the Supreme Court Justices concluded, "and we are constrained to hold the judgement of the circuit court of Cook County must be reversed and defendant discharged." Lenny Bruce was not quite happy with this, and his only comment was, "They're really saying that they're only sorry the crummy Constitution won't permit them to convict me, but if they had *their* choice." (Bruce, *How to Talk Dirty...*, pp. 148-9). Fortunately, they were not as free as he was. He liked to think that, as he frivolously confessed, "Hitler is waiting to book me for six weeks in Argentina" (Bruce, p. 188).

If the language of our journalism obeyed, in this spirit, the law of the land and followed such dialectical legal distinctions, I am afraid that we for our own part would have to begin all over again. The allusiveness of erotica and indeed the whole profane vocabulary are hard to subject to categorical imperatives. They can titillate when trivial, and disgust when tawdry and vulgar; and, possibly, given the unpredictable ways of the sexual personality, they can serve equally well one's modest or promiscuous impulses. There are, regrettably, no laws, and few rules and regulations. The *do's* and *don'ts* on the statute books have proved to be as helpless as the most ambitious of newspaper style-books.

20

Swearing is the Curse

The long march of the f-word through the institutions of the English language has, as we have seen, been making its measured strides forward. The
story up till here: Thomas Bowdler has been long ago consigned to oblivion,
and in the second half of the twentieth century only a sector of the mainstream
press has been holding out against outright four-letterization of publishable
journalese. In the recent obituaries of one famous American journalist–the
veteran Washington broadcaster Martin Agronsky (eighty-four) who was famed
for "riling" presidents of the day–one notorious passage still featured the
deletion of the expletive. It involved Jimmy Carter's ultra-sensitive reaction
to an acerbic dig at his foreign policy–

> Presidents Richard Nixon, Ronald Reagan and Jimmy Carter or their news secretaries
> often called Mr. Agronsky during the program [it was nationally syndicated from 1969
> to 1987 on one or the other of the three major networks]....
>   Mr. Carter called Mr. Agronsky from Camp David, asking him–and emphasizing
> with a four-letter word–to tell Mr. Will [George F. Will, a guest on his program] that
> he would bomb the Iranians into submission as soon as Mr. Will exchanged places
> with the hostages.[1]

But, in the struggle for dictionary correctness, many a nameless lexicographer has won famous victories on a whole wide front of taboo vernacular. No
longer will innocent and blameless students be held to risk anti-Semitic con-
tamination by looking up puzzling phrases embedded in old Dickensian literature (e.g., "to jew down"). Sensitive anti-racists are diligently campaigning
against the lexical incorrectness which perpetuates the memory of yesterday's
hurtful slurs. The *N*-word may never become obsolete, but some expletives
may well disappear (*"Boy!"* the white slave-master called out...) and leave new
readers puzzled or indifferent.

Most guidebooks contain at least a few pages of phrases and vocabulary
which would assist a bewildered tourist caught among the indigenous personnel of some foreign land; and they have also been moving into the era of "dirty

realism." Vague traces of imperial attitudes have long since disappeared. (I once had a Swahili guide-book in Dar-es-Salaam which had me repeating, with grammatical and phonetic precision, to some *"boy"* in attendance, e.g., "Why did you steal these objects from my writing table?" I was traveling light, had no or very few "objects," and none of my hotels in Tanzania had desks or writing tables; and so I escaped the curse of colonialism.) But what would Americans in London do when they got exposed to the full flow of the Cockney–or, for that matter, Australian–street language as-he-(or-she)-is-blankety-blank-spoken. One new handbook has come to the rescue, and is possibly a landmark publication in the profanization of tourist communication abroad.

In a wordplay which suggested linguistic correctness, one London newspaper reported the event of its publication under the headline:

GUIDEBOOK YOU CAN SWEAR BY
"London—A British phrase book littered with four-letter words was published today by guidebook company Lonely Planet."[2]

Visitors to the UK are informed of English (and especially Scottish) football chants, all of which include the f-word. The book also regales tourists with sixty-five different descriptions for being drunk (including *rat-arsed* and *arseholed*, which might not be easily decipherable). Among other phrases explained for visitors are *dog's bollocks* (which is listed as meaning "fantastic!"); *"pillock"* (idiot/fool); and *"skanky"* (ugly/smelly/dirty/foul).

It is often the case that great historic steps forward are modestly undertaken, and new empires of the English tongue are conquered in almost a fit of absentmindedness. The editors of the Lonely Planet guidebook are very far from a cultural awareness of yet another breakthrough for the avant-garde dedicated to demotic truthfulness. Our *Standard* reporter quotes a Lonely Planet spokeswoman, Jennifer Cox, as being close to an *apologia pro lingua sua*: "'We are not saying that people should swear but we want visitors to Britain to know what to expect.' She added: 'The British seem to love swearing and we do seem to swear more than other nations.'" But the embarrassed note of immodesty is more than compensated for by the recognition that an element of national pride or achievement is involved, and even more than that a kindly effort at semantic philanthropy. One is only helping out those fellow-citizens and native speakers who need a bit of assistance: "whose speech is so dependent on the word f*** that they're virtually dumbstruck without it." At least tourists will be returning from London with their vocabularies, if not exactly their minds, broadened by travel.

Apart from the delicate problem of coaching curses for "Yanks at Oxford," there is a greater issue which has long been struggling to get out. I have previously pointed out that these are *new* elements in a cultural backlash which is mistakenly taken to be traditional or old-fashioned–and hence reactionary and nostalgic for the good old days of blue-pencil censorship. What is new in the critique of proliferating profanity is not to be confounded with the Mrs. Grundyism of yesteryear. The very whisper of a four-letter word, or the pursing of the lips as if an expletive was about to be hurled, used to create a social crisis, with embarrassment at "foul language" combined with anger at blasphemous coarseness. What we are witnessing represents, I think, the emergence of a new avant-garde attitude. It is sophisticated, knowledgeable, and with an alarmed sense of concern at the *"dirtying down"* of a language which has to be kept clean, not for the usual reasons of old middle-class morality, but for high professional purposes and semantic integrity. Who can ever write poetry or philosophy, or pen an effective piece of political prose, when the effing four-letterization of vocabulary is turning out to be all intrusive?

I will report here on only one journalistic presentation of this counter-cultural offensive which is committed, as one newspaper headline aphoristically put it, to the post-modern thesis:

SWEARING IS THE CURSE OF OUR LANGUAGE

The news-peg to which this topical outburst was attached was, first, the local publication at long last by T.S. Eliot's old firm of Faber & Faber of the American edition of Jesse Sheidlower's compendium of *The F-Word* (1995); and, secondly, a passage in the Lonely Planet's guidebook, mentioned above, which before appeasing "the notoriously foul-mouthed British" first indicts them as follows:

> Large numbers of British drape their entire discourse around the word *fuck*, with the occasional *wanker* or *bastard* thrown in for color. Those at the cutting edge are moving towards a sort of Zen English in which *fuck* will be the only word–shaped, nuanced, and spat out to convey every thought and sentiment.

Still and all, our newspapers and our books which address themselves to a wide audience "must reflect" (mustn't they?) the language which "large numbers" do in fact use. This is an astonishingly far cry from the world of the *Lady Chatterley* Trial. Then, in 1960, the Prosecuting Counsel (Griffith-Jones) deemed the novel obscene, and used as a clinching argument that it was not a book you would *"wish your wife or your servants to read."* In the end it was judged acceptable in a work of literature to use the word which, henceforth, all good Fleet Street journalists referred to as *"f***."* And precious little indeed is left of the D.H. Lawrence gamekeeper's impression that the aforementioned word was full of quasi-mystic potency and phallic tenderness.

Penguin's triumph over old censorship rules was, in a way, less a victory for ideal profanity than a blow for a mass classlessness. But Lawrence's tremulous personal ideals were, as in most revolutions, not those of the rough and tough men who came after him, from Tynan to Tarantino. Lawrence's was a quiet, almost private gesture on behalf of the purifying sexualization of love, an erotic utopia (if you will), and he had thought originally of calling his novel *Tenderness*. What actually came in the aftermath of emancipation was the universalization of the taboo demotic per se.

It was also politically radicalized. Words mounted the barricades. All speech, like most good things in life, would be free and equal. Obscenities were to be liberated, and never again restricted to a privileged few, set apart as in *Upstairs/Downstairs*. What served Chaucer and Shakespeare (and Lawrence) for ideal literary purposes–and hence a rich culture (for the upper classes) and a robust civilization (for the middle classes)–should be denied to no man. There is nothing that cannot be said "in the presence of the servants," especially when in a desirable democratic society there is willy-nilly no such subjected species. Accordingly, millions have now spoken up, adding their own little four-letter words to the crescendo. To do so almost became an article of faith, a civic duty. To help create a better society wherein all are at long last free and equal as well, the f-word has become a passport to a fairer land, to a kind of cursing Camelot featuring a waltzing Mathilda. It's a vote for the future, a way of being counted. I swear, therefore I am. I also curse, therefore we are all equal.[3]

A.N. Wilson is a popular London journalist, and an English novelist of some repute. In the days when everything used to come down to "class" he has drawn a familiar picture of middle-class English schoolboys who "effed and blinded a bit at their boarding schools" (but would not think of doing so at home). They found out later in life (mostly in military service) what swearing like a trooper actually entailed–"the 'zen' use of f*** as a synonym for almost every verb and noun in the language." Wilson registers–and belatedly appears to regret–the turning points in the contemporary culture represented by the verbal outbursts of Kenneth Peacock Tynan and Sir Peregrine Worsthorne. They, presumably, went on to better things. But,

> the "zen" characters remain stuck in their own weird world. If "f***" is the only word you can use, then your linguistic skills are only one stage up from the mammals who communicate in grunts. It goes without saying that you are cut off from the riches and variety of the English language.

"*Stuck in a weird world*" is an arguable formulation. In the commonplace and everyday world there are many highly successful men and women whose language (and we have documented some) is "peppered with swear words."

In London, the habits of pop realism were transplanted to mainstream-British television by a notorious Carnaby Street spokeswoman, Janet Street-Porter. She has made it–and herself–eminently acceptable; and, as I write, she has just been appointed as editor-in-chief of that stately liberal broadsheet the *Independent on Sunday*. The London staff was stunned by the appointment, and one account of the first editorial meeting recorded–

they were almost more amazed, when she gave her first pep talk to the staff, by the number of times she used the *f*-word. Later in the day, when one of her new lieutenants went in to see her about something, she was on the telephone to the TV company which is producing her new series about English churches. "I don't want any f***ing bells," she was yelling into her mobile. "Bells are f***ing crap."

Is our middle-class schoolboy only being priggish about the ripe language of an ebullient Cockney spirit who famously gave us what she couldn't help calling "*Youf kulchur*"? Wilson demurs, and Ms. Street-Porter's readers in the next few months of Sundays will have to serve as jury. If this is the way you use the langauge, Wilson argues, could you ever be witty? Could you ever say anything surprising or deep? "You would have become your language's servant, rather than the other way about."

Is this, once again, a futile rally in a last-ditch effort to halt the apparently inexorable march of progressive four-letterization? Or, perhaps, a new stage of a trench warfare which has fairer prospects for a tolerable armistice? Every critic on this battlefield has unavoidable doubts and hesitations. Isn't A.N. Wilson, as a prophet of change and the new (and eloquent) wholesomeness, a bit of a hypocrite?

Yes, I curse and swear and blaspheme when the f***ing computer "crashes," when the b*ggering car won't start or when my wife makes us f***ing late for an appointment but it isn't something I am proud of, since it is something I do when I have lost control.

I surmise that the synthesis, in good old dialectical fashion, will embrace both thesis and antithesis. Swearing is the curse of the language; but it is also unavoidable and/or indispensable.

The argument comes out, in the end, to this: the uses of language which elevate both it and its users are those which stretch our ingenuity when we use it "lovingly, wittily, erotically, religiously, playfully." Bawdry is not excluded by the greatest writers, but they do not use it habitually, compulsively, helplessly. Was Dr. Johnson also being "a bit of a hypocrite" when he spoke the word in question in the course of good and lively conversation but kept it out of the pages of his *Dictionary* (1755)? In the anecdote Wilson has to hand: "Dr. Johnson was once asked what were life's greatest pleasures. He replied, 'Sir, drinking and f***ing.' He meant both words."

What meaningfulness did Nixon intend when, in his White House tapes, the crudities of his coarseness escaped bleeping? For a young pro-American English writer the "outing" of the White House was disillusioning, disenchanting, depressing. Here was the most powerful leader in the Western world, "and when his dander was up, he spoke like an uneducated navvy." This is the final testimony from A.N. Wilson, a witness for the new prosecution, concerned about the future of human language and not the presence of domestic servants: "It was demeaning. It was one thing to be a swindler and a shyster. We'd all suspected that Nixon was this all along. But when we heard the tapes, we heard the raw sound of brutalized, irrational fear. It was utterly ignoble." In what direction, pray, lies ennoblement? Some thought the f-word had something to do with tenderness.[4]

In every society all things, great and small, swing to change. Whether they move forward or backward, or in some cases sidewards, depends on the pendulum and its clockwork intricacies. Big wheels that seem to advance the movement turn little wheels that tick the other way. And when the bells ring they toll only for the passing of time which is, mostly, a little fast or, perhaps, a stroke too slow, and signaling no ultimate judgment.

Thus, in the related metaphors of cultural change and social progress, when–possibly–might a so-called backlash set in? The four-letterization of our culture is proceeding apace. Many of the countervailing forces have already been mentioned. There are the reactionaries who do want to turn the clock back. Not, perhaps, to the Inquisition nor to Mr. Bowdler, but to a treasured time when language in public use was clean, and dirt in any of its forms (even to the specks of suggestiveness) was interdicted. The various kinds of Biblical fundamentalists tried to keep faith in their credo–and some in the very beginning were shocked or rather at a loss for words. But one took the liberty of arguing: "God was angry, God was mad, but dammit He didn't bloody well need expletives to tell his darned story! A pox on the cursing classes!"

This corps of uncompromising censors are not to be confounded with the semantic fundamentalists who held that what grew apart in the whole history of culture and civilization–"Day Words" and "Night Words," the sacred and the profane, visible totems and unspeakable taboos–should remain asunder. Who would put them together in a chorus of yawps and guffaws degrades culture, demeans civilization, and takes the proper flavor from the joys and other purposes of both night and day. Neither of these forces has mounted campaigns in the Western world that can be considered here as of moment and importance.

Contradictions in the camp of the avant-garde are a moving factor of another dynamic. Coming from within what is emerging in the mainstream of the world of modern culture, they operate to slow down and trip up the main thrusts of profanity and obscenity. As we have seen, throughout the Western world there is evidence of a built-in reluctance and hesitation. No major organ of Western communication–with the possible exception of "experimental" fiction and "independent" filmmaking–has been courageous enough to go too far, to go the whole way, to do the "full Monty" in the phrase of the nineties. The usual cases which are writ large in our present culture are variants of (if I may) *coitus interruptus*. Four-letterization dictates that the exact number of letters are all in place, but they don't have to be fully spelled. We are half in, and very quickly out.

Where ideas fail or figure only *in absentia*, language languishes. That is to say, where not even a shadow of a concept or an idea, a reflective thought with words being carefully chosen to identify variousness and difference in a perceived piece of reality, the expletive rushes in to ride roughshod. Of a *disagreeable character*, one wants to know: what kind of a s—t is this characterless oaf? Of a *serious crisis*, one is compelled to ask: how distinctive or, perhaps, characteristic are these f***ed-up situations? If everybody is a s—t, it reduces all critical antipathies–traditionally the source of salty brilliance, of unending verbal ingenuity–into a simple standard form of mindless semantic aggression. "*Go t'hell!*" or "*Go f—k yourself!*" are both unlikely prospects (taken literally), and they block a whole range of more colorful and effective invective. Profane put-downs are mostly self-serving and self-defeating. They confound pricking a taboo with making a point.

In high politics low lingo takes over. Woodrow Wilson comes to be seen as full of high-falutin' *b—l-s—t*, and in the Clinton White House it all is being told like it is, according to the maxim: "Screw 'em before they screw you." Even in Westminster, Britain's deputy Prime Minister, John Preston, in Blair's generally well-spoken cabinet has been quoted as saying (to the P.M. himself on a question of salaries), "If you want to be f****** Jesus Christ, don't take your pay rise." And German editors have been similarly poring over political talk in high places, and one researcher has come up with a discovery (promptly reported as a scoop in *Der Spiegel*)–"*Scheisse*" was said once, and in the *Bundestag* by the *Kanzler* of the time, Helmut Schmidt. In the corridors of high finance, the low lingo is hectic and pithy; and four-letter words displace four-sentence paragraphs.[5]

From all the evidence I have assembled it is clear that when a mental vacuum develops, a creeping coarseness thrives. The obsessive obscenities are sustained–in several genres of the novel, in the Hollywood school of dirty realism–by a certain illusion. It is a monumental self-deception that a whole new dimension of reality is being confronted and illuminated in a special, original, and appropriate way. These are the taglines in an underworld of violent and incongruous relationships. As I have argued, the dumbing-down of public discourse goes hand-in-hand with the roughing-up of conventional, acceptable language.

When even the roughest, the most robust of old-time polemicists–from Swift and Heine to Mencken and Karl Kraus–assault reality with hard-hitting sparring techniques, nowadays a spin doctor or any other chic communicator would rather take the opening to deliver a low blow, somewhere in the region below-the-belt. "Kicking ass"–or putting the boot into any other target in the general area–is a favorite form of verbal aggression. A variant in the recent art world of "sensations" is pictorial aggression: a hanging horse (stuffed); floating turds (in formaldehyde); Christian icons in urine or enriched by shapely patties of dung; etc. Moving further afield, one can say that where Nietzsche reconsiders the notions of death and immortality and goes on to argue in a philosophical obituary that God is dead, Quentin Tarantino wants to tell the disagreeable deity just where he can shove it.

On the other hand, when feminists begin to tire of their over-used obscenities, the verbal weariness heralds the end of the "liberating style" of the old feministic agit-prop. When Germaine Greer stops cursing like a trooper, language revives (at least in the case of her own latest books and newspaper articles). Deflowered ideas begin to bloom, a newborn reflectiveness takes shape. Hoaxes,

Part 3

Literary Origins and Popular Consequences

"I have proposed to myself to imitate,
and, as far as is possible, to adopt
the very language of men."
—William Wordsworth *(1802)*

"But did thee feel the earth move?."
—Ernest Hemingway *(1940)*

"The decadence of our language
is probably curable....
Never use a metaphor, simile or
other figure of speech
which you are used to seeing in print...
if you can think of an everyday
English equivalent."
—George Orwell *(1946)*

21

Sources of Malpractice

I am not so sure that Orwell, for all his well-meaning sharpness, got it quite right in his much-praised essay on "Politics and the English Language" (1946); and this for two reasons. He placed far too much faith in the semantic powers of simplicity, brevity, and concision ("Never use a long word where a short one will do"). Consequently he missed the dialectical irony of all radical efforts to reform style and purify vocabulary: namely, that their own theories of sound diction may, in time, contribute to the corruptions of another generation. The compulsory resort to "an everyday English equivalent"–in a subsequent era when "the very language of men" has degenerated into impurities and evasiveness of a different kind–can help create new and synonymous barbarities while extirpating the old.

Orwell's difficulty of half-a-century ago remains: the larger implications of how words, phrases, sentences are effectively arranged for the perceptions of political problems. But, as I want to suggest, a contributing element in our current cultural malaise is the theory and practice of some of our most prestigious writers. Not a few are the immortals of our university anthologies; and thus they have had, even in excerpted snippets, a pervasive educational influence on contemporary readers and, especially, editors. As my three mottoes above hint, there are some literary origins to the distortions of modern political journalism.

For purposes of shorthand brevity I will refer to a great disorientating tradition only by the names of Wordsworth and Hemingway; and the two worthies will serve to encompass (if in different accents) two-way transatlantic malpractices.

What they have in common, in their impact on the journalistic style of our times, is their absolutistic commitments to the speech of common men, to the vocabulary of rhythms of natural conversation, as the proper carrier of discourse and communication. Here is meaning, here is art–and not in the abstractions of formal rhetoric, or the terminology of narrow-spirited pedants.

For Wordsworth it represented the break with classical artificiality, with "gaudiness and inane phraseology."

For Hemingway it was the great heavyweight challenge to "get it right," to pin the truth to the mat, to knock off the excess fat, to be lean and simple and powerful.

This literary aesthetic has impinged on especially American journalism, and this in an extraordinary way: so much so that it is difficult to find an elegant sentence, or a well-fashioned paragraph, or a sharply tuned phrase in the immense output of American daily newspapers. There are, of course, notable exceptions. A columnist like William F. Buckley Jr., paradoxically, still attracts millions–in the American immensity, only a minority–for he uses polysyllabic words and mandarin circumlocutions quite beyond the ken of common man. Another regu-lar commentator like George Will wins a singular reputation for making such recondite references to Samuel Johnson or George Eliot as to titillate North American readers with mild bewilderment. As for William Safire's ingenious exercises in up-to-the-minute etymology, they must often leave the impression that old dictionaries and their prescriptions are quite superfluous in a new grammatical world of fashionable, fascinating, and fast-changing coinages.

Writers like Charles Krauthammer, William Pfaff, and Neal Ascherson, among others, give a special literary pleasure. But an older reader still remains nostalgic for the verbal felicities of a previous generation of columnar stalwarts (Walter Lippmann, Joseph Alsop, Heywood Broun, Max Lerner....)

For the simple, stolid rest there is the pseudo-Wordsworthian homeliness, the neo-Hemingwayesque short slangy expostulation, making do for a full shapely sentence. It is not good enough.

22

From Wordsworth to Orwell and Hemingway

There is a paradox in the increasing use of the street-natural demotic in newspaper journalism. Quotation marks are used when the ascribed remarks are contrived fictions, and they come to be omitted when the actual speech is recorded. In this way, journalism maximizes its sympathy and solidarity with the common man (and woman), with their simple feelings and responses. Thus, the *New York Times* reports: "Many secretaries complain that E-mail has meant less personal contact....Secretaries admit to missing the schmoozing while walking from desk to desk." Then there are "the glitches and the gremlins" which mistakenly go on to produce messages for everybody in the company where they were intended only for the executive few. If, by happenstance, the news in the text is good or especially felicitous–"there are oohs and ahs to be heard resounding through the offices." And if penny-pinching is going the rounds, a Senator is sure to complain that "we are nickel-and-dimes people who put their lives on the line in our nation's interest."[1] Evidently slang is democratic, by definition it is closer to the people. Even onomotopeia serves populistically as a progressive linkage. Journalism wears colored shirts and short sleeves, and casually reflects the tie-less, open-collared, blue-jeaned journalist who is encouraged to "come as you are" and to sound just like everybody else. He (or she) *schmoozes*, utters *oohs-and-ahs* just like all of the real *nickle-and-dime* guys.

A *Washington Post* columnist, giving vent to a perennial, if somewhat archaic, sartorial concern about her fellow-females letting down the side by dressing sloppily, advises that the still-reigning image demands that you "dress for the job to which you aspire"; which is sound enough, but then she adds, "Schlepping around in sneakers and a suit suggests that you're a disgruntled clock-puncher."[2] This kind of slang or argot, explicable to outsiders only with the aid of Leo Rosten and his *Joys of Yiddish*, "schlepps" itself slowly through our newspaper culture, sapping for many disgruntled readers the occasional joys of English.

Some snappy phraseological turns, clever or colorful as they may be, inevitably become buzzwords which are employed obsessively by journalists for a season or two; and they may prolong their shelf-lives by mixing with older elements to give an impression of freshness. The ubiquitous usage of the phrase, "the smoking gun" to denote evidence of a crime which is conclusive, has almost worn itself out – but not quite yet. As the years become stained with increasing crime, pistols, revolvers, and other firearms that the police confiscate get forensically identified as literally smoking guns, offering indisputable proof beyond any doubt. Now our metaphor is joining another to make something new. Thus, a *Washington Post* correspondent acutely observes the consequences of what he calls "the ghostly curse of the Watergate drama" on the local political phraseology: "Watergate lexicon is automatically passed along to the next set of circumstances, no matter how different, usually beginning with the 'gate' suffix and ending with the search for the 'smoking gun.'" Then, President Clinton's lawyers declared that "the smoking gun might be at hand" and "when it proved to be less than lethal, the White House dismissed it as not a smoking gun, but a 'squirt gun.'" Those with a nose for news will note that the smoke has now given way to a water-spray, squirted by malicious critics usually in the press corps who have been known to be so armed, and they have come to be known as "little squirts."*[3]

Can this be the deadend of the modern movement to capture "the very language of men" in everyday prose? Have we been betrayed, or misled, by our classic wordmasters who were such semantic idealists, such well-meaning rebels?

All discoveries of "true paths" are fated to take their wayward turns. If, by accident or dialectic, followers of Wordsworth's populistic instructions have in the course of time proved themselves to be gross, gaudy, and inane, his original example had (unlike Hemingway's) at least a potential self-critical sense which could point the way to find sounder bearings. Aim a little to one side, and this message still makes its point:

> They became proud of a language which they themselves had invented, and which was uttered only by themselves; and, with the spirit of fraternity, they ar-rogated it to themselves as their own.... From a variety of causes this distorted language was

---

* The *Oxford Dictionary of Slang* (p. 240) defines *squirt* as "orig. US. An insignificant but presumptuous person; also, a child." *Longman's Dictionary of Contemporary English* (p. 1082) takes it literally as a "quick thin stream."

Jonathan Green, in his *Slang Down Through the Ages* (p. 158), only couples "squirt" with other alcoholic measures ("a slug...go...snort...sniffler...dash of." etc.) which would take us astray in our pursuit of addiction.

Mencken in his list of "words and phrases" in his one-volume edition of *The American Language* (p. 154) has, between *squire* and *squizzle*, only "squirtish" which he calls obsolete (as well it should be, being only a coinage associated with *slantidicular*, also "now no more").

The older Bartlett offers "a foppish young fellow; a whipper-snapper." J.R. Bartlett, *The Dictionary of Americanisms* (1849; 1989 ed.), p. 329. It warns us that it is "*a vulgar word.*"

received with admiration.... The true and the false became so in-separably interwoven that the taste of men was gradually perverted; and this language was received as a natural language; and at length, by the influence of books upon men, did to a certain degree really become so. Abuses of this kind were imported from one nation to another, and with the progress of refinement this diction became daily more and more corrupt, thrusting out of sight the plain humanities of nature by a motley masquerade of tricks, quaintnesses, hieroglyphics, and enigmas.*

Or, as Orwell said when taking second thought after prescribing a set of firm rules to help "cure the decadence of our language": "Break any of these rules sooner than say anything outright barbarous."**

But surely the one larger prescription it would be unruly to disregard amounts to this: when (as in Wordsworth's day) the high language of the scribes has become formal, stilted, lifeless, then go with the natural speech of the common man. But when the "very language" of common men has become depraved and incapacitated, try the diction of the intellectual few which, after the "motley masquerade of tricks," may be by now capable of some genuine communication.

In linguistics, as in history, no class stays on top for long. Liberators turn to oppressors; the best become the worst, the first the last. Pick your wordmasters in high or low places, wherever you best find them, whenever you most need them. Be patient: a swing of the pendulum, clockwise or otherwise, will not be long in coming.

I simplify of course. The pendulum swings are sometimes not nearly so straightforward as they seemed to be perceived. Most of us think of Mencken's inimitable prose as very special in its embellishment. But he thought of it as the very model of unadorned simplicity, not unlike Orwell taking his cues form King James, and playing out for all they were worth "the stark, salty, unaffected, damn-the-grammarians phrases."

Here is the sage of Baltimore (in 1928) singing the praises, of all people, of President Calvin Coolidge as *"Cal as Literatus"*: "Such a man, when he lets himself go, almost always writes very well. His thoughts may not be profound, but their sincerity makes up for that lack, and they conquer by their freedom from the customary whoopla." It was hard (or so Mencken said in one of his outrageous Monday pieces in the paper) for a simple man, so writing, "to write really bad English."

The language, indeed, seems to have been made for such men. It is extraordinarily rich in homely and pungent phrases, made to shock grammarians and delight the rest of us. All of its so-called rules may be broken without any damage to clarity or eloquence. The more they are broken, the more effective the style, as readers of Mark Twain and

---

*　　"Appendix to the Preface to the *Lyrical Ballads*" (1802), in William Wordsworth, *Works* (ed. Gill, 1984), pp. 616-17.

**　"Politics and the English Language" (1946), in George Orwell, *Inside the Whale* (1962), pp. 155-56.

Carlyle well know. The chief aim of every conscious stylist, in English, should be to write like a simple man, unspoiled by pedagogues. The best English ever written is in the King James Bible. The worst is to be found in the thunderous blather of Dr. Johnson and among the sugar-teats of Walter Pater.[4]

Surely Mencken's thunder was more Johnsonesque than the sweet song of King Solomon.

Or, put another way, one man's stately swing of the pendulum, changing the sounds and sensibilities of the language–from, say the short and simple to the long and complex, or from rich to modest, or from the prickly and the pungent to the fresh and anodyne–is another man's uncertain wobble.

23

The Prose We Write and Speak

When that distinguished *doyen* of the Washington press corps, the late Mr. James Reston, after talking to the White House incumbent and Pentagon "top brass," wanted to tell us that some new pattern is emerging in American foreign policy, he would announce (as he had innumerable times over his three decades in Washington) that *"We are now in a whole new ball game!."* This was supposed to be meaningful to all who know and love their fun and games. Is it really? It may be pithy, but is it in any way revealing or even pertinent? What was the *old* ball game? Was it something like baseball (or, say, cricket): slow moving and calling for great patience and endurance? Or was it as formally stylized as tennis, or perhaps rough-and-tumble like rugby? And that whole *new* ball game—football, or soccer, or basketball: fast breaking and full of sudden surprises?*

This metaphor (if that is what it is) is evidently inexpungible from the American vocabulary. After one round of U.S. midterm elections the *New York Times* (25 November 1986) headlined an analysis by its Washington correspondent: A NEW BALLGAME, AND THE SCORING HAS BEGUN. It quoted Senator Richard Lugar: "I think it's a different ballgame," said Senator Richard G. Lugar, an Indiana Republican, "and the Administration has to understand that.

---

* The English novelist, Kingsley Amis, in his occasional excursions into philology, confessed that he rather liked the baseball metaphor *"a whole new ball game,"* as he wrote in *The King's English* (1997, pp. 9-10).

But I think he got it wrong, not only for confining it to only one sport (and excited TV commentators have been heard to say it in athletic dramas that do not even involve a ball, e.g., ice hockey!), but also for supposing that "the Americanism has driven out native equivalents," *e.g.* a *different kettle of fish* or *a horse of another color.*

The "whole newness" does not necessarily consist in a species-difference, *i.e.* the name of the game, but in a dramatic change of fortune, reversing the competitive advantage of one side over the other.

But Amis was absolutely right about the "the Press *clipping* driving out *cutting.*" My clippings are rarely finely scissors-cut; they are mostly ripped, torn, jagged-edged.

If they do not," he said, "the outlook is for 'one confrontation after another.'"
Sports fans will be having a clouded outlook in any case: since every ball
game, new or old, is a confrontation between opposing teams of players, each
seeking victory.

In all of the recent presidential elections you couldn't quite find out precisely what was happening without looking up some old scorecard from Yankee Stadium. Thus, the Reagan-Mondale and the Bush-Ferraro debates were
described as gladiatorial contests, mostly in terms of boxing metaphors (knockouts, winning points, even-steven draws). In New England coastal and other
more nautical areas, one candidate was seen to have "taken the wind out of his
opponent's sail." In a dispatch from Green Bay, Wisconsin, the *New York Times*
(27 October 1986, p. 24) has this to report:

> Mr Bush, who has frequently used sports metaphors to make political points, at-
> tempted another one as he spoke here, across from the stadium in which the Green Bay
> Packers football team plays. But in trying to make a point about his debate with Mrs
> Ferraro, he confused the Packers with the rival Minnesota Vikings, prompting one
> aide to quip, "We just lost Wisconsin."

They didn't; they lost Minnesota; but it was (to borrow another unavoidable metaphor) a close-run thing.

In the British political vocabulary there is a similar sports-ridden burden,
although the references are (mostly) to local games and hence somewhat obscure to the foreign reader. "Prime Minister Major's cabinet is coming out of
the scrum....The Tory party has been caught again *l.b.w.* ["leg-before-wicket"
which is *out* for the cricketer]....The Opposition has been hitting them for six."
etc. Most readers can make out the point. But these sporting conceits are very
rare, and almost confined to tabloid usage. When Prime Minister John Major,
running far behind Tony Blair in the 1997 electoral campaign, decided to go
down to this level and talk populistically in athletic analogies, it left his
advisors dismayed and won nary an extra vote. For his rhetorical lapses he was
mercilessly ribbed by the satirists even in the Tory camp who envisioned him
saying ("passionate, unscripted, and off-the-cuff'): "I'm going to say, 'Love
me or loathe me. I'm batting for England, so don't tie me down or I'll miss the
catch and score an own goal and then we really will be kicked into touch with
our trousers down.'"[1] Given the penchant of British teams for defeat in competitive matches–they always say they're happy just to "enjoy playing the
game," whatever the outcome–here was a British prime minister on a clear
losing streak. A mish-mash of sporting metaphors scores no runs, wins no
contests, loses out in sticky wickets.

Soccer terminology has won transatlantic popularity in recent years; and
boxing, of course, has supplied a number of hard-hitting phrases with inside
dopesters convinced that the swinging pugilistic phrases are sure to win by a
k.o.—as in the 1995 far-reaching review of Britain's place in the post-Cold

War world wherein the basic debate was "whether Britain can or should 'punch above its weight.'" Both Douglas Hurd, the Foreign Secretary, and Prime Minister Major saw "opportunities for Britain to exploit its language overseas" (*Daily Telegraph*, 14 January 1995). Thus does the White Man's Burden get reduced to a backpack full of soiled slang and messy metaphors.

The looseness of the metaphor does not, of course, remain confined to quick-writing journalists, pressed for fast copy by imminent deadlines, or to fast-talking politicians improvising hastily for the evening news. Academics can be enthusiasts for sports (or for the sports pages); and they pick up bad habits unwittingly or, perhaps, to give a populistic touch to staid prose which could prove to be a mite inaccessible. Thus, Professor Hilary Putnam, the liberal Harvard philosopher, polemicizing (as he thinks) on the highest level against the late Professor Robert Nozick, the conservative Harvard sociologist, writes in his book *Reason, Truth and History* (1993):* "I say I respect Bob Nozick's mind, and I certainly do. I say I respect his character, and I certainly do. But, if I feel contempt (or something in that ballpark) for a certain complex of emotions and judgments in him, is that not contempt (or something like it) for *him*?"

He protesteth too much; and this is always a sign of intellectual weakness and uncertainty, rhetorically camouflaged. The clue is, again, in the "ballpark" metaphor. The lapse into the lingo of the sports stadium betrays him. Some "ballparks," especially in America, are vast coliseums, accommodating a hundred thousand fans, screaming a full range of "emotions and judgments" in the summer sunshine or (covered up) in the wintry snow. Other "ballparks" are small, restricted, with a scramble of players and games intermingling on the local green. Accordingly, the professor's contempt for "*something in that ballpark*" has an outreach of possible implications which can blur, dilute, distort any intended meaning. The whole usage can be treated with something like the contempt it deserves, if that happens to be the academic ball game one is playing.

One fine day an American newspaper sub-editor will be awarded a Pulitzer Prize for his contribution to the language of journalism–as a reward for a simple, uncompromising, absolutist blue-pencil prohibition of the use of "*ballgame*" in any metaphorical size, shape, or form. To be sure, the electoral race of Bush/Gore in the year 2000 was troubled more seriously by the technological difficulties in the final win-or-lose countdown. Faulty or imperfect machines committed intermittent errors by misreading lightly punched holes on the voting ballots (all those dimples! all those chads!). The man the good Florida citizens voted for lost the vote to the man they voted against. In a real ballgame, played out in a real ballpark, did anybody ever doubt that the ball clouted into the bleachers was a home run? Or that the bullet pass caught in the end-zone was a six-point touchdown? One game is full of dramatic and decisive certainties; the other so-called "game" is vulnerable and indecisive.

---

*   Hilary Putnam, *Reason, Truth and History* (1981/1993), p. 165.

Our political journalism continues, as in the past, to make its modest, vacuous contribution to befogging the serious public events which we all, in civic fortitude, try hard to be clear about. In the *Washington Post* one of its resident local experts made an effort to sum up where a confused legal situation was "at" some weeks after the historic election day for the forty-third president of the United States had ended. He wrote in a rich mixture of clichés to suit the historic occasion:

> Barring a bombshell [Florida proved not to be Oklahoma], Friday's absentee ballot deadline appeared likely to come and go with the historic election as uncertain as ever. Mr. Bush, however, will almost certainly contend the ball game is over, with Florida's 25 electoral votes putting him over the 270 he needs to become president.[2]

Jurisprudence is pleased to share all the going buzzwords with journalism; the judge's gowns hide the wearing of hand-me-downs. The *Post* reported that another Texas legal advisor was quick to re-insure himself about the final score, or the referee's decision, or the true victor taking the spoils: "Our basic strategy," the Bush lawyer said, "is we are winning on the law and the votes. They are behind the eight-ball, and we aren't!" As is well known in such pool-playing circles, being behind-the-eight-ball is equivalent to being knocked out, losing in the ninth inning, duffing an easy putt on the eighteenth hole.

I doubt that the other implications which the slang dictionaries list will come into play to further complicate (i.e., to complicate further) an already disastrous situation. One Bush legal strategist may or may not know that an *"eight-ball"* is a widespread derogatory term for an African-American (for the eight-ball is black); it is also a cocktail of crack cocaine and heroin amounting to an eighth of an ounce (3.5) of a drug which is said to be rather popular in Harlem, Watts, and other black ghettoes. A further dictionary listing compounds the possible problem in the Texas governor's camp, namely: "eight-ball, to ruin or frustrate, esp. by cheating." But then, did the Texas governor say it? Or was it the correspondent of the *Washington Post*? Or were they all, perhaps, thinking of "eightball: Olde English '800'; also a popular beer in black neighborhoods..."? Cheers! We'll drink to that.[3]

The bromidic use of this athleticism has a monotonous persistence. In the 1996 Presidential campaign there was not only an exponential rise of sporting metaphors and analogies, drawn from every form of athletic competition, but the mother of them all was also trotted out as if newly conceived. Here is Maureen Dowd, admonishing the Republican candidate for a lackluster campaign which failed to dent President Clinton's lead in the public opinion polls (*New York Times/IHT*, 20 September 1996, p. 9):

WAKE UP, BOB DOLE,
IT'S A NEW BALL GAME

As it happens, Senator Dole brought this sternest of all American political reproofs all on himself–for he had, in one of his many slips of tongue and memory, mentioned the "Brooklyn Dodgers" (an unforgettable New York baseball club that had long ago moved three thousand miles westwards from Ebbets Field):

> If he were really revealing his desire [Ms. Dowd explains] for a better world in which the Dodgers are always in Brooklyn, in which the Avenue of the Americas is always Sixth Avenue, and the differently abled are just people with disabilities, that would be attractive.

The Dodgers' present hometown is, of course, Los Angeles, and in its not unattractive new stadium they play the same old ball game, quite oblivious to its repercussions in the field of the nation's politics.

And where, pray, do American clichés go when they die? They cross the Atlantic and miraculously live on in Standard English whenever a bromide is needed. I note that a London newspaper is upset by recent British court decisions involving Rugby players; they are evidently entitled to damages when a referee sends them, for some misdemeanor, off the field. A leading article views the situation with alarm, and the editor titles his editorial:

WHOLE NEW BALL GAME

Rugby has now become a playing field in which aggressive lawyers claim wrongful dismissal and fast-stepping accountants score for an athlete's financial entitlements. The game may be the same, but by calling in the professionals it has lost its amateur status.

Messy metaphors can also cost money. Here is a London financial editor who is pondering the sad spectacle of the city losing its national character as bank after bank get taken over by foreign companies (the latest being Barings by the Dutch and S.G. Warburg by the Swiss). Few are still left (Schroders, Kleinwort Benson). If the trend to foreign ownership continues, he writes: "London will be in the peculiar position as a world financial stadium where nearly all the teams are playing away [i.e., away from home]. It may not matter, but it is certainly a new ball game."[4] Again, the unanswered questions remain: How different is the new ball game? And if it does not "matter," why then do the differences matter? Why should one, in a complex, interdependent multinational economy, profess to care? Or can the money-game differences turn out to be as raw as rugby scrums or as leisurely as cricket innings? Metaphors are elusive high-flyers, and we are left only with dusty answers, here in low finance as well as in lofty philosophy and politics.

In any event the pundit offers a phrase only to help fill a narrow newspaper column, and the conceit is merely decorative. We are left longing to know, to see, to feel more.

"No way!" says the senator, indicating his adamant objection to President Reagan's El Salvador aid programme. *"Right on!"* says the congressman, revealing his approval of new budgetary appropriations. *"We'll go with that,"* approves the *Washington Post* in its leading article. And the commentators on TV find that after the good news, here comes the bad news that nobody is *"telling it like it is."*

The popular American mind, subjected to this–and I have bulging files of innumerable items–is being slowly reduced to a hash of pop vocabulary, mixed together out of slang and cant, slogans and witless wisecracks, which prevent and indeed sabotage any mature communication of an attitude, idea, or political viewpoint. The professional politician pre-fers the new argot because it serves to make him, or her, a person of the people. The news-paperman highlights it as the fast, colorful quote because this is, after all, good writing, truthful transcription, our natural speech, the way we talk. It is getting it (as Hemingway said) pencil-sharp right: punching straight, one on the jaw, like a real champ.

I can't help thinking again of Wordsworth and Hemingway, the former having made a usable myth of "natural speech," and the latter a fetish of "naturalistic transcription"; and both in their ways forcing their conceits on reality. What people read serves to confirm them in the way they speak. In our modern media-massaged discourse the press' jargon goes a long way towards legitimizing pop slanginess, with fashions changing as fast as the late racing editions. Soon, like a bemused mob of *bourgeois gentilhommes,* we won't even know we've been speaking that kind of prose all our born days.

The dead-heat or neck-and-neck campaign in the presidential election year 2000 (and I write this at its outset) promises more of the same; as yet, there appear to be no quantitative or indeed qualitative changes in the conventional language of political reportage. Beyond the usual vignettes of the hullabaloo and razzamatazz, the first impressions are of the usual mélange: there are the daily snap-shots of men-in-suits, or candidates pretending to come-as-they-are, changing into sweaty short-sleeved polo shirts; pundits make their contradictory readings of the national pulse and heartbeat; and, to be sure, our documents offer the familiar wrap-up in sporting and ballgame metaphors that everybody can immediately understand (who's winning, the Giants or the Yankees…or maybe the Bulls).

Given the matching crazes about sporting events and athletic victories on both sides of the Atlantic, this stadium-situated slang is nothing if not contagious. The English edition of the *Frankfurter Allgemeine Zeitung* (*FAZ*), which is distributed as a supplement to the U.S.-owned *International Herald-Tribune*, publishes a report a report of an excited all-night electoral party in the local *Amerika Haus*:

> as the results trickle in, the air fills with joy and despair, as if the audience were watching a world-class prize-fight. Bush lands a blow in Tennessee–boos!–a right

hook [surely not a left jab] for Gore in Michigan–cheers. But neither comes close to a knockout.

Nor does anyone come close to a clean, crisp perception about a civil process which, gravely considered, is the happy alternative to social strife, class struggles, and (on many unhappy occasions) violent revolutions. It deserves from our journalists and newspaper culture a little better than ballyhoo from the bleachers.[5]

The journalistic conceits over each period of four years become increasingly stereotyped, and it now makes no difference what the "ballgame" is (and this covers athletics with no kind of ball involved, like track-and-field, sprints and dashes, not to mention pole vaults and butterfly strokes). Everybody is keeping score, hand-counting on their fingers. The running mates still run neck-and-neck; and if that's not clear enough on the photo-finish picture, there is always a graphic reference to a k.o. with the gutsy, exhausted loser stretched out on the boxing ring floor. This is how Ms. Peggy Noonan, a contributing editor of the knowledgeable *Wall Street Journal* (where she was writing a weekly column about national party politics), summed up the presidential campaign after the Democratic and Republican Conventions in the summer of the year 2000...with the mental astuteness that only comes from exercising the body regularly in the gym.

> For now the two athletes are separately engaged. One is headed for the shower, the other suiting up. At some point they will meet, and you can't help but hope that they will end their contest as runners do, winded and euphoric or gutsy and exhausted. But one senses that the runner will be dragged, against his will, into the ring. And when it's over there will be swollen faces and bloody eyes. Which would be too bad, because when national contests get violent it's never only the guys in the ring that get hurt.

Are we ringside or trackside, out-of-breath or dripping blood? No matter for now; in a few months' time, the bell will ring or the whistles will blow, and it'll be all over to the roar of the crowd (or, maybe, only roughly half of them).*

Meanwhile, the tension mounts and the myriad factors that may play a decisive role in the final electoral outcome are subjected to everything from hunches to tea leaf readings and sheer confusion. When Senator Joseph Lieberman was chosen to be Al Gore's vice presidential running mate, the speculation ran a bit wild as to the possible/probable impact of his religion–he

---

*   Ms. Noonan's mixed metaphors were, to be fair, quite intentional, as signaled by her column's title: "The Hurdler and the Hitter" with a sub-head questioning whether George W. Bush is "racing to the finish line" or whether Al Gore is "now put[ting] on running shoes–or boxing gloves"? (Peggy Noonan, in the *Wall Street Journal*, 7 August 2000.)

     I hope that English cricket and French bowling never catch on in the U.S.A.–what each of them can contribute to sporting slang, with their spinning bowlers and rolling *boules*, will hopelessly overburden American politics.

is, that rare bird, a modern observant orthodox Jew–on the voting patterns of the electorate. Voters have in the past elected Jewish mayors, governors, and senators, but Lieberman would have been, if Gore should have won, the first U.S. vice president of the Jewish faith. The psephologists have now turned ethnologists. In New York and New Jersey, we are told on the op-ed page of the *Daily News* (by its columnist, Richard Cohen), "the Jewish vote is critical." But, "on the other hand, who knows the extents of anti-Semitism any more? It has never been tested at the polls." Can this be so? "Polls" here is ambivalent: it may mean in-the-voting-booths (and the voters have in fact elected, or rejected, Jewish candidates a thousand times in the last century); or it may mean Gallup-type public-opinion polls on voter prejudices (and Jewish organizations measure this type of thing all the time). Mr. Abe Foxman of the Anti-Defamation League told the *New York Post* campaign-reporters that the level of Internet anti-Semitic postings (slurs, hate messages, warnings that the-Jews-would-be-running-the-country, etc.) seemed to be declining. Evidently "American Online," the largest Internet Service provider, has been intervening and "clearing some of the stuff off." Foxman was hopeful. Even the standard opinion-surveys testing prejudice indicated a slight decline. But the dispiriting fact of the matter is that one poll (taken in 1998) found that about 12 percent of the American people were latent anti-Semites, "and that's 25 to 30 million people." When, if at all, does latent ever become active? And how many millions does it carry along and activate?[6]

These are profoundly earnest issues, and the chronic disorder of ballgame metaphorics has for the moment been mercifully suspended. I am persuaded that Americans will bring serious reflection to bear on the ethnic factors being disputed; but in the first stage, the debate–if that is (hopefully) what it will amount to–appears to be colored with peripheral exotica. The novelist Mordecai Richler has a phrase for it: *pidgin Yiddish.*

Richler uses it in his latest novel, *Barney's Version* (1998, p. 329) and on the same page we find "*boobbe-myseh.Shabbes goy.Mischpocheh... rachmones*"–which, if they ever turn up in the vice presidential literature (unlikely, now that Senator Lieberman lost in the Florida vote), mean, respectively, "an old-wives' tale...a sabbath gentile [usually employed to do the forbidden menial jobs on High Holy occasions]...family...sympathy." Such borrowings are not, strictly speaking, "*pidgin*," defined as "an auxiliary language"–which, in their heyday, the national varieties of Yiddish probably were...with 10-20 percent borrowed from the French in Paris, from the Italian in Rome, from Anglo-American usages in Brooklyn, from the Russian-or-Polish in Minsk and Pinsk. Words, wherever they get to feel at home, tend to intermarry.

My estimate of the percentages of "Yiddishisms" is rather on the high side, impressionistically calculated in various conversations I have heard. More exacting philologists (say, Leo Rosten) who were more familiar with written Yiddish literature and especially Yiddish journalism in New York estimate the

English-American component as something around 4 percent...with Hebrew at 16 percent and German at 72 percent. The preponderance of the German contribution is, of course, historic: for the East European Jews lived for long and important periods in their history in German-language areas (including the Austrian-Habsburg Empire)...*Ashkenaz* being the Hebrew for Germany.

Still, the *Ashkenazi* families who lived in the Pale of Russian-occupied Poland for centuries and subsequently turned up as greenhorn emigrants in Ellis Island not only contributed many colorful words to their "host-languages," but were borrowers as well. So well indeed that when New York newspapers think they are having a kind of cutesy fun with Yiddish phrases, they are, in point of fact, erratically publishing locutions which the Jews absorbed in their *shtetl* near Lodz or Lemberg.

Among such popular Polish words are: *shmatta* (in Polish "*rag*," and was thus indispensable in Manhattan's garment center, a.k.a. the rag trade)–*czajnik* (kettle), the noisy element in the dismissive phrase *hocking ah cheinik*, talking nonsense–*paskudny* for odious, which denigrated in civilized Bronx-Brooklyn values the *paskudnyak* whose villainy (and even hooliganism) was menacing and contemptible. Also of "Slavic origin," referring to a coarse fellow–and who will rise up to defend the Slav character from such mounting political incorrectness?–there is *zhlub* (or *schlub*). Safire in the *New York Times* was worried about its spelling, preferring the former; and he went on to speculate about its large relationship to the coarse zeitgeist: "Jerk and drip are long gone; nerd and dork are passé. Is this the time of the *zhlub*?" How pejorative can that insult be? How to measure the malignancy of foreign put-downs? Is being called "*a zhlub!*" even libellous?

A small ethnic slur implying mere clumsiness or ill manners will probably get you off lightly. But, as ex-President Clinton might say, it all depends on what you mean by "coarse."[7]

Even in those "critical states" where American Jews constitute formidable voting blocs there is only a very small minority who manage to speak, or read, or even understand the old *shtetl* dialect which the grandfathers and -mothers brought with them on the transatlantic steamers to Ellis Island. Certainly it was not substantial or resilient enough to maintain the once-flourishing immigrant press (and the old *Forwaerts*, renamed the *Jewish Daily Forward*, is now published only in English).

Nevertheless, words and phrases of old-world charm turn up increasingly and have a new straggling lease of life as verbal refugees in New York slang. Popular novels with a Jewish milieu like Richler's–and, before him, innumerable authors like Daniel Fuchs (*Low Company*, 1937), Jerome Weidman (*I Can Get It For You Wholesale*, 1937), and somewhat earlier, a Grosset-and-Dunlap star Milt Gross (*Nize Baby*, 1926)–are inevitably dotted with "pidgin Yiddish." Who now understands (I'm only asking!) that vernacular except the very old folk?

Curiously enough, it is to be found more and more as a form of ethnic slang in the daily press of New York. The *Post*–and even the *New York Times*–is nowadays steeped in it, and prints unashamedly it with no quotation marks and without italics. So many stars in stand-up comedy have come from the Bronx or Brooklyn and made their fame in Hollywood or on Broadway, doing their same old Catskills *shtick*, that a reference to *shmoozing* with a *kvetch*– and other Yiddish demotics–adds presumably to the sheer lightness of reading your favorite local newspaper. Yiddishisms seem to flourish in an unusual proportion to the direct decline of the mother tongue: the slang enriching itself as the language dies. As for the by-line writer in the *Post* or the *News* or the *Times*, he had better be obviously Jewish, otherwise nobody'd believe his story was authentic and, what's more, politically correct. He may be giving his ancestral lineage away–discreetly repressed for a generation or two–but evidently he no longer needs to be mortally embarrassed that his father or grandfather had never really learned to speak proper English.

In the current liberal-humanistic defense of Senator Joe Lieberman's nomination as Democratic vice presidential candidate–and there were fears that in a rough campaign he might have gotten hurt badly–we learned that his mother was "a real Yiddishe mama" and was also "a real *mensch*" (*New York Daily News*) and that the senator's twelve-year-old daughter Hana played with *dreidels* in Clinton's White House (she "just loved" Bill who just knew everything that there was to know about Chanukkah).

Such genial sentimentalism may help to bring out the ethnic Jewish vote; but it is also bringing out the murkier language which has marred Manhattan politics in recent decades. Readers are interminably reminded that the Rev. Jesse Jackson, the radical black leader, once referred to New York as "*Hymietown*"; that an angry Hillary Clinton once raged against a campaign manager who was called "*a Jew bastard.*"[8]

24

Dealing with the Grandmother Tongue

The Continuing Domestication of Yiddishisms

At any rate, the melodramatic character of the November 2000 electoral results, if not the dull conventionality of the preceding months of campaigning, gave an opportunity to journalists to re-examine what they were saying in their papers and how they were saying it.

I have referred to the nervous, and perhaps even neurotic, confusions and inconsistencies of the *New York Times'* own rules and regulations on Jewish matters as embodied in the 1999 edition of its *Manual of Style and Usage*. In its two pages under *Y* (pp. 363-64) there is a stuffy item on *Yom Kippur* ("High Holy days preferred, rather than High Holidays of Judaism"). Doesn't the *Times* have a house philologist any longer? The senior editors who put together the latest edition of its house-style book note (p. 363) under *yarmulke*: "Yiddish for skullcap is often preferable in print." However, according to Rosten (in the *Joys of Yiddish*), the *yarmulkah* derives "from a Tartar word, via the Polish for skull-cap." Thus, that orthodox headcovering of sacred memory is not a Yiddish/Hebrew word at all! As for the name of those high holy days, scholars have traced it back to the Babylonian.[1]

The moral of the story is that newspapermen who want to write multicolored prose have to be multilingual, or at least to consult lexicographers and their dictionaries. At the *Times* only Safire seems to crack a book on the language as she is writ and spoke, and give it a long weekend's reflection.

For the rest, there was no general guidance on how to cope with the *mamaloshen* and the editorial intrusion of the ethnic "mother-tongue" of so many New Yorkers (and of so many respected *Times* reporters). The time, if ever, was now ripe for confrontation. Mind you, it could have been a serious intellectual occasion (for the paper prides itself on its "News Analysis"). Or–as it was always more likely to be, alas–it could be jokey, ranging uneasily between coy and twee. It could have had a certain Menckenesque dignity, even a touch of the workaday seriousness of a Theodore Bernstein. Or it could turn out to be cosy and flippant, with undertones of Jack Benny and Eddie Cantor, stand-up comic stars of yesteryear, and overtones of Leo Rosten (whose lexical researches were referred to as "his best fancy-shmancy language"). The sophomoric pun on Rosten's *magnum opus* was inevitable…and the *Times* headline promptly read–

THE OYS OF YIDDISH

It was not a prepossessing beginning, clogging long-awaited lexicographical guidance with schoolboy wordplay. What would the august Adolph S. Ochs, the founding father, have made of reports of Washington statesmen *shmoozing* in the corridors of power or performing their *shtick* in their respective parliaments? Would Turner Catledge or James Reston–not to mention Anne O'Hare McCormick (and, especially, those old-time *Times* models of journalistic elegance, Meyer Berger and Simeon Strunsky), all memorable twentieth-century by-lines who contributed millions of words to the paper's columns–have entertained the editorial usage of ethnic demotics and pidgin slang?

To *shmooze* in Yiddish (and hence in Yinglish) refers to idle chatter, but in German it also has an erotic note, sometimes suggesting sexual foreplay, or at least "petting." (And I've heard of one Austrian ambassador who was nonplussed to hear from a U.N. correspondent that two of the Security Council diplomats were engaged in "*shmoozing*.") A standard German dictionary lists four variants of meaning: (1) flirtatious; (2) passionate kissing; (3) a marriage arrangement; and, last, (4) to talk nonsense.[2]

I regularly received a number of German catalogues which offer me (for cut prices) CDs featuring *schmuse*-songs, recorded with digital remastery, by such artists as Harry Belafonte, the Beach Boys, Pat Boone, et al.–all *schmus*-crooning away. But, then, if this particular word was derived not from German but from the Hebrew (*shmuos*: things heard…rumors), then we're in another…er, well,…ballpark.[3]

Times change. Clyde Haberman who was given the difficult, *oy-vay* assignment began his *Times* piece–one way or another a landmark in Manhattan linguistics–with the latest flourish in attention-grabbing leads, a real shocker, a downright come-on puzzlement.

> What a noodge! She made me shlep to the theater for tickets to a schmaltzy play. While I waited, this nudnik kept kibitzing, I don't mean to kvetch, but his schmoozing was annoying. His shtick made me so meshuga I walked away. But I tripped. Sometimes, I can be a klutz.

The point of this jabberwocky was the highly dubious proposition that New York readers of the *Times* may have comprehended it (all of them? some of them? a few?) and may have thought (even more unlikely) that "every word was standard English." Following on from this questionable supposition, the *Times* man writes with no detectable note of irony that this constituted "pretty solid evidence of how a fair amount of Yiddish, the language of European Jews, has become mainstream in America, land of the free and home of the bagel."

The evidence was dismaying. In the notorious New York Senatorial race which was famously won by Mrs. Hillary Rodham Clinton, she and her Italianate opponent (Rick Lazio) both accused each other of having *chutzpah*, taking for granted that a national television audience would know they meant something like mutually galling brazenness. Neither candidate, as the *Times* reporter hastens to point out with pseudo-genetic finickiness, had "a Jewish bone in their bodies." Such biological details have become news-fit-to-print, already.

Worse was to come, even if it was fuzzily subsumed under the category of what the *Times* rendered as *farpotshket*. Evidently sometime New York Senator D'Amato had tried once to impress a Jewish audience with his qualities as a *shtarker* (a strong-man, a big-shot), by referring to his opponent with a Yiddish expletive. Little did he know that, as Haberman explains, "the word means penis and is so coarse that it won't be printed here." For my part I would have preferred a clue or two, possibly with benefit of dashes or asterisks, as to what the word actually was and to the enormity of the slip-of-the-mother-tongue. But the *Times*' prudish self-censorship extends with admirable fairness to the whole of the multi-culti scene and to each and every one of its coarse vocabularies and obscene excesses. Senator Alphonse D'Amato went on to lose the elections but, as the *Times* sternly admonished, he hadn't helped himself "by behaving like a shmo" (which was "a cleaned-up version of another popular Yiddish word for jerk that also means penis").*

At this point one could become alarmed that the *Times* was here fishing in troubled waters: it was on the verge of implying that a proud language that boasted such extraordinary twentieth-century writers as Sholom Aleichem and the two (I.B. and I.J.) Singer brothers (and Isaac Bashevis had won a Nobel Prize) was now reduced to being of menial service as a mere source of a- and p-words synonyms…which are then promptly deleted.

Unless they are misunderstood. *Dreck* in German means simply dirt; but it is in Yiddish usage a dirty word, and users came-a-cropper when they thought it referred only to *garbage* or *junk*. But, explains Haberman, "dreck means

---

*   This is news indeed. Rosten concedes (*Joys*, p. 359) that *schmo* is used as a "euphemistic neologism" for *schmuck* (which, in turn, can be used as an eminently deletable Yiddish expletive). But he insists that *shmo* is not a Yiddish word but a "Yinglish invention." In point of fact it was the late Al Capp, that madcap inventor of hillbilly hi-jinks in his unforgettable *L'il Abner* comic-strip, who created a cartoonish figure, "an egg-shaped creature that loves to be kicked and gives milk…." He (or she) was named *shmo*.

excrement"–and hence, in a U.S. law trial which ensued, "the Judge, not amused, gave the dirty users 'a klop in kop'…which means hitting-them-on-the-head…or, in free translation, "reading them the riot act."

If Yiddishisms have begun to flavor the activities of, among others, talkative third world diplomats, *shmoozing* in Manhattan cocktail bars, they are in the current phase of upward mobility also detectable in even the highest places, say, the most royal precincts of the English monarchy. It insinuates itself most easily whenever "the German connection" comes up, and the anti-Teutonic slang–kept fresh by the Fleet Street sports writers who don't miss a trick to put down the *Krauts*–is ready at hand to help push the republican anti-monarchical cause. Even the Tory press cannot escape falling into the trap of subversion by genealogy. And given the Battenberg bloodline in the present-day House of Windsor, any mention of Prince Philip–husband of the queen, father of the next king–leads us into old and new colloquialisms.

Graham Turner interviewed (as is his wont) at least a hundred friends and relatives of the Duke of Ediburgh in a long series of articles for the *Daily Telegraph*. Searching for a clue to the aggressive, irascible unpredictability native to his famous explosive temperament, he quoted one unimpeachable source–"one of the Queen's longest-serving aides"–to the effect that he was "*very Germanic,*" and indeed that he was often written off as "*a bit of a Kraut.*" One would think that a Tory portrait of the Queen's consort would loyally try to use a strictly clean Elizabethan prose. But given the fashionable fixations of even the most conservative journalists, good colorful writing has to borrow a bit from here, there, and everywhere, to sport a bit of *chutzpah* and to kid the pants off a royal *schlemiel*. Turner's flamboyantly readable text is sprinkled with what passes for "kosher cockney" and serves to do down some of the Prince's critics who like to dwell on his embarrassing *schlemozzles*: "Such stories, no doubt, are meat and drink to those who like to portray Philip as little more than a gaffe-prone royal klutz, the ultimate brick-dropper."[4]

Klutz in its original Germanic meaning is only mildly pejorative. The *Duden* gives the old platitudinous insult, to be *ein Klotz am Bein*, which is to be a burden on somebody, to be a drag.

In its Yiddish career, as outlined by Leo Rosten (*Joys of Yiddish*, pp. 186-187), it is sharper and, conceivably, "subversive." In the case of a consort to the throne-bearing monarch of the day, it might have in the older days cost a man's head to be so disrespectful.

1. A clod; a clumsy, slow-witted, graceless person; an inept blockhead.
2. A congenital bungler.

As Rosten cracks, "The word even sounds *klutz*-like."

Further in its *klutz*-like American/Yiddish usages, it began by being jocular, as in the Columbia University *Jester* gag of 1918, which has a Hezekiel Klutz who fought in the trenches of Flanders (1914-1918)–and didn't write a book about it. Our novelists then took it over, and it gets rather more acidulous, to judge by the entries in Volume II (p. 369) of Lighter's *Historical Dictionary of American Slang*. The cited quotations are to the effect: A clumsy person, an oaf, who has "a big klutz of a son...who botches everything...who klutzes up the system...who tries to sing and dance but can't escape being klutzy."

The domestication of these Yiddishisms into the proper English sector of the English language appears, by and large, to have had a transatlantic impetus and inspiration. If it penetrates American slang in multifarious usages, it is then *chic* and stylish enough to open up acceptable speech and meaningful prose to London show-biz gossip and even to the more grave vocabulary of high British politics.

There is, of course, an adequate local source. A small Jewish community, based on nineteenth-century emigration from Eastern Europe, populated the Dickensian East End of London, and anybody in the area was entitled to pick up such scraps of *mama-loshen* as were deemed colorful and unembarrassing. The usual homeland pressures on "greenhorns" of assimilation and integration made, in England, for unsurprising conformism to the King's (or Queen's) English. But Jewish writers occasionally peppered their texts with Yiddishisms–among the authors I have published in *Encounter* during my own London years include: Arnold Wesker, Bernard Kops, Ian Sinclair, among others. Still, it was the *goyim* through whom, I think, that the local breakthrough came–to begin with, Colin MacInnes (the half-Australian novelist) and Frank Norman (the Cockney playwright). Above all, it was the Americans of whatever ethnic background–from Brooklyn and the Borscht Belt to Hollywood, from George Jessel to Jackie Mason–who made Yiddish colloquialisms fashionable.

The English looked the other way. Wilde never thought of a joke as a *vitz*, and Shaw never considered any of his plays as a *shtick*. Disraeli's father, a celebrated British man-of-letters in his day, wrote an impeccable "Oxford English"; and so did his son, especially in his early years as a gifted novelist (*Coningsby*, 1844; *Sybil*, 1845). In our own day superb Fleet Street journalists like Bernard Levin and John Gross were unexceptionable models of high Anglo-Saxon style; and, having followed their output for half-a-century, I cannot recall their ever having interrupted their flow of smooth prose (Johnsonian in once case, Orwellian in the other) with a *kosher* or a *shmooze* or a *chutzpah*, or other knowing in-tribe forms of a wink and a nod.

These Yiddishisms (and more) were a late import. With such phenomena as "Americanization" and "globalization" funny things began to happen to the way to Eric Partridge's old dictionary of slang. Traditionally fine and finicky writers felt freely obliged to refer to *shlemiels* (and also to something misspelled called *shemozzle*) and the likes, all emanating from a whole *meshpuchah* of a demotic vocabulary.

A crowning point was reached by the turn of the new millennium; and Yiddish, long since dead as a vital dialect in the London East End, began to have a free-floating influence on the highest political activities in the land. It is not as if a word had been missing and some piece of Anglo-Saxon practice remained unnamed and unidentified. Like so many newly improvised usages in the language of journalism, the sudden emergence of a buzzword contributes merely a diverting sense of noise rather than an illuminating element of meaning. Still, our wordsmiths are convinced–for a season or two, until another brust of faddishness changes the scene–that they have been coming nearer and nearer to the heart of coherence, or explanation, or insight. That's enough, already.

One example. Voted in by the British electorate in 1997, Tony Blair's administration has had the usual amount of political and administrative troubles (a disastrous railroad network; Cabinet ministers who operated close to the line of sleaze; an appalling national health servuce, short on doctors, on nurses, and on everything but pain-killing pills; etc.). To put a good face on things, Prime Minister Tony Blair and his energetic associates conducted intense but not unprecedented public relations campaigns, lacing all information with jiggers of propaganda. The strategy was called "*spin*" (partly, I suspect, from the athletic trick of so-called "English spin," with which a bouncing ball is made to reverse in on itself; and partly from the German/Jewish "*Schpinner*" who makes things up, fantasizing about everything). The cunning manipulators were given the name of "*spin doctors*."

Well, as it happened, the "11th of September" (2001) came along, and the destruction of New York's Twin Tower skyscrapers gave the spin doctors everywhere a special opportunity for their mode of news management. One brilliant and highly paid press consultant in London urgently advised her Ministry to use the sensational Wall Street headlines to get rid of their own worst stories–since the public disclosures of failures and finagling would hardly get much space in the days and weeks to come, so full of tragic tales of terrorism in Manhattan. The tactic was referred to as "*burying the news*." For some critics it was a pernicious new turn in the regrettable phenomenon of "doctoring" government information and lying to the public. Others wearily pointed out that governments have been doing it since the bread-and-circuses of ancient Rome.

An authoritative contribution to this discussion came from Mr. Joe Ashton, a Labour member of Parliament for some thirty years, and in his day a readily quotable source when "dealing" with the press on fast-breaking political stories. He informed the nation in the *Times* (21 February 2002, p. 23) that "there was even a proper Parliamentary word for this" (with *proper* evidently negating the *impropriety*). Surprisingly enough, the word was a *Yiddish* one. According to Mr. Ashton, hitherto unknown in lexigraphical circles specializing in bilingual complications, "It is called 'a tummler,' a Jewish word meaning decoy. A diversion. A distraction created to pick the pockets of the crowd." It happened all the time. Prime Minister Margaret Thatcher was said to be an expert in diversions and distractions (in order, evidently, to sneak through her nefarious governmental policies). On one of these furtive occasions Mr. Ashton recalls, he ran into the Tory chancellor of the exchequer, then Nigel Lawson; and he called attention to the *"classic tummler,"* and Chancellor Lawson "laughed all the way to another election victory."

As it happened Chancellor Lawson was in fact of Jewish origins; but did he laugh in ethnic embarrassment? Or with tribal pride? Or, maybe, because he hadn't the faintest idea what *"tummler"* could possibly signify? It is, as Yiddishisms go, a hard word, a rarity even in the East End, and very problematical even in the expertise of a Leo Rosten. In point of fact Rosten in his popular dictionary lists a dozen various connotations of the word *tummler* (from "a buffoon, commotion, noisy disorder" to "a show-biz life-of-the-party"). Nowhere is there a hint of MP Ashton's sense of the diversionary cunning which Thatcher in her rhetoric, or Blair in his ideology, came to employ in disseminating parliamentary disinformation. Students of anti-Semitism were likely to detect a devious ploy to get the Jews, wittingly or not, involved in yet another disreputable stratagem. They even have especially proper words for that shady sort of thing!).[5]

Why did the *Times* give such pride of place on its leader page to such an outlandish argument? It is usually guided by the semantic sensitivities of its able in-house lexicographer, Mr. Philip Howard, who (unlike his *New York Times* counterpart, William Safire) may not have the ear for Yiddishisms; but there are, after all, lexicons to consult. Slang, especially in the story of the language of journalism, is a self-renewing *patois*, and indefatigable wits keep making up new words or innovative usages all the time. Why discriminate against some unfamiliar Jewish turns-of-phrase? Right or wrong, they seem to be so apt, and appear to be right on-target, and in any case they are free, unprotected, and tolerably multi-cultural. *Nebbish.*[6]

It would be fanciful to ascribe to one single cultural moment in New York City history, a memorable event at the Imperial Theatre on West 4th Street, a turning point significance. Frank Sullivan, the *quondam* cliché expert of the *New Yorker*, taught us all a long time ago that we are rarely at a "crossroads" when pompous pundits pronounce that we are, and even less do "turning points" actually turn when we sense an important change coming on.[7]

Still and all, and for all that, I seem to be convinced with many others on the Broadway scene that, in the longer perspective of linguistic idiosyncrasies, the great success of Jerry Robbins–with Zero Mostel in the starring role of Tevye the Milkman in the adaptation of Sholem Aleichem, *Fiddler on the Roof* (premiere: 22 September 1964)–constituted just such a turning point.

For one thing, the figure of the *Fiddler* –which had been rendered so charming and respectable by the popularity of Marc Chagall's paintings–had suddenly become acceptable on a Broadway stage. He was, only yesterday, everybody's grandfather whose "greenhorn" ways the children of Ellis Island veterans chose to forget. Now, beard and black hat and all, his *klezmer* music would be making it into the popular tunes of Tin Pan Alley's hit parade. Even more than that, Jerry Robbins (né Jerome Rabinowitz) followed Agnes de Mille and confidently accommodated the American ballet to the national ethnicities. Ms. de Mille went West with galloping cowboys in *Rodeo*. Robbins went East and with a stage full of wildly joyous Hassidic Jews from Anatevka reconciled New York audiences to ethnic roots which had previously dared to speak their name on only especially private occasions. Then and there was the beginning of the word. One could sing one's past, and dance it as well.

Now one could even quote it in the morning newspapers, especially for a metropolitan generation so well integrated and assimilated that the usable vocabulary of old *mama-loshen* actually consisted of only a handful of Yiddishisms.

And these, lo and behold, began to insinuate themselves into the language of journalism. Adolph S. Ochs would have given half his fortune–and Eugene I. Meyer the other half of his–in order to avoid the embarrassment of a patois, badly spoken by a tribe of Ashkenazi, the *Ostjuden* of old, still held in such contempt.

The *New York Times* and the *Washington Post*–and in their wake, most of the mainstream press in the boondocks–were reluctantly following the East Coast guidelines. All of them needed a smidgin of extra instruction, perhaps a few night-school hours in the style of H*y*m*a*n K*a*p*l*a*n; and all this, accordingly, made the *mavens* of the grandmother tongue singular and even isolated figures on the bilingual scene, capable of celebrating the "joys of Yiddish," into best sellers. In one of the book reviews (Virginia Kirkus), it was recorded that "Leo Rosten does for the Yiddish language what Cézanne did for the apple." Fruiterers as well as art critics may have been puzzled at the time; but Ms. Kirkus was quick to explain that the apple–in the Big Apple yet!–was being given "body and soul." Isaac Bashevis Singer was still writing it in his uptown Broadway cafeteria table, and with his helped-out fractured English he gave as much aid as he could to his translators.[8]

I have already documented the early incursions of Yiddish into the language of journalism. At this point a few more complex consequences need to be touched upon: (1) the matter of spelling and transliteration and (2) the problem of accurate ethnic inflection as journalistic usages are sounded out in other media (radio and TV, and the spoken word generally).

There are a number of subtle complications in the spelling of popular Yiddishisms. Jewish writers tend to look away from the possible/probable low or medieval Germanic origins of a word or a phrase. The difference is accentuated in whether *sh* or *sch* (as in *schlemihl* or *schlemozzle* or *s(c)hmooz*). Nobody in Berlin where a whole host of local popular expletives smack of the Yiddish ("gonniff!" "meshugge!") dares to offer a confident lexical explanation as to which-came-first, who-borrowed-(or stole)-from-whom....In Hollywood non-Jews confound the tone of words, and feel certain that their arbitrary usages are unexceptionable. Thus, the Butterworth brothers, Jez and Tom, fresh out of London and triumphant with a new hit film, are here—in a *Washington Post* piece—pronouncing about "*joke-oids*" that "look like a joke and sound like a joke, but they're not." This leads to the general thesis that "In American film at the moment [2002], so much of what is called comedy is just shtick." *Shtick* here is pejorative. Does it mean *unfunny*? A "joke-oid," perhaps? Well, Catskill comedians—from Milton Berle to Shelly Berman—for half-a-century made their names by doing their *shtick*; and even top stars like Bob Hope and Bing Crosby were proud to be praised for doing their "*shtick*." Messrs. Butterworth would have been better off just doing their own thing. Playing or messing around with Jews, and their Yiddishisms, can get you into trouble. It is inadvisable.[9]

Leo Rosten's Gallimaufry*

I am not suggesting that my obvious aversion to ethnic-pidgin or lingo-deviance is in any way associated with a long-term fundamentalism which tends to resist all change and innovation in speech habits and literary style. Quite the contrary. In the beginning I shared the enthusiasm of my fellow-New Yorkers over the growing number of Yiddish words and idioms that were "invading" the English we were being taught to speak and write. Even the most fastidious guardians of the old Brahmin Anglo-Saxon proprieties could approve the dictum of the day which held: "But English, far from being a supine language, has zestfully borrowed a marvelous gallimaufry of foreign locutions...and who will deny that such brigandage has vastly enriched our cherished tongue?" This is the argumentative voice of Leo Rosten in 1968, rejoicing as to how "marvelously resilient" the English language (or, perhaps, in the first phase, only the American version) was in accepting the influence of another parlance.

It was also an indication of the extraordinary role being played by Jewish intellectuals in the contemporary American scene. Rosten was modest about his own role in the great outpouring "of Jewish wit and humor into the great flowing river of English." This was before the ingenious codification of "Yinglish" in his best-selling lexicon of 1970. We used to talk and dispute

---

*   According to the *Oxford English Dictionary*, vol. IV, F-G, p. 26-27, "Gallimaufry...A dish made by hashing up odds and ends of food; a hodge-podge, a ragout. A heterogeneous mixture, a confused jumble, a ridiculous medley...A promiscuous assemblage (of persons). 4. Said somewhat contemptuously of a person: A man of many accomplishments; a composite character. Now *rare*..."

such matters at his Manhattan "Chaos Club" meetings, and I sensed that to-wards the end of his life (he died in 1997) he was ready to say in his inimitable manner, "*Enough already!*" He loved the ancestral *mama-loshen*; but when its popularity came, it was not to praise the old parlance but to bury it. As I have contended, the more Yinglish flowered in American usage, the deader the language became of a people who had lived with so much death in the century. "Never in history," Rosten recorded, "has Yiddish been so influential–among Gentiles." And he added, wryly, "Among Jews, alas, the tongue is running dry."

The "revolution in values" which all students of words tend to discern when faced by interesting semantic changes in diction and prose is an unpre-dictable phenomenon which also contains its opposite. We were supposed to get richer but we got poorer. New parlance hinted at new passions, with sug-gestions of fresh meaning and unexpected implications. But it all seemed to dissolve in the American culture's omnivorous appetite for entertainment. All became titillation. A Pentagon officer described the U.S. air-bombardment pattern in the Vietnam War: "You might call it the bagel strategy." A New York daily–of all papers, the august *Wall Street Journal*–headlined a feature on the protesting students of '68: "REVOLUTION, SHMEVOLUTION." Rosten's high-brow spirit warmed to a legendary piece of graffiti which had it: "*Marcel Proust is a Yenta.*"

A half-century has elapsed since–to choose arbitrarily a schmaltzy turning-point–the Catskill comedian style (as personified by U.S. television's first great entertainment star, Milton Berle) popularized a whole vocabulary of Yiddishisms at the center of mainstream conversation and, hence, of newspa-per culture. It was deemed an unqualified success story in the half-illusion which always accompanies phrase-makers, madly intent on allusive reference and apt foreign quotation (from Horace to Sholem Aleichem). Some locutions were already part of English in Rosten's day. Other "foreign-born words" were rapidly becoming part of the scene. And then there were those favorites (stop me if you already heard them) that "deserved to be part of our noble language because no English words so exactly subtly, pungently, or picturesquely con-vey their meaning." Still, for an aging generation of immigrant children there was occasion for sheer pride. A short list:

1. shmaltz…gonif…shlemiel…
2. chutzpa…megillah…shlep…yenta.
3. shmoos…kvetch…shlimazl…tchotchke.[10]

I should add that loan words do not often, as in the case of "Yinglish," carry with them in the process of acculturation the special baggage of old accent and original pronunciation. Native English-speakers did not think it neces-sary to roll their *r*'s in taking over the German "*Kindergarten*" nor to achieve, in the French context, a certain nasality in singing a Maurice Chevalier or an Edith Piaf song. In the case of Rosten's "gallimaufry" (*O.E.D.*: a hash of odds-and-ends; a hodge-podge; a ridiculous medley), the words and especially their accentuation and/or inflection in the wit and wisdom of folkish maxims have also to be taken on board. Love the sayings, sing the whole singsong. I append a small selection which, I am afraid, needs a bit of the Catskill lilt and would sound, the last I heard, half-meaningless in the Bardian posh of Stratford-on-Avon.

Get lost.
You should live so long.
My son, the physicist.
I need it like a hole in the head.
Who *needs* it?
So why do you?
Al*right* already.
It shouldn't happen to a dog.
O.K. by me.
He knows from nothing.
From that he makes a *living*?
How come only five?
Do him something.
This I need yet?
A person could bust.
He's a regular genius.
Go hit your head against the wall.
You want it should sing, too?
Plain talk: He's crazy.
Excuse the expression.
With sense, he's loaded.
Go fight City Hall.
I should have such luck.
It's a nothing of a dress.
You should live to a hundred and twenty.
On him it looks good.
It's time, it's time.
Wear it in good health.
Listen, *bubele*...

For some in the newspaper culture these fragments constitute the happy markers of what still are (but only barely) the joys of a remarkable language. For others, disturbed by a strand of misplaced merriment, they are like the melancholy little pebbles that rest on sunken headstones in some long-abandoned graveyard.

By now (the year 2001) one could find a London scribe (and even a Berlin *feuilletonist*!) citing knowingly any one of a dozen of these phrases in apt contexts. Now that the *New York Times* has "outed" its ethnic roots–with a mournful cry about "*the Oys of Yiddish*"–its ready incorporation of the old East Side ghetto demotic into a colorful daily feature is, more or less, unproblematical...although I suspect that it would be reluctant to go on to share Rosten's high-spirited ethnicity: "What other language is fraught with such exuberant fraughtage?"

Rosten was less interested in the broad vaudeville patter of stand-up Jewish comedians than in hitherto unexploited "nuances of affection, compassion, displeasure, emphasis, disbelief, skepticism, ridicule, sarcasm, scorn" (Rosten, *Joys*, p. xiv).

English-language writers who were devoted to cultivating nuances of other provenance, that is, classical "Anglo-Saxon," were sometimes tempted into a professional backlash. In the case of Leo Rosten, whom I greeted in London twice a year on his Anglophiliac pilgrimages to England–mostly to dine his friends in his favorite club (the Savile) and to doublecheck some footnote (in the sacred reading room of the old British Museum)–it was especially disagreeable.

I can't imagine what got into Kingsley Amis, usually to be found grumbling harmlessly in a corner of the Garrick Club bar, to write as he did about dining out with the Rostens (Amis was married at the time to the novelist Elizabeth Jane Howard). The acerbic English novelist mustered all his prose talents to do the man down. The caustic chapter in his book of *Memoirs* (1991) is a model in its way of non-violent anti-Semitism. When in New York I accidentally called Leo Rosten's attention to the unfortunate pages (in the Penguin edition, pp. 320-323), he was deeply wounded, as only a humorist who loved to laugh could be. None of the dozen English newspaper reviewers ever mentioned the matter (Rosten died in 1997, Amis in 1995).

Something of the same problematical character obtains in the case of what the *Times* calls the "blithe" use of *tochis*, taken to be embarrassingly vulgar, but not altogether so since the word was deemed fit to print. In a free-talking new century in which we have our political guide-lines from the White House as to when and where to "kick ass," then what Rosten records as "unquestionably improper" (*Joys*, p. 406)–the Yiddish word for buttocks, derived from the Hebrew for "posterior"–is losing some of its vulgarity.[10] And so is *bubkes*, which the *Times* reports to be derived from "goat-droppings." Haberman nodded here. Other wordsmiths associate it with *cow-flop* or with that all-time American favorite, *b**-s**t*.

Warming to the subject which in its Anglo-Saxon contexts it had woefully neglected, the *Times* tells us that some misguided linguistic spirits refer to a crotchety old man as an *alter kocker*, "blind to the fact that it means old defecator." How blind can we still be? Why couldn't we see the innocent word *shtup* which means to push or to press "has also become a way to fornicate"? Beware, then, of the *other* words for *any other way*! Down that path lies perdition.

We have been warned. Yiddish in the post-Holocaust era has fallen "into the hands of Hollywood and the Borscht Belt," and it emerges as just "a bunch of curse words." Can't coarseness can be bought elsewhere, more cheaply?[12]

For Yiddish is too important a linguistic tradition to be left to the grandchildren who are only prepared to exploit the rich world of their grandfathers and grandmothers for low demotic purposes, often in gross contexts, sometimes even to camouflage the temptations of scatology. Nor should it be left (Jehovah forbid!) to the *goyim* who, in New York at least, are presiding over the decline of their own highest standards, and seem to be having good fun picking at the corpse of a language which perished in the Holocaust.

I remember with affection my great and revered City College teacher of German, Professor Sol Liptzin. He was conducting at the time a futile campaign to introduce courses in Yiddish language and literature at this institution of higher learning (which included, in its student body, 85 percent young Jews, mostly all sons–and, if one includes Hunter College, daughters–of recent East European immigrants). His recommendation was met in the New York educational establishment of the day with what he thought was "bewilderment" (it was, I surmise, something else). Yiddish was considered to be not a language, only a jargon: did it even have a literature?...In the end, the recommendation was only approved in 1942; and Sol Liptzin went on some years later to write an invaluable 500-page *History of Yiddish Literature*. But my college class (1935-1939)–which included Irving Howe (*né* Horenstein) and many other young would-be Jewish intellectuals (from Irving Kristol and Daniel Bell to Nathan Glazer and Seymour Martin Lipset)–had long since been graduated into the Anglo-Saxon world. Yiddish remained a sentimental memory.

As I write, I note an unusual confession in Saul Bellow's quasi-autobiographical novel *Ravelstein* (2000, p. 167) to the effect: "*Well, I had a Jewish life to lead in the American language, and that's not a language that's helpful with dark thoughts.*" My own dark thought at the moment asks what would have happened to Yiddish *if*–upgraded by an academic patina, enlivened by a new native fluency–literary talents like Saul Bellow and Irving Howe (maybe even Philip Roth and Henry Roth) joined Isaac Bashevis Singer in his cafeteria on Upper Broadway...to live their American lives in the Jewish language?

The Americanization of Yiddish slang follows, as I say, hard on the heels of the Americanization of Jewish writers. Saul Bellow's biographer, James Atlas, places great weight on Bellow's youthful insistence that he was in no way writing "Jewish novels." The breakthrough work for Bellow's reputation–which grew and grew and, very early on, made him a favorite American candidate for the Nobel Prize (which he won in 1976)–was *The Adventures of Augie March* (1953). Atlas follows Leslie Fiedler, Alfred Kazin, and a whole host of other literary critics who argued that the achievement of "American Jewish writers" had a symptomatic, historic importance; for they were acting as surrogates for the whole Jewish-American community in its quest for an identity.

Bellow's *Augie March* was "a novel by an American writer who happened to be a Jew." It took something like half-a-century to raise the alternative question. Could it all have been an achievement of Jewish writers who happened to be Americans? Surely I am not the first to entertain the notion that it was "a close-run thing," that the indubitable literary genius of so many generations of wandering Jews might have induced a modern flowering of Yiddish literature and, perhaps, even of its accompanying journalism.

The Yiddish newspaper press–and everything else associated with it in the American emigration: theater, book publishers, musical folklore–declined and died. The principle factor was, to be sure, great historic forces such as the Holocaust and the desperate post-Nazi establishment of the State of Israel in 1948. My friend Hyam Maccoby (a scholar at London's Leo Baeck College) tells me that "the return to Palestine [the Zionist dream] decided the issue between Yiddish and Hebrew." Was there ever, in the transatlantic hegira, an issue between choosing European Yiddish and American English? If there had been would it be fanciful to imagine the *Times* publishing one fine day a supplement–in Yiddish!–for New York readers who could conceivably still love the language of Bashevis Singer, of Sholom Aleichem, and of...Saul Bellow. After all, the *New York Times* half-owned (with the *Washington Post*) the *International Herald Tribune*; and the *IHT* still publishes an eight-page daily supplement–translated from *the German*!–which represents a readable English-language version of that formidable daily, the *Frankfurter Allgemeine Zeitung*. There are always "cross-roads" in life and letters, and "the road not taken" tantalizes the imagination as to what *might* have been...*almost*.

A pertinent anecdote, as told by the late Irving Howe in his memoirs, *A Margin of Hope* (1982). Howe was completing an anthology of Yiddish stories, and Bellow in New York was assisting in the project. One Yiddish story was as yet untranslated, and Howe watched "in a state of high enchantment" as Bellow transformed it in an afternoon into an English masterpiece. When Bellow's translation of the short story was published in New York it is said that it made the author famous...it was Isaac Bashevis Singer's "*Gimpel the Fool*."*

Alas, the language of such unwritten masterpieces is now used by streetwise Manhattan reporters only to pep up their newspaper *shtick* with a little bit of *shmooze*.

I should add a mention of Stefan Zweig (1881-1942), a formidable figure of Austrian twentieth-century letters. Some time before Zweig fled Vienna (later to commit suicide in exile in Brazil) he expressed hope for a renaissance of Yiddish; I do not know how much of the language he knew, but he supported Max Weinreich's pioneering efforts in Vilna/Lithuania on behalf of what Zweig called a "*jiddische geistige Kultur*." It was the year 1938, and there was just time to dream for a moment of a Yiddish literary utopia, of what a recent writer

---

* James Atlas, *Bellow: A Biography* (2000), pp. 14, 192-3.

affirmed as "an alternative, a third way." As it was, the Nazis destroyed Weinreich's YIVO Institute in Vilna, and Stalin purged Russian Jewish writers (Babel, Mandelstam, et al.). With the death of Isaac Bashevis Singer in 1991, the last of the old Yiddish-writing men of letters had passed away; and Jews in literature now had only "two ways" (the national-language, like the English-writing Bellow, Roth, and Richler; or in the New-Hebrew of Agnon, Amos Oz, and other contemporary Israelis).[13]

I should note that not only has there been an Americanization of the Yiddish slang but, perhaps equally careless and regrettable, a crude nativization of ancestral "customs and mores," even to the tribe's sexual intimacies. On the qualities of Philip Roth's most recent novels, a *Los Angeles Times* book reviewer writes the following in praise of *The Human Stain* (2000):

> American pastoral, American historical, American comical, and now with the appearance of his latest novel, *"The Human Stain,"* American tragical–it's time to circumcise [*sic*] the genre of 'Jewish American' from Philip Roth's name and declare him, simply, bard supreme of the bad end of the American century past. The bad end, for Roth, is the Clinton end, the Lewinsky end.

Whatever this means politically, metaphorically it is with its "circumcision of a genre" on even the more obscure side. Perhaps biologico-comical-tragical...

Could it be that *"de-circumcise"* is being suggested? This might be a Talmudic problem that only the Grand Rabbi of Jerusalem has the subtlety to decide.[14]

In thinking about these matters I found it important to know–but nowadays this troubled awareness is an embarrassment on all sides–something of the mutual contempt in which the two major Jewish tribes had held each other ever since olden times.

The Polish *shtetl* Jews were called *Ashkenazim* (which was a misleading misnomer, borrowed from the Hebrew for "Germany," for the ancestors had lived on Germanic lands). Tribal rivals were the near-assimilated German Jews proper who were called (and still are in Israel) *"Yekkahs."* Naturally, the historic estrangement extended to matters of language and literature. One community could boast (and did) of their mastery in speaking the language of Goethe and Schiller. The other, as Moses Mendelssohn once said in a devastating eighteenth-century judgment on Yiddish, chattered away in a mere "Jargon," and a harmful one at that. *"Charakter-verderbend"* was Mendelssohn's epithet for the corrosive cultural side effects of an underdeveloped dialect. To be sure, there was a "Germanized Yiddish" and actually it was the vernacular spoken by the first Rothschilds making their start in the Frankfurt ghetto. Even learned Jews sometimes stooped (as Prof. Liptzin bitterly remarks) to use it. But the "living Yiddish" resided in the townlets (*shtetl*) of Eastern Europe. There the mild hostility to the Teutonized co-religionists was joined to the antipathies felt for the *goyim* in Russia and Poland and the Ukraine who periodically burst out in violent anti-Semitic rages. Western disparagement may have hurt the pride of would-be Yiddish journalists and storytellers, who were so hungry for approbation in the enlightened world. Still, Eastern literati remained creative and irrepressible until the Holocaust killed off all Yiddish life and letters.[15]

The most graphic portrait of the Ashkenazi, which is also, in my view, a valorous defense of the *Ostjuden*, is from the pen of the distinguished Austrian novelist, Joseph Roth (1894-1939) whose reportages on the subject were made in the 1930s, just before the shadows of Hitlerism inevitably gave a different shade to anything written about European Jewry. (There is also a brief, perceptive chapter on "A Jew Goes to America.")

As I surmise, the "defensism" of Joseph Roth as well as the "defeatism" of I.J. Singer whose great warts-and-all novel of Lodz–*The Brothers Ashkenazy* (1936)–would not have been written in the same acidulous way just a few years later under the lengthening shadow of Hitlerism. The horrific victimization of millions of *Ostjuden* in the Nazi Holocaust shifted, in the standard phrases of our day, the "parameters of praise" as well as "the paradigm" of blame and self-criticism. As Joseph Roth remarked, "after thirty years of residence in New York the Jewish emigrant doesn't know any English, gets along quite well in Yiddish, and can't understand what his grandsons are saying." His story is told, not in the harsh social-realism tones of I. J. Singer, but in the joyous sentimentality of Jerry Robbins' *Fiddler on the Roof*, the hit Broadway musical of the last half of the twentieth century.[16]

A distant echo of all these matters could be discerned in the Times Square quarrels of the last decade (the 1980s/1990s), indeed internecine warfare, between the Frankels and the Rosenthals, scrambling to maintain editorial control at the *New York Times*. (The Ashkenazi lost.)

25

Quotations that were Unquoted

The order-of-battle persists even if the hostilities on the front line appear to have given way to an ethnic armistice. Still, the over-critical or ultra-sensitive New York reader is always on the alert for every suspicious movement along the long frontier between the *New York Times'* formal "house-style" rules and the freshly fashionable demotic. The deeply rooted antipathies among the immigrant tribes, especially in the Bronx and Brooklyn, are too outlandish to be simply assimilated, integrated, and finally closed out. One example, a story suggestively headlined (and thereby reopening yesterday's unhealed wounds):

ON THIS OLD TURF, A TREASURED PAST IS STILL A PRESENCE

Well, the *old turf* has changed so much since the old Ellis Island generation of East European *shtetl*-refugees came to the "*goldene medina*" a century or so ago, that it is in most of the populated neighborhoods practically unrecognizable. The past, if it ever came to be "*treasured*," bore the scars of repression and denial, name-changes and address hopping, alienation and uneasy re-evaluation. And its "*presence*," whatever it happens to be at the moment, is an allegation which, in Manhattan at least, can cause painful, disagreeable alter-cations.

Ms. Judith (*née* Schwartz) Dunford is author of a long and altogether enjoy-able contribution to the *New York Times* (on 6 September 2002); it is one of a long line of sentimental and evergreen pieces that the paper's metropolitan editor assigns every five or ten years or so. (I remember a not dissimilar story by Meyer Berger and a related *Topics of the Times* column by Simeon Strunsky which my father clipped and gave me to read more than half-a-century ago.) They were all gripping and evocative, and were in end effect all the same.... But how could that be? Ms. Dunford, born several decades after my generation, seems to have shared the very same experiences in the streets and the schools in-and-around Tremont Avenue and the Grand Concourse that I and my two younger sisters had "treasured." Each piece of reportage renewed the protection of an old heritage and the reassurance of a new identity. The Jews were not alone in their populistic search for Americanization. I recall–and, curious to tell, everybody before me and after me–the nearby Irish neighborhood (with its pointy neo-Gothic church steeples and forbidding "orphan asylum"). Somewhere to the east was the Italian "little Sicily" zone; not to mention the Negro settlement under the El [elevated] railroad tracks. They were all–not all at once, and to the same degree–radically uprooted and transformed by the general American convulsions which produced a new and different post-Roosevelt society. The patterns are well known–social change (with upward mobility); sociological upsets (trailing middle-class gentrification); anthropological shifts (with enrichening cultural temptations); and, last but not least, the only-in-America economic revolution (bringing sheer prosperity). The melting pot melted, but there were remarkable residues.

Obviously there were shared core experiences which, after a decent interlude of estrangement–and I think of young American university professors of English whose immigrant fathers could not really speak the new *mama-loshen* of a foreign land–made their way into the novels and the newspapers of the day. As with the readers of Ms. Dunford, and all the Bronx chroniclers before her, there were always the belated delights of the shock of recognition. I whooped when I noted that she had borrowed books from the same Tremont public library, a reservoir of the first joys of English so long ago. And what she borrowed on her library card were roughly the same titles–Dumas and Conan Doyle, Edgar Allan Poe and Guy de Maupassant. (I missed her Stephen Leacock; she missed my Fenimore Cooper and Zane Grey.)

But there was one astonishing feature of this specimen of cleanly copyedited Times Square prose. It had not a single Yiddish phrase (if one excepted the "kashe knishes" that constituted the so-called delicious Bronx *nosh* of yore) to help recapture an atmosphere–no *shmooze*, no *shlep*, no *shtick*, not even a *shlemozzle*! My consternation was palpable; I was puzzled. Did Ms. Schwartz-Dunford miss out? Or was her original and surely more fruity text edited out? Could it be that the Leo Rosten revolution had been suspended, suffered its Thermidor, and for a single high semantic moment, a plain unadorned Anglo-American text–with no lox-and-bagels, and no nothing–was being served up as New York fare? Might it be that the mainstream was moving backward?

I got in touch with Ms. Dunford in a jiffy. I put it to her: What had happened to the Yiddishisms in her remembrance of the Bronx past? It was, as any *Times* editor would concede, an *Oy!* problem of some philological importance...certainly for the language of New York journalism as it was caught between *kibbitzers* and *shlemiels*.

Well, I had been mistaken in the reading of the very order-of-battle to which I had been wanting to call attention. The Schwartzes–at least those who emigrated into the walk-ups near Southern Boulevard–were not *shtetl Ostjuden* but *Yekkahs*, that is, not East European but German Jews. As Judith Dunford wrote me, "what Yiddish I know had to be deciphered through German–it's not part of my DNA, so to speak." Her mother, who had come from this side of the Pale, evidently had Yiddish classified as "*streng verboten*, or at least never spoken at home."[1]

As Conan Doyle would have pointed out (since Sherlock Holmes was famously puzzled by the dog that didn't bark), this is a case of the apt phrase that wasn't quoted. The enigmatic discrepancy is, I think, part of the history of the *New York Times*, and of the language of journalism. Also, but rather of lesser importance, it is an element in my own personal history and, possibly, that of Ms. Judith Dunford.

Time for a small change of subject and venue, and a question about how the other American remnants of vernacular are faring in the linguistic pot. What did the Algonquin Indians to the north (actually, in Ottawa, Canada) or the tribes of the Iroquois (in western New York) devise as unsavory references to you-know-what? More than that. Why are we neglecting or discriminating against Neapolitan and Sicilian slang which masses of Italian emigrants brought with them to America...to salt their language on those occasions that cried out for obscenities with old-time force and flavor? The *Times* has yet to devise an editorial house-style for rendering–in a fashion consistent with the rights of a minority culture–the Russian or the Chinese emigration's "good quotes." (But then I concede that printing demotic Cyrillic or idiomatic Mandarin might be a serious alphabetical and proofreading problem for our newspaper culture.) Still there are surely readable and important–and, with a few juicy quotes, flavorsome–news-stories that are being "missed out" somewhere on the streets of New York.

The *Oys* of Russian and Chinese and Korean, among other rich linguistic reserves in the Metropolitan area, await us. The ball is in the *Times'* court, and whole new ball games are in the offing in Times Square. Do I hear anybody saying *nebbish*?*[2]

What we are here up against is a journalistic irony or, perhaps, an intellectual paradox, in any case a surprising complication. The reportage of the "Jewish lives that were lived out in America" (Bellow)–following on from the

---

* According to Leo Rosten, "*nebbish* is one of the most distinctive Yiddish words." So far as I can make out, it expresses, variously, *sympathy* (with the hapless)...*regret* (that the *shlemiel* has gotten himself into another *shlemozzle*).*dismay* (that foolish hope is still being put about)...*pity* (for mortal helplessness)...*contempt* (for those who laughably persist in error). *Nebbish* has even made it into the *Dictionary of American Slang*, where Lighter's volume II has a substantial entry.

Germany's latest *Duden* is uncertain about its origins and even as to whether the Jews borrowed it and embroidered the *Platt-Deutsch*, or the other way around. But since it was (and is) a popular slang word in Berlin and many points east or west, the *Duden*'s entry indicates that it has also served as a big-city punch-line...to suggest melancholy indifference to an absurd situation which is not likely to be set right.

Ellis Island experience–could be distinguished by a kind of pristine authenticity when they are written up *without* any ethnic demotic, without a single Yiddishism of any color or flavor. For a long time the basic Yiddishisms were taken to be unprintable vulgarities, queasy embellishments which might suggest a poor, colorful Brooklyn/Bronx tenement atmosphere but, in effect, they were thought to be sealing a whole immigrant generation back or off into a local ghetto.

Another ethnic wave of immigration from the Old World, the Italian, is scarcely represented in the metropolitan slang vocabulary; it could be that the great shadow of Dante Alighieri blocked the cheap and easy turn to Sicilian defensiveness or Palermo patois. The success of Mario Puzo's stories in his novels and the blockbuster Hollywood movies based on them can be credited only with a very few phrases and one-liners–*Omerta* and a handful of other Godfather's formulae (muttered inaudibly by Marlon Brando). It is revealing that the one quotation that has achieved almost global popularity–the one about Making-You-an-Offer-You-Can't-Refuse–deosn't have a touch of *pizza* about it, nor the slightest Napoli lilt. Straightforward English prose has got a lot going for it.

Time will tell whether the ongoing Italian Mafia story–currently *The Sopranos* (on TV), wherein some New Jersey gangster types try to cope with post-Sicilian problems (*viz.*, psychoanalysis). The Jews had it earlier and easier; after all, Freud and Marx and Einstein were of their very own tribe, and they could without incurring severe identity crises become Freudians (or their patients); Marxists (with choice of a party line or a half-dozen splinter groups); and Relativity-ites (even time and space were no problem). To judge from the most recent Mafia trials (John Gotti and Sammy "The Bull" Gravano, et al.), the Italian contribution to pidgin New Yorkese is very limited. Cinema images have become the clichés. The Italian Godfather is visibly enjoying his spaghetti *al dente* before giving the order to wipe out, and ruthlessly, one or more rival "Families." The Jewish Grandfather will eat his gefillte fiish before trundling off to the eve-of-Sabbath services. Or so appears to be the demotic heritage that is being handed down to Jews and Italians who are living out their American lives in the metropolitan inter-borough area.

For the Anglo-Saxon puritans of the language, shuddering at any new incursions into standard Webster usages–from *wops*, or *kikes*, or whomever–it makes little difference what the sources of corruption are. The sensitivities to everybody's sense of identity, wavering between the old country and the new world, play their own singular role in the politics, the popular culture, and the slang-ridden language of tabloid as well as broadsheet journalism.

26

Dirty Realism in the White House
and Beyond

The final contribution of journalistic culture to the summing up of a news-worthy problem will, in the end, always be passed on to the historians for further research and revised interpretations. It is often difficult to recall the original quotidian twist to the reputations of major American public figures that were popularized in the daily press in thousands of stories bearing a Washington dateline.

True, Harry S. (for nothing) Truman remains the plucky little man from Missouri who grew into presidential stature as the onset of the Cold War challenged America into a duel for world power. On the other hand, Dwight D. Eisenhower did not remain for long the all-conquering hero of the Allied victory in World War II when he served two mediocre terms in the White House. Hardly a reporter or a columnist neglected an opportunity to chide an indolent, golf-playing old gent who bumbled on in press conferences…and who (as I remember) confessed, under some prodding, that the *Decline and Fall* he was reading was not the profound Gibbon history of the end of the Roman Empire but a silly lightweight current best-seller by one Will Cuppy, *The Decline and Fall of Practically Everybody* (1950).

And yet, the auguries change. More and more, historians reveal the hidden Machiavellian scenario beyond Ike's staged public performances, disguising a sly, acute diplomat and savvy politico on the national and the world stage. Something of the same shocking upgrading has overtaken Richard Nixon's reputation, thought to have been hopelessly mired in the squalor of Watergate to which "Deep Throat" and other newspaper sources had consigned him. In his last years of retirement Nixon seemed to be emerging as an elder statesman, a seer who had pioneered new directions in international affairs (the "China Opening"), and an altogether clubbable fellow on the UN circuit.

And what of Bill Clinton? In the last days of his two-term administration, Clinton was subjected by the *New Yorker*'s Joe Klein to a long, thorough twenty-nine-page analysis, summing up in a surprisingly favorable way–at least for the anonymous author of the satirical novel of Clintonia, *Primary Colors: A Novel of Politics* (1996)...the achievements of a poor boy from the Deep South.[1]

Cogitating not only on the Monica Lewinsky affair but generally on President Clinton's consistent popularity in the public-opinion polls no matter what the current political disaster might have been, Joe Klein comes up with a striking explanation, worthy of reflective journalism at its most fanciful:

> the President indulged himself knowing, on some level, that every last pitiful detail was likely to become part of his legacy. After all, his Presidency coincided with the arrival of technologies that made it possible for everyone to know almost everything, a phenomenon whose implications Clinton understood better than any of his peers, and which he often exploited.

Was it, then, a technological trap that was his undoing? Was he fated to be exposed?

> From the start, he was too familiar for comfort. He volunteered that his marriage had "not been perfect." He said that he "didn't inhale." He answered a question, on MTV, about his underwear. Clinton could have said "None of your business" to all these inquiries, but he had a remarkably sophisticated appreciation of the power of vicarious intimacy; he knew that the President now lived in the kitchens and family rooms of the nation as surely as he lived in the White House. One wonders if this President–by snuggling so close, by polling every last public appetite, by trying so hard to please– lost much of his moral authority in the process, and well before Lewinsky. It is possible that the Clinton era will be remembered as the moment when the distance between the President and the public evaporated forever.

The power of vicarious intimacy...a well-turned phrase. Other observers in our newspaper culture have put in in a more traditional way. There but for the grace of god–or of Kinsey, or of Dr. Spock, or whomever–go I....The distance between the two apologias is not great. We are all sinners, and could be worse. Young Monica is the old, eternal Eve. The human stain is indelible.

But there is another style of putting these things, far from the psychology of vicarious powers and secret sympathies or from the theology of guilt and grace. The curse of the demotic is upon us, and we find the all-powerful White House chief-of-staff, Leon Panetta, searching for words to account for the experience of his several years in the Clinton administration which amounted to chaos or, at least, total disorganization.

In the universal history of political leadership–with its center not holding and things falling apart–it is a recurrent theme. Herodotus and Thucydides pondered it; and Plutarch and Suetonius fashioned memorable portraits of the character traits involved in the culture of leadership. Machiavelli tried to advise princes on how to confront and conquer the challenges in public political life (by...espousing the precepts of "Machiavellianism").

Panetta is thoughtful. He senses (as Klein reports) that "Clinton's unwilligness to confront those with whom he disagreed was part of the problem." The man's nature is not to be "confrontational," although he knows the language of confrontation with which he can become strong and decisive. A whole vocabulary, replete with expletives, awaits his command. The final epitaph of failure is etched in a lapidary sentence which puts Leon Panetta (as well as Joe Klein) in the great tradition of famous last words: "I never heard the President tell anyone 'You're full of shit,' even when I knew he wanted to." This kind of/sort of constipation is historic, and represents a faecal high point in the chronicles of governance.

There were doubtless many White House decisions that were argued through with some measure of intellectuality in which such elements as evidence, logic, and rhetorical persuasiveness were marshalled to conclude with a *Q.E.D.* (or something approaching a cogent and coherent conclusion). Yet, increasingly, expletives were assigned a role which was not merely of passing colorful or emotional significance. Many grave decisions—in Somalia, Bosnia, Haiti, among other battlegrounds—were hasty and impulsive, and quickly proved calamitous; and, subsequently, even the president candidly ascribed them to the thoughtlessness of inexperience.

On the ill-fated Haiti invasion Clinton's National Security advisor, Anthony Lake, tried to claim that they had been "double-crossed" by the Haitian General Cedras but, in the end, confessed that "it was our fault" because the *U.S.S. Harlan County*, which had been ordered to carry lightly armed American forces, had been sent out "with zero military support." Conclusion: "*It was a total fuckup.*"

In the calamitous Somali retreat after the U.S. forces had suffered inacceptable casualties (the humiliating murder of eighteen men), President Clinton has admitted: "I think I will always regret that—I don't know whether I could have saved those lives or not...but I would have handled it in a different way if I'd had more experience. I know I would have" (Klein, p. 200). Even "more experience" is not a guarantee of military success. But the failure to converse rationally in terms of strategy and tactics—and to make sober estimates of the way events might develop—must lead to unexpected disasters which, in turn, call for more generalship by expletive. The all-purpose expletives provide the noise to drown out all other quieter conventional efforts to correct errors, revise mistakes, think through a new approach. f-words and s-words become the key concepts—explosive in some situations, and on some shocking occasions silently resonating by their unpronounced absence. Still, we can hear them (as Panetta heard Clinton's imprecations) in the emergent pop vocabulary of profanity and obscenity in high places. Presidents who act as inexperienced commanders-in-chief may well next time try their luck with expostulations like "*Let's not f*** this one up!*." Or, say, in the Bosnian imbroglio which was distorted by all kinds of superficial multicultural considerations, they might resort to rude put-downs to young and callow staff advisors: "*You're full of s—t!*"

Whether these phrases will prove to be better points of departure in the evolution of U.S. policy guidelines only time will tell. Asterisks and hyphens may yet to be found hiding a surreptitious potency in human affairs. Worthy spirits in literature (like D.H. Lawrence, like Henry Miller) devoted themselves to liberating such hidden inner powers. Our public life is not running too far behind…as our body politic "outs" its urges and temptations and tries, in the liberal spirit of the old dirty realism, to tell it like it is.

One has to think again of France and its old *mot de Cambronne*, after which the French suffered great events (lost wars, betrayed revolutions) in its shadow. Sometimes it was a word too much, a *merde* too far. It is a sign of their undoing when men of power fail to make terms with *le mot juste*.[2]

Once the f-word is established–i.e., recognized by newspaper copy editors as a legitimate item in the reporting of news or of the men (and women, more and more) making the news and giving it good quotes to help sustain reader interest–then a number of subsidiary salacities follow on. Prowess in profanity becomes a measurable sub-item; and invidious comparisons begin to develop about "the-hostess-with-the-mostest" and indeed about which cocktail parties salty straight-talking conversationalists can feel most at ease in providing unquotable expletives for putting down the great and the good. This is, generally speaking, only a matter of numbers: which is to say, the more the merrier. One counts the imprecations. But one wonders whether our reporters, otherwise admirably equipped for the occasion–cameramen on call; shorthand notebooks at the ready–can get to pocket calculators fast enough to register every daring trope.

Beyond such dramatic social life where conversations are only half audible and notoriously misheard, there has emerged a rather more dull, if not exactly boring, category in the write-ups of men and women in the loop.

Here is a newspaper correspondent wirting his Sunday column "at the heart of Europe" and informing us of the constitution makers in Brussels and Strasbourg who are engaged in drafting model documents for the upcoming Federal Union of Europe. One might have thought that the language of Magna Carta (1215) or of *The Federalist Papers* (1787-1788), or of the noble Condorcet in Paris on the eve (1788) of *la grande révolution*, would be of prime journalistic interest. (How much protection is being given to human rights? how difficult would it be to put through a basic amendment or two? etc.)

Nowadays, it seems, other curiosities have to be allayed. Our correspondent writes about a MEP (Member of the European Parliament) named Andrew Duff; and what was worth knowing about Mr. Duff, "one of theose admirable British Europhiles who is utterly honest about where he wants to go"?…And where does he want to go? Boldly to go, doubtless, to where no man has gone before? Well, the man is obviously fearless, and the *Sunday Telegraph* dispatch certifies: "Mr. Duff nas never been afraid of the f-word."[3] This may well be a sterling quality of character in a man so utterly honest, but its relevance to the merging "European society"–and to the consitution which will be shaping it–is not immediately apparent. I reiterate my concern: Will the "f-word," hurled back and forth...loud and clear...be guaranteeing frank and realistic debate in the Strasbourg chambers? Will some parliamentarians in Brussels about whom one could not certify such audacity fail the f-word test with disastrous consequences for the constitutional structure of the future Continent? May Mr. Duff's intrepidity be exemplary! If he courageously stands by the f-word and all it stands for, then *Europa* is surely not lost.

Given the invincible popularity of sports, games, and other competitive events in the lives of the great voting public, it is inevitable–at least in Anglo-American societies–that political populism should aspire to the home run or the touchdown or the hole in one or the k.o. knockout, or several other metaphors of triumphalism. Such clichés, as we have observed, often become too jaded for usage in more than one or two electoral campaigns. But there is hardly an alternative in sight, since no politico (or his creative advisor on media communications) would willingly return to the prose of Walter Bagehot when he could be identified with Babe Ruth (or Don Bradman). The knockout punch of Joe Louis or the irresistible slam dunk of Michael Jordan is vastly more seductive than a subtlety by Madison in *The Federalist Papers*. We have been through all that, so what's new?

New is that sex has been rearing its suggestive head in other "cultures" where there is life and love in other ball games, in different ball parks. Consider the most recent inspirations of desperate media communicator, eager to squeeze out a winning percent or two with a daring or startling phrase or image.

In the recent (September 2002) German elections, the contest between *Bundeskanzler* Gerhard Schroeder and his Bavarian rival, Edmund Stoiber, ended in a dead heat, each polling 38.5 percent of the national vote. What propaganda ploy in the heated up run-up campaign to polling day might have played a significant role in the final outcome? Pundits point to the *Bundeskanzler*'s sudden decision that he would not send a single German soldier to fight in President Bush's imminent war against Iraq. (A minister in his cabinet, taking her cue for the "new anti-American line," compared Mr. Bush to Herr Hitler.) There were other bizarre and unfortunate allusions in other party campaigns involving anti-Semitic tones... which experienced Teuton-watchers have heard before. New was the intrusion of sexual metaphors which were truly innovative–but conceivable (for the time being) only in a society where the cultural taboos, unlike in the Anglo-American world, were long since transcended. Germany is different. It dresses (or undresses) differently for swimming on its sandy Baltic beaches. It dubs the Tarantino obscenities differently for dirty realism in its movie theaters or on its TV screens. It has a profane tradition of its own as to how to handle scatology and its vocabulary in acceptable public discourse. (The s-word, like a glottal stop or a vowel shift in post-medieval linguistics, replaces the f-word which has conjugation difficulties when translated.) To go for, or gun for, your political opponent in a democratic election when only a few thousand votes in tens of millions can decide the national prize, you must try and go a little farther than the political puritans who set up the old-fashioned rules about the do's-and-dont's of running for public office. How far is a little farther?

Obviously, many of the electoral promises are what could be called "attractive," even "seductive." Tax cuts, for example; and surely "world peace." Also: *"Keeping Us Out of War"* (which helped candidate Woodrow Wilson to get elected before President Wilson sent General Pershing to help win an Allied victory in 1917-1918). But one Berlin correspondent who was observing the campaign in September 2002 raised an unusual and indeed unprecedented question. What if a party promised happiness to the lovelorn beyond their erotic dreams? The suspicion itself warranted a front-page story in *Die Welt* about the "bedside" manner of the various candidates running for high office. A reminiscent reference or two was made to "Monica Lewinsky" as a factor in the new politology of democratic appeal. But the challenging thesis ran: *"Alle Parteien mit Potenz-Protzerei auf Schmusekurs gehen und Wähler bis unter die Bettdecke verfolgen."* A journalistic observation which suggested that all the German poltical parties were featuring braggarts of potency, who oozed with Schmus, and pursued the vote down unto the bed sheets...

On the Left, the Social Democrats did an electoral placard with a pair of desirable red lips, pursed for a kiss, and telling us that what came before was only "foreplay (*Vorspiel*)" but the "climax (*Höhepunkt*)" was still to come. The paper helpfully suggested that what was still to come, after the climax, was the Chancellor's anxious inquiry, echoung the uncertainties in a thousand boudoirs, "How was I?"

On the Right of Center the CDU/CSU, the Christian Democrats, were accentuating that it was "Time for a Change" and the illustration was of two pairs of happy feet–it was a snappy TV spot, and you could catch the wriggling toes, peeking out from under the bedspread. Whereupon the framed photograph (of Stoiber) on the night table gets changed to a new photo (of the *Bundeskanzler*). The impassioned slogan which summed up the best lesson of the day (or night, as the case might be): "Go along with a changing Germany!" I.e., change lovers, change bedside pictures.

As for the Green Party, which supplied the handful of votes which enabled the Red-Green coalition to take power in 1998 and give it another slim majority for a second four-year term, it was more comfortable with "erotic foreplay" as an element of political ideology. They had in the past latched on to the melodic one-liner in the old Beatles' pop politics: *"Make Love Not War."* In the pacifist anti-war anti-NATO arguments of the 1980s they had intoned:

"*Petting statt Pershing*" which surely had a sexier appeal than the traditional "*Butter not Guns*," quite apart from what was understood to constitute "petting" or, perhaps more importantly, how dietary was the latter-day turning against butter and other high-cholesterol spreads. Now they could be up-to-date. They had pushed through, as a governmental partner in the coalition, the "Homo-Ehe," which legalized gay marriages, of male homosexuals and of lesbians as well. They flaunted the images of their victory: happy, naked pairs of lovers, caressing each other's breasts....

After such explicitness, what was left for the smaller parties, the ex-Communist PDS and the right-wing FDP, to get into the act? The FDP liberals highlighted the voting urn with a voter poised to drop in his ballot into the narrow opening. "*Steck ihn rein!*" they enjoined, hoping against hope that they could be taken to be invasive, or penetrating, and hence macho. The former East German Communist movement now known as the Party of Democratic Socialism (PDS) tried to extend its enlightened progressive image beyond the single-minded sexuality of its rivals. Nudity was not quite for them but, perhaps...a naked lunch. One slogan resonated: "*Heute popp ich, morgen kiff ich, übermorgen wähl ich: PDS.*" It was all so logical and inevitable, as was indeed their previous faith in the dialectics of Marxist historical materialism. First, you have sex with your partner, then you smoke the hashish, then you vote for us...

The results of the election of 22 September 2002 practically wiped out the *PDS* as a small but upcoming political factor on the national German scene.[4]

More than that, the adventurous exercise into sexual metaphorics appeared to be missing the mark; the analogies seemed to be falling short. The analogical virtues of so-called popping and sexual intercourse–of foreplay and penetration, of crossover and coitus–proved not to be wildly successful. Still, over time (as I surmise) with the odd bit of luck, some indelicate metaphors may well be making it into the evolving language of journalism, and its intimate associations with the gross vagaries of pop politics. With a wink and a nudge, we will be recounting the hits and home runs, the knockouts and holes-in-one, and give *scoring*–and the seminal verb *to score*–its old saucy off-color meaning.

How long will the sacred precincts of republican and constitutional governance remain verbally protected and linguistically inviolate in the democratic election of our presidents and prime ministers? Seen in the long perspective this is the historic replacement of thaumaturgical kings, paramount chiefs, and a whole host of charismatic leaders and their medicine men. The postmodern campaign songs that are sung and up-to-the-minute slogans that are chanted are, well, suggestive of demotic change. The Germans have risked a first bawdy breakthrough; the Anglo-Americans may well be not far behind. In an increasingly four-letterized culture, it will be difficult to keep even the most lofty and august of our political rituals free from the sly innuendo and even the coarse expletives that have given a new dimension to public and private discourse in our time. The f-word is not likely ever to be on the ballot and headed for the ballot box; but the voter may well be seduced by the prospect of potency as a political additive.

There have always been incalculable factors in even the most ambitious semantics of diplomatic discourse. It is epitomized in the classical anecdote of the sudden death of a wily Russian diplomat at the nineteenth-century Congress of Vienna and the ensuing puzzlement: "What *did* he mean by that?..." The Japanese need not have cultivated any uncertainties about President Nixon's (off-the-record) remark which, in its leaked form, disclosed that he didn't "give a s—t" about what was happening to the yen in the world's money markets. The s-word was smelly enough to foul up the Dow Jones index; if he had used the f-word instead, as frequently was the case, it may have brought the financial losses on the currency exchanges up or down only a few points. Much depended on arcane subfactors like the rough translation into Japanese of two of the best-known Anglo-Saxon obscenities and whether they had, in the versions published in the morning editions of Asahi or Mainichi in Tokyo, an equally rude venacular impact.

It may be that familiarity breeds equanimity, and experienced Tokyo bankers, wiser for their educational experiences of the street talk in New York and London, know how to evaluate the strength of epithets which increasingly have been coming to dominate in the era of "Pop Diplomacy." Consulting H.L. Mencken or Eric Partridge on the meaning of taboo words and unconventional slang in general might well be more advisable than checking out what could be learned from Lord Keynes and Milton Friedman about the laws of high finance.

In many of the great financial centers, the London "City" for example, the f-word has been winning a fixed place in the know-how–or the low-down, or the inside-info–which plays a role in determining factors like business confidence and a sixth sense about how the share prices might be moving when the markets open up again in the morning. The city editor of the Guardian is evidently of the Mencken-Partridge school of analysts, for she pays special attention to the variable factor of low language in high finance. Among her influential contacts happen to be two powerful chief executive officers–Messrs. Stuart Rose and Philip Green, each in their way "billionaire wheeler-dealers" and distinctly worth listening to....Especially so, when they also happen to be "good chums" and invite each other to birthday parties where only some 200 of their "closest friends" (and a few right journalists) turn up to celebrate the triumphs of corporate governance. Ms. Julia Finch of the *Guardian* listens very carefully. The future of her nation's wholesale and retail clothing industry may be at stake; and she had a sharp eye for detail:

> The two seem unlikely friends, with the only thing they obviously have in common being a substantial ego. While Rose is Mr. Manners–a polished performer who spent

his formative years at M & S and air kisses in true fashion pack style–Mr. Green is the original brash rag trader.

"Brash" may mistakenly be accepted as a code word, especially when textiles and Marks & Sparks (M & S) verterans are involved, a promise of a bit of colorful East End Yiddish which is always good for a choice quote, from the sweet-talking *shmooze* to the fast-moving rag-trader with *chutzpah*. No, not this time. And not on this level. This is the big time; your standing in the major league tables is being determined by quite other non-ethnic statistics. And Ms. Julia Finch is keeping an accurate count–she is listening to "a man who can squeeze more 'fucks' into a sentence than a seasoned squaddie [Brit., army recruit, hence foul-mouthed soldier]." Not necessarily better, and the mathematical counter–tabulating conversations, making annual lists of once taboo words that now grace one's editorial columns–gives way to other categories. Diplomacy is, after all, about words and silences (and a few facial gestures, mostly involving the arched eyebrows, or a curl of the lips). Diplomatic reporting, if for a moment one sets aside the insurgence of a quasi-official vocabulary of obscenities, is feeding more and more on arcane slang and highbrow flippancy. Here is a senior British corrrespondent in the year 2002, flying for a day to Washington, D.C., to cover the war tensions in the Iraq crisis–Prime Minister Tony Blair and Preident George W. Bush are conferring secretly about what to do against Saddam Hussein. In his "Notebook" Andrew Marr asks rhetorically "and what did we, the traveling circus, really learn?" The newspaper reader is forced to decipher the answer: "Marsh gas. The echoes of rumors. To put it bluntly, doodly squat.….We were told who was there, what soup and what wine, down to the year, was drunk. But as to what really went on at Camp David…not a bean, syllable or semi-colon."[5] Between the hard-to-calculate "*doodly squat*" and the exact number of obscene expletives being hurled (in secret) at Saddam Hussein by the exasperated Anglo-American leadership, we are also left without a bean, syllable, or semi-colon.

The kind of diplomacy dares not speak its name, or at least the names its main protagonists have been calling each other. Diplomatic reporters wallow in despair: "If you want to understand [Andrew Marr writes] what has been happening in Iraq, my advice is to junk the political rhetoric, think-tank reports and MI-6 dossiers, and go back for a deep, dark slug of Shakespeare and Webster." Not the Webster (Noah, 1758-1843) of *Webster Dictionary* fame, where the Yankee variations from the English norm received their due entries; but Webster (John, 1580-1625) with his theatricalities of "white devils" and "dark-skinned" characters. Business cycles may well be easier to make out than the curves of power politics. Leave the Bush-Blair story for a moment; return to Messrs. Stuart Rose and Philip Green and their brash bids for majority control of certain basic commodities. Diplomacy, however denatured of its political content due to linguistic corruption, has a residual *gravitas* with its traditional connection with war and peace, with the breaking of nations, the decline and fall of civilizations, and such like. The greatest tragedy in the financial pages of your favorite morning newspaper is "only" a sharp unexpected recession or a "mere" bankruptcy–and there are surely worse fates than being penniless. City analysts can find solace in an easy phrase or a passing joke: "Yesterday Arcadia shares [controlled by Mr. Stuart Rose] jumped up 39 ¾ to 340 1/2 , suggesting the market isn't convinced the two can agree....But stranger things have happened. Smoothie Stu might end up smelling of roses, while poor Terry is left green with envy."[6]

Low language has, thus, been intruding itself into the highest places. In private or "classified" governmental or military discourse its acceptability carries few consequences; strong words are taken to be a sign of manliness (and even more fearsome when mouthed by a woman). In the event of the obscenities being outed–a "leak" to the press–the reaction can still be problematical...although the public spaces are increasingly exploited by entrepreneurs who use the ad-man's prose to turn a dirty trick or two. Prim and proper protests are more and more powerless to effect old-time self-censorship or even a sense of traditional shame. Embarrassment is no longer in losing face or, what is just as bad, losing sales in a profitable sector of the seller's market.

What I have called "the ad-man's prose" is the terrain of so-called *copywriters;* and their literary ambitions or pretensions play a large and unpredictable role in the vulgarization of marketing appeals. The increasingly suggestive tone of the commercial pitch is not taken to be a descent into down-market, rather the opposite. Copywriters who read modern novels–D.H. Lawrence, Norman Mailer, and the like–are not altogether happy with the fame or notoriety that attaches to a classically "great slogan" (*viz.*, walking a mile for a Camel; the silence in a Rolls Royce except for the ticking clock; etc.). More like it is the handsome airline stewardess pleading to *"Fly Me!"*...and all the flirtatious glances of half-dressed female models who are helping to sell Cinzano cocktails or the latest model of a Ford automobile, or a bathroom additive to make hair (and skin and smell) sexy.

Sex has even moved on from there. Anagrams of the f-word are now in. Glimpses of a lovemaking that only yesterday could not speak its name can now peddle expensive deodorants and designer bluejeans. Even that most prosaic of supermarket articles, a sachet of powdered soup, can in the new porno-culture find a sexy place. Unilever makes a popular product called *Pot Noodle*, and a poster for a spicy version of the snack carried the caption:

"HURT ME YOU SLAG."

The London office of the Advertising Standards Authority received hundreds of protests. It seems that not only the copywriters are becoming more subtle and devious; the consumers, in their ultra-sensitivities, are not lagging far behind. *Slag* was "irresponsible"; it called for complaint; it appeared to condone violence; it had unmistakable sado-masochistic overtones.

Unilever argued that the whole thing was only a joke; the poster campaign was only "humorous" and, more than that, was only meant to be seen in conjunction with a television campaign which, it claimed with uncharacteristic obscurity, made clear that the "*slag*" was the product and thus unlikely to persuade anyone "to engage in violent acts." While they were at it they could have argued that their pot noodles were *al dente* and thus above and beyond any foul-mouthed implication.

At the same time the British press was reporting on what some London papers called "a related case"–since all "offensive" imagery is presumably interrelated. An ad campaign for something called "*Hula Hoops Shops*" in which electric eels emerged from taps and lavatories. Many parental complaints said the children had nightmares. In this case the *I.T.C.* (Independent Television Authority) ruled it was wrong to screen the advertisements before 7:30, and to show any kind of sexual innuendo before 9 P.M. The International Psychoanalytic Society may advise otherwise considering the standard Freudian interpretation of wriggling snakes (or eels) as "phallic symbols," lustful or neurotic as the case may be.[7]

In the more political incidents, involving democratically elected officials who have to answer directly to a more or less populistic public opinion, there is a shadow play of a quasi-Victorian backlash, full of sound and fury and signifying almost nothing. Swearing "like a trooper" did not, one surmises, lose Senator Hillary Clinton a single vote in the New York electoral battle....And that now notorious French ambassador to Britain remained in diplomatic office for almost a year after having been quoted as referring to Israel as "*a shitty little country.*" It was a fetid little newspaper scandal for a few editions, essentially because the fecal epithet had been uttered at a dinner party hosted by the Canadian owner of the *Daily Telegraph*, Mr. Conrad Black (who happens to have a Jewish wife, the columnist Barbara Amiel). The French Foreign Ministry, still insisting in conventional denial that its man in London had simply been "misquoted," replaced Ambassador Daniel Bernard and transferred him to Algiers. *La merde* is, presumably, a less explosive epithet in North African politics.[8]

27

Towards a Vocabulary of Pop Diplomacy

Whatever the sport or contest, athletics in general has become the source for most of the pop semantics which color the American political language. The *New York Daily News* features the headline over a political column:

WHISTLE BLOWERS GET WORD:
HERE'S MUD IN YOUR FACE[1]

The muddy word in your face derives, of course, from the football umpire or referee blowing his whistle to stop play; and "whistle-blowing" can now cover the peremptory command to cease and desist, ranging from the force of a legal injunction ("Judge Sirica, the Watergate whistle-blower") to the power of political murder ("the crazed gunman almost blew the whistle on President Reagan's career").

The trouble with over-using metaphors is that naked unadorned reality has a way of catching up on our petty little conceits. "Whistle-blowing" usually puts a stop–on the authority of referees or umpires or judges–to an athletic contest: halts the action, restrains the players, freezes time. But what of the "whistle-blowers" who surged forward night after night on the streets of Belgrade, hooting their opposition to the tyrannical, war-mongering régime of Slobodan Milosevic? They were blowing real whistles. On the 53rd day of the insurgency, the *Washington Post* reported (13 January 1997):"Thousands of whistle-blowing protesters rallied in central Belgrade again Sunday."[2] The whistle-blowers were demonstrably voting with their feet, and making noises all the while just for the fun and sport of it. The din in the Belgrade streets was only the accompaniment to the loud demand for change, for a "revolution," if a "slow and laborious" one. Nothing was stopped; nobody was halted; time marched on. Could it be that the whistle-blowers were trying to blow the whistle on the hated régime? Political metaphors, like too many wet blobs of color on a painted canvas, tend to blur the big picture.[3]

And yet in some newspaper stories the metaphorics involved–a mixture of slang, buzzwords, and verbal visuals–hardly give a picture at all; they add up, rather, to a mere frame of familiar dots and bulges, put together pointillistically. Here, in a *Washington Post* story, is the way "the bad news" is being reported on the confirmation of some new Clinton appointments. The *"bad news"* is only ironical, intended to disappoint those–even among the press?–who were looking forward to *"nasty fights."* One confirmation (Madeleine Albright as secretary of state) would be *"a love-in."* But several others (including the newly-appointed CIA chief, Anthony Lake) were *"sure bets"* for *"lively brawls"* and even for a *"hammering."* The trouble is that many of the Senate hearings would be closed so that some of *"the best stuff"* would not be on view. Ticket-holders should be prepared for *"slim pickings."* It's all because the defeated Republicans were not, at the moment, *"hunting for scalps."*[4]

In the end we are left with a mishmash of a shebang, coming away with the dim feeling that politics are in a different ball game, played in another ballpark, and one can't quite figure out the score at the moment. The old *New Yorker* magazine used to publish overwritten sentences and paragraphs culled from our newspapers and reprinted under its departmental headline *BLOCK THAT METAPHOR!* Nowadays whole columns of newsprint, even full broadsheet pages, would be eligible to be stopped in that way.

Is there any traditional vocabulary left in which to convey careful and precise meanings with a certain amount of prudence, accuracy and, on occa-sion, subtlety? The tongue-tied political scien-tists in the universities are verbally handicapped by their own new academic gobbledygook; and for the rest there is only the diplomatic equivalent of the *biff!-boom!-bang!* of Tom Wolfe's old "New Journalism." In an account of the U.S. military action in Grenada, a caution against too much U.S. interference was recorded: "If we do," explains one diplomat, "we're likely to screw up." The U.S. envoy is even snappier: "We're not looking for a quick fix. We're looking for a lasting fix."[5] Thus, to the throwaway lines of sports writers add a bit of Army argot and streetwise slang, and you could have an entire vocabulary to translate the whole of a *Handbook of Diplomacy & International Politics.*

So does our diplomatic language get looser and shoddier. One of Warren Christopher's foreign-policy advisers in the Bosnian crisis, which led to the U.S. bombing raids on Serbian positions around Sarajevo, was arguing for a "hard line"; and, in the spirit of the day, went so far as to hint that *"robust"*–the ubiquitous buzzword of the moment suggesting a vigorous, energetic, and decisive approach to policy–and, say, *"raunchy"* are pretty close together: "The message is, 'Take us seriously. Screw with us and you pay a big price.'"[6] Lexicographers are in short supply in Washington these days; and one can suspect safely that no one in the State Department took the trouble to check how that message, with its ominous verb *to screw,* actually translated into the Serbo-Croat so that Messrs. Karadzic and Milosevic, then in power, could have some precise idea of how big the price might be for "screwing" with Americans.

Americans have always had a special relationship to the words used in international affairs, to the vocabulary of diplomacy. Our eighteenth-century Revolution and our New World pride in post-colonial independence gave us, or all our forebears, a peculiar sense that "*in the course of human events*" all things, even language, would be different. European diplomats had developed (in French, in English) a style of discourse which formalized and standardized relationships between states and peoples in the various tensions between war and peace, friendship and hostility. I wonder whether any Old World statesmen could have spoken, as George Washington did, of "*entangling alliances.*" In Europe national interests dictated a network of international *ententes*, preferably couched in the protective shield of legal language first devised by cool juridical minds like Grotius and Pufendorf.

Americans tend to lose their cool in venting feelings about the Old World–veering from a distrust of the ancestral continental tangle to sudden bouts of transatlantic attachment and even filial piety. This ranges in our history from the wary isolationism of President Washington to the golden-voiced interventionism of President Roosevelt. In the course of all of this, words and phrases were far more nakedly used to express emotional attitudes than in the well-clad language which marked the moves in the "Great Game" by a Pitt, a Talleyrand, a Metternich, or a Bismarck. Words themselves, so close to passions and temperament, became at times the virtual reality of world affairs, and magniloquent ideals took over from the clear formulation of recognizable national interests, as in President Wilson's "War to End All Wars." Such usages make for what one American commentator on world affairs (although himself resident in Paris) called "optimism in the American style." As William Pfaff wrote (in his *Los Angeles Times* syndicated column) of the U.S. efforts in the election year 1996 to get some solution to the "Bosnian problem": "the New Age American style, which holds that words alone can make it so, and that what counts is whether people, in this case America's voters, feel good about themselves."[7] The "words alone" style has long been present in Washington politics, as I suggest; but the "New Age" release of expletives as an element in the national feel-good factor is new and ongoing.

As soon as that mode of diplomatic expressiveness has become more than occasional, its infectiousness and lasting effects depend, to be sure, on the character of the colorful phrase. Some expletives, enjoying outrage and hushed quotability for a moment, wither away out of sheer irrelevant vulgarity. On the other hand, a pithy, low-falutin' remark by President Lyndon Johnson on the occasion of a state visit to Washington of Prime Minister Harold Wilson has become a standard reference whenever that hoary old transatlantic theme of "the Special Relationship" between the USA and the U.K. comes on to the agenda. Decades later as a new prime minister (Tony Blair) and a new foreign secretary (Robin Cook) were preparing to visit the White House of President Clinton to "refurbish" century-old residues of friendship and alliance, they were realistically reminded that Britain could play only a minor, a very junior role in America's world-political considerations. In a sharp column written by the "World Affairs Editor" of the BBC, John Simpson, enjoining the cheerful, confident Britons to "face home truths," the profanity of the past became bitter personal prelude. A phrase of what came to be notorious in the mid-1960s as LBJ's "toilet talk" remained an unavoidable reminder: "It doesn't make us highly regarded in Washington, of course; President Johnson said of Harold Wilson, 'I've got his pecker in my pocket'" (John Simpson, "Home Truths," *Sunday Telegraph*, 18 May 1997, p. 33). Few variations of the p-word would have the lasting political force of this rather wild sexual conceit in suggesting an historic state of unmanned impotence. Metternicheans might have said, with roughly comparable insolence, that England had become a mere geographical expression.

It is one thing for presidents in the privacy (such as it is) of the White House to indulge in profanity and a whole range of expletives which are officially deleted in the published protocols (*viz.* the newspaper versions of Nixon's tapes) or discreetly self-censored by concerned and sympathetic journalists (e.g., in the case of L.B.J.). It is another when a president feels free to promise in public pronouncements that he would "kick ass." From little acorns... Increasingly every little advisor or minor aide proceeds with threats to "screw" or "bugger," or otherwise "f—" the other side at the tough negotiating table.

I am afraid that I am recording here only the first stages of these regrettable habits which, like nasty little bugs, itch and spread and are uncontrollably contagious. Our diplomatic language, even during the recent term of a stiff and sullen secretary of state who wore starched white collars, gets sleazier in every crisis. A long chorus line of politicians now decide to "*kick ass,*" and several young advisers have been heard recommending "*Screw them before they screw you,*" or, alternatively, "*kicking 'em in the balls.*" Under stress a new generation turns to the rowdy talk it "feels comfortable with." Can there be any room for any language which we are, conceivably, "uncomfortable with"?

This is the comfort station at which we have come to rest at the moment: the feeling, counter-intuitive no doubt, of *being comfortable with* all and sundry, since it is the convenient self-serving standard by which truth (and everything right and proper) is being judged.

Once the tone of sassiness and indeed of off-color emotion begins to resonate in the inner circles of advisers, officials, researchers, and the like, how far are we away from the protagonists of public life going and doing likewise? Prime Minister John Major called half of his Westminster Cabinet "*Bastards!,*" and an English rugby star has referred to the high commissioners of his sport as "*old farts.*" They need no ghostwriters in English public life; the words come trippingly off the tongue; and the good quotes get endlessly repeated on every useful occasion by the London press. Americans may need the pressure of their "spin doctors." I note that the *Washington Post*, in an analysis of a Far East crisis with shifting Sino-Japanese relations, quotes an authority from a Research Institute to the effect that "China is the four-letter word of Japanese politics."

Unlike in the more free-speaking West, this is probably as far as one at the moment can get in the Orient. Still, I wonder how much of that four-ideogram expletive has to be diplomatically deleted?[8]

What I have been describing as the rise of profane discourse to the visible surface and audible center of American public life has not, as is well known, stopped at the gates of the White House. From Nixon to Clinton it would appear that few enough of the multifarious themes of the nation's business have been exempted from its formulation in slang, its discussion in demotic, and altogether in scabrous argumentation. Nothing can be talked about without the f-word, whether it is the high affairs of state or the private lives of the movers and shakers. Here is an example of the latter. It is mid-1996 and President Bill Clinton had just visited the National Geographic Society and had been looking at, among other things, the remains of a mummy whose shapeliness he had noted and admired. It was evidently female, and he had cracked that he might have been tempted to "date" it or her. During what the Washington press corps calls a "post-cocktail chat" the President's senior press assistant joked to reporters that he could understand the President's point. As *Newsweek* tells the story–years after the incident which had never been reported by the dozen reporters present (good for them?)–Mike McCurry insisted that he had been "misquoted" (although he had offered an apology to the lady in question, namely, the First Lady, Hillary Rodham Clinton): Compared to that mummy he's been f————g,' McCurry chuckled, 'why not?'"[9] Mr. McCurry's apology explained to the Clintons that he had "meant no offense." It's just that the language tends to slip away. What it amounts to, as I am suggesting, is not a slippage but an offensive on all fronts.

What reverberates in the corridors of power, up triumphantly from the "dirty talk" of urban street-corners, is inevitably echoed in the salons of the establishment. Hollywood stars are not exactly famous for their unscripted conversation but they have figured importantly in the great political campaigns of recent times, offering glamour as well as cash. More than that, votes can be picked up on the celebrity trail...even if no psephologists can precisely determine who was supporting whose career when Marilyn Monroe cooed her memorable birthday greetings to "*dear Mr. President*" (John F. Kennedy in Madison Square Garden). In any case, presidents and prime ministers often socialize together with the show-business personalities in the limelight at premieres and receptions–and they often get an earful. In London and other Western centers, the *Oasis* group, led by the Gallagher brothers (Noel and Liam), rose to fame and fortune with such best-selling golden albums as *"Definitely Maybe"* and *"What's the Story Morning Glory."* For one obscure reason or another they became, as newspaper pundits insisted, "emblematic" of newly elected Tony Blair's program of *"Cool Brittania"* (such juvenile puns linked pop to power). Accordingly, the *Oasis* stars were invited to Downing Street for one of the New Labour's prime minister parties. Just everybody you could think of was there. As one well-informed newspaperman reported: "Noel [Gallagher] later recalled his ghastly exchange of mutual sycophancy with Mr. Blair. "It was like, 'You're the top,' 'No, you're the top,' 'No, you're [the] f—ing top.'"[10] A good deal of politics and the democratic legitimization of our elected leaders is about praising famous men. They used to be praised in the idiom of de Tocqueville, John Stuart Mill, and Oliver Wendell Holmes. Now the f--word has come along to do service as the absolute superlative of pop and popularity.

These exercises in diplomatic profanity may for the most part be classified as confidential talk within the secret corridors of power. But outside these closed chambers the style is catching on, and two of the leading figures in the State Department's alumni, Messrs. Henry Kissinger and Zbigniew Brzezinski, had been heard going in for the new candor. The saucy tales in the memoirs of the some-time Soviet Ambassador to Washington (*In Confidence*, 1995) had been causing much controversy; and some of the cast of U.S. characters whose diplomacy he criticized were striking back. Had their Cold War anti-Communism done disservice to the cause of détente, Peace, and all the other good things which Anatoli Dobrynin felt his old bosses in the Kremlin stood for? Here is the *Washington Post* reporting, not without a touch of derring-do, on some of the responses:

> "I think he screwed up," says a former secretary of state, Henry Kissinger, when asked about Dobrynin's recounting of American actions at the time of the Yom Kippur War.

> "I think he was a charming bull (expletive) artist," says Zbigniew Brzezinski, whom Dobrynin refers to as "a rather vigorous and pushy academic."[11]

Both of these gentlemen, in and out of office, have been notable in the past for their use of the loftiest abstractions, based on their elevated academic vocabularies perfected at Harvard and Columbia Universities. It is, I suspect, a moot question whether the *Post*, in its selection of a representative publishable quote out of the context of more extensive counter-attacks, was not indulging in some hi-jinks for the morning edition. At any rate the outcome is yet another step towards the legitimization of an earthier diplomatic *newspeak*.

Meanwhile, back at the ranch, the rough-hewn triumphs of Ambassador Richard Holbrook in bullying a Bosnian agreement in Dayton, Ohio, were still being celebrated. Slobodan Milosevic had been persuaded by some strange and diplomatic wiles, practiced only by superpower Americans, to help end a war he triggered. *Time* snaps a picture of "the boss of Belgrade" with "a cigar in one hand and a drink of slivovitz (plum brandy) in the other hand, showing off his command of colloquial English–he praised Holbrook's diplomacy by calling him a 'a bull—— artist.'"[12] Which prompts the question of whether the semantic secrets of the "artistry" will prove to be extendable to the Bosnian combat zones, to the peace-makers in the field, now duly fertilized with *b-s-*. We can only hope.

Familiar is the peacemaker's last sigh: If only the men who come to end the war could only understand each other! Here, too (as *Time* magazine is so well-informed as to report), new linguistic arts are being requisitioned to evade the old "Babel-onian" dangers of not knowing what a wildly gesticulating Montenegrin peasant is actually trying to say to the incoming peacemaking American trooper. Is he offering information? Trying to give a warning? Making some vague threats? Evidently there is an official U.S. military recommendation that in these kinds of communication crises in foreign places, one should turn to a new band of interpreters who represent a non-fighting chance of coming away from a minefield with a smile: "Pick the trash talkers in your group to negotiate.... These are the guys who can establish a rapport."[13] Thus does "*trash talk*"–up till now only a pop-rap favorite in the "ghettos" of New York and Los Angeles–suddenly emerge as the *in*-lingo which can enforce international peace treaties and convert the swords on the Balkan killing fields into ploughshares. But how do you say "*trash*" in Serbo-Croat?

At any rate, the lives and careers of whole corps of foreign diplomats to come may well benefit from these enrichments of old diplomatic approaches– if, that is, they can handle *scat* and *rap* and *trash*, as well as *break* gestures and a whole variety of bullying barnyard epithets.

What used to be known in the 1980s as "Haig-speak" must surely have helped to open the floodgates, and all distinc-tions of discourse are being washed away. It is not unlike the phenomenon one Olympic summer in flamboyant Los Angeles where the blurred lines between classical Greek competitiveness and classy numbers in contemporary show business became so indistinct that tap dancing on a tree-top or juggling dishes underwater were about to become a-*okay* and *right-on* for an Olympic gold. As I write, the British are pushing for the official acceptance in the Sydney Olympics of their pub-obsessed game of darts.

In the ensuing struggle for the leadership of the Tory Party, following the obligatory retirement of the defeated prime minister, John Major, the former home secretary, Michael Howard, emerged as one of the leading candidates. There was much investigative reporting into his record in office by the press and even more by his rivals in the race, with the findings duly leaked to reporters. One or two minor scandals saw the light of day, and the stories in the English newspapers reflected the new step forward (or downward) that had been made in the outing of private profanities. In the feature in the *Sunday*

Times, entitled "Howard's End," there were the fruits of talks with government officials who had worked with the cabinet minister: "Home Office critics hit back that he is dangerous in the wrong way. 'It's not whether he is a s*** that's the question. We may need a s***. It is the way he responds under pressure,' says one. Another insider agrees: 'He never swears, but he panics and he shouts'" ("Howard's End," *Sunday Times*, 18 May 1997 [Focus], p. 13). The four-letter word is the key to political life and death. If he can't *say* one, then he *is* one. Swear words, evidently, are part of the new political vocabulary not least for their vivid descriptive powers but also for the immemorial role they play as a safety-valve in governance which is racked by emotional situations. Expletives can function as stabilizers for the ship of state.

The past is an inexhaustible resource, and when journalism exhausts the news-stories available on the day it can, in inspired moments, turn to the historical record and come up with usefully salty bits. But the price of an extra item of reader entertainment may well be the distortion of an important episode of history which is not usually seen in terms of either sexual sidelights or angry under-the-breath expletives.

For example, the history of the post-1945 Cold War, essentially arising out of the rivalry of the superpower victors in World War II, the USA and the USSR. Most chroniclers recall the slow, indeed reluctant recognition on the part of American foreign policy to discern the threat of Soviet totalitarianism and the expansive-imperialist designs of Joseph Stalin. Only the young George F. Kennan (and his small band of State Department sympathizers) saw the dangers as early as the wartime winter of 1944-1945. James Byrnes, secretary of state, made an insightful speech (in Stuttgart) in 1946. Warnings about the fate of vulnerable Greece and Turkey after the Iron Curtain absorption of Eastern Europe came to a climax in 1947.

When did the President see the Kremlin's hostility and challenge? Truman acted decisively in confronting the Berlin Blockade with an airlift in 1948; and the year before he had also made effective deterrent moves in the Mediterranean.

A somewhat different chronology can emerge when attention is paid to the recorded expletives conventionally deleted by biographers and diplomatic historians. At the Potsdam Conference in the summer of 1945 the new American President–FDR had died in April–conferred with the other victorious Allies (Churchill, Attlee, Stalin). Harry S. Truman was inexperienced on the international scene, exhibited much ignorance and embarrassing naivete; but he came to some characteristically firm conclusions, and especially about the character of Marshal Joseph Vissarionovich Stalin (*b.* Djugashvili). When he was privately asked by a U.S. Navy man what he thought of the Soviet dictator after those intense East-West sessions in the Cecilienhof Palace in Potsdam, he said, "I think he's a son of a bitch." If our standard practice at the time (and for decades to come) was not to delete expletives, then the Cold War might have broken out then and there, or could have been seen to have been mutually declared–since Truman had added that "I guess he [Stalin] thinks I'm one too."

The public myth of "East-West friendship" among "gallant Allies" who were allegedly determined to build a peaceful postwar world, dominated the reportage in the press in the 1940s as it did the diplomatic spirit loyal to the official resolutions of Teheran, Yalta and Postdam. Can it be that the obscenities of four-letter words should have a place in our understanding about what has happened? At least Truman's cuss-word, that classic bit of blue slang, would have inflamed the defenders of the so-called Revisionist Thesis (in history as well as politics), reinforcing their tendentious arguments about how premature American anti-Sovietism instigated the Cold War. I find it curious that it played no such role. For one thing, historians buried the remark; and, for another, the American and worldwide press (including *Pravda* and *Izvestia*) failed to dig it out and pick it up. Some fifty years later I mentioned it, quite casually, in a televised historical film to be shown in Germany. And although the expletive was no longer blue-pencilled, its translation–in German s.o.b. came out as Stalin being a *Hurensohn* (although I also tried the more literal "*Hundesohn*")–inflamed the local ideological spirits and started Cold-War controversies anew. I suspect that *le mot de Potsdam* still has a future ahead of it.*[14]

On the twentieth anniversary of the fall of Saigon (April 1975) and of the panicky last withdrawals of the American presence in Vietnam, a few documents were declassified and released by the U.S. State Department. The language of these cables reveal, yet again, how even the disciplined coolness of professional diplomatic prose can degenerate under the pressure of disarray and disaster. Slips of the tongue are one thing: a slide into verbal chaos quite another.

Time magazine (24 April 1995) has described the last American Ambassador, Mr. Graham Martin, who died in 1990, as "a strange combination of Pollyanna and paranoid." I doubt whether these qualities characterized his entire career; but it is obvious from the style of his cables in the last days of the battle of Saigon–when U.S. Army helicopters were hectically lifting off hysterical evacuees from the roof of the U.S. Embassy building–that the senior person in the disappearing American presence could neither think nor write

---

*   Mencken, in pursuing "son-of-a-bitch" as one of the hardest worked of the "non-profane pejoratives" in common American use, refers to a German traveler who, in 1858, noted that "*hurensohn*" was, just as it was at home, a popular fighting-word among Americans. Almost a century later the "four-word epithet" figured in a controversy over a *Daily News* cartoon (1939) in which Hitler, standing at a bar, about to introduce Mussolini to Stalin, said, "Come, Benito, I want you to shake hands with this son-of-a———." Mencken registered this spelling as a "denaturized form" in contrast to the "collision form," sonofabitch.

clearly. Ambassador Martin had cabled Secretary of State Henry Kissinger in Washington–and this was as late as 28 April, a few days before it was all over– that he foresaw Americans staying in Saigon for "a year or more." Even whis- pering the word *"evacuation,"* he warned, could set off a panic. Yet the last Americans were already leaving, taking with them some Vietnamese employ- ees and sympathizers–and the Ambassador was refusing to allow the felling of a huge tamarind tree which was blocking the helicopters from landing in the Embassy court-yard. (It was hacked down only around mid-day April 29 "when the evacuation was entering its last hours.")

Some of those last cables from the ambassador in Saigon (now Ho Chi Minh City) appear to be written when the balance of his diplomatic mind left some- thing to be desired. Of course, the U.S. press had been grinding its own axe in its almost uniformly critical reports of a hopeless war doomed to failure; and, to be sure, the Washington foreign-policy establishment was no longer of one loyal mind about the crumbling mission to "search and destroy" or to "pacify." Nevertheless, there is a memorable sentence which should be recorded here; for it rivals even the wild petulant prose that German leaders (after their World War I defeat in 1918) indulged themselves with their *Dolchstoss- Legende* to suggest that they had not "lost on the front" but had been "betrayed from behind": stabbed by *a dagger in the back.* Our American version differs only in the choice of the weapon and the place of dastardly incision. As Ambassador Martin wrote: "The sly, anonymous insertions of the perfumed ice pick into the kidneys in the form of the quotes from my col- leagues in the Department [of State] are only a peculiar form of acupuncture indigenous to Foggy Bottom against which I was immunized long ago."[15] Some immunizations, we know, fail to take–and the anti-toxins in time wreak their revenge.

Language registers the tragedy. From Lyndon Johnson's *"undeclared war"* and Robert McNamara's *"body count"* to the Pentagon's *"Operation Crazy Horse"* and Graham Martin's *"perfumed ice pick,"* words were among the battle- field casualties. It was from the start a faltering mission, sounded by an uncer- tain trumpet; and sloppy language was only following the floppy flag, revealing a faulty verbal link to reality. Generals stammered, diplomats grumbled, pro- testers ranted, politicians prevaricated, reporters pontificated. It was a dazed and erratic time. Alone from what they all said–and the deceptive photos and film footage to match–a history of a lost war could be written: not a comedy but a tragedy of errors.

My point in all of this is that it remains a moot question whether diplomatic discourse can maintain itself on a serious and thoughtful level with the inter- penetration of such loose talk, even if the vernacular is occasionally pungent, and even visibly on target. When the ambassador to the UN, Mrs. Madeleine Albright, was named to be the new secretary of state, the chairman of the Senate Foreign Relations committee, the curmudgeonly old combative Jesse

Helms, indicated his approval by saying "She's a gutsy lady." (Ambassador Albright is reported to have winced at being told of the remark.)

When, in turn, the new ambassador to the UN was named by President Clinton, the congressman was just returning from another of his emergency trips abroad on behalf of hostages held in hostile lands; and in an interview, indicating his elation at the appointment, Representative Bill Richardson (a Democrat from New Mexico) expressed his confidence in the world-political role of the USA among the world's nations–"In the end, they know we have the juice to get things done." Whatever "*juice*" may mean in this context, the remark as an explanation of American can-do power took its place mid-way between two other optimistic formulations on the potency of Yankee juices– "We have the balls to do the job" and "Only Americans have the pizzazz* to be a superpower." Why take the trouble to think like Jefferson and Madison and formulate things like Dean Acheson (and indeed Dr. Henry Kissinger), when a "gutsy" phrase will hit the target right on? Old styles in thought and language are too uptight. Mrs. Albright, taking office (in January 1997) as the first woman to be secretary of state in U.S. history, announced her diplomatic credo to be "telling it like it is."

In a time when wars are undeclared and peace treaties rarely signed, everything in international relations tends to be more informal. Diplomats talk casual-like, and the short-sleeved phrases come as they are.[16]

A final example from the White House years of President Clinton. His folksy usages of coarse slang pushed profanity into additional prominence, almost into its shady new role of pop diplomacy. The context was the U.S. military landings in Haiti (1993) when the U.S.-supported Haitian, Jean-Bertrand Aristide, turned out to be "flaky" and the CIA's intelligence profile in fact suggested that he was an unstable manic-depressive. That explained the otherwise inexplicable difficulties that the White House was having in negotiations with him. Still, the U.S. commander-in-chief persisted in restoring the old "abnormal" Haitian president to power. As was reported from the Oval Room, Bill Clinton's shrewdness in judging human nature and aberrant behavior came up with a piece of proverbial wisdom which could serve as a

---

* The origins of "*pizzazz*" seem not to be traceable; but if young new-age diplomats have access to dictionaries of slang their dispatches and public responses can have innumerable alternatives. For *juice* and *pizzazz* as qualities of national power (and thus a formidable notion in international power politics), there is a long list of synonyms from *bang* and *bounce* to *socko, zap, zip,* and *zowie.* Much over-used by now is *guts* (but not yet *gutsy*), and under-used is *moxie* (presumably because it is derived from the name of an old soft-drink). See: *The Slang Thesaurus* (ed. Jonathon Green, 1986), p. 69, and *Modern Slang* (Ayto & Simpson, 1992), pp. 142, 170.

 In any case, Machiavelli who knew a thing or two about the arts of power-political diplomacy might have been delighted by a Prince with *pizzazz,* or even a Doge with *zip* or *zap.*

guideline to future commanders who might be pressed to rely on other foreigners, weak-willed and abnormal, in combined allied military operations: "You know, you can make too much of normalcy,' Clinton said. 'A lot of normal people are assholes.'"[17] How true–and it was to prove an acute observation which would illuminate many of the war crises and peace processes which marked the Clinton years. At least this is one vulgarism that has moved forward from a catchphrase or a salacious slur to a generalization about life and politics that could almost be taken to be a maxim of governance.

For now it is enough of a lexical change to be getting on with the drama of when English journalists abandon their age-old and accustomed expletives in order to accommodate the American way of expostulation.

The *Random House Dictionary of American Slang* (ed. Lighter) devotes fourteen quotation-ridden pages to the entry on "*ass (ME ars)*," including "*ass-hole (ME arce hoole)*." The earliest quote is 1672; but the *Oxford Companion to the English Language* notes that William Caxton (the first English printer, *c.* 1422-1491) preferred to "take the self-censoring route of euphemism," that is, he avoided coarse language, as when he substituted *buttocks* for *arse* in his edition of Malory's *Morte d'Arthur*.

It has been, of course, the favorite seven-letter vulgarism of twentieth-century American novelists from James T. Farrell and Ernest Hemingway to John Updike and Norman Mailer. Although many U.S. Presidents were known to have "cursed like a trooper" (*viz.* Lyndon B. Johnson) President Clinton's may well be the highest-ranking ascription to a**-h**e on record. On the level of party-political polemics, before the expletives get to be deleted, or at least camouflaged, he seems to be getting as good as he gives. The *New Yorker* quotes O. Stone as saying, "Clinton is talking through his asshole."

When both sides get to be even, we may have to be moving on to richer variations of what lexicographers record as an *artsy-fartsy* (or, sometimes, *arsy-varsey*) vocabulary.[18]

Caxton gives way to Clinton. Thus, when a conservative political columnist proposes a "tougher policy," a reply in kind perhaps to Labour's "primal screams along the lines of, 'Get lost, you Tory *****!'"–he recommends a standard Washingtonian "kick-ass" strategy of counterattack against the Blair government: "It would be nice to see the Tories kick some ass for once." The a-word is being Americanized; "*r*'s" are being dropped like Cockney aitches. Cursing does sound a bit better these days with this touch of cosmopolitanism. Still, they've almost lost hold of four or five centuries of tried-and-true coarse aggressiveness with that one.[19]

The least one could say was that, in its wild and inexorable proliferation for the past half-century, the f-word had made its way to all the highest places in the land, indeed in the two lands where English is the official national language and olde Anglo-Saxon rudeness is a constant impertinence in the politest of societies.

Here is an Anglo-American heavy metal rock star, mixing and mingling in the Palace Jubilee concert for the fiftieth anniversary of Queen Elizabeth II's ascension to the British throne. Ozzy Osbourne and his "wild rock wife" Sharon were being presented to the royals when–according to the *Daily Telegraph*, basing itself on an Osbourne interview to *Rolling Stone* magazine*–when there occurred a "foul-mouthed slip." The heavy-metallist said that he had "hissed to the wife to watch her language." But her language evidently had no other effective way to state her true feelings on the grand royal occasion. Sharon, in her proper turn, was being introduced to Camilla Parker Bowles backstage in Buckingham Palace, and she let a four-letter word slip in front of the long-time companion (read: Mistress) of Charles, the Prince of Wales: "My wife [reported Ozzy Osbourne] said to Camilla Parker Bowles 'I think you're f****** great.' My eyeballs nearly flew out of my head." Obscenity may be the natural language of pop stars but evidently they still have funny feelings about its propriety–a cultural or profanity lag, if you will–when it comes to formal pronouncements or élite conversations. Mrs. Parker Bowles may well be marrying the Windsor crown prince; and, as reported, she "remained un-ruffled": "Oh, it's quite all right," she told the slightly abashed Mrs. Obsourne. "We curse quite a lot around here." *Noblesse* (-to-be) *oblige*.

To be sure, Ozzy's a proper little entertainer, and he tells the anecdotes as they wuz; the New York text in *Rolling Stone* merely embellishes the Parker Bowles quote with [*affects posh accent*] and with [*embarrassed laugh*] as the Queen, never noticing the tattoo on the fingers of his left hand (Ozzy kept it hidden in his trouser pocket), remarked that she understood that he was "the wild one"…and Ozzy says he "just went, *Heh, heh, heh.*"

This called for a notable amount of self-control on the part of this particular cult hero; it admittedly is a small setback to the inexorable process of four-letterization which I have ben positing. Osbourne's show in the USA enjoys "a ratings bonanza" and has made of Ozzy *the top TV dad* ("and stars of everyone in his family"). In addition–as the *Rolling Stone* reporter notes for the benefit of such readers who are not aware that the-paper-takes-no-prisoners, *i.e.* never uses asterisks: "the 53-year-old millionaire…shuffles through his Beverly Hills mansion in his tattoos and magenta-streaked shoulder-length hair…firing the word *fuck* every ten seconds…."

Although a poor Birmingham lad of little schooling, Osbourne obviously knew how to behave…basically, sort of. After all, he had been a guest of honor at the White House Correspondents Dinner; he had received a star on Holly-wood Boulevard; and he was now invited by royalty to play and sing and say hello. The restraint was astonishing, the self-censorship nothing less than historic.

---

*   Interview with Ozzy Osbourne, in *Rolling Stone* magazine (New York), 25 July 2002. Hugh Davies, "Four Letters from Ozzy's Wife fail to rock Palace," *Daily Telegraph*, 13 July 2002, p. 3.

Q. Did you try hard not to say fuck when you met the queen?
A. That word was temporarily on hold in my head.

And the music? It was famed for its sinister touch of "satanism" and "witch-craft" (although he confessed he hadn't even heard of "satanism" and Aleister Crowley). But the son of Prince Charles, the teenager Prince William, also the successor in line to the U.K. throne, was cool enough to like Ozzy's *Black Sabbath* and said "It would have been great if you had done *Black Sabbath*." The devilishly clever boy from Birmingham knew his demonology, and knew better: "If I had one '*Black Sabbath*', the fucking royal box would have turned to stone, and the Archbishop of Canterbury would have had to douse them in holy water."

Once there is in the principles of democratic governance a constitutional separation of Church and State, all profane things are possible and all words sayable in the free secular space. The f-word and the s-word (and more) have mounted the commanding heights of our political culture, setting up base camp there, with pup tents and latrines, slit trenches and out-houses, and all the rough idioms that go with them. But even impish Pop cockiness in the precincts of power is somehow aware of the local difference between Palace and Pulpit. (You gotta be careful, or you're gonna get it.) The Royals, as-sembled in Buckingham Palace for the Queen's Jubilee Year, represented not only the legitimacy of British democracy but also the titular Christian head of the High Anglican Church. Not even the Master of Heavy Metal wants to be turned into stone and drown in the depths of holy water.

The young prince was going too far. He too could get into trouble. His tastes in heavy metal rock could be considered unconstitutional at best and heretical at worst; and they used to behead people for that in England. A Black Sabbath? Never on Sunday.[20]

Notes

Introduction

1. John Dos Passos (1896-1970) is enjoying a late, deserved measure of recognition. His *USA* trilogy–consisting of *The 42nd Parallel* (1930), *1919* (1932) and *The Big Money* (1936)–has been reprinted by the Library of America; and the *New York Times'* book critic quoted praise (from Alfred Kazin, Edmund Wilson, among others) which could take him out of the category of "forgotten novelists" and put him among the "great American writers." See "A Second Act for Dos Passos and His Panoramic Writings," Douglas Brinkley, *New York Times*, "Arts & Ideas," 30 August 2003, p. 9.

2. I am following the trail-blazing leads which can be found in a recent German study of the role of "the newspaper clipping in scientific studies," curiously entitled *Cut and Paste um 1900* (ed. Herrmann and Hoffmann, 2002). There are remarkable chapters by Anke Te Heesen, Dieter Hoffmann, Michael Hagner, Lorraine Daston, among others; the documentation, especially the illustrations, is adventurous; and I have followed the trail by consulting their own longer works on the subject. Among them: Steven Shapin and Simon Schaffer, *Leviathan and the Air Pump* (Princeton, 1985); Lorraine Daston and Katharine Park, *Wonders and the Order of Nature, 1150-1750* (New York, 2000).

3. The Collings and other quotes are from Barbara Shapiro, *A Culture of Fact: England, 1550-1720* (2000), pp. 91-93. She gives no more precise source, having borrowed them apparently from Joseph Frank, *Beginnings of the English Newspaper, 1620-1660* (1961), pp. 84, 122, 214, 265.

4. For Robert Hooke's "ideal reporter," see Shapiro, *Culture of Fact*, p. 74. For the pamphleteering in the time of Cromwell, see my *Utopia and Revolution* (1976), chapter 11 ("To Armageddon and Back"), pp. 384-414; and *passim*. See also, for another revival and reconsideration of Marchmount Nedham (who for a time collaborated with John Milton in defending Cromwell's Commonwealth), Paul Rahe's article about "the world's foremost journalist" in "An Inky Wretch," *National Interest*, Winter 2002-2003.

5. Lasky, *Utopia and Revolution* (1976), preface, p. 11.

6. I am indebted to Michael Hagner's sketch of Oscar Vogt in *Cut and Paste*, pp. 116-131.

7. See Lasky, *Utopia and Revolution*, pp. 363-371. The Bayle quote is from his letter to Minutoli, 27 February 1673, in Paul Hazard, *The European Mind: 1680-1715* (tr. May, 1953), p. 100.

Part 1: Towards a Theory of Journalistic Malpractice

1. From A.N. Whitehead to Irving Kristol

1. C.S. Lewis, *The Screwtape Letters* (1942, Fount ed., 1984), pp. 130, 77-79.
2. Steven Henry Madoff, "A Shock for Shock's Sake?," *Time Magazine*, 11 October 1999, pp. 130-132.
3. Roger Kimball, "The elephant in the gallery, or the lessons of 'Sensations,'" *The New Criterion*, November 1999, pp. 4-8. For his own part, Kimball puts the phenomenon – the "new" losing its novelty value – into a longer perspective, and recalls the history of Dada and Surrealism: "Damien Hirst has nothing on Dali...."
    As Kimball notes, "When Dali was active, there were still the remnants of resistance to his pathological antics [the pornography, fascination with decay and mutilation, toying with blasphemy, rebarbative photographs] among people concerned with high culture." Exhibitions like *Sensations* do not "challenge" established taste; they *are* established taste....
4. *Daily Telegraph*, "Chef's £200,000....," 9 December 1999, p. 7. Kimball, "Elephant in the gallery ," *New Criterion*, November 1999, p. 8. *Daily Telegraph*, "£177,000 for Hirst picture," 10 December 1999, p. 7: an "anonymous phone bid" bought the untitled work but the auction house was "unable to confirm" whether the bidder was, as was generally assumed, the artist himself.
5. Colin Gleadell, "Art Sales (New York)," *Daily Telegraph*, 21 May 2001, p. 18.
6. Philippe de Montebello, "The Mayor Is an Astute Art Critic but a Misguided Censor," *NYT/IHT*, 8 October 1999, p. 15.
7. William Safire, "Hubris at the Art Museum....," *NYT/IHT*, 8 October 1999, p. 15. The "Dung" quote was cited by Safire as well as *Newsweek*, "Shock Grows in Brooklyn," 11 October 1999, p. 10. James Bone, "Mayor of New York smells an artistic rat," *The Times* (London), 9 October 1999, p. 14. On the "corrupt" aspects of the Exhibition, see the *New York Times*' stories by David M. Herszenhorn, "N.Y. Accuses Museum of Conspiracy"; David Barstow, "Blurring Artistic Lens: Brooklyn Exhibit's Backers Stood to Gain" and "'Sensations' and Saatchi," *NYT/IHT*, 1 November 1999, p. 3; *NYT/IHT*, 20 December 1999, p. 20.
8. Martin Gayford, "Space Exploration: Rachel Whiteread's Sculptures," *Daily Telegraph* 20 June 2001, p. 21.
9. "Judge Sees Fallacies in the Arguments of the Mayor," *New York Times*, 3 November 1999, p. B5.
10. Michael Kimmelman, "In the End...Critic's Notebook," *New York Times*, 3 November 1999, pp. E 1-4. David Barstow, "Mayor Says Judge Rushed Decision in Museum Case," *NYT*, 3 November 1999, p. B3; David Barstow, "Giuliani Ordered...," *NYT*, 2 November 1999, pp. 1, B5. Stephen C. Munson, "The Monotony of 'Sensations,'" *Commentary*, January 2000, pp. 61-65.
    Arguments slur and stutter, and nobody can breathe deeply enough for second thoughts. Art critics with a monthly deadline have more time to write thoughtfully and more knowledgeably. In addition to Roger Kimball's critique in the *New Criterion*, mentioned previously, there is Stephen C. Munson in *Commentary*. Both analyze dismissively "the sort of hype [which is] the staple of the huckster and an omnipresent part of our mass culture....{The works] were largely derivative of the pop, conceptual, minimalist, and neo-realist movements that first emerged in the 1960s and that have undergone several recyclings since then...."
11. "Connections" by Edward Rothstein: "Faust Learns the Painful Truth," *New York Times*, 13 January 2001, p. B-13.

12. "Saatchi buys hell on earth," Catherine Milner, *Sunday Telegraph*, 6 February 2000, p. 8.

    The reports in the German press, always attentive to "Holocaust news," were mixed. Some were, as expected, shocked by the "frivolous" exploitation of a great tragic event. Others defended the exhibition (also sight unseen) on the grounds that the history of art is replete with masterpieces about the horrors of war and torture (e.g., Goya), of intolerable suffering (Jesus on the cross), etc.

    Paul Spiegel, the chairman of German Jewry, was quoted as saying: "Every realistic representation of the Holocaust's horrors serves to shock people, and also to alert them..." Siegfried Helm, "*Wir lassen kleine kulturelle Handgranaten hochgehen* (We're exploding little cultural hand-grenades)," *Welt am Sonntag*, 20 February 2000, p. 43.

13. William Rees-Mogg, *Times* (London), 30 January 1995. Heren obituary, *Times*, 27 January 1995.

14. For the texts of Robert Elegant and Stanley Karnow, see *Encounter* (August 1981, pp. 73-90). For Julian Pettifer, a brief story was in London's *Evening Standard*; and Pettifer subsequently clarified and confirmed his self-criticism in a personal letter to me. See also: Günther Lewy, *America in Vietnam* (1979).

15. Geneva Overholser, "We Have Bad News, And More Bad News," *Washington Post/IHT*, 18 July 1996, p. 9.

2. The Little Lie and the Big Story

1. K.P. Klingelschmitt, *Tageszeitung*, 17 December 1996; *TAZ*, *Weihnachten* (Christmas) 1996, pp. 1, 10; Reinhof Reis, *Der Tagesspiegel*, 23 December 1996, p. 23. *FAZ*, 24 December 1996, p. xxx.

2. John Evangelist Walsh, *Unravelling Piltdown: The Science Fraud of the Century & Its Solution*, (Random House, 1996), quoted by Richard Bernstein in his *New York Times* review, *IHT*, 25 September 1996, p. 11.

3. Tom Wolfe, *Hooking Up* (2000), p. 68-71, 88.

    The latest details on the Piltdown forgery-hoax are in Professor Brian Gardiner's article in *Nature*, the British weekly science journal, 23 June 1996. See also the accounts in the *Washington Post/IHT*, 24 May 1996, p. 1, and the *Daily Telegraph*, 23 May 1996, p. 9. The result of the earlier investigations into the fraud were summed up in: J.S. Weiner, *The Piltdown Forgery* (Oxford University Press, 1955). My article in German was in *Der Monat*, September 1955, "Londoner Tagebuch," pp. 567-70.

    The late Frank Spencer, who was a professor of anthropology at Queens College, New York, added to the cast of villainous characters by pointing an accusing finger at Sir Arthur Keith (1866-1955), an anatomist whose papers revealed that he had been "in" on the 1912 dramatic premiere of *Eoanthropus dawsoni*. One newspaper obituary recorded that "his [Spencer's] conscientious sifting of the evidence [in his 1990 book, *Piltdown, a Scientific Forgery* (1990)] had yielded the most convincing solution of the hoax thus far produced...." (*Daily Telegraph*, on the death of Professor Frank Spencer, 4 June 1999 p. 31.

3. Difficulties in Grappling with Reality

1. See my own article in *Commentary* Magazine, January 1952, p. 1-6: Melvin J. Lasky, "Why the Kremlin Extorts Confessions: The Most Jealous God, the Cruelest Inquisition."

2. "Chinese Filmmakers Dare to Correct Mao," Reuters dispatch in *IHT*, 25 October 1996.

3. *Dpa* dispatch, "Kein Schnapp-Kuss: Doisneau's Foto war gestellt," *FAZ*, 1 December 1996.

4. See the reflections of one critical (and self-critical) journalist who had covered the Vietnam war, Robert S. Elegant, "How to Lose a War," *Encounter*, August 1981, pp. 73-90. For his troubles Elegant was publicly denounced – the charge was his "Goebbels-style war propaganda" – by Morley Safer in an NBC TV broadcast shortly thereafter.
See also: Günther Lewy, *America in Vietnam* (1979), which is a meticuloulsy scholarly work, and two more widely-read books by William Shawcross, *Sideshow* (1979) and Michael Herr's *Dispatches* (1978). Another more balanced viewpoint: Peter Braestrup's 2-volume *The Big Story* (1977) as well as Philip Knightley's history of "the War Correspondent as Hero, Propagandist, and Myth Maker" entitled *The First Casualty* (1975).

5. See the accounts of the Michael Born trial in Koblenz which were published in the *Frankfurter Allgemeine Zeitung*, especially Michael Hansfeld, "Der Connaisseur nimmt die Kröten in Kondensmilch," *FAZ*, 14 October 1996, p. 39.

6. I have been summarizing here the discussion in the *Süddeutsche Zeitung* which was instigated by two glittering articles: Andreas Bernard, "Born der Wirklichkeit: Gibt es ein wahres Fernsehen im falschen?," 9 October 1996, p. 13, and, especially, Peter Sartorius, "Lügen wie gesendet: Über den journalistischen Umgang mit der Wirklichkeit," 12/13 October 1996, p. 13.

7. "Angus McGill saunters through town in search of the swinging sixties spirit: When *everyone* loved London," *Evening Standard*, Wednesday, 2 July 1980. Horace Judson's *Time* cover story was published in the issue of 15 April 1966, pp. 30-34, "You Can Walk Across It On the Grass."The BBC quiz program which I heard (and, regrettably, failed to note the time and date) was broadcast in the early 1970s. Paul Krassner, "The Summer of Love Plus 30: You Want to Smoke a Banana?," *Los Angeles Times/IHT*, 25 June 1997, p. 9.

8. "TV chiefs 'still turning blind eye to hoaxers,'" *Daily Telegraph*, 31 August 1999, p. 27.

9. See Steve Atkinson, "Diana's Fury at Sneak Sex Video," *Daily Mirror*, 8 October 1996, p. 7. "Sun Diana Video Exclusive A Hoax," 9 October 1996, *Daily Mirror*, p. 1-3. "The Story Behind Princess Diana Video Hoax," *Daily Mirror*, 10 October 1996, p. 2.

10. Donna Britt, "15 Years Later, a Lie Still Rankles," *Washington Post/IHT*, 13 June 1996, p. 9. Mike Sager, "Janet's World," *GC (Gentlemen's Quarterly)*, June 1996, pp. 200-209, 210-211.Bill Green, The Ombudsman's report to the *Washington Post* on "the Janet Cooke affair," *ms.* (June 1981), 144 pages. (I am grateful to my friend, Robert Kaiser, managing editor of the *Washington Post*, for sending me a copy of this document.) John Updike, *Brazil: a Novel*, 1994, p. 1.

11. Robert Sam Anson, "Secrets and Lies," *Vanity Fair*, November 1997, pp. 42*ff.*, Seymour Hersh, *The Dark Side of Camelot* (Little Brown, 1997). Evan Thomas *(et al.)*, "The JFK-Marilyn Hoax," *Newsweek*, 6 October 1997, pp. 24-26.

12. *IHT*, 10 November 1997, p. 7.

13. Richard Cohen, "It's Only an Asterisk," *Washington Post/IHT*, 12 November 1997, p. 9. William Safire, "Uncovering the Story of the Full Monty," *NYT/IHT*, 17 November 1997, p. 11.
Safire mentions as a possible source of the term *"full monty"*: Field Marshal Montgomery "who cut a splendid figure in full regalia." This would give an extra sartorial twist, a special cladding to the phrase which, after all, was popularized by the film about male night-club strippers. Its title signified "taking all one's clothes off, to go the whole way, to be totally naked."

Similarly, "the asterisk" is almost established as the short signal or emblem of upcoming obscenity.

14. Gore Vidal's review of Seymour Hersh's book appeared in the *New Yorker*, 1 December 1997, pp. 85-92, under the title, "Coached by Camelot: Why do we still want to defend J.F.K.?"

15. For the Martin Walser texts, see the brochures of the *Dolf Sternberger Gesellschaft* (Heidelberg, 5 November 1994). The Walser speech was also in *Der Spiegel* (Hamburg, November 1995)

The defense of the *Süddeutsche Zeitung* against Walser's attack on its historic and disastrous interview is by Jürgen Busche (*SDZ*, 8 November 1995). The press always takes such things badly. Critics are accused of treason to their own intellectual class and admonished (as Busche to Walser) to remember the "healing powers of controversy." In the end the journalist falls back on the bromidic analogy of punishing the messenger who brings the bad news. Doubtless, a foolish reprisal; but what if the messenger had been caught tampering with the nature of the message? Who would be blameworthy in that case?

The text in German reads: "Wer bist du überhaupt, daß du frei sein willst?... Tatsachen haben es schwer in Deutschland, anerkannt zu werden....Wenn wir in der Vergangenheit sind, fehlt die Hauptsache, die Gegenwart. Wenn wir in der Gegenwart sind, fehlt die Hauptsache, die Vergangenheit. Wir sind nie da, wo wir gerade sind."

16. For the Bubis-Walser controversy, see Roger Cohen's dispatch to the *New York Times*, "Debate Shows Issue of Holocaust Guilt Still Haunts Germany," *NYT/IHT*, 30 November 1998, p. 6. For Bubis' "ingenious experiment," Mariam Lau's article in *Die Welt*, "Verdächtigungsrhetorik," 1 December 1998, p. 10. All the leading organs of German public opinion during these weeks – especially *Der Spiegel*, *Die Zeit*, and the *FAZ* – were crowded with agitated commentaries.

Part 2: Sex and Other Ongoing Titillations

5. The Ennui of Obscenity

1. *Sunday Telegraph*, article by Kenneth Rose, 23 June 1996, p. 32.

2. *FAZ*, 4 October 1994, p. 36.

3. The Ophelia/nunnery references are at *Hamlet*, Act III, I; 24, 141. J. Dover Wilson in his seminal work on *What Happens in Hamlet* (Cambridge, 1935) argued famously on behalf of the obscene implication.

Many other Shakespeare scholars dissent. The editors of the new Arden *Hamlet* (1982), in my opinion, protesteth too much. *Nunnery*, they write (Arden ed., p. 282) "was sometimes used sarcastically for a house of unchaste women, and awareness of this may add a bitter undercurrent as the dialogue proceeds; but to insist on it (as in Wilson, pp. 128-134) at the expense of the literal meaning, itself so poignant in the context, is perverse...."

Perverse is the baseless academic self-confidence that one can know precisely what was meant in difficult, century-old texts.

4. *NYT/IHT*, "Letters to the Editor," 7 October 1994, p. 5.

5. Fiona Pitt-Kethley, "Posterior Analytics," in *The Times*, 23 Nov. 1995.

6. Mike Allen, "Reading Bush's Lips...," *Washington Post/IHT*, 2 October 2000, p. 3.

7. Maureen Dowd, "Minor-League Mouth," *NYT*, 6 September 2000, Op-Ed, p. A27. Deborah Orin, "@#$% Times...," *New York Post*, 6 September 2000, p. 22. Matthew Campbell, "Bush panics as robot Gore learns charm," *Sunday Times*, 17 September 2000, p. 23. Rush/Molloy, "Gnashville over Bush," *New York Daily News*, 7 September 2000, p. 18. Thomas M. DeFrank, "W. gives words his own twist," *New*

York Daily News, 7 September 2000, p. 27. Mark Steyn, "Dubya's expletive ex-poses....," *Daily Telegraph*, 8 September 2000, p. 20. John Leo, "Bush has basis for that insult," *New York Daily News*, 9 September 2000.

8. Sean Day-Lewis, "Crime and Punishment in LA-155," *Daily Telegraph*, 31 July 1996.

9. Richard Woods, "Magnificent 14 Prepare to Sail the Globe," *Sunday Times*, 28 July 1996, p. 9.

10. *Financial Times*, "Dealing with the Popo Problem," 29 July 1996.

11. Thomas Sutcliffe, in *The Independent*, 1 September 1997, p. 2 (supplement).

12. H.L. Mencken, *American Language: Supplement One* (4th ed., 1945), p. 654.

13. *Stern* advertisement, 28 August 1997, No. 36, p. 8.

14. "Jeffrey Bernard isn't just unwell...," *Evening Standard*, 5 September 1997, p. 10.

15. Charles Laurence, "Schindler's List," *Daily Telegraph*, 15 October 1997, p. 19. Emilie Schindler (with Erika Rosenberg), *Where Light and Shadow Meet* (W.W. Norton, 1997).

16. Hugo Gordon, "FBI knew in advance of Oklahoma bomb," *Daily Telegraph*, 21 October 1997, p. 15. The quotation from the German "neo-Nazi" tape is in Ambrose Evans Pritchard's book, *The Secret Life of Bill Clinton* (1997), which sums up his investigative journalism during his years in the U.S.A. as the *Sunday Telegraph*'s Washington correspondent.

17. Lin Cook, "Not the Peter Cook I knew," *Evening Standard*, 29 August 1997, p. 44. The unauthorized biography Mrs. Cook was protesting was by Harry Thompson (1997).

18. David Hume, "Of National Characters," *The Philosophical Works of David Hume*, ed. T.H. Green and T.H. Grose, (London, 1882), also "Of National Characters" in Knud Haakonsseen, ed. David Hume: *Political Essays* (Cambridge 1994), pp. 78-82.

19. "Nothing explains everything": Nothing explains everything? I do not mean to be cryptic here; I mean, of course, no-thing, i.e. no *idea* or concept or all-explanatory theory or credo. It is, I am afraid, not the very best way of putting the point; and if I were consistently to follow my own precepts I would have "edited it out." But somehow I want to keep these pages open to the possibility of philosophical digression; for journalism must be thoughtful...or it is nothing at all. I follow here a writer called P.L. Heath (I know, alas, nothing more about him) whose contribution on the subject – in the *Encyclopedia of Philosophy* (1972, pp. 524-525) – produced one of the finest short essays that I know:

NOTHING is an awe-inspiring yet essentially undigested concept, highly es-teemed by writers of a mystical or existentialist tendency, but by most others re-garded with anxiety, nausea, or panic. Nobody seems to know how to deal with it (he would, of course), and plain persons generally are reported to have little difficulty in saying, seeing, hearing, and doing nothing. Philosophers, however, have never felt easy on the matter. Ever since Parmenides laid it down that it is impossible to speak of what is not, broke his own rule in the act of stating it, and deduced himself iinto a world where all that ever happened was nothing, the impression has persisted that the narrow path between sense and nonsense on this subject is a difficult one to tread and that altogether the less said of it the better....

It goes on to consider the views on *nothing* or *no-thing* from Parmenides and Plato to Heidegger, Tillich and Sartre. The author touches lightly on Heidegger who alone among philosophers has extended the symmetry between the contemporary notions of being and nonbeing to the point of

...equipping *Das Nichts* with a correlative (if nugatory) activity of noth-ing, or nihilating, whereby it produces *Angst* in its votaries and untimely hilarity in those, such as Carnap and Ayer, who have difficulty in parsing 'nothing' as a present participle of the verb 'to noth.'

Nothing, whether it noths or not, and whether or not the being of anything entails it, clearly does not entail that anything should be….It remains a question to some why anything, rather than nothing, should exist. This is either the deepest conundrum in metaphysics or the most childish, and though many must have felt the force of it at one time or another, it is equally common to conclude, on reflection, that it is no question at all.

I try to re-read it every year.

20. The Alan Dundes book in German translation had two editions but, regrettably, did not make its mark in the *feuilleton* discussions of the day: Beltz Verlag (1985) and DTV (paperback, 1987).

A treatment of the subject by a German writer is: Ernest Bornemann, *Sex im Volksmund* which was published in Hamburg by Rowohlt Verlag (1971). Dundes includes in his original American edition (published by Columbia Unievrsity and Wayne University Press (1984; 1989), a useful bibliography with further references to the psychoanalytical literature (Lou Andreas-Salomé on "Anal/Sexual"; C.G. Jung; Alfred Adler; Karl Abraham; Geoffrey Gorer; et al.). It also offers some rare items which strike one as scraping the bottom of the barrel…e.g. Josef Zintl, "Prosodic Influences on the Meaning of *Leck Mich am Arsch* in Bavarian," published in a journal called *Maledicta* (volume 4, pp. 91-95).

Hans-Martin Gauger, the linguistics professor at Freiburg University, is the lone German academic defender of Alan Dundes and his theses of the "differentness" (and indeed the "exceptionalism") of the German language in its special way, a *Sonderweg*, of dealing with excremental themes. I found his sophisticated essay in *Merkur* (January 1999, pp. 40-49) on "*Sprache und Sexualität*" to be both witty and surprising; most of the time quite convincing. But his last-ditch defense of a culture's scatological realism – and he insists that Dundes' material "just can't be pushed aside" – is that it has its "praiseworthy aspects" which remain unnamed. They reside possibly in those mysterious philosophical realms bordering on Heidegger's Black Forest where negatives are negated and turn out to be life-enhancing positives.

I imagine that some fine day all that "turd spotting" in toilet-bowl inspection which is supposed to have gone on for centuries in *Mittel-Europa* under Teutonic influence will show itself in the happy German statistics of increasing digestive well-being and, in general, gastro-intestinal health.

21. The Reich-Ranicki *vs.* Maischberger TV controversy was reported on the *Welt am Sonntag*; Reich-Ranicki's letter of scatological correction was published on 15 October 2000, p. 10.

22. Stephen Burgen's book on "European Invective" – although it's a popular, very breezy read, entitled *Your Mother's Tongue* (Gollancz, 1996) – is useful and entertaining. His last chapter is devoted to "The Scatological Imperative" (pp. 208-218) which by delving into a dozen other languages and their excremental vocabulary serves in its way to qualify Dundes' exclusive attention to German obsessions. It leads him to a quotable conclusion: "…But are the words really losing their impact? Perhaps, but if we tire of one set of particular words, we'll find others…because 'bad language' is just another manifestation of our love of words and wordplay….Invective is pure mainly in the sense that so much of it is undiluted ideology." Whatever he means by that it hints at the war between scatology and ideology, and that with the breaking of all the taboos there would be nowhere left to go: "…Overuse has blunted a vernacular that was honed for use in extremis, not for slashing at the everyday."

On the matter of Neanderthal Man, see the summary of the recent German attempt to find more anthropological evidence in the still-extant pre-historic caves near Düsseldorf and in the new book by Schmitz and Rissen, *"Neanderthal: Die Geschichte geht weiter"* (2000), and an article "Das Modell Urmensch," in the *FAZ*, 10 August 2000, p. 51. The *DNA* testing might reveal how "humanoid" the N-Man was, and his exact place in the evolutionary scale.

So far there has been no evidence, as in the "Piltdown Hoax," of the "Ideology-Scatology" role played in the research or the revised re-interpretation.

23. The "fecal" aspect of the case for and against cacophony as the Weasel-Word of the Year was reported in a front-page story in the *Frankfurter Allgemeine Zeitung*, 22 January 2003, p. 9. See also *Die Welt*, 22 January 2003, p. 28; *Der Tagesspiegel*, 22 January 2003, pp. 1, 21; and indeed all other German newspapers of that day for the additional details of the *Unwort* competition.

The journalists in their stories and the editors in their leading articles are almost to a man in outrage against the progressive "desecration" of their native language, so highlighted by the annual register of buzz-words, cant phrases, profanities and inanities which they thoughtlessly feed their frenzied viewers and readers. It is a record which, at the very least, discloses the peculiar perils of our contemporary verbal obsessionism.

Yet a follower of the German national media (the inter-regional press, the twenty-odd TV channels) sees no sign of an earnest self-critical effort to stop the rot. One newspaper columnist (on *Die Welt*) muttered sullenly about the verbal misdemeanors of the Railway System, the *Bundesbahn*. His foreign friends now arrive on something called the *"Inter-City Night,"* formerly known cosily as the *"Schlafwagen,"* the old sleeping car of the European express services. And if he's a bit late they arranged to join up at the *"Meeting Point,"* formerly known as the *Treffpunkt*. Nothing to get overly excited about. But, at this rate, the philologists estimate a half-century before the mother tongue, once the pride of the "Indo-Germanic" branch of languages, would be reduced to the everday status of pidgin.

An even more pessimstic perspective is given in Professor Walter Krämer's lexicon of *"Denglish"* (which mostly consists of Teutonized Americanisms). His dire prediction is that on New Year's Day of the year 2022 Germany, previously known to its natives as *"Deutschland,"* became the 51st state of the United States. He voices the slight hope that the German language might be getting some UN protection as a "minority cultrual right" which might fend off its terminal fate as a *"Pidgin-Dialekt."* Krämer, *Modern talking auf deutsch* (2nd ed., 2000), pp. 5, 262.

25. An example of *"Indogermanisch"* etymology in an Internet entry on the resemblances between German, English, and Old Greek. (See www.etymologie.info/et/etsam_k.html.)

26. Leo Rosten, *The Joys of Yiddish*, p. 14. *Cassell German-English Dictionary*, p. 314.

27. John Corry, *My Times: Adventures in the News Trade* (1994), pp. 155-157.

28. For A professional critique of the *Times Manual*, see Anne Bernays/Justin Kaplan, "Fashions for the Times," in *Columbia School of Journalism Review*, November-December 1999, pp. 76-77.

The authors are struck by the advice that the word "holocaust" has to be capitalized only when it refers to Nazi destruction of Jews during World War II. This prompts the remark (perhaps ironical) that "...This is a distinct advance in sensibility over the *Times* of World war II: in its report on Dachau the paper omitted any mention that Jews were primary victims." Which, in turn, called forth a comparison with the 1976 edition of the stylebook: "...[It was] extremely delicate if not to say reticent when it came to Jews and Jewish-related topics." Its only entry was *"Jewess"* – and its recommendation was *"Do not use. See woman."*

In the current 1999 edition the racial and multi-cultural progress is undeniable: there is a substantial item, including separate entries for *Sephardi* and *Ashkenazi*.

The definition of the former is incomplete and therefore only half-correct. The *Times* overlooked the Israeli usage which refers to present-day North African Jewry as well as Jews who had once lived in Spain and Portugal and founded the great Portuguese Synagogue in Amsterdam. I know Israelis who regret the "cultural-anthropological confusion" between refugees from backward Yemen, poor and scraggly, and those older Sephardi who were taken to be distinguished patricians from the Iberian kingdoms.

29. *Columbia Journalism Review*, November-December 2000, p. 101.
30. Nancy Gibbs/Timothy Roche, "The Columbine Tapes," *Time*, 20 December 1999, pp. 18-29.
31. I am quoting from the *New York Times* story by Michael Janofsky on the *Times* Internet service for 14 December 1999.
32. *Daily Telegraph*, 13 December 1999, p. 5.
33. William Safire, "NATO Entangled in Its Own SWAG," *New York Sunday Times Magazine*, 25 April 1999; *IHT*, 26 April 1999, p. 10. The Old Testament, *Job 24:5* (King James tr.). *New York Times' Manual of Style and Usage* (rev. ed., Siegal/Connally, 1999).
34. Melvin J. Lasky, "The Poets Laureate of Wild Assholes with Revolvers," in *The Republic of Letters* (ed. Saul Bellow & Keith Botsford), No. 4, 1998, pp. 3-4.
35. *Daily Telegraph*, 2 November 1995.
36. "Jury Backs Dismissed Teacher," *New York Times*, 20 November 1996, p. B11. James Kelman, *How Late It Was, How Late*, (London, 1994). This novel won the Booker Prize in 1994.
37. Pamela Druckerman, "Bloomberg Demands Expletives Deleted, Traders Say: $!*@&," *Wall Street Journal*, 28 June 1999, p. A-1.
38. "Das Streiflicht," *Süddeutsche Zeitung*, 3-4 July 1999, p. 1.

6. *"O Propheta"*

1. Thomas W. Ross, "Taboo-Words in Fifteenth-Century English," in *Fifteenth-Century Studies* (ed. Yeager, 1984), p. 137.
2. *Daily Mail*, 15 July 1995. See also: *The Autobiography of Margot Asquith*, (ed. Mark Bonham Carter, 1995), which is rightly celebrated for being witty, indiscreet, entertaining...and inaccurate.
3. "Nicholas Soames," *Daily Telegraph*, 1 March 1997, p. 14.
4. "Gibbon," *Guardian*, 16 November 1994.
5. "Sadistic Secrets," *Sunday Times*, 18 May 1997, p. 9.
6. Stephen Pile, in the *Daily Telegraph*, 10 October 1998, p. A12.
7. Adam Nicolson, "Farewell, angry reader," *Sunday Telegraph*, 15 June 1997, p. 39.
8. *The Times* (London), 24 July 1996, front-page story by Joe Joseph.
9. The *Letters of Wilkie Collins* have been published by Macmillan Press (ed. Baker & Clarke, 1999); N.J. Hall has brought out an edition of *The Letters of Anthony Trollope*, published by Stanford University Press in 1983; both are quoted in Bevis Hillier's article in *The Spectator*, 7 August 1999, pp. 27-32.

7. Chaucer and a Choice of Taboo Words

1. "Last Days of Dylan Thomas," *Sunday Times*, 13 June 1999, p. 8 (News).)

8. Strong Odors, Blurred Pictures

1. Joe Joseph, "Where did all these sex experts come from?," *Times*, 17 November 1998, p. 55.

2.   Matthew Bond, in the *Times*, 25 October 1996, p. 47.
3.   Mary Blume, "Charles Pathé and the Birth of a Cinema Empire," *IHT*, 12-13 November 1994.
4.   *The Oxford Dictionary of Quotations*, Oxford, p. 20, cites Wodehouse's novel, *Young Man in Spats* (1936), Oxford, p. 576. Aldous Huxley, *Brave New World* (1932); Michael Kennedy, *Concise Oxford Dictionary of Music* (1996), "Skryabin," p. 602.

9. Obsessions with the *S*-Word

1.   Gillian Reynolds, "Radio," *Daily Telegraph*, 8 June 1999, p. 21.
2.   Benedict Nightingale, in the *Times*, 12 April 1995.

10. The Case of the Missing F**r-L****r Word

1.   *Standard*, 7 April 1995, p. 13.

11. Asterisks: From Byron to Madonna

1.   Adam Sherwin, "Eminem took drug as part of his show," *The Times* (London), 10 February 2001, p. 23. The New York report on ex-Mayor Koch is on p. 19.
2.   My quotes are from an Associated Press dispatch from Pittsburgh in October 1998. My attention was called to it at an international press conference by the Editor of the *Kuwait Times*. He was "culturally perplexed" by the extra-curricular meanings of "*stain*" and "*asterisk*" as published in his own English-language newspaper (he gave me the cutting of 21 October 1998). I tried to fill him in.

The "damned spot" quote is, of course, from Shakespeare, *Macbeth*, V, i, 38. The "echoes" I refer to include the Biblical "*Leave not a stain in thine honor*" (*Ecclesiastes* 33:22); and, again, from an English poet:

> *From the contagion of the world's slow stain*
> *He is secure, and now can never mourn*
> *A heart grown cold, a head grown grey in vain.*

(Shelley, *Adonais*, XL)

Journalists can play with these echoing quotes without implying in the slightest that Ms. Lewinsky had anything more in mind when she refrained from removing that notorious tell-tale stain by dry-cleaning that famous blue dress.

> *To my true king I offer'd free from stain*
> *Courage and faith; vain faith, and courage vain.*

(Macaulay, A Jacobite's Epitaph)

As for the asterisks in *M*A*S*H*, that widely popular long-playing television comedy about the U.S. Army, this is as good a place as any to note that I was mistaken in suspecting that the G.I. slangsters had inserted something blue and saucy – as in *Snafu* and many other ingenious acronyms – into that four-letter word. But my brief search has come up with no evidence. The comical doctors and patients in the canvas tents of *M*A*S*H* are merely characters in a "mobile army surgical hospital."

Although, if one wants to follow the verbal trail, mash has a dozen usages bordering on extra-medical meanings from flirting to kissing and hugging and/or sexual harrassment. See *Random House Webster's Concise College Dictionary*

(1999), p. 514. *Historical Dictionary of American Slang* (ed. Lighter), vol. II, pp. 519-521.

3. Christopher Clarey, "It's Time for the IOC to Make Amends to Victims of Drugging," *IHT*, 14-15 November 1998, p. 20.
4. Grafton, *The Footnote** (1997), pp. 233-234.
5. The second Belafonte anecdote is also in Grafton, footnote 17 on p. 235, taken from H.L. Gates, Jr., "Belafonte's Balancing Act," *New Yorker* Magazine, 26 August-2 September 1996, p. 135.
6. M.P. Parkes, *Pause and Effect*, p. 91.
7. *Webster* defines "the character * used in printing as the first in series of the reference works to indicate the omission of letters and words, in linguistic works to mark hypothetical forms belonging to a reconstructed ancestral language, and in various arbitrary uses...."

    The *Oxford* gives its first usage as 1612...possibly a little too late for Shakespeare who might have been, under pressure, among the very first to mask sexual references by adapting one of the new printing marks. See also Gordon Williams' studies on the subject: *Dictionary of Sexual Language and Imagery in Shakespearean and Stuart Literature* (1994) and *A Glossary of Shakespeare's Sexual Language* (1997). *Webster's Third New International Dictionary Unabridged* (1993, p. 134). *Shorter Oxford English Dictionary* (1973), vol. I, p. 121. *Oxford English Dictionary*, vol. I, p. 520.
8. David Crystal, *The Cambridge Encyclopedia of the English Language* (1995). P. 395. G. Wilson Knight, *Lord Byron's Marriage: The Evidence of the Asterisks* (1957).
9. See "Godfather of the f-Word: Kenneth Tynan," in vol. I of *The Language of Journalism,* pp. 387-411.
10. The report on Madonna's opening concert (in Barcelona) was by Kathleen Wyatt, in *The Times*, 11 June 2001, p. 18.

12. Who's Afraid of the Big, Bad F-Word?

1. "Sixsmith stands by story...," *Daily Telegraph*, 25 February 2002, p. 6. *Daily Telegraph*, City Comment, 28 February, p. 36. *Storyville*, "The team that dare not speak its name," *The Independent on Sunday*, 3 February 2002, p. 10. "Bono ist der Star auf dem Wirtschaftsgipfel," *Die Welt*, 2 Febryary 2002; "Nein, Strassenkrawall...," *Die Welt*, 4 February 2002, p. 10.
2. *Storyville*, in *The Independent on Sunday*, 10 Febryuary 2002, p. 9.
3. Rachel Johnson, "The mummy diaries," *Daily Telegraph*, 18 January 2003, p. 12.

13. Tiger, the *Times*, and a Dreaded Black Asterisk

1. While I am in the neighborhood, I might as well acknowledge in this place the guidance on these matters of footnotery which this professional scholar formulated in his wise and instructive little book.

    As Grafton writes: "footnotes have never supported, and can never support, every statement of fact in a given work. No apparatus can prevent all mistakes or eliminate all disagreements...." Accordingly, I have gone on researching...although a possible primary source has escaped me...and a particular page number in a magazine or newspaper remains missing. If I have left (as I hope) a general impression of researched accuracy, then an incomplete reference or two should be of no great matter. They, believe me, are all there, as given (barring a few typos)....

    As for the larger claim of scholarly footnotes to attest to truth and authenticity, I recall my difficulties as a young military historian in Alsace-Lorraine in the last year of World War II. We were all assigned "small action studies," to catch history on the fly (as "jitney Tolstoys," as we were dubbed), mainly by being close to the combat and reporting what we saw and heard. Still our commanding Colonel of the Historical Division (a strict and fussy West Pointer) demanded footnotes. I dissented, arguing that if I had been prevaricating in the text I could easily support it by fibbing an appropriate and convincing footnote thereto. I lost the argument. My accounts of Alsatian battles in the last campaign for the liberation of all France were accepted for the Official Victory of General Eisenhower's "Crusade for Europe" – at least most of them were – when I provided proper footnotes. They were only inconsequential references to what I saw and heard, where and when, and what I was told by the frontline combattants as to what they saw and heard....

2. *New York Times*, editorial, 18 November 2002; "Calls for Woods to Boycott Masters," *Daily Telegraph*, 19 November 2002, p. S-1.
3. My quotes are from the Associated Press dispatches from Atlanta (by Doug Ferguson and Jim Armstrong), dated 20 November and 4 December 2002.
4. Anne Applebaum, "Meanwhile...," *Washington Post/IHT*, 12 December 2002, p. 9.
5. John Leo, "Teed off About Tees," *New York Daily News*, syndicated from the *U.S News and World Report*, 2 December 2002, p. 49.
6. Frank Ahrens, "Laying Out the Future of the New World Times," *Washington Post*, 14 March 2003, p. EO1.
7. Michael Wilbon, "Forcing a Social Conscience is Unconscionable," *Washington Post/IHT*, 21 November 2002, p. 19. Wilbon (with photograph) was available on the Internet at *www.washingtonpost.com*.
8. Selena Roberts, "Augusta's Power Felt Far Beyond Its Gates," *New York Times*, 9 April 2003, p. S5. "Augusta master adamant," *New York Post*, 10 April 2003, pp. 31, 88-89. Mark Steyn, "All the News That's Fit to Bury," *National Post*, 17 April 2003.

14. Morphing the A-Word

1. Roberto Calasso, *The Ruin of Kasch* (1994), p. 154. See also his *The Marriage of Cadmus and Harmony* (1993).
    Marshall McLuhan, *The Gutenberg Galaxy* (1962) and *Understanding Media* (1964). Jean Baudrillard, *Cool Memories II 1987-1990* (1996), *Selected Writings* (1988), *System of Objects* (1996).
    Umberto Eco, as befits a Professor of so-called Semiotics – "the study of signs and symbols as elements of communicative behavior...the analysis of systems of communication, as language, gestures, or clothing" (*Random House Webster's*, 1999, p. 741) – has sent out, especially in his novels, a thousand tantalizing signals. See: *The Name of the Rose* (1983), especially his *Postscript* (1984) thereto; *Foucault's Pendulum* (1989); *Travels in Hyper Reality* (1989). I might also mention *The Search for the Perfect Language* (1997); *Kant and Platypus: Essays on Language and Cognition* (1999); his *Theory of Semiotics* (1976); and *Semiotics and the Philosophy of Language* (1984).
    Readers of Signor Eco may find, possibly, some significance in Webster's third meaning of "semiotic" – "of or pertaining to symptoms of disease." But "symptomatic" of what? and of which "disease"?

15. Terms of Endearment and Agreement

1. Sue Mott, "Saturday interview," *Daily Telegraph*, 11 May 2002, p. S7.
2. Sue Mott, "Joys that Channon swears by," *Daily Telegraph*, 16 Ocober 1999, p. S6; "The gospel according to King," 23 October 1999, p. S6; "Legend and Honour is bruised by women," 25 October 1999, p. S4.

16. The Mergenthaler Option

1. Brough Scott, in the *Sunday Telegraph*, 16 June 1996.
2. "*Wizard of Id*," *IHT*, 16 June 1995.
3. *Daily Mirror*, 13 August 1996, p. 11.
4. Victor Lewis-Smith, "It's hard work watching porn," *Evening Standard*, 16 August 1996, p. 31.
5. *Daily Mail*, "Stunned Agassi shown the door," 16 August 1996, p. 68.
6. *Daily Mirror*, "Noel Looks Back at Me in Anger" and "What was said" in a "Foul-Mouthed phone tirade," 13 August 1996, p. 13.
7. "Papal Views/Newspaper of Vatican City," *NYT/IHT*, 24-25 December 1996, p. 2.

17. A Matter of Illegitimacy

1. Magnus Linklater, "Mind Your Language, Mr. Blair," *The Times*, 12 December 1996. Personal letter, 7 February 1997.
2. Matthew Engel, "Pigs should fly," *The Guardian*, 24 January 1998.

18. The Guard that Failed

1. The American reviewer was Herb Greer, writing in the London periodical *The Spectator*, 20 January 2001.
2. Tony Wright, "Bad Language: Poor English murders clear-thinking – and academics, politicians and journalists are the culprits"; Polly Toynbee, "Whimpering nation: we see every mishap as a portent of doom;" Matthew Norman, "Diary," 6 April 2001, pp. 7-8.
3. Peterborough (ed. Sam Leith), "Helena blows her top," *Daily Telegraph*, 18 May 2001, p. 26.
4. Ian Mayes, "Expletives and excess: in the use of four-letter words," 31 October 1998, in: *Corrections & Clarifications* (2000), pp. 82-83.
5. My references to and quotes from the *Guardian*'s Style Book are based on the comprehensive text available in the Internet at its website: *www.guardianunlimited.co.uk./styleguide/*.
6. Atticus in the *Sunday Times*, 15 December 2002; letter, 22 December 2002, p. 18.

19. The Desperate Search for "The Good Bits"

1. Christopher Clarey, *NYT/IHT*, 27 August 1999; Robin Finn, *NYT/IHT*, 11-12 September 1999, p. 20; Rachel Alexander, *Washington Post/IHT*, 11-12 September 1999, p. 1, 18.
2. Robin Finn, in *NYT/IHT*, 3 September 1999, p. 20.
3. William Gray, "Toshack's 'goats' furious at insult," *Daily Telegraph*, 28 April 1999, p. 31.
4. Joe Joseph, *The Times*, 24 June 1996, p. 1.)
5. Stoichkov quote in Ian Thomsen, *IHT*, 19 June 1996, p. 26.
6. *Daily Telegraph*, 16 February 1995.
7. Patrick Collins, "Cult of Dishonesty," *The Mail on Sunday*, 21 September 1997, p. 92.
8. "Cursing Henman," *Daily Mail*, 12 July 1997, p. 77.
9. "Faldo fury," *Daily Telegraph*, 13 July 1997, p. 3.
10. "Spielberg: Smaller than life," *Sunday Telegraph*, 13 June 1997, p. 35.
11. *Der Spiegel*, interview with Tom Jones, 9 January 1995, pp. 164-5. *Die Woche*, Ursula Ott, "*Sex für 1 Mark,*" 6 June 1996, p. 29. *Duden*, 8 volumes, (Duden Verlag, rev. ed.1996). *Frankfurter Allgemeine Zeitung*, 4 October 1994, *Feuilleton*.

German criticism, otherwise ultra-classical in their cultural prejudices, object to the flight – in the old *Duden* as well as in the 1854 work of the Grimms – into an unblushing (and perhaps incomprehensible) Latin, when the sexual revolutionaries raise too many verbal demands. Gibbon would have understood the problem. [See above, *"O Propheta...,"* in this section].

The matter of recognition (and approval) through inclusion was raised in several famous American articles in 1960s by Dwight Macdonald where the celebrated Manhattan radical of his day took a conservative position. He argued that if one put sloppy or undesirable usages into our dictionaries, we would be left with an increasingly decadent language. (See Dwight Macdonald, "The Decline and Fall of English" (in *Life*) and "The Strong Natured" (in *The New Yorker*), reprinted in *Against the American Grain: Essays on the Effects of Mass Culture* (1963), pp. 289-316, 317-333.

12. Quoted from Lenny Bruce, *How to Talk Dirty*, pp. 127-8.

20. Swearing is the Curse

1. *New York Times/IHT*, "Martin Agronsky Dies: Riled Presidents on TV," 23 July 1999, p. 2.
2. *The Standard*, London, 20 July 1999, p. 5.
3. On the D.H. Lawrence and *Chatterley* references, see C.H. Rolph's Penguin edition of the London trial transcript, *The Trial of Lady Chatterley* (1961). The prosecutor's reference to "the servants" is on p. 17. "Phallic tenderness" is Lawrence's own phrase, p. 20.
4. A.N. Wilson, "Swearing is the curse of our language," *The Standard* (London), 21 July 1999, p. 13.
5. The *Spiegel* report was in No. 44, 1 November 1999, pp. 263-65. The quote from John Preston, the British deputy Prime Minister, is in the *Daily Telegraph*, "Blair's Feuding Cabinet," 1 November 1999, p. 4.

Part 3: Literary Origins and Popular Consequences

22. From Wordsworth to Orwell and Hemingway

1. *New York Times*, 25 September 1995. *New York Times/IHT*, 10 June 1996, p. 4.
2. Robin Givhan, "It's High Time Women Quit Sneaking Around," *Washington Post/IHT*, 20 June 1996, p. 11.
3. *Washington Post/IHT*, 20 June 1996, p. 1.
4. *H.L. Mencken on Politics: A Carnival of Buncombe* (ed. Moos, 1960), pp. 134-35.

23. The Prose We Write and Speak

1. Craig Brown, "My diary of the broadly successful 1997 Conservative election campaign," *Daily Telegraph*, 14 June 1997, p. 14.
2. Charles Babington, "Florida Court Decision…," *Washington Post/IHT*, 18-19 November 2000, pp. 1, 4.
3. See, under "eight-ball," *The Cassell Dictionary of Slang* (ed. Green, 1998), p. 390. *Slang* (ed. Paul Dickson, 1998), p. 169. *The Oxford Dictionary of Modern Slang* (p. 64) explains the origins: "From the disadvantage, in a variety of a game of pool, of having the black ball (numbered 8 and which one is penalized for touching) between the eyeball and the obejct ball."

The fullest listings are, of course, to be found in Lighter's *Random House Historical Dictionary of American Slang* (vol. 1, pp. 699-700). It doesn't attempt to explicate the rules of the game in which the eight-ball is consigned to play such a dark role. (Who today, I wonder, is agitating to change them and make all billiards politically correct?) But it emphasizes that its slang usage refers to a black person and is "used contemptuously." Lighter's colorful selection of citations includes one quote which had totally escaped me and which I found resonating. It was from a book which had been "central reading" for my New York generation growing up in the 1930s. It was a snippet written by James T. Farrell – whom I had revered as a novelist and as a mentor/friend – from *Studs Lonigan: A Trilogy* (1932-1935) wherein a *Studs* character says: "...He'd have to get away from the eight-balls and tin-horn kikes."

The pseudo-metaphor on the rebound from the green-baize pool-table is a favor-ite buzz-word – mindless, graceless, and almost meaningless – for our political commentators who are unable, or unwilling, to think of something more penetrating to say. Lighter's *Dictionary* preserves a sentence from the *New York Times*, evaluat-ing Presdient Dwight D. Eisenhower's administration in 1959: "...Ike has spent so much time standing behind a golfball that he has got the American people standing behind the eight ball...." Did the *Times* editors know their words would become a dictionary quote, anthologized as a citation, and hence immortal? As Kojak used to say on CBS/TV, "We've been eightballed, baby!."

4. *Daily Telegraph*, 3 May 1995.
5. Walther Wille, "Election Party at Frankfurt's Amerika Haus," *FAZ* (English ed.), 9 November 2000, p. 2.
6. Richard Cohen, Op-ed page column in the *New York Daily News*, 8 August 2000, p. 37, and Foxman interview, *New York Post*, 9 August 2000, p. 6.
7. On the subject of *Yiddisch in Berliner Jargon*, see Andreas Nachama's brochure, so entitled (1994). On the Polish elements, see the excellent book by Eva Hoffman, on "the life and death of a small town [Bransk] and the world of Polish Jews" called *Shtetl* (1997), p. 136. William Safire, "Language," *New York Times Magazine/IHT*, 25 June 2001, p. 14.
8. See Michael Daly, "Dreidel spells out thrill...," *New York Daily News*, 9 August 2000, pp. 24-25.

I can also recommend a stimulating book (from which I have learned much): Mark Steyn: *Broadway Babies Say Goodnight: Musicals Then and Now* (1999). In his chapter on "The Jews" (*vi*, pp. 74-87) he is often excessively flippant and gag-ridden, but incisive for all that. His research is full of surprising history and cultural insights which the coverage of Broadway in the American mainstream press rarely found a peg to report.

On Al Jolson and other (mostly Jewish) vaudevillians in blackface, Steyn writes: "...blackface was a code, one race's pain speaking in the form of another."

Again, "...the first talking picture, *The Jazz Singer*, is about a cantor's son (and in what other country could that have happened in 1927?)...." All in all, Steyn gives a new dimension to conventional journalism's discussion of America's "Melting-Pot Culture."

24. Dealing with the Grandmother Tongue

1. Rosten, *Joys of Yiddish*, pp. 426, 446.
2. See: *Pons Wörterbuch der deutschen Umgangssprache*, (ed. Küpper, 1987), p. 728.)
3. The German catalogue which lists *Schmuse*--songs is the *Merkheft* (2000) from Zweitausendeins Versand.
4. Graham Turner, "Prince Philip at 80," (4-article series), *Daily Telegraph*, 21-24 May 2001.

5.   A London lexicographer is similarly oblivious in his British compilation to the "proper parliamentary word"; his entry in its entirety:

"*tummler* n. (20 C.) 1. (US) the 'life and soul of the party,' a person who talks a great deal but accomplishes little. 2. (US, show business) the MC of a (Jewish) hotel in Catskill Mts, NY (cf. BORSCHT BELT). (Yid/Ger. *Tummel*, disorder)," *The Cassell Dictionary of Slang* (1998, ed. Jonathon Greene), p. 1233.

"We have always buried bad news" (Joe Ashton), *The Times*, 21 February 2002, p. 23. Leo Rosten, *The Joys of Yiddish* (1970), "*tummler*" pp. 417-418.)

6.   I should note that Mr. Joe Ashton has held the seat for so-called "Bassettlaw" for some 30 years now. In true British eccentricity the place doesn't actually exist—something like "Brigadoon"—but it still embraces a number of real-existing ex-mining villages, the largest being Worksop (*sic*). Labour has held the seat in every national election since 1929.

The Times, surprisingly enough, gave Joe Ashton a pride-of-place on its editorial page, although the man has had well-known "*tabloid problems*." These have comprised many "politically incorrect views," such as: lowering the homosexual age-of-consent; objecting to quotas for women (eager to have good political jobs); the legalization of suicide (with the usual euthanasian guarantees); a demand for more "Pop movies" (*e.g.*, "*Carry On*"-films); last but not least, his being found by the police in an unorthodox 'massage parlor'..."—which ended his long parliamentary career. Source: *BBC News*, Internet, 23 February 2002.)

7.   On the cliché, see Frank Sullivan's series of articles of fictitious interviews with "Mr. Arbuthnot," an expert on the cliché, published the *New Yorker* from 1935-1952.

8.   See Mark Steyn, *Broadway Babies Say Goodnight: Musicals Then and Now* (1999). On Jerome Robbins, see Greg Lawrence, *Dance with Demons: The Life of Jerome Robbins* (2001) and Christine Conrad, *Jerome Robbins: That Broadway Man, That Ballet Man* (2001). The Kirkus quote is included in the pocketbook edition of the original McGraw Hill title in 1968, *The Joys of Yiddish* (back cover).

9.   Butterworth interview in *Washington Post/IHT*, "A Director Jettisons the Hollywood Formula," 8 February 2002, p. 20.

10. Leo Rosten's famed H*Y*M*A*N K*A*P*L*A*N pieces were written for Harold Ross' *New Yorker* magazine in the 1930s and first printed together in book form as *The Education of H*y*m*a*n K*a*p*l*a*n* in 1937, decades before the "greenhorn" words received their first citizenship papers. There is also *The Return of H*y*m*a*n K*a*p*l*a*n* (1959).

See: Rosten's preface to *The Joys of Yiddish*, first published in 1968. His collection of "Yiddishisms," which became in time "*Yinglish*," was immense; and it was my passing pleasure to have contributed to it with cuttings from London and Berlin; the Bronx and Brooklyn he covered himself, and with meticulous care for footnotery. The Pentagon's "Bagel," *Newsweek*, 25 September 1967, p. 63. "Schmevolution," *Wall Street Journal*, 12 January 1968....He also cites my sometime English co-Editor, Frank Kermode of *Encounter* Magazine, who used "*kvell*" in London's *The Listener* (28 December 1967, p. 849.).

I told Rosten that, for my part, I didn't know exactly what it meant. Nor did, as I suspected, Professor Kermode, who, as a brilliant literary scholar, had an admirable addiction to hard words with secret meanings.

11. I have already mentioned Andreas Nachama's short but stimulating book on *Yiddisch im Berliner Jargon* (1994). He deals there (pp. 71-72) with "buttocks" (*das Gesäss*), and explains the differences in meaning when, in Hebrew nouns, vowels are not included but sounds are added with the aid of diacritical signs. *Tokus* or *tochus* takes on almost philosophical significance.

His explication comes between *Tacheles* (which is now a tourist center in the new Berlin)…and *Tinnef* which in Hebrew amounts to *dreck*. It would therefore constitute a special lexicographical problem for the *New York Times* which airily continues to avoid earthiness as the essence of dirty realism.

12. Clyde Haberman, "The Oys of Yiddish," *New York Times* (Week in Review), 22 October 2000.

13. The problems of meaningful translation are illuminated by two American translators – Saul Bellow and Irving Howe – in their respective collections, *Great Jewish Short Stories* (New York, 1966) and (with Eliezer Greenberg) *A Treasury of Yiddish Stories* (New York, 1953). See: a report on the revival of the "YIVO in Vilna" which looks back on "*eine jiddishe Alternative*": Eva Kirn-Frank, "Litauisches Jerusalem," *FAZ*, 24 November 2000, p. 46.

At the very least our mainstream press would not have had an opportunity to dumb-down the language of journalism with the likes of the *New York Times'* "Oys of Yiddish."

Notable too is a more recent anthology, entitled *Jewish American Literature* (ed. Chametzky, et al., 2001) and a thoughtful long review of it in the *L.A. Times* (Books), 18 February 2001, pp. 6-7, by Nessa Rappaport. She touches upon our problem of translation by invoking Cynthia Ozick who, in her story "Envy, or Yiddish in America," invokes in turn echoes of Emma Lazarus' lines inscribed in the Statue of Liberty ("Give me your tired, your poor,/Your huddled masses…" etc.).

A beleaguered Yiddish poet in America, Edelshtain by name, pleads with a young American woman whom he has just met to become his translator:

"All you can hope for, you tattered, you withered, is translation in America."

As Rappaport concludes in the *Los Angeles Times* (whose readers may still have a recondite interest in such matters) –

"For Yiddish immigrants, America is a refuge; for the Yiddish language it is death."

14. My quotes are from the *Los Angeles Times* ("Book review" section), 3 December 2000, p. 8.

15. Liptzin, *Yiddish Literature*, pp. 2, 26-28.

I should mention here what has been called the last tragic masterpiece of the Yiddish language: incomprehensible to all but a few, and quite untranslatable for the many in the major languages. I refer to Izchak Katznelson's *Dos Lied vunm oysgehargetn jidischn Folk* (1942-1944). It was composed en route to the Auschwitz concentration camp, well-hidden until the end of the Hitler régime, and then first published in Switzerland. (The poet himself perished in the gas chambers in 1944.)

It was an Austrian Catholic editor, the historian Friedrich Heer, who first called my attention in Vienna to this astonishing text which he compared to the Biblical *Hiob* ("Job") as written by a *Zaddik*, a legendary wise man. Despite the valiant efforts of the well-known German lyricist Wolf Biermann on behalf of Katznelson's poem, I cannot detect a resurgent appreciation of this memorable "last song of the slaughtered Jewish people" in any language.

See the bi-lingual editions of Hermann Adler (Zurich, 1951) amd Biermann (dtv, Munich, 1996). A translation into English, *The Song of the Murdered Jewish People*, translated and annotated by Noah H. Rosenbloom, was first published in Israel by publishers named the "Ghetto Fighters House" (1980). There is also a "requiem" of Katznelson's *Song* which was put to music by a young composer named Zlata Razdolina. It was performed by the Moravian Philharmonic Olomouc (Czech Republic) and conducted by Victor Feldbrill in 1998.

I fear that the *New York Times* has by now helped to make Yiddish into a Manhattan "fun talk," and just too comical to take the accents of even an Auschwitz poet seriously. I can't recall a mention of Katznelson in the pages of the *Times* in half-a-century.

16. See: Joseph Roth, *Juden auf Wanderschaft* (Amsterdam/Cologne, 1976), which was a shade erratically translated as *The Wandering Jews* (London, 2000).

25. Quotations that were Unquoted

1. Personal (email) letter, 26 October 2002.
2. *Duden: Das Grosse Fremdwörterbuch: Herkunft und Bedeutung der Fremdwörter* (Mannheim, 1994), p. 936. Also: *Wahrig Deutsches Wörterbuch* (1980), p. 2663.
    Leo Rosten, *The Joys of Yiddish* (1970), pp. 264-66. J.E. Lighter, *Random House Historical Dictionary of American Slang*, vol. II (1997), p. 643.

26. Dirty Realism in the White House and Beyond

1. As Rev. Jesse Jackson put it, he went "from poverty-stricken Arkansas to Oxford [which] gave him almost the entire range of human experience, and so wherever he lands he's at home...." That "almost" is rich; for the man, as is well-known, never landed in the horrors of Vietnam; and surely the Auschwitz-Holocaust element in "the range of human experience" never cast a shadow in Little Rock or in his nearby hometown of Hope.
    The analogy which the Rev. Jesse Jackson offered to explicate Bill Clinton's transcendent kinship to all – well, *almost* all – of suffering humanity is worth preserving. "...And so wherever he lands he's at home. If he's riding in the golf cart, he's mindful of his fellow-golfers, and he's also mindful of the caddy and cook." Joe Klein, *The New Yorker*, p. 203.
    I should think that if the man were to land a hole-in-one, he sure would apologize to all and sundry.
2. My quotations are from Joe Klein, "A Reporter at large: Eight Years. Bill Clinton and the politics of persistence," *The New Yorker*, 16 & 23 October 2000, pp. 188-217.
3. Daniel Hannan, "What do the people of Europe want?," *Sunday Telegraph*, 29 September 2002, p. 32.
4. *Axel Bruggemann, "Wahl unter der Bettdecke (Elections between the Bed Sheets)," Die Welt (Berlin), 4 September 2002, p. 1.*
5. Julia Finch, "Interview," *Guardian*, 24 August 2002, p. 26. Andrew Marr, "Notebook," *Daily Telegraph*, 11 September 2002, p. 16.
6. "City comment: the Rosy glows, Green-eyed Monsters," *Daily Telegraph*, 20 August 2002, p. 34.
7. "Pot Noodle criticized for bad taste advert," and "Pot Noodle advert lands in hot water," *Daily Telegraph*, 19/28 August 2002, p. 6, 5.
8. "Ambassador in Israel gaffe moved," *Daily Telegraph*, 7 September 2002, p. 20.

27. Towards a Vocabulary of Pop Diplomacy

1. *New York Daily News*, 12 August 1986, p. 43.
2. *Washington Post/IHT*, 13 January 1997, p. 7.)
3. *NYT/IHT*, 14 January 1997, p. 2.
4. "A Breeze on Confirmations," *Washington Post/IHT*, 14 January 1997, p. 3.
5. *U.S. News & World Report*, 6 August 1986, p. 28.
6. *Washington Post/IHT*, 22 September 1995.
7. William Pfaff, "International Trouble-Makers Could Do Some Good In Bosnia," *Los Angeles Times/IHT*, 11 July 1996. For a brief history of such transatlantic oscillations, see Melvin J. Lasky, "Europe and America: Transatlantic Images," in

Encounter, January 1962, pp. 78, and reprinted in *New Paths in American History*, ed. A.M. Schlesinger, Jr. (1965).

8. "A Bolder Japan," *Washington Post/IHT*, 16 October 1996, p. 1.

9. "Clinton's 'Human Pinata,'" 9 March 1998, p. 29. The McMurry story, unreported by the dozen journalists present, was first published by the *Washington Post*'s media critic, Howard Kurtz, in a new book entitled *Spin Cycle* (1998).

10. "Profile Noel Gallagher: Cradle Rocker," *Sunday Telegraph*, 28 May 2000, p. 41.

11. *Washington Post*, 30 October 1995.

12. *Time*, 25 December 1995-1 January 1996, p. 52.

13. *Time* Magazine, 25 December 1995-1 January 1996, p. 82.

14. Mencken, *American Language, Supplement One* (1952), p. 677.)

    One can't hear the hyphens, so that Truman's "collision form" could be taken as signaling in one way or the other the collision course between Truman and Stalin in the forthcoming "Cold War." See Charles Mee, Jr.'s *Meeting at Potsdam* (1975), p. 263. My s.o.b. quotation from it was in a short film history of the Potsdam Conference, made by Dr. Bernhard von Gersdorff for the Chronos video history of World War II, entitled "Potsdamer Konferenz" (1995).

15. *Time*, 24 April 1995, p. 28.

16. *Washington Post/IHT*, "Way to UN," 14-15 December 1996, p. 1; BBC World News Report, 14 December 1996.

17. Quoted in: George Stephanopoulos, *All Too Human: A Political Education* (1999), p. 219.

18. *Random House Dictionary of American Slang* (ed. Lighter), vol. 1, pp. 37-50. *The New Yorker* Magazine, 17 May 1993, p. 17.

19. Phillip Oppenheim, *Sunday Times*, "Hague's not the problem...," 9 May 1999, p. 18. *Random House Dictionary of American Slang* (ed. Lighter), vol. I, pp. 39-50.

20. Interview with Ozzy Osbourne, in *Rolling Stone* magazine (New York), 25 July 2002. Hugh Davies, "Four Letters from Ozzy's Wife fail to rock Palace," *Daily Telegraph*, 13 July 2002, p. 3.

    On the subject of Aleister Crowley (1875-1947), there is a vast literature, mainly appealing to those who are predisposed to "magical ceremonies" and/or drug-induced orgies. He attracted many disciples for his so-called black satanic creed, making for his reputation as "the Great Beast." He fancied himself as " the wickedest man alive," which was a puerile exaggeration.

    I found Charles R. Cammell's biography, *Aleister Crowley: The Man, the Mage, the Poet* (1962) mildly interesting, and only in the English context of bohemian hocus-pocus. Still, where Bloomsbury played with eccentricities, California made it all into a cottage industry for the next top-of-the-pops gig. Notable further studies include: John Symonds, *The Great Beast: The Life and Magick of Aleister Crowley* (1973); and the two latest biographies: byLawrence Sutin: *Do What Thou Wilt: A Life of Aleister Crowley* (2000) and Martin Booth: *A Magick Life: A Biography of Aleister Crowley* (2001).)

Index